Yankees
BY THE
Numbers

Also by Bill Gutman:

It's Outta Here: The History of the Home Run from Babe Ruth to Barry Bonds

Lance Armstrong: A Biography

Parcells: A Biography

Twice Around the Bases: A Thinking Fan's Inside Look at Baseball
(with Kevin Kennedy)

What if the Babe Had Kept his Red Sox: And Other Fascinating Alternate Histories from the World of Sports

Won for All: The Inside Story of the New England Patriots' Improbable

Run to the Super Bowl (with Pepper Johnson)

Yankees
BY THE
Numbers

A COMPLETE TEAM HISTORY OF THE
BRONX BOMBERS BY UNIFORM NUMBER

BILL GUTMAN

Skyhorse Publishing

Skyhorse Publishing books may be purchased in bulk at special discounts
for sales promotion, corporate gifts, fund-raising, or educational purposes.
Special editions can also be created to specifications. For details, contact
the Special Sales Department, Skyhorse Publishing, 555 Eighth Avenue,
Suite 903, New York, NY 10018 or info@skyhorsepublishing.com.

www.skyhorsepublishing.com

10 9 8 7 6 5 4 3 2 1

All baseball cards featured in the book reprinted with the
permission of the Topps Company, Inc.

Library of Congress Cataloging-in-Publication Data

Gutman, Bill.
Yankees by the numbers : a complete team history of the New York
Yankees by uniform number / Bill Gutman.
p. cm.
ISBN 978-1-60239-763-7 (pbk. : alk. paper)
1. New York Yankees (Baseball team)--History. 2. Baseball uniforms--
Numbers--New York (State)--New York--History. I. Title.
GV875.N4G97 2010
796.357'64097471--dc22
                                                    2010002456

Printed in the United States of America

This book is for Yankees fans everywhere. For newer fans, it's a chance to experience a taste of the team's long and glorious history, and the men who helped make it. For older fans, it's plain and simply a grand trip down memory lane. Enjoy.

CONTENTS

INTRODUCTION

It should come as no surprise that baseball's most famous team was also the first to wear numbers, permanently, on the backs of their uniform jerseys. With all of the World Series triumphs and great players who have donned the pinstripes over the years, it's almost a forgotten piece of trivia to know that the New York Yankees also introduced uniform numbers to Major League Baseball. The Yankees had been in existence since the formation of the American League in 1901 (they were known as the Highlanders back then) and by 1929 had already solidified their reputation as baseball's best team, coming off three straight American League pennants and a pair of World Series triumphs. Yet when they took the field for the 1929 season, something was different. There were large numbers on the backs of their uniforms.

The concept wasn't entirely new. Cleveland had tried it back in 1916, but the numbers were on the sleeves of the jerseys, not the backs. The idea didn't take. Nor did it when the St. Louis Cardinals tried it briefly in 1923. But once the mighty Yankees appeared with numbers emblazoned on the backs of their shirts, other teams took notice and began doing the same. Within three years, all 16 teams had numbers and the old expression, *you can't tell the players without a scorecard,* suddenly had veracity. The Brooklyn Dodgers of 1952 were the first team to duplicate the numbers on the front of their jerseys, while the 1960 Chicago White Sox became the first team to add the players' names above the numbers of the backs of their jerseys. Ironically, the Yankees, despite being the first with numbers, stayed with their pin-striped tradition and never added names to the back or numerals to the front of their uniforms.

There are two others pieces of numeric information about the Yankees that fans should find interesting. Many people have wondered over the years why Babe Ruth wore No. 3 and Lou Gehrig No. 4. They were the Bronx Bombers' two best players back then, but their numbers didn't come by choice. The first numbers were issued to correspond with the team's batting order. And since the Babe hit in the three spot and Gehrig batted cleanup, there you go. The Yankees' first 10 original uniform numbers were as follows:

Earle Combs

Mark Koenig

Babe Ruth

Lou Gehrig

Bob Meusel

Tony Lazzeri

Leo Durocher

Johnny Grabowski

Benny Bengough

Bill Dickey

Next came the pitchers, and finally the bench players. That first year there were 32 numbers issued. While the coaches also began wearing numbers in 1929, no Yankee manager wore a number until 1947, when Bucky Harris became the team's skipper. The only exception was when a coach or player (who already had a number) became manager in mid-season. Bob Shawkey (29) took over for a sick Miller Huggins in 1929 and catcher Bill Dickey (8) replaced Joe McCarthy in 1946, succeeded later that same year by coach Johnny Neun (32). McCarthy, the Yankee skipper from 1932 until early in the '46 season, never donned a uniform with a number.

The Yanks hold yet another distinction. The team has retired more numbers than any other ballclub, speaking again to the many great players and managers who have appeared in pinstripes over the years. Sixteen players have had their uniform retired over the years. Yet only 15 numbers hang in Monument Park in Yankee Stadium. That's because one number has been retired twice. As an early point of reference, the retired numbers are: 1 (Billy Martin), 3 (Babe Ruth), 4 (Lou Gehrig), 5 (Joe DiMaggio); 7 (Mickey Mantle), 8 (Yogi Berra and Bill Dickey), 9 (Roger Maris), 10 (Phil Rizzuto), 15 (Thurman Munson), 16 (Whitey Ford), 23 (Don Mattingly), 32 (Elston Howard), 37 (Casey Stengel) 44 (Reggie Jackson), and 49 (Ron Guidry). All are highly recognizable names. And the team isn't through yet. Think Derek Jeter, Alex Rodriguez, and Mariano Rivera for starters, with other possibilities like Paul O'Neill, Joe Torre, Jorge Posada, and Andy Pettitte waiting in the wings. For a young player, finding a number with the Yankees that he really wants to wear may soon become a rather gargantuan task.

Yankees by the Numbers is a book for both Yankee fans and baseball lovers alike. You'll read about the best players in franchise history since uniform numbers were introduced, discover plenty of anecdotes and stats, and get a glimpse of the many other players who have come and gone but had the honor of wearing the famed Yankee pinstripes over the years. The majority of stats will be for the time a particular player was with the Yanks, unless there's a reason to also mention numbers from another phase of his career. Though the coaches and manager are listed—with their numbers—before each chapter, they are not all mentioned in the body of the text. Only those who have played a major role in a certain era will be discussed in any detail.

For the top players in the game, their uniform was, and is, a real source of identification part of their baseball being. For the journeymen, numbers often come and go, and some have worn several numbers for the same team, in this case the Yankees. With the long history of this highly successful, epic franchise, the cast of characters is a large one. Much of the fun in putting this book together comes from not only in revisiting the top players from each era, but looking for those little-known facts and anecdotes about those who have arrived, then departed quickly, sometimes leaving an indelible mark, but other times just slipping into anonymity and winding up all but forgotten. But they were all New York Yankees and, as such, they had a number and merit a mention. So here we go. It's both a trip down memory lane and a treatise on the most current Bronx Bomber ballclubs. Enjoy.

#1: BILLY THE KID STEPS TO THE PLATE

There's really only one place to begin. Sure, the form of the book dictates that the opening chapter be those Yankee players who wore No. 1. With the exception of three utility players who had the number for a single season, there have been just six main men who have sported the number over the course of the franchise history. All were fine players, but there's only one who's eminently qualified to be in the leadoff spot here. He's none other than battling **Billy Martin**, who donned No. 1 as both a player and manager, and eventually saw the number retired in his honor in 1986.

"Billy the Kid" had a star-crossed Yankees career rife with controversy, brawls, hirings, and firings . . . and winning baseball. As a player, Alfred Manuel Martin was a scrappy second-baseman, a 170-pounder soaking wet, and essentially a singles hitter who was ready to put it on the line every night. He was managed by Casey Stengel when he played for the Oakland Oaks of the Pacific Coast League in 1948. Ol' Case became so enamored with the youngster's hellbent-for-leather style that when he became the Yankees' skipper a year later he convinced the team go out and buy Martin, who made his Yankees debut in 1950. It wasn't long before the thin second-baseman became known as "Casey's Boy," and teamed with the other great Bombers who were in the midst of five straight pennants and World Series triumphs. Billy formed a close friendship with Yankee superstars Mickey Mantle and Whitey Ford, and the three became drinking buddies, often going out on the town together in a modern version of the Three Musketeers.

On the field, Martin was little more than a .250 hitter (.257 lifetime) who had his best year in 1953 when he hit .257 with 15 homers and 75 runs batted in. In the World Series that year he had a record 12 hits

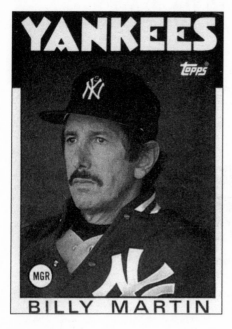

BILLY MARTIN

in just six games, including a pair of homers and eight RBIs, as the Yanks beat the Brooklyn Dodgers for their fifth straight championship.

Martin's first Yankee honeymoon came to an abrupt end on June 15, 1957, a month or so after he and some of his teammates visited the famed Copacabana nightclub in Manhattan to celebrate Mickey Mantle's birthday. A fight ensued. The subsequent publicity wasn't good and management decided that Martin had to go, if only to protect stars Mantle and Ford. So the kid was sent to baseball purgatory in Kansas City. Four years later his playing days ended and soon after he embarked on his managerial career, his heart was still in one place . . . New York.

By 1969, Billy the Kid resurfaced as the manager of the Minnesota Twins, piloting them to a 95–65 first-place finish. Not only did they lose in the playoffs, but Billy's managerial tenure in the Twin Cities was short-lived. After a nasty fight with one of his players, pitcher Dave Boswell, he was canned. He then managed almost three years in Detroit (1971–73), moving on to Texas for the final 23 games of the '73 season. He stayed through 95 games of the 1975 season when Yankees owner George Steinbrenner summoned him back to New York. Eighteen years after being traded to Kansas City, No. 1 was back home with a Manager of the Year (1974) prize as part of his résumé.

There was little doubt that Billy the Kid got the most out of his players. His teams played hard and they won. When he joined the Yankees they were building an outstanding team. After familiarizing himself with his ballclub during the remainder of the 1975 season, he then piloted the Yankees to an American League pennant in 1976 and a World Championship in 1977.

But there was already an ill wind blowing over Yankee Stadium. Martin clashed with several players, including team captain Thurman Munson and, most notably, free agent slugger Reggie Jackson, who came to the ballclub in 1977. The team was tagged with the infamous nickname, "The Bronx Zoo." However, all seemed forgiven when the Yanks won the World Series, led by Jackson's five home runs, three coming in a single game. Then the next year the manager imploded.

With the Yanks trailing the Boston Red Sox in July 1978, Martin suspended Jackson for bunting against orders and then, in a rambling news conference, he referred to his star player and his owner by saying, "One's a born liar and the other's convicted." (Steinbrenner had made illegal contributions to Richard Nixon's presidential campaign.) A day later, Martin resigned and Bob Lemon stepped in to skipper the team to yet another championship. Strangely enough, Martin was rehired in July of the following year, much to the delight of the fans, who always loved battling Billy. But shortly after the season he was fired again, this time after punching out a marshmallow salesman. All in all, he would have five different tenures as Yankee skipper, several of them brief, the last coming in 1988. He might have gotten a sixth chance had he not been killed in an automobile accident on Christmas night of 1989. Not surprisingly, alcohol was involved.

Billy the Kid's tumultuous Yankee career over eight seasons saw his teams win 556 games while losing just 385. While he won more than 1,200 times in all his managerial stops, he'll always be remembered as a Yankee, No. 1 forever in the hearts of Yankees fans. For all of his faults and personal problems, he was a winner as both a player and manager.

Now let's hit rewind a bit. **Earle Combs** (1924–1935) holds the distinction of the being the first New York Yankees player to bat with a number on his jersey. That's because Combs was the team's leadoff hitter in 1929, the first year the Yankees wore their numbers. But he was a lot more than that. Combs was the first great Yankees centerfielder, preceding the likes of Joe DiMaggio, Mickey Mantle, and Bernie

Williams. Besides being an outstanding flychaser, he was a solid hitter who set the table for the likes of Ruth, Gehrig, Meusel, and Lazzeri batting behind him. A solid 6-foot, 185-pounder, Combs had a .325 lifetime batting average with a career high of .356 in the incredible "Murderers' Row" season of 1927. That same year he slammed out 231 hits, a club record until Don Mattingly netted 238 in 1986.

Combs's career ended a bit prematurely when he ran into the centerfield wall at old Sportman's Park in St. Louis on July 24, 1934, suffering a fractured skull as well as shoulder and knee injuries. He was a player-coach the next year, playing in just 89 games and hitting .282, only the second time in his career he finished under .300. After that he became a full-time coach, eventually giving up No. 1 and wearing both 30 and 32 until he retired for good in 1944.

Frankie Crosetti holds a unique distinction, having spent 37 straight years in a Yankees uniform, the first 17 as a player and the final 20 as the team's third-base coach. That's the longest continuous time in a New York uniform for anyone. "The Crow," as he was known, was a typical good-fielding, light-hitting shortstop who played from 1932–1948, though he lost the regular shortstop job to Phil Rizzuto in 1940. When Crosetti first joined the Yankees, he donned No. 5, and we all know who that number is most associated with. He wore it through 1936, then took uniform No. 1 in 1937. In 1945, he flip-flopped with second baseman **Snuffy Stirnweiss**, taking Stirnweiss's No. 2 and giving No. 1 to the younger player. The Crow remained No. 2 through the end of his coaching career in 1968.

How, you probably ask, can a big league baseball player end up with the nickname of "Snuffy?" In the case of George Henry Stirnweiss the answer was a sinus condition that gave him a constant case of the sniffles. Stirnweiss wore No. 2 his rookie year, but with Joe Gordon ensconced at second, became a part-time shortstop. The next year Gordon was in the service and Stirnweiss (who was rejected by the Army due to a gastric ulcer) became the second baseman. The year after that, in 1945, he switched to No. 1 and took the American League batting championship with just a .309 average, putting together his greatest season partly because many of the game's top stars were aiding in the war effort. It was the third lowest average ever for an American League batting champ.

With the war over and Gordon back, Snuffy shuffled over to third base and saw his batting average drop by 58 points. He would never hit more than .256 again.

There were two more prominent Yankees that wore the leadoff number through the years. They were a pair of Bobbys, **Bobby Richardson** and **Bobby Murcer**. Richardson spent his entire career (1955–1966) with the Yankees and became one of their slickest second sackers ever. When he joined the team, Billy Martin was established at second and as the wearer of No. 1. Like so many utility players, Richardson had what you might call secondary numbers. He wore No. 17 for two years, then No. 29 in 1957. When Martin was traded to Kansas City, Richardson was given No. 1 though he didn't win a full-time job until 1959. The next year Bobby proved his mettle on the biggest stage of

Courtesy of the New York Yankees

Bobby Murcer

9

all—the World Series. Even though the Yanks lost in seven to the Pittsburgh Pirates (on Bill Mazeroski's walk-off, Series ending home run), Bobby Richardson stood out, collecting 11 hits and 12 RBIs, including a grand slam. He became the first player from the losing side to be named the Most Valuable Player.

Bobby had his best offensive year in '62 , batting .302 with 209 hits, 8 homers, and 59 RBIs. Not bad for a singles hitter with a .266 lifetime average.

Richardson played one more season before hanging them up at the tender age of 31. A devout Christian all of his life, Bobby later coached baseball at the University of South Carolina and eventually became an ordained minister, stepping to the plate once more to officiate at teammate Mickey Mantle's funeral.

Bobby Murcer's Yankee career vacillated between elation and disappointment. He had two tours of duty with the Bronx Bombers, then moved into the broadcast booth and eventually became one of the most beloved Yankees figures of all-time. But it all started under a blanket of unrealistic expectations. An Oklahoma native, Bobby was signed as a shortstop by scout Tom Greenwade in 1964. Mickey Mantle was also signed as a shortstop by the same Greenwade and also hailed from Oklahoma. That immediately made people look at the 18-year old as the next Mantle. That was nearly impossible.

Murcer had cups of coffee in '65 and '66, just as the Yankee dynasty was crumbling. He then went into the service for two years and when he returned in 1969, Mantle had retired and Murcer turned in No. 17, which he'd worn briefly, for No. 1. He began the season as a third baseman, but after making 11 errors in 31 games he was switched to the outfield. He soon became the centerfielder .

While he never approached the greatness of his idol, Bobby Murcer became a solid player and run producer, and a very good outfielder. He had 90 or more RBIs in five different seasons, had a high of 33 homers in 1972, and had batted .331 the year before. While no Mantle, Murcer was carving a reputation as a Yankee of real substance. Then the disappointments began.

For openers, new Yankees manager Bill Virdon decided to install Elliott Maddox in center and move Bobby to right. It didn't bode well. That year, the Yankees played their home games at Shea Stadium while Yankee Stadium was being renovated. The combination of a deeper right field and the swirling winds limited Bobby to just 10 home runs. The final blow came on October 22, when he was traded to the San Francisco Giants for Bobby Bonds in what was considered a blockbuster deal.

Murcer would play two years in San Francisco, then the next two and a half with the Chicago Cubs. In his mind, he was a Yankee and nothing else would suffice. Then on June 26, 1979, the Cubs suddenly traded him back to the Yankees for a minor leaguer. He was 33 years old, but had come home. Though No. 1 was still available, the Yankees assigned him to uniform No. 2 and, at age 33, he would be a part time player for the rest of his career.

He had one more great moment when he drove in four of the Yanks five runs, including the game winner, in the team's first game after captain Thurman Munson's tragic death in 1979. Murcer was one of Munson's closest friends.

He would play through June 1983, when the Yanks released him. But he soon moved to the broadcast booth where his folksy charm and friendly demeanor won him even more fans. He stayed until struck down by a brain tumor in 2007. He recovered enough to make a few brief appearances early the next year but died on July 12, 2008, at the age of 63. Still, he had proven himself more than worthy of No. 1, which was never worn again by a player until retired for Billy Martin in 1986.

Other than these front liners, uniform number one was worn only by **George Selkirk** for part of the 1934 season, by **Roy Johnson** in 1936, and by a long-forgotten player named **Tuck Stainback** for a portion of the 1944 season. Otherwise it was Combs to Crosetti to Stirnweiss to Martin to Richardson and finally to Murcer. Not a bad lineup at that.

THE MOST AND LEAST-WORN NUMBERS

Numbers, numbers everywhere. This is a book that will contain all the Yankees who have worn numbers for 80 years. With 15 numbers retired, some are obviously cut off at the pass and cannot be worn again. Others are always up for grabs and sometimes passed between one player after another for short periods of time. Here are the 10 most worn numbers by Yankees players as well as the 10 least worn.

Most Worn Numbers

No. 26 – Worn by 63 Yankees	No. 39 – Worn by 56 Yankees
No. 28 – Worn by 59 Yankees	No. 18 – Worn by 54 Yankees
No. 27 – Worn by 58 Yankees	No. 17 – Worn by 52 Yankees
No. 29 – Worn by 57 Yankees	No. 22 – Worn by 50 Yankees
No. 38 – Worn by 56 Yankees	No. 36 – Worn by 49 Yankees

Least Worn Numbers

No. 91 – Worn by one Yankee (Alfredo Aceves)

No. 77 – Worn by one Yankee (Humberto Sanchez)

No. 76 – Worn by one Yankee (Craig Dingman)

No. 75 – Worn by one Yankee (Ben Ford)

No. 72 – Worn by one Yankee (Juan Miranda)

No. 69 – Worn by one Yankee (Alan Mills)

No. 4 – Worn by one Yankee (Lou Gehrig)

No. 67 – Worn by two Yankees (Clay Christiansen, Darrell Einertson

No. 99 – Worn by three Yankees (Charlie Keller, Matt Howard, Brian Bruney)

No. 66 – Worn by three Yankees (Steve Balboni, Jim Deshaies, Juan Miranda)

The logic is simple here. None of the most popular numbers have been retired and the least popular numbers are the ultra-high numbers that are rarely used. The only exception is No. 4, which Lou Gehrig wore the first year in 1929 and right up to his retirement in 1939. It was retired upon his death two years later and was never worn again. Only one player, Gus Niarhos, ever wore No. 37. But two managers did, Bucky Harris and then Casey Stengel; and Ol' Case had it retired ten years after he left the Yankees (1970).

#2: THE CAPTAIN INTO THE 21ST CENTURY

Derek Jeter came to the Yankees at the tail end of the 1995 season for his first big league cup of coffee. He was given No. 2 and hit just .250 in 48 at bats. Nothing special. The next year, the Yankees had a new manager in Joe Torre and a team expected to contend for the American League pennant. During spring training the 22-year-old Jeter was competing with veteran Tony Fernandez for the starting shortstop job. When Fernandez broke his elbow a week before the season began, Jeter was named the starter and, despite some reservations about whether he was ready, he quickly became a star and the American League Rookie of the Year. As of 2009 he continues to be the Yankees shortstop, still a star of the first magnitude at the age of 35, and the Bronx Bombers' captain. He batted .334 with 18 homers, 66 RBIs, and whacked 212 hits during the season before batting .407 in the 2009 World Series. After the season, he was honored as *Sports Illustrated*'s Sportsman of the Year.

With a squeaky clean image and an almost regal demeanor on and off the field, Jeter has become a New York icon and the epitome of class at the same time. He has always been careful to steer clear of controversy to the point where he's considered a "bad" (i.e. boring) interview. His mantra is to lead by example with his clutch play and strong sense of the game, as well as an immeasurable number of those often elusive baseball "intangibles" that go far beyond the basic stats.

It's easy to put together clips for a Jeter highlight film; the only problem would be picking from the many great moments during a career that has seen the Yankees win five world championships (1996,

1998–2000, 2009). But perhaps the play that epitomizes Jeter the most was his dive into the third base stands in the 12th inning against Boston on July 1, 2004, after he raced over to make a clutch catch several feet in front of the railing. He emerged with a cut chin and bruised eye and face . . . and with the baseball in his glove. (P.S. The Yanks won in 13.)

This is a guy who can flat out play. He followed up his Rookie of the Year season with incredible consistency on a very high level, batting .349 in 1999, .339 a year later, and .343 in 2006. With 2,747 hits through the 2009 season, he is not only the Yankees' all-time hit leader (passing Lou Gehrig), but is also en route to becoming the first Bronx Bomber ever to amass more than 3,000 hits. In 2009, at the age of 35, he led all American League players in All-Star Game votes and became the oldest American Leaguer ever to start the Midsummer Classic at his position. And many say he's fielding better than ever, as he proved by exhibiting improved range to his left and winning a fifth Gold Glove, making him the oldest shortstop to ever claim that prize. There's little doubt that he'll easily find his way to Cooperstown five years after he hangs up his uniform.

Derek Jeter

A MILESTONE FOR THE CAPTAIN

Derek Jeter was honored in the summer of 2009 when he passed the legendary Lou Gehrig as the Yankees' all-time hits leader. The mark is a tribute to Jeter's talent and longevity, and before he's through he'll undoubtedly be the first Yankee ever to get 3,000 hits. Jeter is certainly in select company. Here are the top 10 all-time Yankees hit leaders (through the 2009 season).

Derek Jeter.............................2,747 hits

Lou Gehrig..............................2,721 hits

Babe Ruth...............................2,518 hits

Mickey Mantle ....2,415 hits

Bernie Williams.......................2,336 hits

Joe DiMaggio...........................2,214 hits

Don Mattingly ....2,153 hits

Yogi Berra...............................2,148 hits

Bill Dickey...............................1,969 hits

Earle Combs ....1,866 hits

On June 3, 2003, Derek Jeter was named the 11th captain of the Yankees, the first since Don Mattingly retired in 1995. For Yankees fans, it's hard not to think of their shortstop as the same enthusiastic young kid who took over the job in 1996 and immediately showed maturity far beyond his years. It's almost as if he hasn't changed. And there's little doubt that his No. 2 will hang on the wall at Monument Park someday in the future, retired alongside all of those other great Yankee numbers.

In 1969, another No. 2 was named the New York Yankees' all-time greatest third baseman. Granted, it was before the days of Graig Nettles and certainly before a guy named A-Rod, but **Red Rolfe** (1931, 1934–1942) could certainly play the game. And while this long forgotten Yankee had a relatively short career with essentially seven peak years, Red Rolfe did his uniform number proud. Rolfe graduated from Dartmouth College in 1931 and was signed by scout "White Ties" McCann for a nice bonus at the time. After pinch-running in one game in 1931, he was farmed out so that he could be converted into a third baseman. He returned in 1934 and the next year he began the seven-year run that made him a Yankees great.

Rolfe was on six pennant winners (including four World Series championships in a row from 1936–39) and usually batted in front of top hitters like Joe DiMaggio, Lou Gehrig and Bill Dickey. He led the league with 15 triples while batting .319 in 1936, hitting three homers and a double in a June 11 game that year. Then in the ensuing World Series he batted .400. Three years later he led the league in runs (139), hits (213), and doubles (46) while batting a career-high .329. Troubled by stomach ulcers and some other ills, he retired after the 1942 season at the age of 34.

The first ever No. 2 on the Yanks' history goes back to the first year of numbers, 1929. Shortstop **Mark Koenig** donned the uniform and batted second. A switch hitter who didn't have a great stick, Koening was an adequate fielder who had come to the team in 1925, making him the shortstop on the famed Murderers' Row ballclub of 1927. By 1929, Koenig was sharing the shortstop position with a pugnacious young player whose name would become part of baseball lore—Leo Durocher.

Though Koenig had hit .285, .319, and .292 between 1927 and 1929, he was hitting just .230 midway through the next season and was shipped to Detroit. By 1932, Koenig was a 27-year-old backup shortstop with the Chicago Cubs. But he took over the job for the final month or so of the season and hit a torrid .353 as the Cubbies won the National League pennant. When the team voted Koenig only a half share of their upcoming World Series check, it angered their opponents and Koenig's former team, the Yankees. Legend has it that Babe Ruth's called shot in the Series was a direct result of his ire over the way his popular former teammate was being treated. Koenig could never duplicate his Yankee days and retired in 1936 at the age of 31.

When Koenig was traded in 1930, utility infield **Yats Wuestling** wore No. 2 for his entire 25-game Yankee career, his last of two seasons in the majors. Another infielder, **Lyn Lary**, claimed the uniform in 1931 after young Red Rolfe had worn it for a single contest that year. He stayed with the Yanks until he was shipped to Boston after appearing in just one game for the Yanks in 1934. His one claim to fame as a Yankee? In

1931, he batted .280, hit 10 homers, and drove in 107 runs, most ever for a Yankee shortstop.

Between Rolfe and Jeter, a period of 53 years, uniform No. 2 was worn by a succession of players who were coming or going, wore a more memorable Yankee number, were veterans at the end of the line or utility players and stop gaps. It was quite a collection. Some made solid contributions while others slipped away almost unnoticed, and a few just didn't live up to expectations.

First, those who flip-flopped. In 1945, Frankie Crosetti and Snuffy Stirnweiss changed uniforms, the Crow going from No. 1 to No. 2 and Stirnweiss the opposite way. Bobby Murcer also wore No. 2 in his return to the Yankees in 1979 after a five-year absence, while third sacker **Graig Nettles**, who you'll read about as No. 9, had to give up that uniform in 1983 as the Yanks prepared to retire the number in the honor of Roger Maris. So Nettles also borrowed No. 2 for part of 1983, his last year as a Yankee.

Jerry Kenney came to the Yankees with great expectations. A 6'1", 170-pound third sacker, he got a cup of coffee in 1967, wearing No. 14 in a late-season, 20-game trial that saw him hit .310. When he returned from the minors two years later he was given No. 2 and became more or less the regular third baseman. That same year Bobby Murcer returned from the service to play short and was issued No. 1. Murcer, of course, eventually became a star outfielder, while Kenney slowly saw his star set.

Finally, in November of 1971 the Yanks shipped Kenney, along with three other players, for a pair of Cleveland Indians.

Next came a parade a veterans and utility players. The first was former National League batting champion **Matty Alou**, acquired before the start of the 1973 season. Alou, whose brothers Felipe and Jesus were also very good players, was a .300 lifetime hitter; the Yanks hoped, that at age 34, he could help. He played 123 games in the outfield, at first base, and as the designated hitter in the first year of its existence, and batted a solid .296. Late in the season he was sold to St. Louis, played one more year and then retired.

For the next three years, (1974–76), No. 2 belonged to **Sandy Alomar**, the father of future big leaguers Roberto and Sandy, Jr. A light-hitting infielder also in the twilight of his career, Alomar was yet another veteran who provided little but backup help as the team improved. He was part of the Yanks' pennant-winning 1976 club, but had only one at-bat in the entire postseason, after which he was traded.

Paul Blair was a different story. One of the best centerfielders in baseball, Blair had been with the Orioles for 13 years beginning in 1964. Though not a huge stick at the plate, he had a penchant for getting big hits on the biggest stage, the World Series, and his eight Gold Gloves spoke to his defensive ability. When Blair batted just .197 as a 32-year-old in 1976, the Orioles decided to move him, trading him to the Yankees.

In his two full seasons with the Yankees, Blair was a part-time centerfielder who hit .262 and then a paltry .176 in 1978. But he could still play center with the best of them and, lo and behold, he played in two more World Series. Not surprisingly, he came through again when it counted. In the '77 Series, his clutch single brought home the winning run in the 12th inning of Game One. And a year later, with the Yanks winning once more, Blair batted .375.

DALE BERRA

He was released after just two games in 1979. A year later he rejoined the Yanks as a minor league base running and fielding instructor. When the team needed a temporary outfield replacement midway through the 1980 season, Blair answered the call, donned No. 27, and played in 12 games, mostly as a defensive replacement, where he still excelled.

Others who wore No. 2 were **Darryl Jones**, **Tim Foli**, **Dale Berra**, **Wayne Tolleson**, and **Mike Gallego**. Jones played just

18 major league games for the Yanks in 1979, while Foli was a 61-game infield fill-in in 1984. Dale Berra was Yogi's kid and considered a top infield prospect when the Pirates drafted him in 1975. Berra wasn't a very good fielder, however, and after a bout with drug problems, he was traded to the Yankees in 1985. It looked like a good fit because Yogi was the team's manager that year . . . until he was fired 16 games into the season. "Boo Boo" was little more than a weak-hitting, end-of-the-bench guy during his two years in the Bronx, then played one more season in Houston before calling it quits at age 30.

Tolleson and Gallego were both utility infielders. The former played the final five years of his career (1986–90) in New York as an infield sub who hit below the Mendoza Line his final two seasons, while the latter fared somewhat better. Gallego came over to the Yanks as a free agent in 1992 after seven years at Oakland, and a year later produced the best year of his career. Playing in 119 games he hit .283 with 10 homers and 54 RBIs. But he faded after that and left as a free agent after 1994. He finished pretty much as he started, as a career utility player.

Then, in 1995, along came Derek Jeter and the real history of uniform No. 2 resumed . . . in spades.

#3: THE ONE AND ONLY BABE

ALL TIME NO. 3 ROSTER	
Player	Year
Babe Ruth	1929–34
George Selkirk	1935–42
Bud Metheny	1943–46
Roy Weatherly	1946
Eddie Bockman	1946
Frank Colman	1947
Allie Clark	1947
Cliff Mapes	1948
Retired for Ruth	1948

Was there ever anyone else who wore No. 3 with the Yankees? There are probably many fans who don't think so. That's how strongly the number is associated with the one and only **George Herman Ruth.** There are still many out there who believe the Babe to be the greatest player ever to put on a pair of spikes. The argument is simple. Besides being arguably the game's greatest slugger, the Babe was on track to become a Hall of Fame pitcher before his ability with the bat became more important than his ability to throw a fastball.

Most everyone knows the numbers—the 714 lifetime homers, the 60 he hit during the great 1927 season, the .342 lifetime batting average—and the fact that he was baseball's greatest attraction in the 1920s, the first decade after the so-called dead ball era. The Babe astounded baseball with his frequent, long, and majestic homers. He belted 54 of them in 1920, his first year with the Yankees, then followed with a 59-homer season a year later. The Yanks were still playing in the old Polo Grounds then, sharing the bathtub-shaped field with the National League Giants, but the Babe was the only show in town, hitting home runs at a pace never even imagined.

People also know that the Yanks bought the Babe from the Red Sox for the then princely sum of $125,000 prior to the 1920 season. But what they tend to forget was that Ruth was 94–46 as a pitcher before converting to the outfield. He had a pair of 20-win seasons in Boston, and was also 3–0 in a pair of World Series with a combined 0.87 ERA. And that's the reason many call him the greatest. He virtually did it all. By 1930 he was earning the mighty sum of $80,000 a year, more than the president of the United States. When asked about that, he gave his now classic answer:

Courtesy of the New York Yankees

Babe Ruth

"So what? I had a better year than he did."

Babe and New York City of the Roaring Twenties were a perfect fit, and he lived life to the hilt. His antics often drove Yankee skipper Miller Huggins nuts, and the manager once had to suspend the big guy. But the public loved the Babe and he loved to strut his stuff in front of his fans. Unlike today's sluggers, the Babe used a big, 42-ounce bat. Because he had small hands for a man his size, he'd have the handles made thinner than normal, something that might have increased what we know today as bat speed.

When he entered the 1929 season with No. 3 on the back of his uniform, he immediately became identified by that number and would continue to be forever. The on-field highlights can fill an entire book: The 60th home run on the last day of the 1927 season off Tom Zachary of Washington, the famed "called shot" home run against the Cubs in the 1932 World Series, his .625 batting average in the 1928 World Series (10-for-16 with three homers), leading the league in home runs a record 12 times, and his three home runs in one game for the Boston Braves in 1935, when he was just a shell of his former self and ready to retire. The only thing the Babe still had was his picture-perfect swing and his great power. At the time of his retirement he held an amazing 56 Major League batting records.

The Babe's biggest disappointment was never being asked to manage the team he loved, the one that played in "The House that Ruth Built." The Yankee brass knew he wanted the job, but the prevailing thinking wondered about a guy who could never manage himself . . . how in the world could he manage 25 other men? So Babe wasn't hired. Thanks to his second wife, Claire, and an astute business manager, Babe's post baseball life was comfortable. But in 1946 he was stricken with cancer and he died on August 16, 1948.

The Babe is the Babe is the Babe. Despite the proliferation of home runs in recent years (the specter of steroids and other performance enhancers notwithstanding), most people still consider Babe Ruth the game's greatest slugger. Remember, he played the first six years of his career as a pitcher during the so-called dead ball era. Some people don't realize the Babe didn't hit all of his fabled 714 home runs with the Yanks. He hit some while with the Red Sox and a few with the Boston Braves at the tail end of his career. In fact, it might be a good trivia question to ask how many the Babe belted with the Yanks. Here's the answer along with the other top Yankees home run hitters.

Babe Ruth .... 659 home runs

Mickey Mantle.............. 536 home runs

Lou Gehrig .... 493 home runs

Joe DiMaggio............... 361 home runs

Yogi Berra .... 358 home runs

Bernie Williams .... 287 home runs

Graig Nettles .... 250 home runs

Jorge Posada .... 243 home runs

Alex Rodriguez .... 238 home runs

Derek Jeter .... 224 home runs

Remember, not all of the Yankees sluggers have spent their entire career in New York. Alex Rodriguez, for example, has hit 238 homers with the Bombers, but 583 overall. And Reggie Jackson, who has 563 total homers, isn't even a blip on the Yanks' top ten list, but is remembered for his timely October blasts when he wore pinstripes.

Only 14 short years had passed between Babe leaving the Yankees and his death in 1948. That same year the Yankees retired his No. 3. But during that time, a handful of other players wore the famous number. Let's take a look at who they were.

First, let's talk about shoes. Or to be more precise, filling shoes. Imagine being issued uniform No. 3 for the Yankees in 1935, the immediate year after the mighty Babe had departed? And imagine if your nickname is "Twinkletoes" and you're following the "Bambino," "the Sultan of Swat," the one and only Babe. Well those were the shoes **George Selkirk** had to fill. The story goes that the first time he came to bat at the Stadium in 1935 wearing No. 3, the fans booed. Imagine how Twinkletoes felt?

In truth, Selkirk was a fine player who would wear No. 3 for eight years, during which time the Yankees went to six World Series and won five of them. He had a lifetime average of .290 and hit over .300 five times. He best season came in 1936 when the Yankees were led to the World Series by Lou Gehrig and a rookie named Joseph Paul DiMaggio, as Selkirk hit .308 with 18 homers and 107 RBIs. Tommy Henrich eventually replaced Selkirk in the outfield beginning in 1941, and he retired after the '42 season.

Oh, one more thing. Why Twinkletoes? The name was given him for the odd way he ran on the balls of his feet.

From 1943 to 1947 the classic No. 3 hit rock bottom. It was worn by the likes of **Bud Metheny, Roy Weatherly, Eddie Bockman, Frank Colman**, and **Allie Clark**, none of whom would come close to having a brick in monument park. Then in 1948, young outfielder **Cliff Mapes** was given No. 3. In the minors, Mapes pitched, caught, and played the outfield. Unfortunately, he didn't do any of them well enough to make a mark and his Yankee career lasted only three years and change, all as a part timer.

But Mapes only wore No. 3 during that first year. The Babe died in August, and after the season the Yankees decided to retire the number. Mapes, however, was not only the last Yankee ever to wear No. 3. He also became the first Yankees player to don uniform No. 13, pulling on that jersey before the '48 season ended. The next year, he appeared wearing No. 7, which he kept until he was sold to the St. Louis Browns 45 games into the 1951 season. Before that year had ended, a young rookie outfielder from Oklahoma was wearing the jersey. His name: Mickey Mantle. So Cliff Mapes had the distinction of wearing two numbers that would ultimately be retired. Unfortunately for him, he wasn't the retiree either time.

Let's face it. As far as the Yankees and their fans are concerned, there will always be only one No. 3. Forever. George Herman "Babe" Ruth.

#4: THE IRON HORSE. BASEBALL'S TRAGIC HERO

The Yankees' cleanup hitter on Opening Day in 1929 was a 25-year-old first baseman named **Lou Gehrig,** who was presented with jersey No. 4. When all was said and done, Henry Louis Gehrig would immortalize that number in the same way that the Babe put his stamp on No. 3. In fact, he's the only player in Yankees history to wear his number. In a twist of irony, he is almost remembered more for his tragic death from amyotrophic lateral sclerosis (Lou Gehrig's Disease) and his courageous speech at Yankee Stadium, in which he called himself "the luckiest man on the face of the earth," than for his exploits on the diamond.

But, oh, what a hitter he was. The man dubbed "The Iron Horse" for his strength and endurance played in a then record 2,130 games (since broken by Cal Ripken Jr.), was an RBI machine, and a vicious line-drive hitter who simply loved the game. As much as the Babe was

flamboyant, Gehrig the man was dull. He came to the ballpark, played great and went home. The next day he did it all over again. His wife, Eleanor, once said that her husband was just a "square, honest guy."

The square guy, however, excelled at hitting a round baseball. Just look at some of the numbers and you'll get the idea of how incredible and consistent he was. Big No. 4 had a lifetime batting average of .340. He whacked 493 home runs,

Courtesy of the New York Yankees

Lou Gehrig

hitting a high of 49 twice. Not quite Ruthian, but remember, Gehrig was a different kind of hitter. Gehrig had a compact, level swing and put a tremendous charge into the ball. To that end, he averaged 147 RBIs in his 13 full seasons and set a still-standing American League record of 184 in 1931. Three years later he won the Triple Crown with a .363 average, 49 homers, and 165 runs batted in. Gehrig went to the World Series seven times and batted .361 in the Fall Classic, with 10 homers and 35 RBIs in 34 World Series games.

That still wasn't all. He loved to scrub the bases clean and set a record that still stands with 23 career grand slams. He also amassed more than 400 total bases in a season five times. The Babe only did that twice. And to show he was no slouch in other phases of the game, he worked to make himself into a fine first baseman and he was quick enough to steal home 15 times in his career. In both 1927 and 1936, he was named the American League's Most Valuable Player.

The first sign that something might be wrong began in 1938. Lou was 35 years old, but still looked in great shape. The year before had been a typical Gehrig season, with 37 homers, 159 RBIs, and a .351 batting average. He still played every game in '38, but there was a dropoff to 39 homers, just 114 ribbies, and a .295 batting average. Those would still be considered great numbers today, but for the Iron Horse it was an off year. Age? Maybe. But he didn't seem to have the same strength. During the offseason, he became noticeably weaker, and when he had only four hits in the first eight games in 1939, he looked finished. That's when he told manager Joe McCarthy to remove him from the lineup. His consecutive game streak was over.

The shock that hit the sports world that April only grew when Gehrig's condition was finally diagnosed in June. Very few people had heard of ALS then and couldn't believe a seemingly indestructible player like Gehrig had been struck down in the prime of his life and career. "Lou Gehrig Day" on July 4, was a solemn occasion, but Gehrig's brave speech, which ended when he said, "I may have been given a bad break, but I've got an awful lot to live for," elicited huge cheers. But, unfortunately, nothing could stop the progression of his disease. That same year, he was unanimously elected to the Hall of

Fame, the usual waiting period thrown aside. At the same time, the Yankees decided that no other player would ever wear No. 4 again. So Gehrig's became the first Yankees number to be retired, some nine years before the Babe's. All those gestures were important, because Gehrig didn't survive for long. He died on June 2, 1941, a few weeks shy of his 38th birthday.

There's little doubt that Lou Gehrig was one of the greatest hitters ever. Had he not become ill his record would have been even greater. An incredible run producer, he stands fifth all time in RBIs with 1,995, and had he remained healthy, he may well have leapfrogged everyone and stood ahead of the 2,297 that has Henry Aaron in the top spot. But that's just speculation. One thing is for sure, he was more than just a home run hitter. He knocked in runs with singles, doubles and triples, as well. Believe it or not, Gehrig is the all-time Yankees leader in three-base hits, rather surprising for a guy considered a slugger and not a speed demon. By way of comparison, here are the Bombers' top 10 triple producers.

Lou Gehrig 163

Earle Combs............................ 154

Joe DiMaggio 131

Wally Pipp 121

Tony Lazzeri 115

Babe Ruth 106

Bob Meusel 87

Tommy Henrich 73

Bill Dickey 72

Mickey Mantle......................... 72

Check out the guy in fourth place. Wally Pipp was the guy who got the headache that enabled young Lou Gehrig to take over at first and begin his playing streak of 2,130 consecutive games. Since Pipp left the Yanks after 1925, he never wore a number, but he couldn't have been too shabby a player in his own right.

#5: THE YANKEE CLIPPER

ALL TIME NO. 5 ROSTER	
Player	Year
Bob Meusel	1929
Tony Lazzeri	1930–31
Frankie Crosetti	1932–36
Nolen Richardson	1935
Joe DiMaggio	1937–42, 1946–51
Nick Etten	1944–45
Retired for DiMaggio	1952

He was first in the hearts of Yankees fans and the last player to be introduced on Old Timers' Days at Yankee Stadium. In later years, as part of his introduction, he was described as the greatest living ballplayer. That was **Joseph Paul DiMaggio**. And when he emerged from the dugout the fans went wild, whether he came out wearing his pinstriped No. 5 or in a suit and tie when he was too old to play the game. He always looked great with his classic profile and well-groomed gray hair. In a sense, he was the perfect retired ballplayer just as he had been the perfect player during his Yankees days, especially those between 1936 and 1942, before he lost three seasons to the service during World War II.

What other ballplayer married the world's most glamorous movie star (Marilyn Monroe), had songs written about him ("Joltin' Joe DiMaggio" and "Mrs. Robinson"), and remained a viable commercial spokesman (Mr. Coffee) long after his playing career ended? "DiMag" didn't even play in the media-crazed world of today, but he was never far from the headlines or the public eye. And for those who don't remember him, what a ballplayer he was, the natural extension of Babe Ruth and Lou Gehrig as the Yankees resident superstar who led them to multiple pennants and World Series titles.

By 1935 the Babe was gone and Gehrig carried on as the team's leader and offensive force. But when the season ended the Yanks had only been to one World Series since 1928. That, to their loyal fans, was tantamount to sacrilege. But they wouldn't have long to wait to taste championship wine again. The team had already put dibs on a young outfielder with the San Francisco Seals of the Pacific Coast League. The Yanks bought his contract for $25,000 and five minor leaguers prior to the 1935 season. The only stipulation was that Joe D. play one more year in San Francisco. He did, and hit .398 while leading the league in RBIs and outfield assists from his centerfield position. The next year the graceful, 6'2", 190-pounder was in center for the Yankees and a new version of the dynasty was born.

DiMag was not only an immediate star, but a superstar from Day One. As a rookie in 1936, he batted .323 with 29 homers and 125 RBIs. He set rookie records with 132 runs scored and 15 triples, and also led all American League outfielders with 22 assists. Gehrig had another great year and the rejuvenated Yankees won the pennant and the World Series, the first of four straight. A year later DiMag joined baseball's elite with a .346 average, 46 homers, and 167 RBIs. Two years later, with Gehrig departed due to his fatal illness, Joe D. hit .381 and was now the leader of the Yanks. By 1941 he was a living legend. He set a record some feel will never be broken—hitting in 56 consecutive games—and won the Most Valuable Player award despite the fact that Boston's Ted Williams hit .406. (P.S. After falling short in 1940, the Yanks won the World Series yet again.)

Joe DiMaggio

Courtesy of the New York Yankees

SLUGGERS, YESTERDAY AND TODAY

One reason DiMaggio was able to put together his great hitting streaks is that he rarely struck out. Unlike modern sluggers who swing from the heels, even with two strikes, and sometimes accept a strikeout like a badge of honor, DiMag always wanted to put bat on ball. Like many of the players back then, he changed his hitting technique a bit once he had two strikes. His aim was to put the ball in play, not in the seats. As a result, he struck out only 369 times in his entire career, only eight more than his total home runs, 361. Look at some of the strikeout stats of today's sluggers, starting with all-time leader Reggie Jackson's 2,597 whiffs!

Like so many players of his generation, DiMaggio lost three peak seasons during the war years. He wasn't quite the same player when he returned, hitting just .290 and .315 his first two years back. But in 1948 he turned back the clock, batting .320 with 39 HRs and 155 RBIs, reminding everyone just how great he was. He was injured for a good part of the 1949 season, appearing in just 76 games, but hit .346 as the Yanks won yet another title. Though his average dipped to .301 the following year, he still hit 32 homers and drove in 122 runs. He was 36 years old in 1951 and wearing down rapidly. When he could manage just a .263 average in 116 games, this proud man decided to call it quits

After his retirement, he made headlines with a short-lived marriage to Hollywood sex kitten Marilyn Monroe. As for the Yankees, they didn't really skip a beat. They already had Joe's successor in center, a strong, young kid from Oklahoma named Mickey Mantle. But as great as Mickey would be, there was just one Joe DiMaggio. He played the game with style, grace, and tremendous skill, a guy who always made the tough catch look easy.

Someone once asked Joe why he played all out every single game. His answer was simple. "There might be one person in those stands seeing me play for the first time and I want him to remember me at my best."

That was "the Yankee Clipper." He was elected to the Hall of Fame in 1955. By then, the Yankees had already honored him. Shortly after his retired, the team retired No. 5. After DiMaggio, no other Yankee would ever wear that number again.

But a few Yankees had worn it before him.

There was a player who wore No. 5 for just a single season yet is the second greatest player after DiMaggio to wear the number. That's because 1929, the first year the Yanks wore numbers, was **Bob Meusel's** last with the team. But he was the number five hitter on opening day and thus given the No. 5 jersey. Meusel was a star throughout the 1920s, a lanky, 6'3" outfielder who played the game with such ease that some thought he didn't give 100 percent all the time. He joined the Yankees in 1920 and batted .328 as a rookie. A year later he hit .318

with 24 homers and 136 RBIs. In 1925, with Babe Ruth out of the lineup much of the time due to illness, Meusel led the American League with 33 home runs and 138 RBIs.

When the Yanks reeled off three straight pennants between 1926–28, Meusel was considered the third best player behind Ruth and Gehrig on Murderers' Row. All told, he had five 100-RBI seasons, hit 40 or more doubles five times, became one of only two major leaguers to hit for the cycle on three separate occasions, and even once stole second, third and home in a single game. In 1927 he hit a career best .337 with 47 doubles and 103 RBIs. When his average dipped to .261 in 1929, the year he donned No. 5, the Yankees sold his contract to the Cincinnati Reds, where he played one year before retiring at age 33.

Frank Crosetti wore No. 5 as a rookie in 1932, and kept it through the 1936 season before switching to his more familiar No. 1. In 1935, shortstop **Nolen Richardson** played 12 games with the Yanks and was given No. 5 because Crosetti wasn't with the team during that part of the season. Hall of Fame second baseman **Tony Lazzeri** wore No. 5 in 1928 and '30. Lazzeri wore No. 6 in 1929 and might have changed jerseys when he moved up in the batting order, but since he went back to No. 6, he will be discussed more in the next chapter.

The only other player to wear No. 5 was first sacker **Nick Etten,** a player who benefited from the fact that many of the game's top stars were in the service during the early to mid-1940s. Etten spent eight long years in the minors and finally found a full-time job with the Phillies in 1941 when he was 27. He surprised everyone with a .311 average, 14 homers, and 79 RBIs. Two years later, in need of players to replace those departing for the service, the Yankees traded for him, sending four marginal players and $12,000 to Philadelphia.

What's surprising is that the Yankees gave him No. 5 instead of simply holding it for the superstar DiMaggio. But apparently it was just a matter of being practical. Etten played three full years (1943–1945) at first base for the Yankees and was close to being a butcher in the field, making 17 errors one year. But he hit surprisingly well, thanks somewhat to the diluted pitching.

When DiMaggio returned in '46, Etten was given No. 9, but with many good pitchers returning from the war he hit just .232 in a part-time role. The following spring, the Phillies bought him back and when the year was over he retired. Nick Etten had his moment in the sun playing for the New York Yankees while wearing one of the most famous numbers in the team's history, but a number that ultimately belonged to and will always belong to only one man—the Yankee Clipper.

#6: FROM CLUELESS JOE TO THE LEADER OF A DYNASTY

The first Yankees player ever to wear No. 6 may still be the best of all. But to many, **Tony Lazzeri** is simply someone they may have read about as part of the Bronx Bombers history. Fans today remember the number for a manager, a guy who wore No. 6 for a dozen years, during which time the Yankees won four World Series over a five-year span, appeared in two others, and made the playoffs each year. But his stay in New York didn't begin as a honeymoon. When **Joe Torre** was unexpectedly named the Yankees' manager by owner George Steinbrenner prior to the 1996 season, the *Daily News* greeted him with a headline: CLUELESS JOE.

The play on "Shoeless Joe" Jackson referred to Torre's questionable reputation as a skipper during stops with the Mets, Braves, and Cardinals. Though there were certainly managers with worse records, the media and many others simply felt the easygoing Torre was the wrong man to manage in Steinbrenner's fishbowl, where the mantra was always the same: Win, win, win, win . . . or else. Coupled with a talented team, gamers like Derek Jeter, Paul O'Neill, and Tino Martinez, and a top-flight pitching staff—including the incredible Mariano Rivera setting up John Wetteland in the pen—the Yanks won it all in 1996, and took home three straight titles from 1998–2000. His 1998 team won 114 regular season games. In the space of five years, Clueless Joe became one of the top skippers in the game.

No one questioned Torre's baseball acumen. He was an outstanding player, close to Hall of Fame level, a catcher and third baseman who could hit. Playing with the Braves, Cardinals, and Mets—also the first

three teams he would manage—Torre had a .297 lifetime batting average from 1960–1977, hit 252 home runs, and collected 2,342 hits. His best season was in 1971, when he won the National League batting title with a .363 average for the Cards, adding 24 homers and a league-leading 137 RBIs. He was named Mets manager in 1977 when he was still on the active roster, then formally ended his playing career on June 18 of that year.

Torre's Mets teams did poorly, and he had a mark against him for giving his approval to trading the great Tom Seaver in 1977. GM Frank Cashen fired him toward the end of the 1981 season. He then skippered the Braves from 1982–1984, winning a division title his first year, but the team got worse over the next two seasons and he was fired again. After six years as an Angels broadcaster, the Cardinals hired him with 58 games left in the 1990 season. He lasted through 47 games of the 1995 season when he was handed his third pink slip. Torre's St. Louis teams played close to .500 ball but never finished better than second in the division and posted losing records his last two years. As a three-time loser, his chances of another managerial job seemed slim.

That's why it was so surprising when the Yankees came calling and why the New York tabloids jumped all over him. Imagine everyone's surprise when the team won it all. Joe Torre proved the perfect manager for the Yankees in one respect. With a flamboyant owner in George Steinbrenner, a sometimes ruthless press, and a collection of diverse personalities (especially after 2000), Torre proved a diplomatic and calming influence on the players, taking the heat and deflecting it like a sun shield, diffusing potential controversies before they affected team play, and playing the press like a maestro.

But in the end, there's no substitute for winning. The Yankees lost both the 2001 and 2003 World Series. A string of playoff failures followed, the Yankees getting bounced in the first round several times. In 2007 the Yanks were derailed by Cleveland and many felt Torre would again be fired. When the Yanks offered a one-year pact at a reduced salary (he was by this time the highest paid manager in the game) with incentives, he surprised everyone by walking away, saying he had been disrespected. No. 6 had managed the Yankees for an amazing 12 years, compiling a 1,173–767 record and taking his team to the World Series six times.

Now let's put No. 6 back in the hands of the players.

Here's a quick question to test your baseball acumen: Who was the first player ever to hit 60 home runs in a season, including the minor leagues? The quick answer, and logically so, would be Babe Ruth in 1927. Wrong. Two years earlier, a 21-year-old second baseman playing for Salt Lake City in the Pacific Coast League walloped 60 homers and drove in an incredible 222 runs. When the Yankees saw that kind of production from **Anthony Michael Lazzeri,** they immediately forked over $55,000 and five players to obtain him. (Not to cheapen his accomplishment, the only caveat was that the old PCL played an elongated, 197-game schedule back then, taking advantage of the favorable weather.) But Tony Lazzeri was the real deal. A year later he was the Yanks second baseman and he fit right into the great team that would become known as Murderers' Row a year later. As a rookie, "Poosh 'Em Up" Tony batted .275 with 18 homers and 114 RBIs.

When the 1929 season opened, Lazzeri was given No. 6 to correspond with his spot in the batting order. Strangely enough, even though he was already a star, he played the game of musical numbers for a few years. He switched to No. 5 the next two seasons, then wore No. 23 in 1932. A year later he was No. 7 before switching back to No. 6 for his final four Yankees seasons. So No. 6 he is.

Lazzeri remained a staple of the Yankees through the World Series year of 1936, a sure-handed fielder, very smart player, and productive hitter. In fact, between 1926 and 1937 (when he tailed off to a .244 batting average and only 70 RBIs) he was the seventh most prolific home run hitter in the league and ranked sixth in RBIs. On May 24, 1936, he became the first player in major league history to hit two grand slams in one game, driving in a league record 11 runs. But after the 1937 season, the future Hall of Famer was released, and over the next two seasons played sparingly for the Cubs, Dodgers, and Giants before retiring.

In the four years between 1929 and 1934, when Lazzeri reclaimed No. 6, a pair of lesser players wore the number. Part-time outfielder **Dusty Cooke** wore it the first two years, while speedy flychaser **Ben Chapman** claimed it the next two.

The Yanks have had two players named Gordon with the nickname of "Flash." The first, **Joe Gordon**, was one of the finest second baseman of his time, a guy who did No. 6 proud. Baseball finally recognized him in 2009 when the Veterans Committee elected him to the Hall of Fame, but in the late 1930s and early 1940s, Yankee fans appreciated everything Joe Gordon did.

This version of Flash came to the Yankees in 1938. The Yanks saw his talent immediately when Gordon hit 25 home runs and drove home 97 as a rookie. Not bad for someone hitting just .255. Though Gordon never hit for average, he became a power-hitting second sacker who was the equal of anyone. He would average 25 homers and 101 RBIs over the next four seasons, a perennial All-Star who became the American League's Most Valuable Player in 1942 when he hit a career best .322 with 18 homers and 103 RBIs.

After hitting just .249 in 1943, Gordon went into the service for two years. He returned to play 112 games in 1946, but hit only .210. Thinking he was starting to fade, the Yankees traded him to Cleveland for pitcher Allie Reynolds, one of those deals that turned out great for both teams. Gordon retired after the 1950 season having hit 246 of his 253 homers as a second sacker, a record for that position at that time.

During Gordon's two years in the service (1944–45), infielder **Don Savage** wore No. 6, before leaving baseball and leaving the number free for Gordon in his final year with the Bombers. Third baseman **Bobby Brown** was given the jersey in 1947 after wearing No. 7 during a brief call-up the previous year. He was a solid hitter who had close to stone hands playing third (and sometimes at short) and, for that reason, was platooned for most of his career. He shared third during these years with Billy Johnson and later Gil McDougald, but still played in four winning World Series, hitting a combined .439 in 17 games, though he didn't start them all.

Oh yes. In 1951, when Brown played 103 games, he shared his No. 6 with a Yankee rookie. His name: **Mickey Mantle**. Mickey, of course, would switch to his famed No. 7 a year later, and once Bobby Brown left the team that year, young **Andy Carey** (1952–60) took over third base, as well as No. 6. Carey, however, turned out to be adequate at best, rarely spectacular, but got to play in four World Series and was on the winning side twice.

One more thing about Andy Carey. It's said that because he had such a big appetite the Yankees stopped a longtime practice of allowing players to sign for their meals.

When Carey was dealt to Kansas City early in the 1960 season his No. 6 was given to 21-year-old infielder/outfielder **Deron Johnson**. He was looked at as a kid with power, but played just six games for the Yanks that year and 13 more in 1961 before being traded as part of the Kansas City shuttle that gave the Yanks pitchers Art Ditmar and Bud Daley. Johnson would play for a number of teams until 1976, finishing with 245 home runs.

Then along came **Clete Boyer**. The youngest of the three Boyer brothers (third baseman Ken and pitcher Cloyd were the others), Clete originally signed with Kansas City in 1955 when he was just 18 years old. He didn't play much for the Athletics over the next three years, but his fortunes were about to change. In February 1957, the Yankees made a huge deal with the A's that wound up involving 13 players. Among the players coming to the Yanks were pitchers Art Ditmar and Bobby Shantz. Then on June 4, Clete Boyer was shipped to the Bronx as a player to be named later.

In Boyer, the Yankees felt they were getting a potentially spectacular third sacker with the glove. Whatever he could contribute at the plate would be a bonus. And that's how it turned out. In 1959 and 1960,

Boyer wore No. 34 as he wrested the position from Andy Carey. He donned No. 6 in 1961and began establishing himself as one of the two flashiest third sackers in the league. The other was the Orioles' Brooks Robinson.

Boyer was part of a great Yankees infield that included shortstop Tony Kubek, second sacker Bobby Richardson, and first baseman Joe Pepitone. Boyer loved to play third and rewarded his team with often spectacular plays, diving to both his left and right to make stops and throwing runners out with a powerful arm. In 1962 he had his best offensive year with the Yanks, hitting .272 with 18 homers and 68 RBIs. He then batted .318 in the World Series that year as the Bombers defeated the San Francisco Giants in seven games.

By 1966, the latest Yankee dynasty had collapsed and the team was in a rare rebuilding mode. After the season the Yanks traded Boyer to the Atlanta Braves. Boyer took advantage of a more homer-friendly stadium and produced a season in which he hit a career high 26 round trippers and drove in 96 runs. But he still hit .245. Clete would continue with the Braves until 1971, when he retired at 34. He later became a Yankee instructor and coach, and was their third-base coach from 1992–1994.

Journeyman **Charley Smith** (1967–68) manned the hot corner and wore No. 6 for two seasons during the Yankees' down years, but his batting average never reached .230 and he was soon gone. And waiting in the wings to bring the luster back to No. 6 was **Roy White**, a 5'10", 160-pound outfielder who would spend more than a decade in pinstripes, lasting long enough to help the Yankees regain their baseball stature and return to their championship style.

White played at Compton High in Los Angeles was signed by the Yankees in 1962. He was called up for 14 games as a 21-year-old in 1965. Like most young players who might or might not make it, he was issued a high number. He would wear No. 48 for the next four years, finally becoming a regular in 1968, as the Yanks climbed above .500 for the first time in four years. White hit .267 with 17 homers and 62 RBIs that year and switched to No. 6 the following season. He was now the Yankees' leftfielder.

Maybe the best way to describe White is simply that he was solid, a very good ballplayer, the kind of guy every good team needs to complement its stars. He could almost do it all. He had occasional pop in his bat, walked a lot, could steal bases, and drive in runs. His only shortcoming was a weak throwing arm, and that's why he was usually in left. In 1970, he hit .296 with 22 homers and 94 RBIs. A year later he was at .292 with 19 homers, 84 RBIs, plus a then league record 17 sacrifice flies. He twice led the league in plate appearances, once in runs scored, and once in walks. He also had 233 steals in his career. That's the kind of player he was.

White played through some of the Yankees' lean years and was finally rewarded by being an integral part of three pennant winners (1976–78) and two World Championship teams. In 1979 he hit just .215 and was granted free agency, playing three more years in Japan.

Ken Griffey Sr., came over to the Yankees in 1982 and wore No. 6 before switching to No. 33 for his final four seasons in pinstripes. Third sacker **Mike Pagliarulo** wore No. 6 his second season with the team after wearing No. 48 as a rookie in 1984, then settled on No. 13 for the remainder of his Yankee career (1984–89). Catcher **Rick Cerone** wore it for a year in 1987, his second stint with the club. (He was No. 10 from 1980–84.) The last three players to wear it before Torre came along were all veterans whose best days were behind them.

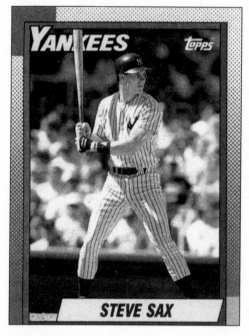

STEVE SAX

Surly slugger **Jack Clark** came to the Yanks in 1988 after productive years at San Francisco and St. Louis, put on No. 6, and hit 27 homers with 93 RBIs. But he hit just .242 and rubbed a lot of people the wrong way. He was traded after the season, along with the perennial chip-on-his-shoulder. The next year, second baseman **Steve Sax** (1989–91) was signed as a free agent after having a fine career with the Dodgers since 1981. A good hitter and top base stealer, batting .332 in 1986 and swiping as many as 56 bases in a single year, Sax had one problem with the Dodgers, the throwing disease. He often couldn't make the routine throw to first and was considered a defensive liability.

By the time he reached the Yanks and put on No. 6 he had overcome his throwing problems and produced three good seasons with New York, becoming an All-Star twice. He hit .315 his first year and .304 in the last year with the team. He also swiped 117 bases during that time and even led all AL second basemen in fielding percentage one year. Sax was just 29 when he joined the Yanks and seemed primed for a fine second career with the Yanks, but after the 1991 season the team inexplicably traded him to the White Sox for three pitching prospects, none distinguishing themselves long-term in New York.

In 1995 veteran infielder **Tony Fernandez** came to the Yankees as a free agent after a stellar career with the Toronto Blue Jays, which included being part of their 1993 title team. He was given No. 6 and the shortstop job, but managed to hit just .245 in 108 games as the Yankees made the playoffs. The next year he was competing with young Derek Jeter for the starting job when he broke his elbow and ended his Yankees career.

After Fernandez broke his elbow in the spring of 1996, the Yankees' new manager took over No. 6. If Joe Torre mends his fences in New York, the number may someday join the other retired numbers in Monument Park.

#7: THE MICK. WHO ELSE?

ALL TIME NO. 7 ROSTER	
Player	Year
Leo Durocher	1929
Ben Chapman	1930–31, 1934–36
Jack Saltzgiver	1932
Tony Lazzeri	1933
Jake Powell	1936–38
Tommy Henrich	1939–42
Roy Cullenbine	1942
Billy Johnson	1943
Oscar Grimes	1944–46
Aaron Robinson	1946
Bobby Brown	1946
Charlie Dressen (coach)	1947–48
Cliff Mapes	1949–51
Bob Cerv	1951
Mickey Mantle	1951–68
Mickey Mantle (coach)	1970
Retired for Mantle	1969

He came out of Spavinaw, Oklahoma, and acquired the nickname "The Commerce Comet" after starring in baseball and football at Commerce High School. But soon after his major league debut and, later, as his reputation grew, he came to be known simply as "The Mick." It was often said that no one ever looked better in a big league uniform than **Mickey Mantle**. A muscled 5'11", 200-pounder, the handsome, blond-haired Mantle came to the majors at the age of 19 in 1951. A switch hitter with enormous power from both sides of the plate and the fastest runner in the big leagues, he was already predicted by many to be the best ever. But while The Mick had a great Hall of Fame career, he also had a lifestyle that he later admitted probably held him back. In spite of that, he made No. 7 his own and no Yankee will ever wear it again. Nor could anyone wear it in quite the same way as Mickey Mantle.

Though Mickey came up as a shortstop, it was soon obvious that wasn't his position, especially after he committed 47 errors in just 89 games while playing for Independence in Class D ball. But when he moved up to Class C Joplin and hit .383 with 26 homers and 136 RBIs, the sky seemed the limit. "He should lead the league in everything," Yankees manager Casey Stengel said before the 1951 season. "With his combination of speed and power he should win the triple batting crown every year. In fact, he should do everything he wants to do."

Talk about great expectations. Now an outfielder, the Mick had to play right field his rookie season because the great Joe DiMaggio was in his final year as the Yankees' center fielder. In the World Series that

Courtesy of the New York Yankees

Mickey Mantle

year he tore the cartilage in his knee when he tripped over a drainpipe in the outfield, the first of many injuries that would hamper his career.

The first years weren't easy. The fans weren't always on his side. But that stopped for good in 1956 when the Mick went from very good to great. He fulfilled Stengel's prophecy that year by winning the Triple Crown with a .353 batting average, 52 home runs, and 130 runs batted in. A year later he hit .365 with 34 homers and 94 RBIs, his power production down somewhat because pitchers walked him a league high 146 times. He was the American League's Most Valuable Player both years.

Mickey was playing with great Yankees teams that seemed to be in the World Series every year and was a bona fide superstar at the age of 25. He also became fast friends with teammates Whitey Ford and Billy Martin, and the trio spent many a night on the town sampling the best watering holes that New York City had to offer. Martin was traded after the much-publicized brawl at the Copacabana in 1957, but Mickey's habits didn't change. His father, uncle, and other male members of his family had died of cancer before the age of 40, which gave Mickey a kind of fatalistic view of life. He was going to live every minute, no matter what.

He had a beautifully long swing that made his misses almost as impressive as his hits. The fans simply couldn't take their eyes off him, especially when he hit those long, tape-measure home runs. On May 23, 1963, he slammed one lefthanded that came within a foot of being the first fair ball ever hit out of Yankee Stadium. It hit about a foot below the top of the facade over the third deck. Experts estimated that if unimpeded, the ball would have traveled some 602 feet.

Then there was the 1961 season. Within a couple of months of the beginning, it became obvious that both Mickey and Roger Maris were engaged in a home run race the likes of which hadn't been seen in years. By midseason everyone knew that both sluggers had a chance to top the coveted record of 60 set by the one and only Babe. Maris was relatively new to New York and had a hard time handling the press and fans. He just wasn't outgoing. The Mick had his "aw shucks" charm and a decade of dealing with both the good and bad. And as the season continued to unfold, the fans began openly rooting for Mantle. After all, he was the true Yankee, the guy who descended from Ruth, Gehrig, and DiMaggio. Maris was the outsider who hadn't earned the right to break the record.

In the end, it was Maris who did it, hitting No. 61 on the final day of the season. As for Mickey, he was on the bench. He had developed a bad cold in September and then an abscessed hip that landed him in the hospital. He wound up playing eight fewer games than Maris and had 76 fewer at-bats. He still finished with 54 homers, 128 RBIs, and a .317

batting average. Maris had 142 ribbies to go with his 61 homers, and while he hit just .269 he won a second MVP Award.

It was a great season for both sluggers, but by finishing second, the Mick had found his way into the hearts of all Yankees fans. For the remainder of his career, he would be greeted by cheers and ovations almost every time he came to the plate. Though the Mick was not yet 30 years old at the end of the 1961 season, he would have just two more big years. In 1962, he had 30 homers and 89 ribbies, hitting .321 while playing in just 123 games. Yet he was given a third Most Valuable Player Award. A year later he broke his ankle in June and was able to play in just 65 games. Then in 1964 he bounced back with a .303, 35- HR, 111-RBI season as the Yanks went to their fifth straight World Series. It would be his last .300 season, and he'd never hit more than 23 homers or drive in more than 56 runs again. The injuries just kept getting worse.

Mickey really struggled in 1967 and '68. The Yanks even played him at first base because he couldn't cut it in center anymore. He hit just .245 and .237 those final two years, dropping his lifetime average below .300 to .298, something that really hurt him. Finally, just after the start of spring training in 1969, Mickey Mantle called it quits.

A great career had ended, one that produced 536 home runs and saw him retire as the greatest switch hitter in baseball history. In his latter years he became even more of a beloved figure. He talked to kids about the dangers of drug and alcohol abuse and in 1994 made news when he received a liver transplant. Sadly, doctors then found a cancerous tumor. Despite a valiant fight, Mickey Mantle died on August 13, 1995, at the age of 63.

Since his death, the Mick's legend has grown. His No. 7 was retired in 1969 and five years later he was elected to the Hall of Fame. But his was certainly a star-crossed career. Take away the many injuries and the late-night carousing and people still wonder what could have been. Those who saw him in his prime—beating out a drag bunt with his great speed, hitting long, majestic home runs from both sides of the plate, chasing down fly balls in the vast expanse of Yankee Stadium— will never forget him. And, yes, no one ever looked better in a baseball uniform than Mickey Mantle, No. 7 forever.

MICKEY'S DREAM

No one loved playing baseball for the Yankees more than Mickey Mantle. He hated to give it up, but hated not being Mickey Mantle on the field even more. Years later, Mickey told people about a recurring dream. He'd be outside Yankee stadium and hear his name announced by Bob Sheppard. "Now batting, No. 7, Mickey Mantle. No. 7." The problem was Mickey couldn't find a way into the Stadium. He tried and tried, but the doors were always locked. It's apparent what Mantle wanted, one more at bat, one more chance to hit one of his majestic home runs and to hear the roar of the crowd as he circled the bases.

It's not easy to go past the Mick when discussing No. 7. But like most other immortal Yankees numbers, there were those who came before or after. In the case of No. 7, the first guy to wear it would make a great trivia question. When the Yankees took the field in 1929 with new, fresh numbers on their backs, the shortstop who was batting seventh was none other than **Leo Durocher**. Yep, the same Leo who later became know as "The Lip" during a controversial, tempestuous, and ultimately successful managing career that saw him wind up in the Hall of Fame.

As a player, Durocher was a good-field, no-hit shortstop who was signed by Paul Krichell, the same scout who inked Gehrig. Leo got a two-game taste of the big leagues in 1925, then didn't return until 1928 when he played in 102 games and batted .270 without a single home run. The next year he was again the starting shortstop and issued No. 7. He would end up playing in just 106 games and hit .246 without a homer. The Murderers' Row veterans teased him mercilessly. Ruth called him "the All-American out" and Leo being Leo, he fought back. The next year, he was dealt to Cincinnati and his Yankee career was over but, as everyone knows, Leo Durocher was far from finished in baseball.

In the early years after the advent of numbers, players often switched several times as teams tried to continue corresponding uniform numbers to the batting order. That's why, for example, **Tony Lazzeri** began as No. 6, switched to No. 5 for a couple of years, moved to No. 7 one year, and then went back to No. 6 again. Ruth and Gehrig never switched spots in the order, but many of the others did. Thus **Ben Chapman** started his Yankees career (1930–36) as No. 7 in 1930, two years later donned No. 6 for a couple of seasons, then switched back to No. 7 until he was traded.

Chapman started out as an infielder but in 1931 was moved to left field and immediately became a Bronx Bomber. He batted .315, hit 17 homers, and drove in 122 runs. On top of that, he led the American League in steals with 61. Solid production. He would be the league's top base thief for the next two seasons, though his power production dropped each year. Ben Chapman's Yankees career ended suddenly on June 13, 1936, when he was traded to the Washington Senators for outfielder Jake Powell, who was expected to supply more power. He didn't. Chapman hit .332 the remainder of the season with Washington, played until 1946, and retired with a .302 lifetime average.

As for **Jake Powell,** he took over No. 7 but didn't exactly do it proud. Showing promise by hitting .302 in 87 games with seven homers after coming over from Washington, he went into a three-year funk that saw him never hit over .263, and never top three home runs or 45 RBIs. The Yanks rid themselves of Powell after the 1940 season, selling his contract to San Francisco of the PCL.

Outfielder **Tommy Henrich** was signed by the Yankees in April 1937 for $25,000 as the Bombers outbid seven other teams for his services. Henrich wore both Nos. 37 and 22 that year and hit .320 in 67 games.

Though he never became a huge star, he was a steady performer who could be counted on in the clutch. It was Yankee announcer Mel Allen who gave him the nickname "Old Reliable," and he became a fixture in the outfield. In his second year, he wore No. 17, and in 1939 was given No. 7, which he wore until he entered the Coast Guard following the 1942 season. When he returned in 1946 his number was occupied and the Yanks gave him No. 15, which he wore until his retirement after 1950.

A .282 lifetime hitter, Henrich's best year was 1948, when he hit .308 with 25 homers and 100 RBIs. Rather than being remembered for his numbers, he's known as a guy who helped the Yanks win four World Series with his steady, clutch play.

A parade of part timers, short termers, and players who wore several numbers had a chance to wear No. 7. All before Mantle, of course. Infielder **Jack Saltzgaver** wore No. 7 in 1932 but was given No. 12 when he returned from the minors two years later. **Roy Cullenbine** donned the jersey for just 21 games in 1942, while third sacker **Billy Johnson** had it for a year in 1943. Johnson would return after the war and play from 1946–1951 wearing No. 24. Infielder **Oscar Grimes** wore No. 12 in 1943, then alternated between No. 8, No. 7, and No. 8 again from 1945–1947. Third sacker Bobby Brown was No. 7 in 1946 before changing to No. 6 for the rest of his Yankees career, and outfielder Cliff Mapes wore it for three undistinguished years. Young slugger **Bob Cerv** was given No. 7 for 12 games in 1951. He would wear Nos. 41 and 17 between 1952 and 1956, and between 1960 and 1962. The reason he gave up No. 7 was simple. Mickey Mantle was there to stay.

#8: A PAIR OF HALL OF FAME CATCHERS

In baseball's earlier days, catchers were always bruised and battered. They didn't have the advantage of the hinged mitt and had to catch with both hands. Most of them wound up with broken and gnarled fingers on their bare hands. Then there were those sometimes bone-crushing collisions at home plate.

Back then, only a handful of catchers were considered truly great. You could almost count them on the fingers of one hand. Well, the New York Yankees had two, and because their careers virtually overlapped, the Bronx Bombers had an all-time great behind the plate almost continuously from 1929 into the early 1960s. And they wore the name number, now retired, making the Yankees the only team to retire a number in honor of two players. **Bill Dickey** and **Yogi Berra** each wore No. 8, put up great numbers, did yeoman service behind the dish, and played in a ton of World Series with great Yankees teams.

William Malcolm Dickey doesn't sound like a rough-and-tumble catcher from baseball's early days, but he was as tough as he had to be to survive and thrive. Dickey played with the Yanks from 1928–1943, then returned after the war for one more season in 1946, when part of his job was to tutor the rookie Berra. During his playing days Dickey excelled. He then took over the catching job shortly after the start of the season the first year of numbers. Because **Johnny Grabowski** was the starter on Opening Day, he was given No. 8. Dickey wore No. 10 that year. Grabowski hit just .203 before losing the job to the 22-year-old Dickey, who promptly became an integral part of the team, batting .324 with 10 homers and 65 RBIs. In 1930, Grabowski was gone and Dickey inherited the number.

Dickey would go on to bat over .300 in 11 seasons, with a high of .362 in 1936, when he added 22 homers and 107 RBIs. The next year, he

Courtesy of the New York Yankees

Yogi Berra

hit .332 with 29 homers and 133 RBIs. In fact, the Yanks would win four straight World Series between 1936 and '39; Dickey batted over .300, hit more than 20 homers, and drove in over 100 runs in each of those seasons. At 6'2" and 185 pounds, he was unusually tall and thin for a catcher back then, but he became an adept handler of pitchers and a guy who made the difficult job of catching look easy.

The '43 Series was a memorable one for Dickey, who belted a key two-run homer off the Cards' Mort Cooper in Game Five to break a scoreless tie and give the Yanks a win. He was 36 years old then, but still good enough to hit .351 in 85 games. Following the season, he went into the Navy for two years. When he returned he still caught 59 games at the age of 39. He also did double-duty as he replaced Joe McCarthy as manager that May. It wasn't a good year for the Yanks and after the season he was released from both jobs.

Dickey later scouted and was a long-time first base coach for the Yanks. When he returned to coach, he wore No. 33 and kept that number until he left for good after the 1960 season. He was elected to the Hall of Fame in 1954, having retired with a .313 lifetime batting average, 202 home runs, and all that great work behind the plate.

While Dickey's playing days were coming to an end in 1946, 21-year-old Lawrence Peter Berra was just getting started. Born in St. Louis, Berra got his nickname from Bobby Hofman, a boyhood friend and future big leaguer, who saw a movie about an Indian snake-charmer—a "yogi"—that he thought walked like his friend. It was a nickname for life.

The Yankees ultimately signed him for the princely sum of $500. But Yogi enlisted in the Navy when he was 18 and didn't return until 1946, when he began the season with the New London team in the minors. After a seven-game trial with the big club in 1946 (in which he wore No. 38), Yogi returned and caught 83 games the next year, this time donning No. 35. When he hit a solid .280 with 11 homers and 54 RBIs, the Yanks knew they had the right guy. A year later he was given Dickey's old number, 8, and his Yankees career began in earnest. At 5'8", 194 pounds, Yogi looked like the typical catcher. He soon became an outstanding catcher and handler of pitchers. At the plate he was a free swinger, often going after pitches out of the strike zone. But more often than not, he hit them, rarely striking out. In 1950, he whiffed just 12 times in 597 at bats. He also hit .322 that year with 28 homers and 124 RBIs. He was also the last guy opposing teams wanted to see swinging the lumber in a clutch situation.

Yogi was selected to the All-Star team for 15 straight years. He played on 14 pennant winners, was on the winning side in the World Series 10 times, and holds the record for hits in World Series competition with 71. He was named the American League's Most Valuable Player in 1951, 1954, and again in 1955.

Courtesy of the New York Yankees

Bill Dickey

In 1955, the Yankees brought up Elston Howard, their first African-American player and a fine catcher in his own right. Manager Casey Stengel often wanted both his catchers in the lineup at the same time. The only way to do that was to play one out of position. Thus both Howard and Yogi began seeing time in the outfield, a way of saving their legs from squatting down dozens of times every single day. By 1960 Yogi was playing the outfield as much as catching, and soon was playing it more. He was only an adequate outfielder, but the team was willing to make the tradeoff. They even had a third catcher then, John Blanchard, so all of them split playing time and through it all Yogi continued to hit.

He was part of the great 1961 team that set a record with 240 home runs, still good enough to hit 22 of his own, but it would be his last big year. His final season was 1963. At age 38, he played in just 64 games but managed to hit .293. Yogi was still dangerous with a bat in his hands. A year later, fans got a surprise when Manager Ralph Houk became the team's general manager and Yogi got the job of field boss. He skippered the Yanks to yet another pennant, but after the team lost to the Cards in the World Series Berra was dismissed.

THE HARMONICA INCIDENT

When Yogi Berra was fired after the 1964 season, word was that he couldn't control the players because he had been a teammate to most of them. Critics pointed to the infamous "harmonica incident" in which young infielder Phil Linz began playing "Mary Had a Little Lamb" on the harmonica as the team rode the bus to the airport after they had lost four straight to the White Sox. Yogi told him to stop, but Linz didn't hear him. He looked at Mickey Mantle who, with a twinkle in his eye, told Linz that Yogi had said play to louder. That's what Linz did and an enraged Yogi raced to the back of bus and knocked the harmonica from Linz's hand. It was a rare show of temper from Yogi and might have sealed his fate as manager of the Yankees.

So he was gone, but not for long. The newly formed Mets, in just their fourth season, hired Yogi as a player/coach in 1965. He appeared in just four games as a player and had a pair of singles in nine at-bats. Then his playing days ended for good, but not before he compiled a .285 batting average and swatted a then record 358 home runs for a catcher. He later managed the Mets to a pennant in 1973 and was hired by George Steinbrenner to skipper the Yanks again in 1984. He led them to a third-place finish and was fired again just 16 games into the 1985 season. That began a 13-year period of estrangement between Yogi and the Yanks, until he and Steinbrenner mended fences in 1998. He finally returned to the Stadium to throw out the first pitch of the 1999 season and has been a fixture there ever since.

In 1972, Yogi was elected to the Hall of Fame, and that same year the Yankees decided to retire the number, in honor of not only Yogi, but Bill Dickey as well. Those two guys could catch with anyone.

The only other players to wear No. 8 were **Johnny Lindell** in 1944 and '45, but he would be better known for wearing No. 27; **Aaron Robinson** in 1945 and '47; and **Frank Colman** briefly in 1946. No. 8 really seems to be a catcher's number, but only Robinson qualifies. He was a backup for several years and also wore No. 25 in 1943 and No. 7 in 1946.

#9: ROGER MARIS. A LONG TIME COMING

For **Roger Maris** it was never about the glory. A modest, small town guy from North Dakota, Maris had no aspirations beyond being a solid baseball player and earning a steady living for his family. That became impossible in 1961, when Maris and teammate Mickey Mantle began to make a run at one of baseball's most cherished records, the Babe's 60 home runs, set back in 1927. The fact that both sluggers played for the New York Yankees made the chase even more prominent and it became a national story. The closer Maris came, the more difficult it became for him as the media descended upon him like an ominous cloud. Suddenly, the guy who just wanted to be left alone and play baseball was sitting smack in the middle of the world's biggest fishbowl.

Prior to 1960, it looked as if Maris would get his wish. He signed with Cleveland at the age of 18 in 1953 and made it to the majors four years later. Early in 1957, he was leading the league in homers and RBIs, but he broke three ribs sliding and wound up his rookie season hitting .235, with 14 HRs and 51 RBIs. In June 1958, he was traded to Kansas City, and finished the year with a .240 average, 28 home runs, and 80 RBIs. It was almost the kind of season he envisioned. An appendectomy the next year limited him to 122 games—and then his life changed. On December 11, Maris was traded to the Yankees in a swap of seven players. And when the 1960 season opened, he was the starting right fielder on the best team in baseball. He was also given No. 9, which had previously been worn by Hank Bauer, one of the players who had gone to Kansas City.

In his first game, Roger belted a pair of homers to go with a single and double, and he was off to the races. He soon found the short right field porch at Yankee Stadium to his liking and finished the season with a .283 average, 39 home runs, and a league-best 112 RBIs. Though Mantle won the home run crown with 40, Maris was named the American League MVP. He was no longer an average player—he was a star—and the stage was set for 1961.

Once it became apparent that two Yankee sluggers had a shot at Ruth's record, the fans in New York made a shift. The majority began openly pulling for Mantle, the homegrown Yankee, the heir apparent to Ruth, Gehrig, and DiMaggio. In the second half of the season, there was often open hostility toward Maris. It not only hurt him, it caused him an increasing amount of stress, so much so that his hair actually began falling out in clumps. The pursuit of a great record was becoming a nightmare for Roger Maris.

ROGER MARIS
Outfield
New York Yankees

The pressure increased in September when Mantle went out of the lineup with a hip abscess and suddenly Maris was alone. Maris had 58 home runs when the team took the field in Baltimore to play its 154th game. That night he would hit his 59th, but because it was the first year of the 162-game he went on to break the record later in the season, hitting his 61st in the final game, prompting Commissioner Ford Frick to threaten putting an asterisk next to his record.

His final numbers read .269, 61 and a league-best 142 RBIs. Once again he was the league's MVP and the Yanks won the World Series. But critics quickly decided that Mantle's line of .317, 54, 128 was better because the Mick had hit 48 points higher than Maris. He just couldn't win.

Unfortunately, Roger Maris wouldn't go on to further Yankee glory and couldn't seal his legacy. He had a good 1962 as the Yanks won again, batting .256 with 33 homers and 100 RBIs, but then the injuries started and his power numbers began dropping. A wrist injury curtailed his production and the fans booed, not realizing he was playing with a broken hand in 1966. That winter he was traded to the Cardinals for a journeyman infielder named Charley Smith. That's how far his value had diminished.

Maris had two steady, though far from spectacular years with the Cards, playing right field and helping his team reach a pair of World Series, the sixth and seventh of his career. After 1968 he retired. In appreciation of his contributions to his new team, owner Gussie Busch set him up with a profitable beer distributorship in Florida. So Maris was done, holder of a great record that many people still didn't even recognize as legitimate.

Some tend to overlook that in addition to his power, Maris was an outstanding fielder with a strong throwing arm, as well as a fine baserunner. He excelled in all phases of the game. The Roger Maris story had a bittersweet ending. He finally mended fences with the Yankees and began going back to Old Timers' Days. In 1984, the Yankees finally made the most appropriate gesture they could to a man who never really got his due, retiring No. 9 in his honor. It didn't come too soon. A year later, Roger Maris died from lymphatic cancer.

Only three other significant Yankees who wore No. 9 between 1929 and its retirement in 1984. Otherwise, the number bounced between one player and another, some wearing it until they received a more permanent numeral. Career backup catcher **Benny Bengough** was the first to wear it, since he was the Opening Day catcher in 1929. The next year he wore No. 10, his final season in pinstripes. Between 1930 and 1933, **Bubbles Hargrave, Cy Perkins, Art Jorgens**, and **Joe Glenn** all took the field wearing No. 9. Bubbles, he of the unusual nickname, was a part-time catcher who finished his career with the Yanks in 1930, while Perkins, another part-time backstop, saw action in just 16 games in 1931. Joe "Gabby" Glenn, the third of this trio of backup backstops, hung around six years, never playing in more than 45 games in any one season.

Arndt Ludwig Jorgens was —guess what?—a backup catcher. Jorgens had an undistinguished 11-year career with the Yanks lasting from 1929–39; his biggest claim to fame could be that he was baseball's first player born in Norway. He also played musical numbers, starting with No. 15 in 1929, wearing No. 28 a year later, and No. 10 the year after that. He wore No. 9 for four years (1932–35), then doubled it and donned No. 18 for his last four. In 11 years, Jorgens hit the grand total of four home runs and drove home just 89 runs.

Joe D. wore the number as a rookie in 1936 before getting his classic No. 5, and for two years after that No. 9 was worn by **Myril Hoag**. Hoag also wore Nos. 27 and 28 before his final two seasons.

Then in 1939, along came "King Kong." No, it wasn't the famous movie starring Fay Wray and a mechanical ape. That *King Kong* debuted in 1933. This one was only 5'10" and weighed 190 pounds. Real name: **Charlie Keller.** He debuted with the Yanks in 1939, put on uniform No. 9, and became a star. The 22-year-old played right field alongside DiMaggio in center and in hailing distance of George Selkirk in left, and he promptly hit .334 with 11 homers and 83 RBIs in just 111 games. He then batted .438 (7-for-16) in a World Series sweep of the Reds, slamming three homers, a double, and a triple, and driving home six runs. Some rookie. It was his great strength that resulted in his rather ignominious nickname. The press loved it, but Keller didn't, and he seldom would answer if someone addressed him with it.

Nevertheless, Keller's powerful lefty swing was deemed just right for the Stadium's short right field porch and he was told to try to pull the ball more to get his power numbers even higher. He belted 21 homers and drove home 93 runs in 1940. He also had 15 triples and led the league with 106 walks while still batting a respectable .286. The next year, Tommy Henrich joined the outfield in right. Keller moved to left. All three outfielders topped the 30-home run mark, making them the first trio of American Leaguers to do that. Keller had 33 of them and

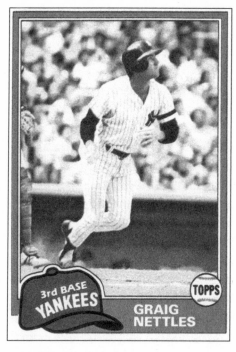

GRAIG
NETTLES

drove home 122 to go with a .298 batting average.

King Kong continued to play at a high level through 1943, when, like so many other ballplayers, his career was interrupted by the war. He joined the Navy and didn't return until late in the 1945 season.

Something else was new when he took the field. His uniform had No. 12 on the back and he would wear it for the remainder of his Yankee career, though he did return to No. 9 briefly for part of his final Yankee season of 1949.

The Yanks released him after the 1949 season. He then played two years in Detroit, then returned to the Yanks briefly in 1952. But he played in just two games and fanned in his only at-bat. For that final, short cameo appearance in pinstripes, King Kong Keller donned No. 28 and then No. 99.

In the nine seasons between Charlie Keller leaving for the Navy in 1943 to **Hank Bauer** donning the number in 1952, the jersey almost became a throwaway with 11 different players appearing with No. 9 on their backs. In 1944, three players wore No. 9 during the course of the season. **Ed Levy**, an outfielder/first baseman, had played 13 games for the club in 1942 and wore No. 17. He returned in '44 for 40 more games and was given uniform No. 9. In June, Levy was traded to Milwaukee of the American Association for ourfielder **Hersh Martin**, who took over the number and wore it for two years. Martin would hit .307 with 9 homers and 47 RBIs in 85 games during 1944. He played in 117 games in '45, then was gone.

Tuck Stainback was another veteran player who spent the war years with the Bombers. His first two years (1942–43) he wore No. 16, then saw action in 30 games with No. 9—the third player to wear it—in 1944. In his final season with the team he wore No. 18 and managed just five homers in 95 games. In 1946, Aaron Robinson and Nick Etten both saw time in uniform No. 9. Robinson also wore Nos. 7 & 8 the two previous seasons, while Etten had worn No. 5 from 1943–45, then had to return that one to Joe DiMaggio.

George McQuinn was a veteran first sacker who came to the Yanks at age 37 in 1947. It took a while since McQuinn was originally in the Yankees farm system and finally became established with the old St. Louis Browns in 1938, when he was 28 and began forging a solid career. Despite his age, he wore No. 9 proudly (after starting the '47 season as No. 51 briefly), putting together two All-Star years in what would be the final seasons of his career. In his final season, he played in just 94 games, still made the All-Star team, and set a then record by recording 14 putouts at first base.

Charlie Keller revisited his old No. 9 for a year in 1949, and third sacker Bobby Brown wore it in 1951 when rookie Mickey Mantle wore his No. 6 for part of the season. **Dick Wakefield** and **Hank Workman** both wore No. 9 in 1950 and **Jim Brideweser** took it over for part of 1951. Wakefield would play just three games for the Yanks while Workman played just two. Infielder Brideweser was with the Yanks in a limited role from 1951–53. He wore No. 27 the final two years. In 1953, Brideweser came to bat just three times . . . and had three hits, giving him a perfect 1.000 average for the season.

Finally, No. 9 got some stability when **Hank Bauer** took it over in 1952. Bauer had joined the Yanks in 1948, wearing No. 25 during his first four Yankee seasons. Once he became an established star, he was given No. 9. Either way, Bauer was a tough, uncompromising player, a former Marine who had fought on Okinawa and not a man to be trifled with. If he saw a teammate loafing he'd growl, in that raspy voice, "Don't mess with my money." He was used to those Yankees World Series checks (he'd eventually cash nine of them) and expected to get one every year.

Bauer was a strong hitter with power, though he often batted leadoff, and had 18 home runs leading off games in his career. He was also a three-time All-Star (1952–54), a good outfielder with a strong throwing arm. Playing in the Casey Stengel era, Bauer was often platooned with lefty swingers Gene Woodling and Enos Slaughter, among others, something that made the former Marine chafe.

Hank was a .277 lifetime hitter with 164 homers. In 1950, he hit .320 with 13 homers and 70 RBIs in just 113 games. His best power year was 1956, when he clubbed 26 and drove home 84 in 147 games. In his final World Series in 1958, Bauer hit .323 with 4 homers and 8 RBIs. He also completed a record 17-game World Series hitting streak that began in the '56 Series and lasted through '58. In December 1959, Bauer was part of the deal with Kansas City that brought Roger Maris to the Yanks. Maris inherited Hank's No. 9 and Bauer finished his career with two years at KC. He later managed the A's and Orioles, skippering the Birds to a World Series title in 1966, as the former Marine got to cash yet another October check.

Steve Whitaker was a good-looking young outfielder who came to the Yanks in 1966, when the team had crashed. He was given No. 28 and

HANK BAUER

played in 31 games. A year later he was in 122 and hit just .243 with 11 homers. The team gave him No. 9 in 1968, maybe hoping it would inspire him. It didn't. He hit a paltry .117 and was gone. A year later, in 1969, outfielder **Dick Simpson** joined the team and lasted all of six games, three fewer than the number on his back. Before the year ended, No. 9 was passed along to outfielder **Ron Woods** (1969–71), who came over from Detroit in a trade for the once-promising Tom Tresh.

Woods was yet another jour-neyman who stayed with the team

for three years. In June 1971, he was traded to Montreal in exchange for former Mets hero Ron Swoboda. But it was time for No. 9 to regain some of its lost glory.

The Yankees made a November trade in 1973 with the Cleveland Indians, giving up four prospects in return for backup catcher Jerry Moses and third sacker **Graig Nettles**. It was the 28-year-old Nettles that they really wanted. He had played the outfield, first, and third when he was a part timer at Minnesota for three years. In his three seasons with the Indians he had settled in at third and shown some pop in his bat, though he never hit for average. In 1971, he slammed 28 homers and drove home 86 while hitting just .261. When his numbers dropped a year later, Cleveland deemed him expendable and, in all honesty, the Yankees didn't know quite what they were getting.

They didn't know that Nettles would turn into an All-Star and one of the cornerstones of the Bronx Zoo championship teams of the late 1970s. He would also become one of the most spectacular fielding third baseman ever to come down the pike. As it turned out, Nettles was a guy who loved the pressure of a pennant race and the post-season. He had great balance and lightning-quick reflexes, often diving to make brilliant stops, then righting himself to throw out the runner with his strong arm. His play brought constant comparisons with the great Brooks Robinson, widely considered the best fielding third baseman of all-time. Though he would never hit for average, his southpaw swing was tailor-made for Yankee Stadium and he would hit 20 or more homers in each of his first seven seasons in pinstripes.

Nettles was at his best in the pennant-winning years from 1976–78. His batting averages were just .254, .255, and a career high .276. But he hit 32 homers to lead the league in '76, following it up with 37 and 27 the next two years. He also drove home 93, 107, and 93 runs in those three years, was an All-Star each time (six in his career), and became the best fielding third baseman in the league.

By 1983 the Yanks weren't contenders and Nettles was 38 years old. He was coming off a .266, 20, 75 season and the Yanks decided to move him while he still had value. They sent him to San Diego for pitcher Dennis Rasmussen, and Nettles promptly became part of another pennant winner in '84. He would finish his career in Montreal in 1988 at the age of 43, the author of 390 career home runs and countless great plays at third base. His 11 seasons in pinstripes made him a true Yankee and the last player ever to wear No. 9. One year after he left, the number was retired in honor of Roger Maris.

#10: SCOOTER

They told him he was too small, but he wouldn't listen. When they suggested he go home and forget baseball, he just sucked it up and tried harder. In the end, he wound up being an All-Star, a Most Valuable Player, a World Series winner seven times over and, finally, a Hall of Famer . . . not to mention a beloved broadcaster and New York Yankees icon. That was **Phil "Scooter" Rizzuto**, the diminutive shortstop with the big heart and valuable member of the great Yankees teams of the 1940s and '50s. He went directly from the playing field to the broadcast booth in 1956 and remained for another 40 years.

Rizzuto first joined the Yankees in 1941 after being named Minor League Player of the Year the season before. Frank Crosetti was winding down as the Yankees' shortstop, so the Scooter's timing was perfect. He was issued uniform No. 10, a jersey that really hadn't been worn by any of the team's stars before; he kept it his entire career. Just 5'6" and 160 pounds soaking wet, Rizzuto had been sent home from several tryouts while in his teens. He was finally signed by the Yanks prior to the 1937 season when he was 20 years old. Four years later, he was standing out at shortstop at massive Yankee Stadium.

He was never a great hitter, though he batted .307 as a rookie and .324 in his MVP season of 1950, but it was his glove and leadership that made him such an integral part of those powerful Yankee teams. There's little doubt about Rizzuto's fielding prowess. He led the league in double plays three times and was the leader in total chances per game on three occasions. He was also tops in fielding percentage on two occasions and played errorless ball in 21 consecutive World Series games. From 1949 to 1952, *The Sporting News* named Rizzuto the top shortstop in the majors. Offensively, the Scooter had just a .273 lifetime average with 38 career homers. But he was a master bunter, using it as a weapon to get a base hit, execute the sacrifice, or engineer the squeeze.

In 1950, he put it all together with a .324 season in which he had 200 hits, a career-best 7 home runs, and 66 RBIs. The Yanks won another pennant and swept the Phillies in the World Series. For his efforts, Phil Rizzuto was named the American League's Most Valuable Player.

By 1954 the Scooter had really slowed down, hitting just .195. He was a part timer after that, and on August 25, 1956, which was Old Timers' Day, he was suddenly released. To soften the blow, the team offered Scooter a broadcasting job. He was a complete novice at a time when not many former players sat alongside professionally trained announcers. But he turned out to be the perfect foil for pros like Mel Allen and Red Barber, and as the years passed, his unique, almost childlike way of calling games won over listeners. He slowly became a broadcasting fixture in the Bronx.

A SCOOTER ALL HIS OWN

Phil Rizzuto was far from the prototype baseball announcer. He was often a show all his own with a style to match, and the fans loved him. Anyone listening to the Scooter heard his trademark "Holy cow!," his wishing happy birthdays to friends, calling hot dogging players "huckleberries," talking about his wife, Cora, and his family, and discussing food and eating cannolis in the booth that fans would send up to him. He'd sometimes miss plays and joke that he was going to put a "ww" in his score book. That meant *wasn't watching*. He also had a genuine fear of thunderstorms and would run for cover when they sprung up. When the boomers began overhead, he couldn't be found in the booth. In later years, he would leave the game in about the sixth inning to beat the traffic driving home. The remaining broadcasters would kid about the Scooter driving over the George Washington Bridge, especially if the big play unfolded late. But he became an institution and fans never wanted him to leave. He finally retired in 1996 after some 40 years behind the mike, still upset that he was ordered to broadcast a game instead of attending Mickey Mantle's funeral. But he was also 80 years old by then, so it was time.

PHIL RIZZUTO

shortstop NEW YORK YANKEES

Then there was the Hall of Fame. For years, Scooter and Brooklyn Dodgers shortstop Pee Wee Reese were two of the best in the game and compared with one another. Both were excellent fielders and team leaders. And while Reese had just a .269 lifetime average, all his power numbers were better than Rizzuto's. Reese was elected to the Hall of Fame in 1984. A year later the Yankees honored the Scooter by retiring his No. 10. But the Hall still didn't come calling. Finally, in 1994, the Scooter was voted in and he enjoyed every minute of it, giving a warm and humorous acceptance speech at Cooperstown.

Prior to Rizzuto in 1941, there was a real smorgasbord of Yankees players wearing No. 10. From 1929–1931, catchers Bill Dickey, Benny Bengough, and Art Jorgens wore the number. Then in 1932 and part of 1933, pitcher **George Pipgras** donned No. 10. Pipgras had joined the Yanks in 1923 and benefited from the big bats of Ruth, Gehrig & Company. He had a lifetime 102–73 record, but his 4.09 ERA was high for the day. Pipgras had his best year in 1928 when he was 24–13 with a 3.38 ERA in another pennant-winning year. A year later, when numbers started, he wore No. 14, then the next two years No. 12 before putting on the No. 10 jersey his final two Yankee seasons.

Catcher **Tony Rensa** played eight games as No. 10 after Pipgras was sold in 1933. Then in 1934, infielder **Don Heffner** began wearing No. 10 and would keep it for four years while playing infrequently. After the 1937 season, he was traded to the St. Louis Browns for **Bill Knickerbocker**, who took his place on the roster and the No. 10. Knickerbocker was dealt after the 1940 season, and the next spring

Phil Rizzuto claimed the number that would always be associated with him.

While the Scooter was in the service from 1943–45, **Roy Weatherly** and **Mike Garbark** had temporary custody of No. 10. Both were typical wartime players who might not have made it otherwise and neither was with the team for long.

Yankees fans must have done a double-take when they looked out at shortstop in 1957 and saw rookie **Tony Kubek** standing there. They were used to seeing Phil Rizzuto for so many years and now they were looking at a player some nine inches taller, at 6'3". Kubek was 21 years old and wearing No. 34 as he began his first season, which would end with him being named Rookie of the Year. Kubek would hit .297 as a rookie, but might have won the award due to his versatility. Manager Casey Stengel played him at short, third, and in the outfield, and the newcomer responded beautifully. In the World Series that year he slammed two homers in Game 3 against his hometown team, the Milwaukee Braves. So the next year he got a promotion to Rizzuto's old No. 10.

Kubek would only play for nine years, retiring after the 1965 season, and was just a .266 lifetime hitter with little power. But by 1960 he was playing shortstop nearly full time and formed one of the league's best double-play combinations with second baseman Bobby Richardson. The Bombers really didn't need much power from him because he played in the days of the power-packed Mantle-Maris teams. In essence, he was an outstanding role player.

Kubek continued to play at a high level, but in 1965 he just didn't feel right in the field. He went to the famed Mayo Clinic and learned he had three fused vertebrae in his back and that a hard collision on the field could leave him paralyzed. He felt he had no choice but to retire at the tender age of 29.

In December 1966, the Yanks made a trade with Cleveland to bring 31-year-old shortstop **Dick Howser** to the Bronx. Howser had been the American League Rookie of the Year with Kansas City back in 1961, and while he had been oft-injured since then, the team hoped he might be able to fill the spot for a few years. He would wear No. 10 but wind up being just a part timer for two years, hitting .268 his first year but then an anemic .153 in 85 games in 1968. He was done as a player, but his Yankee saga didn't end there. He would stay on as a Yankee coach for the next 10 years, then spend one season as head coach at Florida State University. In 1980, he got a call back to the Bronx, this time as the Yankees manager.

Howser's Yanks promptly won 103 games during the regular season to cruise into the playoffs, but in the ALCS they were swept by the Royals. After the season, Howser was dismissed, though the public story was that the popular manager resigned to go into the real estate business. It was not Steinbrenner's finest hour, as he became the only owner in history to fire a manager who had just won 103 games. Rumor was that at once point Steinbrenner tried to get Howser back, but the manager refused.

In August 1981, Howser was hired to manage the Royals and was once again successful, eventually leading the team to its only World Series triumph in 1985. In July of the following year, the popular manager first began feeling symptoms of what would be diagnosed as a malignant brain tumor. He passed away on June 17, 1987, at the age of 51.

Backup catcher **Frank Fernandez** wore No. 10 in 1969 after wearing No. 38 the previous two years, then veteran **Danny Cater** took it over for two more years. Cater had a couple of solid seasons at the plate for mediocre Yankees teams, then was traded to Boston after the 1971 season for relief pitcher Sparky Lyle, who would play a huge role in the Yankees' resurgence five years later. Long time minor leaguer

Celerino Sanchez wore No. 10 in both 1972 and '73, didn't cut the mustard, and was gone. Then along came **Chris Chambliss**.

Chambliss was a 215-pound first baseman and a good all-around player, though when he debuted with Cleveland in 1971, he didn't hit with much power. Then in late April 1974, he was traded to the Yankees with pitchers Dick Tidrow and Cecil Upshaw for four players. Chambliss was given No. 10 and the first base job. He had some of his best years with the Yanks and while he never hit as many as 20 home runs in a season, he certainly had his share of big hits.

In 1975, he hit .304 with 9 homers and 72 RBIs. But the next year, as the Yanks moved toward a division title, he would hit .296 with 17 home runs and 96 runs batted in. Then the Yankees met the Kansas City Royals for the American League title. In the fifth and final game, the Yanks blew a 6–3 lead in the eighth inning when George Brett slammed a three-run homer. It was still tied when Chambliss led off the bottom of the ninth. He promptly took reliever Mark Littell's first pitch over the right field wall for a walk-off, pennant-clinching home run.

The team would lose to Cincy in the World Series that year, but come back to win the next two with Chambliss driving home 90 runs each time. The Yankees traded him to Toronto in November 1979, with catcher **Rick Cerone** the key guy coming back to the Bronx.

The Yankees needed Cerone following the tragic death of their captain Thurman Munson in a plane crash that August. So the 26-year-old Cerone was handed uniform No. 10 and the catcher's job. He produced a career season, hitting a solid .277 with 14 home runs and 85 RBIs as the Yanks won 103 games before losing to Kansas City in the ALCS. After that, Cerone's production fell off sharply, and for the remainder of his Yankee career he would share the job with other catchers until he was traded to the Braves for pitcher Brian Fisher at the end of the 1984 season. He made brief returns to New York in both 1987 and 1990. He couldn't ask for his old number either time. For in 1985, No. 10 was permanently retired in honor of Phil Rizzuto.

#11: STARS EARLY; A POTPOURRI LATE

Hey, here's a low Yankees number that hasn't been retired and so far isn't likely to be. It's still up for grabs and looking for someone to make it his own. Three of the first four players to wear the number are now in the Hall of Fame. No player who has worn it since comes close to making a trip to Cooperstown.

The first player to wear No. 11 was star pitcher **Herb Pennock**, a stylish southpaw whose career began with the Philadelphia A's way back in 1912. He didn't have much success and was traded to the Red Sox in 1915, pitching mostly out of the bullpen for a few years. Pennock didn't have a great fastball and it wasn't until he found his control that he also found success, beginning in 1919. He was traded to the Yanks in 1923, and with those big bats behind him he thrived. He won 19 games that first year, 21 the next. In the pennant-winning years from 1926–28 he won 23, 19, and 17. The next year, the Yanks began wearing numbers and Pennock donned No. 11. He was also 35 years old by then.

He stayed with the Yanks until 1933, switching to uniform No. 16 for two years and then to No. 12 for his final two seasons.

WHO NEEDS A DOCTOR?

In the days before modern medicine, players often did strange things when they were hurt. Pennock was no exception. In 1928, he suddenly found himself with a sore arm. He couldn't go to the local hospital for an MRI or CAT scan so he listened to a tale that said bee venom might help. Unbelievably, Pennock thrust his arm into a swarm of bees and was stung repeatedly. The only thing that happened was that his arm swelled up and was extremely painful. Said Pennock, "All I can say is that nature intended self-respecting bees to spend their time getting honey out of flowers and not go drilling into a pitcher's arm." The bee stings notwithstanding, Herb Pennock won 241 games and was eventually elected to the Hall of Fame.

When Pennock switched his number to 16 in 1930, fellow pitcher **Waite Hoyt** changed his from No. 12, which he wore the year before, to No. 11. Welcome the second Hall of Famer to the uniform. Hoyt would only appear in eight games wearing No. 11 before being traded to Detroit, but the righthander was great for the Yanks during the 1920s, going 22–7 with the Murderer's Row Bombers of 1927 and 23–7 the following year. He also won 19 twice, 18, 17, and 16 games. From 1921, when he was traded to the Yanks from Boston, through 1928, he won 145 of the team's 750 victories and six of their 18 World Series triumphs.

Waite Hoyt and his 237 wins were elected to the Hall of Fame in 1969, and after his retirement he became one of baseball's best early broadcasters, beginning with the Cincinnati Reds in 1942.

A pitcher named **Ownie Carroll** kept No. 11 warm for 10 games after Hoyt was traded in 1930, then two years later **Vernon "Lefty" Gomez** took it over, also pitching his way into the Hall of Fame. The sometimes daffy Gomez joined the Yanks in 1930, going just 2–5 with No. 22 on his back. A year later, wearing No. 20, he blossomed with a 21–9 record. Once it looked as if he'd be around a while, he was given No. 11 and wore it for the remainder of his Yankees career.

Gomez was one of baseball's all-time zany characters, witnessed by his teammates' nickname for him. It wasn't Lefty; it was "Goofy." What other guy would stop a World Series game while he stood on the mound watching an airplane fly overhead? And what other guy would tell his teammates he had an idea for a great invention—a rotating fishbowl that would save gold fish the trouble of swimming around? But while he was amusing everyone with his antics, he was baffling the opposition with his crackling fastball. In 1932, he was an impressive 24–7 and two years later led the American League in wins (26), ERA (2.33), and strikeouts (158), the Triple Crown of pitching.

What derailed Lefty was arm problems. They slowly robbed him of his fastball, forcing him to become more of a finesse pitcher. "I'm throwing as hard as I ever did," he said, later in his career. "The ball's just not getting there as fast."

Arm problems limited him to nine games in 1940, but he rebounded to produce a 15–5 season in the World Series year of 1941. Then the next year, he struggled again and the Yankees sold him to the Boston Braves after the season. They, in turn, also released him and he wound up pitching just one game for Washington before calling it quits at age 34. But his 189–102 record, helped by a perfect 6–0 slate in five World Series ensured his eventual election to the Hall of Fame.

With Gomez gone in 1943, another hard-throwing lefty named **Tommy Byrne** was given No. 11. He pitched for one year and then went into the service. Byrne would return for two separate tours with the Bombers, but never wear No. 11 again. Catcher **Rip Collins** took over No. 11 the next year. He played in just three games and his big league career was at an end. Then along came a pitcher named **Joe Page,** who would quickly restore past glory to No. 11.

Page was a big, 6'2", 205 pound lefthander with an overpowering fastball who just couldn't seem to cut it as a starter. He joined the Yanks in 1944 at the age of 26 (wearing No. 16 that first season) and struggled for three years, starting more than relieving and always walking too many hitters. Then early in the 1947 season, manager Bucky Harris put him into a game against the Red Sox with two on and no one out. After Ted Williams reached on an error to load the bases, Page threw three balls to Bobby Doerr. It looked like disaster, but Page dug down, struck Doerr out, and got out of the inning. That's when Joe Page, relief specialist, was born.

For three years, Page was the top relief pitcher in baseball and while his wasn't a long career, in those three years he became the prototype of the modern closer, a guy who could come in and shut down the opposition. Unlike today's closers, Page usually pitched more than one inning. In fact, he threw a lot more than his predecessor on the Yanks, Johnny Murphy. From 1947 through 1949, Page pitched in 171 games and logged 384 1/3 innings. He helped the Yanks win two World Series and was the go-to guy in every tough situation. He also won 34 games during those three peak years.

The workload gradually wore Page down and in 1950 he wasn't the same pitcher. He was released in May 1951 without making an appearance, attempted an aborted comeback with Pittsburgh in 1954, and retired for good. But for those three great seasons, Joe Page showed the baseball world what a potent weapon a great relief pitcher could be.

Johnny Sain is a guy remembered as both an outstanding pitcher and highly successful pitching coach. He came to the Yankees from the Boston Braves in August 1951 in a trade that sent a young pitcher named Lew Burdette to Boston. While Burdette wasn't a known commodity then, Sain was.

JOHNNY SAIN
pitcher NEW YORK YANKEES

The righthander had pitched for the Braves as a reliever in 1942, then went into the service for three years. When he returned in 1946, the team made him a starter and he proceeded to reel off four 20-win seasons in five years. When Sain came to the Yankees and pulled on No. 11, he was 33 years old. It was the following two years, 1952 and '53, that the crafty righty became an indispensable part of two World Series-winning teams. He started and relieved almost equally, going 11–6 and 14–7 with

16 combined saves. In 1954 he became the equivalent of a closer and saved 22 games. The Yanks traded Sain to Kansas City in May 1955 and that would prove to be his final season.

As a pitcher, Sain relied on outstanding control and letting the hitter hit. As a pitching coach for the A's, Yankees, Twins, Tigers, Angels, White Sox, and Braves he was loved by all his hurlers and made many of them 20-game winners. A good number never won 20 again after he left. He changed teams so often because managers either feared he was after their job or didn't agree with his way of coaching . . . or he didn't agree with a team's pitching philosophy. Former Yankee Jim Bouton spoke for many when he said, "Johnny Sain is the greatest pitching coach who ever lived."

Sain wore No. 11 his entire Yankees career. When he left, infielder **Jerry Lumpe** wore it for three-plus seasons from 1956 to '59, then was put on the Kansas City shuttle and dealt with pitchers Johnny Kucks and Tom Sturdivant in return for outfielder **Hector Lopez** and pitcher Ralph Terry. Lopez was given No. 11 immediately and would wear it through 1966, his last year as a Yankee and as major leaguer. He batted .293 with 22 homers and 93 RBIs in 1959, playing 112 of his 147 games with the Yanks. That would be his best season, but he was a solid hitter. As for his fielding, check out his nickname: Hector "What a Pair of Hands" Lopez. Yes, it was said with sarcasm. But, hey, when you play in five World Series, who can complain?

Rightfielder **Bill Robinson** came to the Yankees from the Braves in 1966 in exchange for Clete Boyer. He was a 6'3", 205-pounder who had played just six games for the Braves as a rookie a year earlier. The Yankees thought they might have themselves a five-tool player for years to come and gave him No. 11. Only it was three-and-out as Robinson just couldn't hit, finishing below the dreaded Mendoza Line in two of those seasons, and hitting a total of 16 home runs. He was sent packing after the 1969 season.

Bernie Allen, a former star quarterback at Purdue, came to the Yanks and No. 11 in 1972, near the end of his career. Essentially a backup infielder, he was sold to Montreal after playing in just 17 games in 1973.

He had a familiar problem—he couldn't hit. For the next eight years, No. 11 was worn by **Fred "Chicken" Stanley**, a backup infielder who also didn't hit much. The old expression *good field, no hit* certainly comes into play often. Stanley stuck around from 1973–1980, never playing regularly, but providing some good moments in the field, often as a late-inning defensive replacement. He also got to play in three World Series.

Between 1984 and 1990, No. 11 was worn by utility players, veterans who had better days elsewhere and were strictly backups. They were **Billy Sample** (1985), **Gary Roenicke** (1986), **Lenn Sakata** (1987), **Don Slaught** (1988–89), and Rick Cerone, in a third go around (1990). For five years the number remained unclaimed until, in 1996, came a Steinbrenner reclamation project—**Dwight "Doc" Gooden.**

Most fans know the Gooden story. Signed by the Mets he joined their rotation in 1984 and, at age 19, took the baseball world by storm. With a moving, electric fastball and a curve that fell off the table, Gooden looked absolutely special from Day One. He finished that first season with a 17–6 record, a 2.60 earned run average, and an amazing 276 strikeouts in 218 innings. He became the youngest player ever to be named Rookie of the Year, the youngest to play in an All-Star Game, and the first teenager to ever lead the majors in strikeouts. When he was even better the next year, finishing at 24–4 with a 1.53 ERA, 268 strikeouts, and a unanimous Cy Young Award, it looked like he was the real deal, on a fast track to Cooperstown.

While he had a few more good years with the Mets, Gooden's career was ultimately derailed by drug and alcohol abuse. He was suspended for 60 days in 1994 and stayed out of baseball the next year. He was signed by the Yankees in February 1996. He was 31 years old by then, no longer the fastballing "Doctor K," no longer on any track to Cooperstown. In a sense, he was one of baseball's sad stories of talent unfulfilled.

But the Doc knew how to win and the Yankees' newest No. 11 shocked everyone by pitching a no-hitter against the Mariners on May 14. More of a finesse pitcher, he wound up the season at 11–7, with with an inflated ERA of 5.01. The next year he was 9–5 with a 4.91, a far cry from his incredible work of a decade earlier, and after the season, he left as a free agent. The Yanks brought him back for a last hurrah in June 2000. Wearing No. 17 and pitching mostly in relief, he was 4–2 in the final work of his career. He finished with a career mark of 194–112.

Second baseman **Chuck Knoblauch** was No. 11 from 1998–2001 after coming over from the Twins in exchange for four prospects. Knoblauch had been an All-Star in Minnesota and contributed to three World Series winners in New York. He was especially effective his first two years in pinstripes, a real sparkplug as a leadoff man with power. He hit 35 homers and drove home 132 runs in those years while playing a slick second base. The next year, he began to develop Steve Sax disease and suddenly had trouble making routine throws to first. By 2001, unable to correct his throwing problems, he was playing left field. His production at the plate also dropped off and the Yanks allowed him to leave as a free agent.

Backup catcher **Chris Widger** wore No. 11 for 21 games in 2002, while **Erick Almonte**, **David Dellucci**, and **Curtis Pride** all split time in the jersey during the 2003 season. Veteran slugger **Gary Sheffield**, who was Dwight Gooden's nephew, came as a free agent in 2003 and wore No. 11 for three years. Sheff put together two incredibly consistent seasons (.290, 36, 121; and .291, 34, 123), but had his third sabotaged by injury. After appearing in just 39 games in 2006 he was traded to Detroit. But he had some big moments and was a Yankee Stadium favorite during those two big years.

Backup first sacker **Doug Mientkiewicz**, a great glove, wore No. 11 in 2007, then veteran third baseman **Morgan Ensberg** had it at the beginning of 2008. When he was cut, minor league call-up **Brett Gardner** took over No. 11 and the speedster continued wearing it as he split centerfield duties with Melky Cabrera in 2009.

#12: THE NUMBER OF THE FIRST DH EVER

Many old baseball junkies know that the Yankees' **Ron Blomberg** was the first player ever to step into a batter's box as a designated hitter. But how many remember his number? It was No. 12, the only number Blomberg wore as a Yankee, beginning in 1969 and then from 1971–76. Back in 1967, the Yankees made the strapping, 6'1", 205-pounder the nation's top pick in the amateur draft, thinking they might now have a power-hitting first baseman for the next decade and a half. There were just three problems: Blomberg couldn't field, couldn't hit lefthanded pitchers, and really couldn't stay healthy. He was an iron butterfly, a guy who looked like he had muscles on muscles, yet kept pulling and straining them.

After a four-game cup of coffee in 1969, Blomberg came up to stay in 1971. He quickly showed he could hit righties with a .322 average in just 64 games. He also had 7 HRs and 31 RBIs, playing all of his games in the outfield. A year later, he was in 107 games and started 95 times at first, committing 13 errors. That convinced the team he wasn't the first baseman of the future. So when the designated hitter rule was implemented in the American League a year later, Blomberg was a natural . . . against righthanded pitchers. He hit .329 in 100 games, with 14 homers and 49 RBIs, pretty good production.

A likeable guy and a strong lefthanded hitter, he had a .311 season in '74, playing 90 games, the majority as DH but a few in the outfield. The team kept him away from first. But then the injuries started. He just couldn't stay healthy. He played in just 34 games in 1975, then just a single game a year later before missing the entire 1977 season. In essence, he missed the first pair of pennant winning seasons and was then released. He had a short-lived comeback with the White Sox in '78 and then retired at the age of 29.

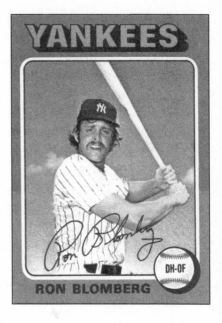

RON BLOMBERG

As always, the early days saw the game of musical numbers being played. Pitcher **Waite Hoyt** was the first to wear No. 12 in 1929. A year later he switched to No. 11 and there's more about him in Chapter 11. Another pitcher, **George Pipgras**, also played musical numbers. He wore No. 12 in 1930 and 1931 before switching to No. 10 in 1932, the chapter in which he was discussed. The same with lefty **Herb Pennock**, who debuted with No. 11 in 1929 and wore No. 12 in 1932–33.

Infielder **Jack Saltzgaver** started his Yankees career wearing the magical No. 7 for 20 games in 1932. When he returned in 1934, he donned No. 12 and kept it through 1937 as he played out his utility role. Then, in 1938, along came first baseman **Babe Dahlgren**, purchased from the Red Sox and given No. 12. Dahlgren would also play a part in one of baseball's most remembered moments.

On May 2, 1939, Lou Gehrig's great consecutive game streak finally ended. Already weak from the illness that would take his life, he told manager Joe McCarthy to take him out of the lineup. Trotting out to first base to begin the game wasn't No. 4. After 2,130 games, there was a No. 12 standing on first: Babe Dahlgren, starting a game he would always be remembered for.

Dahlgren homered that day, but he'd be no Gehrig, hitting just .235 in 144 games. He was sold to the Boston Braves after the 1940 season and had his best year with Pittsburgh in the war year of 1944, driving in 101 runs.

During the war years, No 12 was worn in quick succession by **Buddy Roser** (1941–42), **Oscar Grimes** (1943), **Mike Milsevich** (1944), and **Joe Buzas** (1945). At the end of 1945, returning vet Charlie Keller took the uniform and wore it again from 1947–49, though he is best remembered for wearing No. 9. Pitcher **Vic Raschi** wore No. 12 in his cup-of-coffee year of 1946 before switching to No. 17 and becoming a star. Another short timer, pitcher **Ralph Buxton**, wore No. 12 briefly in 1949, and a rookie named Billy Martin pulled the jersey on in 1950 before taking over his classic No. 1. Then along came **Gil McDougald**.

McDougald joined the Yanks as a 23-year-old second baseman in 1951 and deservedly hit .306 with 14 homers, 63 runs batted in, and 14 stolen bases. For his effort he was deservedly named Rookie of the Year, getting more votes than a freshman outfielder named Mantle. In the World Series that year, the Yankees' newest No. 12 became the first rookie ever to hit a grand slam. He would go on to have a solid career with the New Yorkers.

He came up as a second baseman, but ended up playing both third and short, and playing them well, perfectly suited to Casey Stengel's penchant for platooning and moving players around. McDougald was a solid .276 lifetime hitter and usually had double-digit home runs, consistently between 10 and 14 until his final two seasons.

McDougald played at just the right time. His 10-year career spanned 1951–1960, and the Yankees went to the World Series eight times during that period. His contributions to those teams should not be forgotten. Unfortunately, he is often remembered today for his part in one of baseball's most tragic accidents. It happened on May 7, 1957, when the Yanks were facing the Cleveland Indians and their great young pitcher, Herb Score. McDougald hit a hard liner that caught Score flush in the eye, leaving him with serious injuries and ultimately derailing his career.

Utility player **Woodie Held** wore No. 12 for a single game in 1957. Then from 1961 to 1993, when **Wade Boggs** joined the Yanks, there were a succession of utility players, part-timers and veterans sharing the number with none of them really putting a stamp on it. That's especially surprising given the Yanks penchant for handing out lower numbers to players they feel will be special or long term stars. But right after McDougald, No. 12 went to utility infielder **Billy Gardner** (1961–62), then to backup catcher **Mike Hegan** (1964), infielder **Phil Linz** of harmonica fame in 1965, and infielder **Ruben Amaro** (1966–68).

Outfielder **Billy Cowan** had his time in 1969 before Blomberg took it that same year and wore it through 1976. Veteran first sacker **Jim Spencer** (1978–81) was a lefthanded platoon player who had one solid season with 23 homers before moving on, while **Dave Revering** played even less at first in 1981–82. Another veteran, **Roy Smalley**, came to the Yanks from the Twins in 1982. That year he was given No. 55 for the first part of the season and No. 34 later. In 1983 and '84, he wore No. 12.

In Smalley, the Yanks were getting an All-Star who had just one problem – his back. He had developed a lower back condition known as spondytitis, a chronic imflammation of the spine and back. Though he could still hit well, the disease was taking away his range in the field. In 1984 the team sent him to the White Sox. Smalley ended up finishing his career back in Minnesota and retired at the age of 34, yet another what-could-have-been.

Backup catcher **Joel Skinner** took over No. 12 from 1986–88 and another catcher, **Ron Hassey,** also wore it for in 1985 and part of 1986. Infielder **Tom Brookens** was No. 12 for just 66 games in 1989 and **Carlos Rodriguez** had the number for 15 games in early 1991. Then along came "The King." **Jim Leyritz** was a 26-year-old rookie when he joined the Yankees in 1990 and donned uniform No. 12. Leyritz came up as a third baseman, but he ultimately proved much more versatile than that. The Yanks soon discovered that he could also catch, play first, and the outfield. Leyritz was fearless and confident, and had some power at the plate and a strong throwing arm. Though he was with the club from 1990–96, and again for parts of the 1999 and 2000 seasons, he always seemed to be in the middle of the action and loved the limelight.

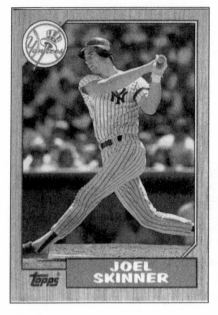

JOEL
SKINNER

A .264 lifetime hitter whose batting average fluctuated between .182 (1991) and .309 (1993), Leyritz slowly became known as a guy who would come through in the clutch and get the big hit. After his anemic .182 sophomore year, Leyritz wanted to change his luck and that meant changing his uniform. He decided to move up a notch from No. 12 to lucky 13. He would wear No. 13 until being traded in 1996, then wear 12 again when he returned in 1999, and then finished up with No. 13 in 2000. He was definitely a two-number guy.

Despite his many big hits, the Yanks broke Leyritz's heart by shipping him to the Angels after the 1996 season, getting just minor leaguers in return. Over the next three years he would bounce around from Anaheim to Texas, Boston, and San Diego. He had a brief homecoming with the Yanks in 1999 and shortly afterward called it a career. . . .

When Leyritz changed his number in 1992, part of the reason was to make room for the first superstar to wear No. 12 as a Yankee. He was 35 years old when he joined the Yanks, already one of the great hitters of his generation and, as a member of the Boston Red Sox, an arch enemy. But free agency and pragmatism are great equalizers. Third baseman Wade Boggs was suddenly a Yankee.

Boggs was originally drafted by the Red Sox in 1976 but had a hard time making the majors because he didn't hit for power and was inconsistent in the field. The Sox finally brought him up in 1982, when he was 24, and: he promptly hit .349 in 104 games. And while he didn't qualify for the batting title, it was still the highest average for a rookie in league history. A year later, playing full time, he won his first batting title with a .361 mark. He dropped to .325 the next year, but then won four straight hitting crowns with marks of .368, .357, .363, and .366, establishing himself as one of the great pure hitters of his time. He even clubbed 24 homers in '87, a year in which many claimed the ball was "juiced." But Boggs was the real deal. He had 200 or more hits seven years in a row and gradually worked to make himself into a very good third baseman. After his fifth batting title in 1988, Boggs had a .356 lifetime batting average, third best of all-time behind Ty Cobb and Rogers Hornsby.

Though he hit over .300 the next three seasons, his production began to dip. Then in 1992, he suddenly fell way back to .259. He was 34 years old, and maybe the Sox thought he was seriously on the downside. He became a free agent that year and the Sox let him leave. In walked the Yanks. Needing a third sacker, they signed their former enemy to a three-year deal. Wade Boggs was in pinstripes and wearing No. 12.

Boggs would stay with the Yanks for five years and hit over .300 four times, including .342 in the strike-shortened 1994 season. He also banged 11 homers, second most of his career and even won a pair of Gold Gloves for his play at third. In 1996, he finally realized another dream, being part of a World Series-winning team. Boggs hit .311 that year and fans remember him jumping on the back of a policeman's horse for a victory lap of Yankee Stadium. He would play one more year in pinstripes before finishing his career in hometown Tampa, where he got the 3000th hit of his Hall of Fame career.

Another former Red Sox star, **Roger Clemens**, wore No.12 briefly when he joined the team in 1999. But he switched to No. 22 after Tony Tarasco was sent down early in the season and would keep that number for five years. In 2000, lefty pitcher **Denny Neagle** came with high hopes, pulled on No. 12, but then went just 7–7 and left as a free agent. In 2001, utilityman **Clay Bellinger** was No. 12 after wearing No. 35 the previous two seasons. Then he was gone and the intriguing **Alfonso Soriano** took over the number in 2002.

Soriano was a tall (6'1") shortstop from the Dominican Republic who was playing in Japan when the Yankees signed him in 1998. He got a nine-game cup of coffee the next year, wearing No. 58, and was called up for 22 games the next year, donning No. 54. The problem was that the Yanks already had a shortstop, and no one was about to move Derek Jeter out of his position. So in 2001, the Yanks made Soriano a second sacker and gave him No. 33. He responded with a .268 season, including 18 home runs, 73 RBIs, and 43 steals. He looked like a coming star.

In 2002, he appeared with No. 12 on his back and put together an All-Star season, hitting .300 with 39 homers and 102 runs batted in, as well as leading the league with 41 stolen bases. It was production almost unheard of from a second sacker. When he hit 38 homers the next year, with another 91 ribbies and a .290 average, it began to look as if he might be a superstar in the making. Then came a very tempting offer.

The Yankees suddenly had the opportunity to acquire Alex Rodriguez from Texas. Who could resist the talent and allure of A-Rod? But to get, you've got to give. On February 16, 2004, the team reluctantly parted with Soriano and a player to be named later and got A-Rod and his huge contract in return. Since then, Soriano has played for Texas, Washington, and the Chicago Cubs. He continues to play at a high level as a left fielder, though is sometimes erratic and has never quite become the superstar he looked to be. But for two seasons he certainly was spectacular in pinstripes.

Since A-Rod decided to wear No. 13, two veterans took over No. 12 the next two seasons, outfielder **Kenny Lofton** and infielder **Tony Womack**. Neither played up to expectations; each stayed just a year. Utility infielder **Andy Phillips** was No. 12 in 2006 and 2007, while young **Alberto Gonzalez** wore it for portions of the 2008 season. In 2009, infielder **Cody Ransom** took the number. Ransom had been signed as a free agent the season before, wearing No. 29 and hitting .302. He had his chance early in 2009 while Alex Rodriguez was rehabbing from hip surgery and was given the third base job. But Ransom stopping hitting. He was below the Mendoza Line when A-Rod returned and was batting just .190 when designated for assignment. Pitcher **Josh Towers** also wore the number briefly late in the season after rehabbing an injury.

ROOKIES OF THE YEAR

When Gil McDougald was named Rookie of the Year in 1951, he became the first Yankee to receive that honor. Since them, seven other Bronx Bombers have won the prize.

Gil McDougald................................. 1951

Bob Grim.. 1954

Tony Kubek 1957

Tom Tresh 1962

Stan Bahnsen................................. 1968

Thurman Munson........................... 1970

Dave Righetti................................. 1981

Derek Jeter 1996

The first six winners came during a 19-year period, one Rookie of the Year almost every three seasons. Over the last 39 years, only two Yankees have won the award, one Rookie of the Year almost every 20 seasons. What's the difference? Can you spell free agency?

#13: A-ROD: FOR BETTER OR WORSE

He's known to everyone as A-Rod, but a more apt description might be Lightning Rod. **Alex Rodriguez** is undeniably one of baseball's all-time talents, a player who when on his game can do it all and do it better than anyone. But since coming to New York in 2004 after establishing his reputation in Seattle and enhancing it in Texas—at least in the numbers he put up—he has become a magnet for the media in New York, a place he obviously wanted to be. Baseball aside for a moment, since coming to New York, A-Rod has been involved in a messy and public divorce; had dalliances with celebrities such as Madonna and Kate Hudson; had an ill-timed opt-out of his contract announced during the World Series until he returned with an even bigger one; had his named leaked out as a guy who tested positive for performing enhancing drugs in 2003; and finally endured hip surgery that, for a while, threatened his 2009 season. All this happened as he

Alex Rodriguez

inexorably climbed the home run ladder with the expectation that he would someday surpass Barry Bonds as baseball's all-time king of the four baggers.

Whew! That's one skewed résumé, especially when playing alongside fellow superstar Derek Jeter, whose image has always been polished by Mr. Clean. There's also been a love-hate relationship with the fans of the Big Apple. With all his achievements, A-Rod has had some notable playoff failures where he just didn't hit and a number of seasons where his work in the clutch has been lacking.

Rodriguez was a boy wonder in Seattle when he took over the regular shortstop job in 1996 at the age of 20. All he did that year was lead the league in hitting with a .358 average, wallop 36 home runs, and drive in 123 runs. He was a tall, 6'3" shortstop who could make all the plays and was named Major League Player of the Year by *The Sporting News*. He starred in Seattle for four more years, blasting more than 40 homers three times and also hitting above .300 on three occasions. There was little doubt that he was a full-fledged superstar by the age of 24. He became a free agent after the 2000 season and signed an unprecedented 10-year, $252 million contract. Yet in Texas he was still under the radar. The team didn't win even though A-Rod won a pair of Gold Gloves, an MVP prize, and hit 52, 57, and 47 home runs. But Rangers owner Tom Hicks realized he'd never build a winning team with A-Rod atop his payroll and dealt him to the Yanks for Alfonso Soriano on February 16, 2004. The Rangers even agreed to pay part of A-Rod's salary for the remaining years of his contract. And Rodriguez had his wish. He'd be with a team that had a chance to win every year and he could now perform in the high-profile fishbowl of New York.

But because Jeter was the Yankees' captain and shortstop, A-Rod had to move to third base. He quickly became a proficient third sacker, though not a Gold Glover. But it was his bat the Yankees wanted. The Bombers had won four World Series between 1996 and 2000, but none since, despite making the playoffs every year and going to the Series twice more (2001 and 2003). A-Rod was supposed to help get the team back over the hump, but had a disappointing first season with just 36 homers and a .286 average. A great season for many was sub par for him.

If 2004 was down, the next year up (.321, 48 HRs, 130 RBIs), then down again (35 homers) for him, then spectacular. In 2007, he slammed 54 homers, drove home 156 runs, and hit .314. In early August, he became the youngest player in baseball history to reach the 500 home run mark. In both 2005 and 2007 he was the AL MVP. But by the end of the 2007 season there were problems. A-Rod's personal life was being put under the microscope and detractors were quick to point out that since the final four games of the 2004 playoffs he was 8-for-59 in post-season play, a .136 average, and that he was hitless in his past 18 post-season at-bats with runners in scoring position. He also had a clause in his contract that would allow him to opt out and become a free agent, in spite of already being the highest paid player in baseball.

The announcement came from his agent, Scott Boras, during Game Four of the World Series that year. A-Rod was opting out, once again looking for greener pastures. But just a short time later, A-Rod personally reached out to the Steinbrenner family and said he didn't really want to leave New York, blaming the decision on his agent. Soon he had a new contract, one laced with incentives that could be worth up to $300 million. So he was back.

The opt-out led to more boos from the fans, and in 2008 he had another sub par season (for him) with just 35 homers and 103 RBIs to go with a .302 average. Then, in 2009, things would get worse. Shortly after spring training began, it was revealed that A-Rod would need hip surgery. Doctors would fix the hip so he could play in 2009 but said he might need more extensive surgery after the season (which now he apparently does not). Then there was the infamous list from 2003 that supposedly had the names of 104 players who tested positive for banned substances. A-Rod's name was somehow leaked, and at a media-frenzy press conference, he admitted using a substance he called "boli" while at Texas. Most felt boli was an anabolic steroid. Suddenly, like so many other sluggers of his generation, many looked at his achievements as tainted.

So the A-Rod saga continues. After missing the first month or so of the 2009 season, A-Rod wound up having a great year, hitting 30 homers and driving in 100 runs in just 124 games. He also hit in the playoffs, belting six homers and driving in 18 runs, finally getting that monkey off his back. And he won his first World Series ring. No. 13 continues to be a Lightning Rod and will probably always be. Now there's the question of whether his ultimate achievements will be looked upon as tainted because of his admitted use of PEDs. And what will that mean for his Hall of Fame chances and the odds that No. 13 will someday join the other retired numbers in Monument Park? At the beginning, it all looked so easy for Alex Rodriguez. But it was never quite the same once he left Seattle.

There have always been some players superstitious about wearing No. 13, and there usually aren't as many players wearing a number that's synonymous with bad luck. Pitcher **Spud Chandler** took on No. 13, in his rookie year of 1937, but quickly changed to No. 21 the next year when Pat Malone left the team and wore that for the remainder of his Yankees career. After an 11-year gap, outfielder Cliff Mapes pulled on the uniform in 1948, also in his rookie year. The next season he became a pre-Mickey Mantle No. 7, which he kept for several seasons. It would then be another 22 years before a player would accept the number.

In 1970, outfielder **Curt Blefary** came to the Yanks from Houston in exchange for the colorful Joe Pepitone. Blefary had some good power years in Baltimore before spending a year with the Astros, and the Yanks hoped the southpaw swinger would find the short field porch to his liking. Ble-

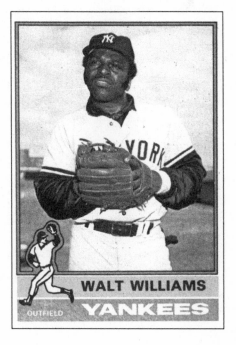

WALT WILLIAMS
OUTFIELD YANKEES

fary put on No. 13 and totally flopped. He was a part-timer in 1970 and played just 21 games the next year before being shipped to Oakland in exchange for Rob Gardner.

Walt "No Neck" Williams came to the Yanks in 1974 and appeared in No. 13. A speedy outfielder, he had some good seasons with the White Sox, but he played sparingly and hit just .113 in 43 games. A year later he did better, hitting .281 in 82 games, but it wasn't enough. After the season, he was released and retired. Young outfielder **Bobby Brown** was brought up for 30 games in 1979 and wore No. 58. When he made the team out of spring training the following year, he took on No. 13 and showed some promise, hitting .260 in 137 games with 14 homers and 47 RBIs. But when he regressed the following year, he was traded to Seattle as part of a multi-player deal that brought the Yanks lefty pitcher Shane Rawley. Young shortstop **Keith Smith** played two games in 1984 wearing No. 20, then four more in '85 wearing No. 13.

Just when it looked as if No. 13 would never house a real live ball-player, along came third sacker **Mike Pagliarulo**. The lefthanded

hitting third sacker was drafted in 1981, got called up in 1984, and became the team's regular third baseman that July at the age of 24. He wore No. 46 his rookie year, as he hit .239 with 7 homers and 34 RBIs in just 67 games. "Pags" was a hard worker with good pop in his bat and the Yanks hoped they had their third baseman for the next decade. In 1985, he changed to No. 6 and whacked 19 home runs while hitting that same .239. The next year, Pags appeared wearing No. 13 and hit 28 homers with 71 RBIs. But again, his average was just

.238. The Yanks liked his power and defense, but wanted that average to get higher. Instead, it continued to go down.

When Pagliarulo hit a career best 32 homers in 1987 with 87 ribbies, the team ignored his .234 average, but the next year he slumped to .216 with just 15 homers and the handwriting was on the wall. After hitting just .197 in 74 games with only four homers the next year, the Yanks gave up on him. On July 22, he was shipped to San Diego.

After Pags left in '89, infielder **Mike Blowers** took over the number for the rest of the season. Then in 1991, **Torey Lovullo** wore it for a year, and outfielder **Gerald Williams** the year after that. The King, Jim Leyritz, took it over for four years until 1996. Third sacker **Charlie Hayes** came over from the Pirates late in the 1996 season, and wore No. 33. He played 20 games in the regular season, then was essentially the starter in the playoffs and World Series. Figuring he'd stay awhile, Hayes switched to No. 13 in 1997, hit just .258 with 11 homers and was traded after the season. Was No. 13 a jinx after all?

In the next six years the number was worn by such luminaries as **Mike Figga** (1998–99), **Willie Banks** (1998), **Jeff Manto** (1999), Leyritz again in 2000, **Jose Vizcaino** (2000), **Michael Coleman** (2001), and **Antonio Osuna** (2003). Today it continues to be all A-Rod.

#14: SWEET LOU, PROFESSIONAL HITTER

Before he became one of baseball's best known and mercurial managers, **Lou Piniella** was a solid, professional hitter and a winning ballplayer just a couple of notches below the game's best. "Sweet Lou" came to the Yanks in 1974 from Kansas City, traded with a player named Kenny Wright for veteran reliever Lindy McDaniel. The Yanks got the better of that one, a guy who had been Rookie of the Year in 1969 when he hit .282 with 11 homers and 68 runs batted in. Piniella would hit over .300 twice in the next four years, but when he slumped to .250 in 1973, the Royals chose to move him.

He would remain a fixture with the Yanks, wearing No. 14, for the next 11 years, participating in four World Series and playing a major role in the 1977 and '78 championship teams. Though he was a solid, 6'2", 200-pounder, Piniella wasn't a power hitter. He hit 11 home runs four times and 12 once, and never topped 70 RBIs with the Yanks. But he would hit over .300 five times with the Yanks, including highs of .330 and .314 in the championship years of 1977 and '78. Rather, he was a slasher and a clutch hitter who could handle the bat. He played without fear, led by example, and was extremely popular among his teammates. A very solid outfielder with an above-average throwing arm, he cut down 10 or more baserunners three times.

By 1980, Sweet Lou was 36 years old and slowing down. He still had a valuable bat, but became more of a platoon or part-time player. In both 1983 and '84, he doubled as player and the team's hitting coach and then retired with a solid .291 lifetime average and .319 mark in World Series play. But the Yanks and baseball at large hadn't seen the end of Lou Piniella. He remained the team's batting coach in 1985, and when Billy Martin was fired for the umpteenth time after the season, Piniella became the Yankee skipper.

The Yanks finished second his first year at the helm, then fell to fourth in 1987. Word was that Martin, still in the front office, was a constant critic of Sweet Lou's skippering. So the fickle Boss changed horses again, bringing Martin back in '88 and making Lou the general manager, a job he disliked intensely. No need to worry. After just 68 games, Steinbrenner fired Martin once again and convinced Piniella to return to the dugout. But when the team finished fifth, Lou was gone for the last time . . . at least in New York.

He emerged again in Cincinnati in 1990 and his club promptly won the World Series. He also managed in Seattle, Tampa Bay, and is currently with the Chicago Cubs.

For the first two decades in which numbers were worn, there was quite a collection of forgettable Yankees showing up with No. 14 on their backs. Pitcher **George Pipgras** was the first in 1929, but he promptly dropped down to No. 12 the next two seasons. Taking over the uniform in 1930–31 was righty **Hank Johnson**, who was with the team from seven seasons then was traded to the Red Sox in 1932. Southpaw **Ed Wells** was a guy who always pitched better in the minors than the majors, but had a four-year stint with the Yanks from 1929–32. He wore No. 19 his first season, No. 17 the next two, and then No. 14 in 1932, his last with the team. Wells went 12–3 in the pennant-winning year of 1930, but the Yanks didn't use him as they won the World Series.

Lefthanded pitcher **Russ Van Atta** joined the Yanks as a 27-year-old rookie in 1933, pulling on uniform No. 14 and having one of the best major league debuts any player could have, finishing the year at 12–4. But some of the promise disappeared after he cut his pitching hand badly during the off-season. He was never quite the same after that and was used mostly in relief until he was sold to the St. Louis Browns in May 1935. The next character to wear No. 14 was **Irving Darius Hadley**, called "Bump" by his friends and teammates.

A 5'11", 190-pound righthander, Bump Hadley got his odd nickname from a storybook character named Bumpus, who was also short and chunky. This Bump, however, could throw hard; the problem was his difficulty finding the plate. In his rookie year of 1927, Bump looked like a coming star, compiling a 14–6 record for the Washington Senators. He had several more pretty good seasons before the Yanks got him in 1936.

Bump donned No. 14 and went to work for the best team in baseball. Benefiting from the potent Yankee lineup, the Bump compiled a 14–4 record and led the league with a .778 winning percentage. He did this despite compiling a 4.35 ERA and walking 89 compared to 74 strikeouts. But it was on May 27 of the following year that Bump Hadley threw one high and tight to Detroit's great veteran catcher Mickey Cochrane, fracturing his skull and effectively ending his Hall of Fame career in one of baseball's tragic accidents.

The Bump would continue to pitch for the Yanks through 1940 and have three more winning years. His last hurrah came in the 1939 World Series, when he relieved Lefty Gomez in the second inning of Game 3 and went the rest of the way in a 7–3 Yankee win. The Giants bought him after the 1940 season, and he pitched one more year before retiring. Thanks to his wildness and

LOU PINIELLA
OUTFIELD
YANKEES

some bad St. Louis teams, his lifetime mark was just under .500 at 161–165.

Infielder **Jerry Priddy** (1941–42) was a "priddy" fair ballplayer who spend his first two years of his career wearing No. 14 for the Yanks. Though he hit .280 in 59 games in 1942, he was deemed expendable and moved to Washington in a minor deal. He had his best years with St. Louis and later Detroit before retiring after the 1953 season. Pitcher **Butch Wensloff** was a 27-year-old rookie who joined the Yanks in 1943, wore No. 14, and compiled a 13–11 record during one of the thin war years. After that he went into the service and then worked in a war plant. He returned in 1947 to pitch in 11 games, but had arm problems and retired the following year. **Monk Dubiel**, who inherited No. 14 from Wensloff, was another of those wartime pitchers who came to the majors late. When the better players returned, he was shipped to the National League, where he hung on with several teams until 1952.

Righthander **Floyd "Bill" Bevens** pitched four consecutive years for the Yankees (1944–47) and wore three different numbers, 21, 16, and 14. His biggest moment came in 1947 when he was wearing No. 16, and that's the chapter in which it will be described. From 1946 to 1948, No. 14 was worn by such luminaries as **Cuddles Marshall** (1946), **Ted Sepkowski** (1947), **Rugger Ardizoia** (1947), and **Lonny Frey** (1948–49). Then, for the next 14 years, No. 14 would house two excellent players from the great pennant-winning years of the 1950s and early 1960s. They were **Gene Woodling** (1949–54) and **Bill "Moose" Skowron** (1955–62).

Woodling got an eight-game cup of coffee as a 20-year-old with Cleveland in 1943. After that he spent two years in the Navy, hit just .188 with Cleveland in 61 games in 1946, went to Pittsburgh a year later and played in just 22 games before spending the 1948 season back in the minors. A lefthanded hitter who used a Stan Musial-type crouch, the Yankees purchased his contract from the Pacific Coast League San Francisco Seals in September 1948. The next season, he was in the New York outfield as the Bronx Bombers embarked on a run of five straight World Series triumphs.

BILL SKOWRON

NEW YORK YANKEES — FIRST BASE

Woodling was a victim of Casey Stengel's platoon system and often split time with Hank Bauer. Both players complained from time to time, and sometimes Ol' Case put them both in the outfield together. Woodling was an outstanding fielder and clutch hitter (with the nickname of "Old Faithful") who batted .283, .281, .309, and .306 from 1950–53. He had just mediocre power, with his 15 homers and 71 RBIs in 1951 his best numbers a Yankee. But he was a big part of those five straight titles. The Yanks moved him to Baltimore following the 1954 season, the biggest name in a record 17-player deal.

One of baseball's genuine nice guys, Bill Skowron came to the Yanks in 1954, two years after being named *The Sporting News* Minor League Player of the Year. Not quite six feet tall, and weighing 195 pounds, he wasn't that big to have the nickname "Moose." But Skowron was a power-hitting first sacker who would play in seven World Series during his nine-year Yankees tenure.

A strong right-handed hitter, he would bat over .300 his first four seasons in New York, though he was often the victim of Casey Stengel's platoon system. He had his best overall year in 1960, when he batted .309, clubbed 26 homers and drove in 91 runs. A year later, the Moose contributed 28 dingers to the team's 240. Then, after hitting a solid .270 with 23 homers and 80 RBIs in 1962, the Yanks suddenly traded the 31-year old Skowron to the rival Dodgers for pitcher Stan Williams, who never really panned out.

Utility man **Harry Bright** wore No. 14 in 1963 and part of '64, then pitcher **Pedro Ramos** took it over at the end of 1964 and for the next two years. Ramos was from Cuba and was signed by the Washington Senators in 1953, long before the Communist revolution led by baseball lover Fidel Castro. "Pete" was a good pitcher playing for bad Washington teams and led the American League in losses for four straight years (1958–61). He was dealt to Cleveland in 1962, and on September 5, 1964, the Yankees picked him up for $75,000 and two players to be named later (pitchers Bud Daley and Ralph Terry). The Yanks were in a pennant fight and needed a reliever. What they got was an ace, an early version of today's closers. Ramos was outstanding. He was 1–0 with a 1.25 ERA and eight saves in 13 games down the stretch. Unfortunately, he was ineligible for the World Series.

He became the Yanks, stopper the next two years with 19 saves in '65 and 13 the next year, but the Yankee dynasty was crashing and the team finished in the basement in '66. After the season he was sent to the Phillies for Joe Verbanic and cash. Thanks to those bad Washington teams, Ramos' lifetime record was just 117–160.

Utilityman **Jerry Kenney** was No. 14 in his cup-of-coffee year of 1967, then wore No. 2 from 1969–71. In 1968 and '69, third sacker **Bobby Cox** wore the number but was just a .225 hitter with little power. They were his only two years in the majors. And yes, he's the same Bobby Cox who will be going to the Hall of Fame someday for his highly successful career managing the Atlanta Braves. Then in June 1971, the Yankees gave No. 14 to a genuine New York hero. They traded outfielder Ron Wood to the Montreal Expos for outfielder **Ron Swoboda.**

Swoboda was one of the heroes of the "Miracle Mets" in 1969, a team that took the city by storm when it went from ninth place in 1968 to win the World Series over the powerful Baltimore Orioles. In truth, Swoboda was just a mediocre player with occasional bursts of power, but he was also a powerful personality whom the fans loved.

With the Yanks, Swoboda was a part-time outfielder who didn't play a lot, and he hit just four home runs in two and a half seasons. In his final year of 1973, he batted just .116 in 43 at-bats and at year's end was out of the majors at the age of 29.

The next year, Sweet Lou took over the number through 1984, then it got a rest until reserve infielder **Mike Blowers** wore it for part of 1991. In the second half of the 1991 season, second sacker **Pat Kelly** took over the number and wore it through 1997. He was granted free agency after the 1997 season. In April 1997, the Yanks made a deal with the San Diego Padres, sending outfielder Ruben Rivera and Rafael Medina to the West Coast for a minor leaguer and infielder Homer Bush, as well as a player to be named later. That player came in May. When Japanese pitcher **Hideki Irabu** arrived in New York, the Yanks said they were getting the Nolan Ryan of Japan. He left two years later with owner George Steinbrenner referring to him as a "fat toad."

The reason the Padres shipped Irabu to New York was because they couldn't sign him. They had the rights, but Irabu insisted he would only pitch for the Yankees. Pitching for the Lotte Orions in the Japanese Pacific League in 1993, Irabu threw a fastball that was clocked at 98 mph. By the time the Padres acquired his rights he was known at the greatest strikeout pitcher in Japanese baseball. All that advanced hoopla prompted the Yankees to sign him to a four-year, $12.8-million contract.

Standing 6'4" and weighing upward of 240 pounds, Irabu pitched in just 13 games in 1997 and had just a 5–4 record with an elevated 7.09 ERA. In 1998, Irabu started 28 times, pitched some strong games and wound up with a 13–9 record and a 4.06 ERA. But at the same time he was also showing a propensity for American junk food and beginning to put on weight.

The next year, it began to come apart for the latest No. 14. His weight ballooned along with his ERA. In 27 starts he still won fairly often, coming in at 11–7 because of the solid Yankees team behind him. But he had a 4.84 ERA and incurred the wrath of Steinbrenner when he failed to cover first on a grounder during spring training. Thus the fat toad remark. That about did it. After the season the Yanks swapped him to Montreal for pitcher Jake Westbrook. Irabu would win a grand total of five games over the next three years with Montreal and Texas.

Since Irabu, No. 14 has been passed around to a variety of players, only one of which has become a star, but who has done it with a different number. Infielder **Wilson Delgado** donned it for part of the 2000 season, followed by another utility infielder, **Enrique Wilson**, who had some good moments while playing for the Yanks from 2001– 2004. Veteran **Joe Oliver** wore it for all of 12 games in 2001. In 2005, utility infielder **Andy Phillips** had No. 14 for part of the season. He also wore No. 18 that year. But Phillips was another musical numbers guy. He wore No. 39 during a five-game stint in 2004 and then switched to No. 12 his final two years of 2006 and 2007.

But No. 14 continued to be a popular stopoff for utility players in the first decade of the new century. The versatile **Miguel Cairo** wore it in 2006. In his two other Yankees seasons (2004 and part of 2007), Cairo was No. 41. Pitcher **Matt DeSalvo** wore No. 14 briefly in 2007 and infielder **Wilson Betemit** donned it in 2007 and 2008, and infielder **Angel Berroa** had it briefly in 2009, as did veteran outfielder **Eric Hinske**, who helped a bit down the stretch. Rookie second sacker **Robinson Cano** wore No. 14 for part of 2005, then switched to No. 22 later in the season. He kept that number the following year and then made a permanent change to No. 24 in 2007 and continues to wear it today.

SOME YANKEE STADIUM FIRSTS

Here are some Yankee Stadium firsts, the following from the first incarnation of Yankee Stadium that opened in 1923:

First home run: The one and only Babe Ruth, a two-run shot off Boston's Howard Ehmke in a 4–1 Yankee victory on April 18, 1923.

First error: Also the Babe. Though he was a good outfielder, the Babe dropped a fly ball in the fifth inning of the same game, April 18.

First World Series home run: Believe it or not, Casey Stengel of the New York *Giants,* an inside-the-park shot in Game 1 of the 1923 World Series.

First night game: May 28, 1946, a 2–1 loss to Washington.

First player to have his number retired: Lou Gehrig. His No. 4 was retired on Lou Gehrig Appreciation Day, July 4, 1939.

#15: THURMAN MUNSON. ANOTHER TRAGIC CAPTAIN

When **Thurman Munson** was named just the second ever captain of the Yankees in 1975, no one thought he would share the same fate as the team's first captain—dying young. Munson, the Yankees' All-Star catcher and team leader, was killed while practicing landings in his private plane on August 2, 1979, at the age of 32. The Yankees immediately retired his No. 15, and no player occupied his locker at the old Yankee Stadium. It stood, with his name still above it, alongside Derek Jeter's. At the new Yankee Stadium, the locker was placed in the museum within the Stadium for visitors to see. Thurman Munson was that special a player.

The Ohio-born Munson overcame a difficult childhood to become a three-sport star in high school and earn a football scholarship to Kent State. But when the Yankees drafted him in June 1968, he dropped out of school and signed for $75,000. A year later he was called up for a 26-game look-see and given No. 15, which became available when Tom Tresh was traded to Detroit in June. The very next season, Munson became the team's starting catcher, a position he'd hold until his untimely death. He also became the American League's Rookie of the Year and showed everyone that he was more than ready to handle the job at age 23.

Success on the field didn't always make Munson a happy camper. He was often surly and combative, and that may have made him a better ballplayer. He could hit, and was an outstanding receiver with a quick release to cut down baserunners. In 1973, he began flashing more power at the plate, hitting .301 with a career-best 20 home runs and 74 runs batted in.

By 1975, the Yankees were again becoming a top team, on the brink of a three-year period when they would go to the World Series each time and win twice. Munson was at his best from 1975–77, hitting over .300 and driving in 100 or more runs each season. In 1976, Munson was the league's Most Valuable Player and then hit .529 in the World Series. He was at the top of his game going into the 1977 season, the captain and leader of the New York Yankees. The Yanks had a great team in 1977 and '78, especially after adding outfielder Reggie Jackson. But Reggie and Munson didn't get along, and while the 1977–78 Yankees were a mix of volatile personalities that became known collectively as the Bronx Zoo, they came together on the field to win a pair of World Series. In 1977, Jackson was the hero, blasting five homers in the Fall Classic, including three in one game. But Munson's steady play continued to anchor the team. He had another fine year in '77, but fell off a bit the following year, still hitting .297 but with only six homers and 71 RBIs.

The fans continued to love him and he was still a dangerous clutch hitter. Munson was just 32 when the 1979 season began, yet some thought he was beginning to show signs of wear and tear from so much hard time behind the plate.

After 97 games, he was still hitting a solid .288, but his power production was way down. He had just three homers and 39 RBIs. Munson had earned his pilot's license a few years earlier and in '79 bought a twin-engine Cessna so he could fly home to Ohio and visit his wife and children more often. On August 2, he had his fatal accident, which stunned the Yankees and the entire baseball world.

Tributes poured in. The team had lost its captain and leader, a guy who was far from a perfect human being,

as he would readily admit, but who was an outstanding player, maybe a tad short of Hall of Fame caliber. But Thurman Munson was a guy you'd want to go to war with and definitely want on your side. Not surprisingly, his No. 15 was retired shortly after his death. He had done it proud.

Looking back, the number established itself quickly, after those first few years. Pitcher **Hank Johnson** was the first to wear No. 15 in 1929 before switching to No. 14 for the next two seasons and No. 17 for one after that. Backup catcher **Art Jorgens** also wore No. 15 in 1929. He stayed with the Yankees until 1939 also wearing Nos. 28, 10, 9, and 18, making him almost a whole team by himself. In 1930 and '31, the number was taken by pitcher **Roy Sherid**, who had started out with No. 31 in 1929. It really was difficult to tell the players without a scorecard in those early years. Then in 1932, No. 15 was stabilized when it was given to **Charles Herbert "Red" Ruffing**, a man some call the greatest right-handed pitcher in the team's history.

Largely forgotten by today's fans, Ruffing has an incredibly interesting story. His big league career is a tale of two cities—Boston and New York—one bad, one more than good. In August 1923, the Red Sox got Ruffing from Danville of the Three-I League, and a year later, at the age of 19, he had his first taste of the majors. The year after that, he became a mainstay of the Red Sox rotation. There was just one problem. The Sox had become one of the worst teams in the bigs thanks to owner Harry Frazee selling off his best players (starting with Babe Ruth in 1920) to pay debts and finance his Broadway shows. In a nutshell, Ruffing took a beating. He lost 18, 15, 13, 25, and 22 games between 1925 and 1929. His 93 losses during that period were the most in the majors. At that point he was more Hall of Shame than Hall of Fame.

Then in May 1930, the Yankees got Ruffing for outfielder Cedric Durst and $50,000. Ruffing was 0–3 at the time of the trade. For the rest of the season he was 15–5. His Yankees days had begun. He had one off year in 1933; otherwise he was great. In 1936, he began a string of four, 20-win seasons as the Yanks copped four straight pennants and World Series wins. By 1940 he was 35 years old but still good enough to win 15, 15, and 14 the next three years. Ruffing showed his clutch side in the World Series. In seven Fall Classics, he had a 7–2 record and 2.63 ERA.

In 1943, despite his missing toes from a mine accident when he was 15 and now being the sole support of his wife and two children, Ruffing was drafted into the Army. He returned in July 1945 (wearing uniform No. 22 for the remainder of the season), still good enough to go 7–3. The next year, at age 41, he was back in No. 15 and started the season at 5–1 before breaking his kneecap. He was released at the end of the year and finished in 1947 with the White Sox. Despite the lean years in Boston, Ruffing wound up 273–225, good enough to be elected to the Hall of Fame in 1967. As a hitter, he finished at .269, with 36 home runs—behind only Wes Ferrell and Bob Lemon among pitchers—and 273 runs batted in, the most for any pitcher in major league history.

FINISH WHAT YOU STARTED

In the days when pitchers routinely went the distance, Red Ruffing had more complete games than any other Yankee. Here's the top five slots, occupied by seven pitchers. The only one close to a modern-day moundsman is Whitey Ford. These guys weren't begging to have a closer. They did it themselves.

Red Ruffing............................ 261 complete games
Lefty Gomez........................... 173 complete games
Jack Chesbro .... 168 complete games
Herb Pennock........................ 164 complete games
Bob Shawkey .... 164 complete games
Whitey Ford............................ 156 complete games
Waite Hoyt.............................. 156 complete games

The reason Red Ruffing wore No. 22 when returning from the service in 1945 was **Hank Borowy**. A righthander who attended Fordham University and signed with the Yanks in 1939, Borowy didn't get to the majors until 1943. With Ruffing gone to the service, the 26-year-old Borowy was given No. 15 and put in the starting rotation. Over the next three years he pitched well, with records of 15–4, 14–9, and 17–12. In 1945, he was 10–5 for the Yanks in July when he was suddenly sold to the Cubs for $97,000. Maybe the Yanks figured with players returning from the war there wouldn't be room for him. He went 11–2 for the Cubs to complete his best season at 21–7.

Ruffing took the number back in 1946, but after his injury, it was passed along to Old Reliable Tommy Henrich, who had worn No. 7 (and is discussed in that chapter) before the war, then No. 15 from 1946 until his retirement in 1950. Outfielder **Archie Wilson** played three games as No. 23 in 1951 and four games as No. 15 in 1952. Then in 1953, first sacker **Joe Collins** took over the number through 1957. Collins was one of the pieces manager Casey Stengel moved around during the platoon years of the '50s, years when the Yanks were in the World Series almost every year.

Collins platooned at first with several right-handed swinging teammates for eight years, and while never a great player, contributed to seven Yankees World Series teams. He wore No. 42 in 1948 and No. 41 the next year, when he played a total of 12 games. In 1950, he became the first sacker against right-handed pitchers, keeping No. 41 through 1952. Then he switched to No. 15 until he retired. Collins hit four World Series home runs, all of which came in clutch situations.

Outfielder **Jim Pisoni** wore No. 15 for a total of 37 games in 1959 and '60, failing to get his batting average over the Mendoza Line either year. In 1961, reserve outfielder **Jack Reed** took over the number. Reed was used mainly as a late-inning defensive replacement, but stayed with the team three years, switching to No. 27 in 1962 and '63.

When Jack Reed took No. 15 in 1961, it was because he was there when **Tom Tresh** wasn't. Tresh wore No. 15 during his nine game cup-of-coffee. The next year the Yanks needed a shortstop when the incumbent Tony Kubek went into the service. There was a spring training competition between Tresh and Phil Linz, which ended when Tresh was named the starter. He wanted No. 15, because that was the number his father, Mike, wore when he caught for the White Sox. Tresh then made the number stand out when he batted .286, hit 20 homers, and drove home 93 runs to be named American League Rookie of the Year. Tresh was a switch hitter with power and, anticipating Kubek's return, the Yanks even played him in the outfield for 43 games.

The next year, Tresh was a full-time outfielder and hopefully a coming star. But something strange happened. He continued to show power, but his average began dropping. While he would hit 25, 26, and 27 homers in three of the next four seasons, the most runs he would drive in was 74, a far cry from the 93 his rookie season. Despite 27 homers in 1966, he hit just .233. He hurt his knee the next spring and needed surgery. He came back to play 130 games but hit just .219, and when he failed to top the Mendoza Line with a .195 average in 152 games and just 11 homers in '68, his star began to set. Some say the knee was never the same and after hitting just .182 in 45 games in '69 the Yanks traded him to Detroit for Ron Woods. He finished the season with the Tigers and then retired at the age of 31. Tresh had his moments, but never quite lived up to the great expectations of his rookie year.

After Tresh was traded in June 1969, the Yankees called up a young catcher and gave him No. 15. Thurman Munson would be the last to wear it. It was retired in his honor in 1980 to help celebrate the life of the ill-fated Yankees' captain.

#16: THE CHAIRMAN OF THE BOARD

Here we go again, another Yankees number that's been retired. But then again, what else do you do with the number of the best lefthander in franchise history, a Hall of Famer with the top winning percentage of any pitcher in MLB history? That's how good **Edward Charles "Whitey" Ford** was. Known as "The Chairman of the Board" to the media and "Slick" to his friends, the 5'10" 180-pound southpaw won 236 games while losing just 106 in a Yankees career that lasted 16 years, not counting two spent in the military. Along the way the Queens native won a Cy Young Award, was the victor in a record 10 World Series games, and set a record by throwing 32 consecutive scoreless innings in the Fall Classic.

Whitey didn't wear No. 16 when he was called up by the Yanks in the middle of the 1950 season at the age of 21. He wore No. 19 that year, but it wasn't his number that mattered, rather it was his talent. Both starting and relieving, he won his first nine decisions and ended the year with a 9–1 mark and 2.81 ERA. He started 12 games that year and completed seven of them, then got his first World Series win when he threw 8 2/3 innings of shutout ball in Game Four of the sweep against the Phils.

As happened so often then, Ford was drafted into the Army and spent the next two years working for Uncle Sam. When he returned in 1953, he was given No. 16 and showed he hadn't missed a beat, going 18–6 as the Yanks won their fifth straight pennant and World Series. Ford was an instant ace. Manager Stengel, who liked to platoon, mix, and match in those days, often didn't pitch Ford on his regular four-day turn. He sometimes held him out so he could pitch against the better teams. Still, the crafty lefthander won 16, 18, 19, 11 (injured part of the

year), 14, 16, and 12 games during Stengel's tenure, and the team continued to
win, as well.

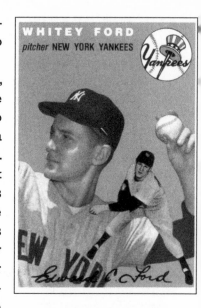

Though Ford possessed a good fastball,
he was a lot more than just a thrower. He
had impeccable control and the ability to
mix his pitches, combining the heater with
a good curve and outstanding changeup.
He was also a fine fielder and had a quick
pickoff move. The consummate pro, he was
at his best in the biggest games. When he
was on the mound, Whitey Ford was always
ready. Through the 1960 season he already
had seven World Series victories and four
rings. And in the '60 Series against Pittsburgh, he had thrown two complete game
shutouts. After the season, however, Stengel was fired and Ralph Houk
became the Yankees' skipper. Houk decided to pitch his ace every four
days and Ford responded with the greatest season of his career.

Whitey started 39 times that year and threw a career high 283
innings, best in the league. He was almost unbeatable with a 25–4
record and a career-best 209 strikeouts. The Yankees won yet another
pennant and Ford won the Cy Young Award (when there was just one
for both leagues) as the best pitcher in baseball. As the Yanks swept
the Cincinnati Reds in the World Series that year, the redoubtable lefty
won two more games without giving up a run and broke Babe Ruth's
longstanding record when he completed 32 straight scoreless innings.
There was no doubting his talent any more.

Two years later he was almost as good, compiling a 24–7 record
with a 2.74 ERA and 13 complete games. He was already 34 years old.
He continued to pitch well for two more years, winning 17 and then
16. By then, the Yankees' dynasty was also crumbling and Whitey was
just a part-time pitcher his final two years of 1966 and '67. In his final
season, he started just seven times and was 2–4, but with an ERA of
1.64. He was still stingy with the runs.

GETTING AN EDGE OR CHEATING

Late in his career there were always stories of Whitey "cutting" the baseball, a way in which some pitchers got an edge. They would put a scuff mark or small scratch on the ball and it would dip or drop just a little more than usual. No pitcher likes to admit wrongdoing or any kind of doctoring of the baseball. Some have been caught redhanded with a tack in their glove or sandpaper in their pocket, and that's embarrassing. Whitey was never caught but years later admitted he had a little burr cut into his wedding band that he used to doctor the ball. "This pitch wasn't like the spitter or mudball," he said. "It just sank slightly more than my ordinary pitches."

Ford left the game in 1967; his pal Mantle left the next year. Both were inducted into the Hall of Fame in 1974 and deservedly so. Each played a major role in one of the greatest Yankees eras of them all. Seven years after Whitey Ford retired, the Yankees also had a retirement ceremony, for his No. 16. It would never be worn again for the simple reason that there could never be another Chairman of the Board.

Before Ford the No. 16 had been passed around, especially in the early years when players often wore several numbers during their Yankees tenure. It may surprise some that **Tom Zachary,** the pitcher best known for giving up Babe Ruth's epic 60th home run in 1927, was also the first Yankees' player to wear No. 16 in 1929. And that year, he also became the first and only pitcher to go undefeated for a season winning 12 games or more. Zachary, in his first Yankees season, was a perfect 12–0.

The Yanks picked Zachary up off waivers in August 1928. He was just 3–3 in seven appearances, but started Game Three of the World Series against the Cardinals that year and went the distance in a 7–3 Yankees win. The next year, he appeared with No. 16 on his back and won all 12 of his decisions, appearing in 26 games and starting 11. In May 1930, the Yanks put Zachary on waivers and he was picked up by the Boston Braves. Incidentally, he wore No. 18 that year.

Hall of Famer **Herb Pennock** wore No. 16 in 1930 and '31 after being the first to wear No. 11 in 1929. Then in 1931, pitcher **Wilcy Moore** took over No. 16 as Pennock decided to switch to No. 12. Moore was a 30-year-old rookie in 1927 and appeared in 50 games, only 12 of them starts. He was 19–7, winning 13 games in relief and saving 13 more. In 1929, he wore No. 18, but was already experiencing the arm problems that would curtail his career. He went to the Red Sox in 1932, then came back to the Yankees in August of 1932 and stayed through the 1933 season wearing No. 16.

Gordon Rhodes, another of those unheralded pitchers, saw action with the Yanks from 1929 through part of the 1932 season, and was another guy who wore multiple numbers. He started with No. 21 in 1929, then switched to No. 19 the next two years, and finally to No. 16 in 1932 until he was dealt to Boston. Righthander **Jimmie DeShong** wore No. 16 while pitching mostly relief in 1934 and '35. Righthander **Monte Pearson** came to the Yanks prior to the 1936 season in a trade with the Indians that sent Johnny Allen to Cleveland. He would wear No. 16 through 1940 and play on those four World Series winners (1936–39).

Outfielder **Johnny Lindell** was No. 16 for just a single game in 1941. Though he would stay with the Yanks through part of the 1950 season, he would be much better known for wearing No. 27. **Tuck Stainback**, a backup outfielder, had No. 16 for two years in 1942 and '43, then switched to No. 1 for the 1944 season and finished his Yankees days as No. 18 a year later. Pitcher **Mel Queen** was with the Yankees for parts of four seasons, wearing No. 16 in 1944, but starting with No. 36 two years earlier, then wearing No. 17 in his final seasons of 1946 and '47. Relief ace **Joe Page** donned No. 16 his rookie year of 1944 before switching to the number he is remembered for, No. 11. **Herb Crompton** and **Frank Hiller** are two more forgotten names who wore the number in 1945 and '46 respectively, while **Ernie Nevel** had it briefly in 1950 before switching to No. 26 for a single game a year later. The only other player to wear No. 16 was pitcher **Bill Bevens**, who pitched for just four years (1944–47), but deserves a special mention. The righty wore Nos. 21 and 14 before switching to No. 16 late in the 1946 season.

Bevens was just 7-13 that year, but the Yanks won the pennant and the big righty got the start in Game 4 against the Brooklyn Dodgers at

Ebbets Field. And on that day Bevens was nearly unhittable, but wild. Going into the bottom of the ninth, the Yanks led, 2–1, and Bill Bevens was three outs away from pitching the first no-hitter in World Series history. The Dodgers' only run had come on two walks, a sacrifice, and a ground out. To begin the ninth, Bevens walked his ninth batter of the game. Then, with two outs, the runner stole second and mananger Bucky Harris ordered the next batter walked intentionally. It was the pitcher's spot, and Dodger skipper Burt Shotton sent up veteran Cookie Lavagetto to pinch hit. Lavagetto swung late and drove the ball down the right field line . . . and off the wall. Both runners came around to score. Not only had Bevens lost his no-hitter, but he had lost the game as well.

The Yanks, as usual, rebounded to win the Series, but for Bevens it was a last hurrah. After the season ended, he never pitched in the majors again. And in a further irony for the 35-year-old Lavagetto, his game-winning hit would be the last of his career. One pitch, one hit, and baseball history was altered forever.

#17: THE SPRINGFIELD RIFLE AND MICK THE QUICK

Despite the Yankees' full array of superstars, the No. 17, worn by some fine players, is another that has never had that singular figure who becomes an icon worthy of Monument Park. Even in the early years, when the numbers were passed around constantly, none of the big names ever grabbed hold of it, even for a season or two. It wasn't until 1947, when righthanded pitcher **Vic Raschi** began wearing No. 17, that the number became really significant for the first time. Raschi was part of the Yanks' "Big Three" during the beginning of the Casey Stengel years when the Bombers won five straight pennants and World Series between 1949 and 1953. The other two members of the pitching triumvirate were Allie Reynolds and Eddie Lopat, with the trio going 255–117 during those five championship seasons. Raschi's contribution was a 92–40 slate.

Raschi came out of West Springfield, Massachusetts, and thus his nickname, "The Springfield Rifle." The Yanks signed him prior to the 1941 season when he was 22 years old. But the war came and Raschi didn't join the Yanks until 1946, when he was 27. He wore No. 12 during his two-game stay, but when he returned the next year he was issued No. 17 and that became his permanent number.

He started 14 games that year and went 7–2. The next year, he joined the rotation full time and proceeded to go on a six-year run in which he was a good as any pitcher in the league. Raschi was a 6'1", 205-pounder who was strong and tough. He stuck mostly with his great fastball, but occasionally threw a slider and change to keep the hitters honest. The big guy also looked menacing on the mound. He would scowl at hitters and was always unshaven when he pitched.

Raschi went 19–8 in 1948, and over the pennant-winning years he won 21, 21, 21, 16, and 13. He led the league with 37 starts in 1949 and had 21 complete games. He also led with 34 starts and 164 strikeouts in 1951. In 1949, it was his 21st victory against Boston on the last day of the season that clinched the pennant for the New Yorkers. He also went 5–3 in six winning World Series, and his earned run average was a sparkling 2.24. He was never afraid of taking the ball in a big game and almost always pitched well.

After the 1953 season in which he went 13–6, the Yankees decided to cut his salary. They were spoiled by his 21-win seasons and looked for any excuse to make a cut. Raschi flat out refused and on February 23, 1954, he was sold to the St. Louis Cardinals. He was 34 years old then and on the downside. He went 8–9 with the Cards in '54, then split the 1955 season between St. Louis and Kansas City before retiring. Because he got a relatively late start, he won just 132 games, but lost half that amount, 66, for an impressive .667 winning percentage.

Flash forward to December 11, 1975. The Yankees, liking their pennant chances in '76 after a long drought, traded productive outfielder Bobby Bonds to the California Angels for pitcher Ed Figueroa and centerfielder **Mickey Rivers**. Though Figueroa would become a 20-game winner for the Yanks, Rivers was the guy they wanted. He was a lightning-fast leadoff hitter and centerfielder, a 27-year-old coming off a .284 season with a league-best 70 stolen bases, most in the American League since Ty Cobb in 1915. One of Rivers's nicknames was certainly apropos. They called him "Mick the Quick."

But then there was also the other nickname. Gozzlehead. It was a nickname bestowed upon him when he was growing up in Florida. It originally referred to his looks, but later it came to exemplify the way he acted. Rivers could sulk, said things that were tantamount to Yogisms—"I'd like to hit .300, score 100 runs, and stay injury-prone"—and was very careless with money, often spending time and money at the local race tracks. He was a complete character, a player who walked slowly to home plate, looking slightly bent over and walking gingerly on his tip toes. But once he hit the ball he took off like a shot, running out triples like no other player in baseball at the time.

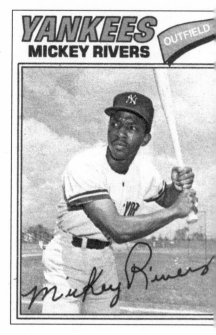

Rivers, indeed, became a spark plug of three Yankees pennant winners and two world championship teams. Wearing No. 17, he fit perfectly into the Bronx Zoo with the other diverse personalities. He batted .312 in his first Yankees season of 1976, showed more power with eight homers and 67 RBIs, and swiped 43 bases. A year later, he hit .326 with 12 home runs and 69 ribbies. He didn't have a strong throwing arm, but his speed made him an outstanding center-fielder in mammoth Yankee Stadium. After the '76 season, his team-mates named him the Yankees Most Valuable Player.

By 1978, some of Rivers antics were beginning to weigh on the Yankees. So when he slumped in that year and hit just .265, the hand-writing may have already been on the wall. He was still hitting a solid .287 after 74 games of the 1979 season when the Yanks decided they had seen enough. On August 1, 1979, he was suddenly dealt to the Texas Rangers in a multi-player deal. The only notable player the Yanks got in return was outfielder Oscar Gamble.

Mick the Quick would play for the Rangers through the 1984 season, when he retired at the age of 35 with a .295 lifetime average.

Both Raschi as the consummate professional and Rivers as the talented but sometimes flake made No. 17 memorable during their time.

Others did, as well, but either for a shorter time or with less flair or success. Let's take a look at the potpourri of players who have worn the number, beginning with **Fred Heimach** in 1929. Heimach was a veteran lefty who began play in 1920 and came to the Yanks in 1928. He was there two years, going 11–6 in 1929, before finishing his career with Brooklyn.

Another southpaw, **Ed Wells**, had a four-year Yankee career beginning in 1929 when he wore No. 19. He wore No. 17 the next two years and finished in 1932 with No. 14 on his back. Wells was 13–9 in 1929 and 12–3 the next year, wound up finishing his career with the St. Louis Browns, and is largely forgotten.

Pitcher **"Deacon" Danny MacFayden,** was acquired from Boston in June of 1932 for Hank Johnson and took over Johnson's No. 17. He stayed through 1934, won just 14 games, and moved on, bequeathing the number to yet another hurler, **Walter George "Jumbo" Brown**, as the parade of mediocrity continued. Jumbo, however, earned his nickname. He stood 6'4" and weighed a mammoth 295 pounds. When he came to the Yanks in '32, he hadn't been in the bigs for four years. He wore No. 19 for two years, didn't pitch in 1934, and came back his final two years as No. 17.

Tommy Henrich was a guy who could have made No. 17 memorable, but he wore it only in his second season of 1938. Old Reliable was better remembered for wearing Nos. 7 and 15. Outfielder **Jake Powell** wore No. 17 in 1939 and 1940 after wearing No. 7 his first three years with the club. He swapped numbers with Henrich. Maybe the Yankees felt Tommy was going to be the bigger, longterm star. Outfielder **Buster Mills** also wore No. 17 for just 34 games in 1940. The parade of forgettable No. 17s continued as pitcher **Charley Stanceu** wore the number for 22 games in 1941. He would return for just three games in 1946 as No. 20. Outfielder/first baseman **Ed Levy** was next, wearing No. 17 for just 13 games in 1942, then returning for 40 more in 1944, for which he donned No. 9.

Next came wartime pitcher **Bill Zuber**, who wore No. 17 from 1943 through June of 1946, when he was sold to the Red Sox. Pitcher **Mel Queen** was up in even years, 1942, '44, and '46, wearing Nos. 36, 16, and 17, respectively. He stuck around until July 1947, again wearing No. 17, until he was sold to the Pirates. That's when Raschi took over and had his great run through 1953. After that, the names become more familiar, beginning with Hall of Famer **Enos "Country" Slaughter**, the original Mr. Hustle.

Slaughter forged his reputation with the Cardinals, playing in St. Louis from 1938 to 1953. He was the original Pete Rose, running to first on a walk and going all-out every minute of every game. He and Stan Musial were the heart of some great Cardinals teams of the 1940s. The Yanks traded for him right before the start of the 1954 season in exchange for three players, including outfielder Bill Virdon. Slaughter was just ready to turn 38 years of age.

Even at 38, he still hustled and, donning No. 17, became an important spare part on some fine Yankee teams, pinch hitting and playing both left and right field. Slaughter hit just .248 in 69 games in '54, and in May 1955 was traded along with veteran pitcher Johnny Sain to Kansas City for a minor leaguer. But in August 1956, the Yanks took him back off waivers and, at age 40, he hit .350 in the World Series that year against the Dodgers, including a home run. He was primarily a pinch hitter the next two years, but still managed to hit .304 in 1958. In September 1959, the Yanks sent the 43-year-old Slaughter to the Braves to help them in a pennant chase. He finally retired after the season and was elected to the Hall of Fame in 1985, mainly for his work with the Cardinals.

Another 39-year-old veteran, **Elmer Valo**, played eight games with the Yankees as No. 17 in 1960, while young **Lee Thomas** played just two games wearing No. 17 the following year. Burly **Bob Cerv,** mostly a reserve outfielder, wore No. 17 for parts of 1960, '61, and '62. Why parts? The Yanks kept dealing him and then getting him back. But they already had a history. Cerv had played for the Yanks from 1951–56 before being sold to Kansas City that October.

He never played in more than 56 games nor hit more than five homers despite being a big, strong guy. But the Yanks never saw him as a regular, and after the 1956 season he was sold to Kansas City.

Two years later, big Bob suddenly became one of the top sluggers in the American league, hitting .304 with 38 home runs and 104 RBIs.

On May 19, 1960, the Yanks sent third sacker Andy Carey to KC and brought Cerv back to New York. That's when he began wearing No. 17. But once again he couldn't break into the Yankee outfield. At season's end he was drafted by the expansion Angels, only to be traded back to the Yankees the next May. This time he stayed until June 1962, when he was purchased by the Houston Colt 45s only to be released a month later.

Bobby Murcer wore No. 17 for 11 games in his first year of 1965 and another 21 the next year before going into the service for two years and returning as a regular in 1969 with No. 1 on his back. Reserve outfielder **Tom Shopay** wore No. 17 for eight games in 1967 and then played another 28 two years later as No. 27 before being shipped to Baltimore. Infielder **Gene "Stick" Michael** stabilized the number by wearing it between 1968 and 1974, playing mostly shortstop during one of the team's rare down periods. Michael was a good-field, no-hit player who had a hard time getting above the Mendoza Line with Pittsburgh, the Dodgers, and the Yanks from 1966–68. Then in 1972 he suddenly jumped to .272, but a year later was back to .214. His lifetime average was just .229. He later served as both manager and general manager of the Yankees and is still with them today as a Vice President.

Mickey Rivers was next, and when Rivers was dealt to Texas in 1979, **Oscar Gamble** came in return and took over No. 17. He would wear it through 1984. But that wasn't the first time the sometimes enigmatic Gamble wore the pinstripes. He debuted with the Cubs at 19 in 1969, then went to the Phils and Indians through 1975, then came to the Yanks in exchange for pitcher Pat Dobson the next year.

As the Yankees rolled to the pennant in '76, Gamble played in 110 games and had 17 homers to go with 57 RBIs. The problem was his batting average, which tumbled to .232. At season's end, after being swept by the Reds in the series, the Yankees decided they needed a shortstop and sent Gamble to the White Sox for Bucky Dent.

Without him, the Yanks won a pair of World Series. Then on August 1, 1979, the Yanks, tired of Mickey Rivers' antics, traded him to Texas in return for Gamble, who was hitting .335 in 64 games. So he was back and in 36 games hit .389 with 11 homers and 32 RBIs. For the season, he was a .358 hitter, best in the league, but his 274 at bats didn't qualify him for the batting title. Gamble would stay with the Yanks for the next five years through 1984, play more than 100 games just once, and continue to be plagued by inconsistency. When the Yanks didn't offer him a contract he signed with the White Sox, hit just .204 in 1985, and then retired.

Once Gamble left the team, the No. 17 became a nomad, going from one player to another on an almost yearly basis right through 2009. It became a rarity for a player to have the number two years in succession. Let's take a look at the passing parade of No. 17s.

Outfielder **Victor Mata** was the first in 1985, and one of the most forgettable. He wore No. 17 for just six games and seven at-bats in 1985 after wearing No. 55 for 30 games the year before. **Mike "The Hit Man" Easler** inherited No. 17 in 1986. Easler made his reputation elsewhere, his best season being with Boston in 1984, when he hit .313 with 27 homers and 91 RBIs. The Yanks got him in a trade for another veteran, Don Baylor, and the 35-year-old Easler responded with a .302 average, 14 HRs, and 78 RBIs in 146 games. Yet, with the Yanks in a rebuilding mode, he was traded to the Phils as season's end, only to come back in another minor deal the following June. He played the final 65 games of his career in pinstripes wearing No. 34.

Infielder **Paul Zuvella** wore No. 17 in 1987 after wearing No. 26 a year earlier. Yet he played in just 35 games total as a Yankee and couldn't hit above the Mendoza Line. A year later, infielder **Rafael Santana** inherited No. 17 and hit .240 in his only Yankees season. After a year in mothballs, No. 17 came out again in 1990 on the back of veteran **Claudell Washington**, who came over from the Angels at the end of April in a deal for pitcher Rich Monteleone and outfielder **Luis Polonia**. Washington had also been with the Yanks from 1986 to 1988, at which time he wore No. 18. He then left as a free agent and signed with the Angels.

So the uniform moved on. Outfielder **Scott Lusader** wore it for 11 games in 1991, then passed on that same year to **Pat Sheridan**, who hit .204 in 62 games. Utility infielder **Andy Stankiewicz** was No. 17

CLAUDELL
WASHINGTON

in 1992, hitting .268 in 116 games. He returned for just 16 games the following year wearing No. 35 and failed to get a hit. Veteran infielder **Spike Owen** wore the jersey in 1993 and hit just .234 in 103 games before moving on during a period when the team was looking to build a title team again.

Veteran outfielder **Luis Polonia** came as a free agent in 1994 and donned the oft-worn No. 17. It was the second of three Polonia stints in New York. Essentially a singles hitter who could steal a base, Polonia was with the Yanks for parts of 1989 and 1990 (wearing No. 22), traded by Oakland with pitchers Greg Caderet and Eric Plunk in exchange for All-Star Rickey Henderson. But Polonia was no Henderson and was shipped out early in 1990. He would return for two more stints in 1994 and again in August of 2000, but never became a force. He finished the 2000 season wearing No. 19, got to play in the winning World Series against the Mets, then retired.

Ruben Rivera took over No. 17 after Polonia was traded in 1995. A tall, speedy outfielder, he was considered a real prospect, but got in just five games that year. The next season he was called up long enough to play in 46 games, this time wearing No. 28. Then he was sent to San Diego in a multi-player deal involved mostly minor leaguers. In February 2002, the Yanks took another chance and signed him as a free agent. And that's when Rivera got major ink from the New York press, but it wasn't for his exploits on the field. Rivera, it seemed, decided to appropriate one of teammate Derek Jeter's gloves and sell it to a memorabilia collector for $2,500. This after signing a $1-million contract with the team. It was a serious no-no. Ultimately, the glove was returned, and after just one month back with the Yankees, Rivera was released.

Then along came "The Gambler." Taking his nickname from his country music namesake's hit song, **Kenny Rogers** was a good lefthanded pitcher who would win 219 games in his career. Starting with Texas as a reliever, he became a starter in 1993, won 16 games, then threw a perfect game the next year and won 17 the year after that (1995). That's when the Yankees signed him as a free agent, bringing him to New York in 1996 and giving him No. 17. When he left two years later, he was a guy everyone thought couldn't handle the big stage and bright lights of New York.

His regular season record in two seasons was 12–8 and 6–7, mediocre at best. But in the playoffs he was absolutely horrendous. After the 1997 season, he was traded to Oakland with cash in return for third baseman Scott Brosius.

But none of those players enhanced the reputation of No. 17. Infielder **Dale Sveum** lasted just part of one season with No. 17 in 1998, hitting a meek .155 and being released in early August. The next two years, the number was worn by outfield prospect **Ricky Ledee**, who some said had a swing like Don Mattingly, but unfortunately not the results. In 1990 he was shipped to Cleveland in return for veteran slugger David Justice.

Pitcher **Dwight Gooden** donned No. 17 for part of the 2000 season, his last in the majors. He was 4–2 in 18 games before retiring. In his early stint with the Bombers, in 1996 and '97 he wore No. 11. Outfielder **Gerald Williams** took over the number for parts of 2001 and 2002 as the parade of players continued. He had also been a part-time player from 1992 to 1996, wearing Nos. 13, 36, and 29, but just didn't show enough to earn a full time job or stick around. Another outfielder, **Darren Bragg**, was No. 17 for just five games in 2002, and infielder **Alex Arias** wore it for the final six games of his big league career in 2002.

Next it was catcher **John Flaherty**'s turn. "Flash" wore No. 17 from 2003 to 2005, doing a nice job backing up Jorge Posada. A solid catcher with an average bat, he had been in the league since 1992 and played for several teams.

After Flaherty, No. 17 went nomadic again. Utility infielder **Nick Green**, a have-glove, will-travel type, wore the number in 2006. Then in 2007, pitcher **Jeff Karstens** wore it for part of the year and donned No. 58 for another portion of the season. That gave career minor leaguer **Shelley Duncan** his chance to wear No. 17 in 2007. Duncan hit some mammoth homers, but was back in the minors most of the next two seasons. Young **Justin Christian** had No. 17 in 2008, catcher **Kevin Cash** briefly the next year, and then veteran utilityman **Jerry Hairston Jr.**, a valuable acquisition in 2009, became the latest to have No. 17 on his back. So it continues to be a number in search of a star, and knowing the Yankees, that's sure to happen one of these days.

#18: LOSING PITCHER; PERFECT GAME

Had it not been for one autumn afternoon in October, **Don Larsen** would have been remembered (if anyone remembered him) as just another of baseball's many losing pitchers, a guy who never won more than 11 games in a season and lost as many as 21. But on October 8, 1956, not only did Don Larsen win a game, he won a World Series game, and he won it with the greatest pitching performance in World Series history. For the two people who don't know by now, on that day the big, 6'4" righthander with the no-windup style pitched a perfect game, retiring 27 Brooklyn Dodgers in order as the Yankees won, 2–0, en route to yet another World Series triumph.

Larsen had come to the Yanks a year earlier from the Baltimore Orioles, a team that had been known as the St. Louis Browns up until 1954. They moved to Baltimore that year and Larsen, a second year pitcher, promptly went 3–21, becoming the losingest pitcher in the league. Two of his wins, however, came against the Yanks, and in November the Yanks acquired him, along with infielder Billy Hunter and pitcher Bob Turley (who would prove a more valuable acquisition) in a deal that involved 17 players. Larsen spent the first half of the 1955 season at Triple-A Denver, going 9–1. He was promoted to the Yanks midway

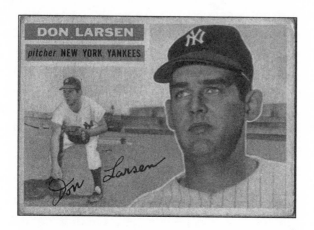

through the season, given No. 18, and then compiled a 9–2 record in the second half, both starting and relieving.

Larsen again made the team out of spring training in 1956 and became a more valuable pitcher that year, both starting and relieving in almost equal numbers, with 20 starts and 18 appearances out of the pen. Larsen now worked out of a no-windup style that he said gave him better control, and finished with an 11–5 record with a 3.26 ERA as the Bombers won yet another pennant and geared up for a World Series rematch against the Dodgers, a team that had finally beaten them a year earlier.

Larsen got the start in Game Two that year and was knocked out in the second inning. So when he got the call again in the fifth game at Yankee Stadium, there were plenty of skeptics, especially with the Series tied at two games each. This one was pivotal.

Using his no-windup delivery, Larsen began setting the Dodgers down, 1–2–3, 1–2–3, 1–2–3. The only close call in those first three innings came in the second when Jackie Robinson hit a shot that deflected off third sacker Andy Carey's glove right to shortstop Gil McDougald, who threw him out. The Yanks got one off the Dodgers' Sal

Maglie in the fourth, and in the Dodgers' fifth, Gil Hodges hit a drive to left-center that Mickey Mantle ran down, making a nifty backhand grab. The Yanks got a second run in the fifth as Larsen kept up the 1–2–3 rhythm right to the ninth. By then, in keeping with the superstition of the day, none of his Yankees teammates were talking to him.

In the ninth, the big righty set down Carl Furillo, then Roy Campanella. One batter now stood between Larsen and perfection, Larsen and immortality. And when pinch hitter Dale Mitchell took a called third strike, it was over. Yogi Berra leapt into Larsen's arms and into history. It was the first and only no hitter and perfect game in World Series history.

Larsen and No. 18 were the toast of baseball that winter. But spring comes, as always, and the what-have-you-done-for-me-lately mentality takes over. Big Don was 10–4 in 1957, but didn't emerge as a big star. He was 9–6 the next year and won another World Series game, but just 6–7 the year after that. By then, the Yankees knew he would never become a big winner for them, and in December 1959 they made another of their seemingly endless trades with Kansas City, sending Larsen to purgatory.

At Kansas City, without the big Bomber bats behind him, Larsen had a putrid 1–10 season. He would hang on with several clubs until 1967 and retire with a lifetime mark of 81–91. But his one achievement remains a high-water mark and he's often feted at Old Timers' Days, when he and Yogi Berra reunite to create one of the great moments in baseball history.

Prior to Larsen, No. 18 was another number without a real identity. In fact, while Larsen's perfect game is now part of Yankees lore, few if any associate pitcher and number. As always, the early years saw players who changed numbers several times and just made No. 18 a pit stop. For example, the first to wear it was pitcher **Wilcy Moore** in 1929. He wound up in the minors the next year, spent a year in Boston, then came back to the Yanks as No. 16 for part of 1932 and then 1933. In 1930, pitcher **Tom Zachary** took over the number. A year earlier, the man who gave up Ruth's number 60 with Washington was the first Yankee to wear No. 16. And in 1931, Hall of Fame pitcher **Red Ruffing** was No. 18. A year, later he would move to No. 15 and begin to make his mark. Two marginal players, **Lou McEvoy** and **Bill Henderson**, also wore No. 18 for part of the 1930 season. Then, in 1932, right-handed pitcher **Johnny Allen** pulled on uniform jersey No. 18.

Allen hit the ground running as a 27-year-old rookie in 1932, compiling a 17–4 record for the pennant winning Yankees. Allen followed that with a 15–7 season in 1933, then came down with a sore arm the next year and was just 5–2. He bounced back to go 13–6 in 1935, but the Yanks had enough and that December packaged him off to Cleveland for Monte Pearson and a player named Steve Sundra.

Backup catcher **Art Jorgens** has been mentioned before since during his 11-year Yankee career (1929–39) he wore Nos. 15, 28, 10, 9, and 18. He took over No. 18 the final four years of his career. Though he was with five Yankees pennant-winning teams, he never once appeared in a World Series game. Pitcher **Steve Peek** wore No. 18 in 1941, just long enough for the fans to get a peek, and then the next two years outfielder **Johnny Lindell** took over the number. Lindell wore No. 16 in a one-game cameo in 1941, then put on No. 18 the following year and wore it for two seasons. He then moved to No. 8 for another two years before wearing No. 27 his final five years in pinstripes. So he'll be noted more in Chapter 27.

Weak-hitting reserve outfielder **Tuck Stainback** wore No. 16 for two years in 1942 and '43, switched to No. 1 in 1944, and finished as No. 18 a year later. Wartime pitcher **Johnny Johnson** was No. 18 in 1944, never won a game but saved three. A pair of tall right-handers, **Karl Drews** and **Randy Gumpert**, both gave No. 18 a try between 1946 and 1948. Drews wore the uniform for three games in 1946, then returned as No. 19 the next two years, while Gumpert had it for part of '46 and then for the next two years. Neither pitcher was particularly successful and both were sold within a month of each other in 1948. A first sacker with the unlikely name of **Fenton Mole**—his teammates sure must have had fun with that one—wore No. 18 for all of 10 games in 1949.

The parade continued. Righthander **Bob Porterfield** began his career with the Yanks, wearing No. 18 from 1948–1950. He never won more than five games in a season, switched to No. 23 in 1951 when recalled from the minors for two games, then was moved to Washington for lefty Bob Kuzava. Righty **Dave Madison** wore the number for a single game in 1950 when Porterfield was in the minors, while another righthander, **Bob Muncrief** borrowed the number for two games in 1951, his final games of a mediocre 12-year career. It was the same for **Jack Kramer**, also in 1951. He was signed in May, released in August, but pitched in 19 games. Righthanders **Ray Scarborough** and **Jim McDonald** were next. The former was purchased from the Red Sox in August of 1952 and released in August of '53. He wore No. 18 his first year, No. 19 his last. The latter pitched mostly relief as No. 18 from 1952–54. Then Larsen inherited No. 18, in reality the next mediocre pitcher to wear it.

For nearly 15 years, a wide variety of hurlers wore the number and few were winners. Young **Eli Grba** was with the Yanks two years, wearing No. 47 in 1959 and No. 18 a year later, when he went 6–4 in 29 games. But that was it. He was taken by the Los Angeles Angels in the expansion draft of 1961. **Fred Kipp** came over from the Dodgers in a trade in April 1960, pitched just four games as No. 18 and was gone, his career over.

When relief pitcher **Hal Reniff** was issued uniform No. 18 in 1961, he would wear it for almost seven seasons. A six-foot, 215-pound right-handed reliever, affectionately called "Porky" by his teammates, Reniff came out of the Yankee bullpen 247 times without ever starting as baseball began evolving more into a game of specialties. He had 18 saves in 1963 and appeared in a career high 56 games three years later. Reniff also pitched in two World Series ('63 and '64) and was unscored upon in four games. He was finally sold to the Mets in June 1967 as the Yankee dynasty crumbled and he retired after that season.

When the Yankees traded for lefthander **Steve Barber** in July 1967, the bloom was already off the rose, though the Yanks didn't know it at the time. Barber was one of a kiddie corps of pitchers who joined the Baltimore Orioles in the early 1960s. He had an explosive fastball, but his biggest problem was controlling it. Nevertheless he became a

20-game winner and looked to have a future. He was off to a great start in 1966 (10–5) when arm trouble shelved him for the rest of the year.

After that, Barber began losing and was just 4–9 when the Orioles shipped him to the Yanks, where he was given No. 18. He didn't fare much better in New York, going 6–9 the rest of the way for a 10–18 season mark. When he was just 6–5 the following year, still plagued by wildness and arm problems, the Yanks left him open to the expansion draft and the Seattle Pilots claimed him.

But Barber's Yankees stay was pale in comparison to another lefty, **Mike Kekich**. Like Barber, the results didn't approach the talent level, but Kekich also gave the staid Yankees a taste of scandal that today would dominate the news for weeks at a time. On the pitching side, Kekich first full year was 1968 when he pitched to a 2–10 record for the LA Dodgers. Yet the scouts felt he was a guy who could be very successful if he put it all together, and the Yanks sent outfielder Andy Kosco to the Dodgers for Kekich in December of '68. In 1969, he was in the Bronx as he Yankees went about rebuilding a team that had crashed.

Wearing No. 18, Kekich spent the next four years trying to find it as he went 4–6, 6–3, 10–9, and 10–13. Like so many southpaws, he struggled to find his control, but every now and then would throw a great game, and the team continued to hang on that tantalizing word – potential. Then in early 1973 a story broke that caught the team and the baseball world by surprise. Kekich and teammate Fritz Peterson, another southpaw, had literally switched families. Each had fallen in love with the other's wife. Kekich had moved in with Peterson's wife and kids, and Peterson was living with Kekich's wife and kids. It was like a soap opera, and that wasn't in keeping with the Yankees image. In June, Kekich was exiled to Cleveland for Lowell Palmer, but his career still didn't take off. An elbow injury ended it in 1977 and he retired with a record of 39–51. As a footnote, both players obtained divorces and married the other's ex-wife. Peterson and his wife are still married, though Kekich eventually divorced Peterson's former wife. But for a couple of weeks in 1973, all of New York was abuzz with the story of the family-swapping lefthanders.

With the departure of Kekich No. 18 began to be passed around once again. You could almost look at it as a number with a jinx attached to it since so many pitchers who wore it had losing records and the position players came and went in revolving door fashion. As soon as Kekich left in 1973, righthander **Dave Pagan** wore the uniform for just four games. Pagan came back for parts of the next three years wearing No. 53 and had a Yankees record of just 2–4. First baseman/outfielder **Mike Hegan** also donned the jersey in 1973. The son of longtime Indians catcher Jim Hegan, Mike never quite made it past substitute status in two tours with the Yanks.

Trying their luck with non-pitchers, the Yankees assigned No. 18 to outfielder **Larry Murray** in 1974 and again the next year, though he was up twice in '74 and also wore No. 52. In 1976, he appeared as No. 47. Those three seasons consisted of 20 total games. Outfielder **Dave Bergman** was next, wearing No. 18 for seven games in 1975 then coming back as No. 54 for five more games two years later before he was sent to Houston. Bergman went 1-for-21 at the plate as a Yankee. But he did go on to a 17-year career with several other teams.

Lefty reliever **Tippy Martinez** wore No. 18 briefly in 1976 and had been No. 40 during brief trials in 1974 (10 games), 1975 (23 games, 8 saves), and early in '76 before switching numbers. But Martinez went to the Baltimore Orioles in a 10-player trade that June and missed out on the Yankees' first pennant since 1964. The southpaw went on to an outstanding career with the Orioles and played on some great Baltimore teams in the late '70s and early 1980s. One of the players who came to the Yanks in the same deal, veteran catcher **Ellie Hendricks**, wore No. 18 for just 12 games in 1976 and '77, while infielder **Dennis Sherrill** pulled the jersey on for two games in 1978. He would for three more in 1980 as No. 57. By that time No. 18 must have seemed more unlucky than No. 13.

Infielder **Brian Doyle**'s short stay in the majors can be explained very simply. He could never crack the Mendoza Line, hitting under .200 in all four of his seasons, three of which were with the Yanks. Doyle's lifetime batting average was a paltry .161, but in the playoffs he can proudly say he was a .391 hitter.

In 1981, **Larry Milbourne** took over Doyle's utility role and No. 18. Milbourne was a vet who came over from Seattle and hit .313 in 61 games. But the Yanks played yo-yo with him. After playing 14 games in 1982, he was dealt to the Twins, who turned around and traded him to the Indians. At the end of the year he went to the Phils and in July of 1983, the Yanks bought him back, long enough to play another 31 games wearing No. 39. He hit just .200 that year, was traded to Seattle after the season, and then retired.

The revolving door continued. Outfielder **Mike Patterson** was No. 18 for just 11 games in 1982 after wearing No. 56 in four games a year earlier. Then infielder **Rodney Scott** was given No. 18 for just 10 games in 1982. He hit .192 and was gone. **Andre Robertson** lasted almost five seasons as a utility infielder, started out with a 10-game cup of coffee as No. 55 in 1981, then wore No. 18 through 1985. Robertson played as many as 98 games in 1983, but never hit much, his career slowed by a bad car accident on the West Side Highway late in 1983. His .248 that year was his best. Then in 1985, he suddenly hit .328 in 50 games. Yet he didn't make the club out of spring training the next year and was dealt to the Braves June 30, 1986, with Ken Griffey Sr. for Claudell Washington and Paul Zuvella. Robertson never made the majors again.

The veteran Washington then wore No. 18 for three years, until 1988, and then would return briefly in 1990 as No. 17. Utilityman **Jamie Quirk**, who had a 17 year career and played every position except pitcher and centerfielder, wore No. 18 for 13 games in 1989, but was released in May. Then infielder **Randy Velarde** took the number and had the most sustained success in years, wearing it through the 1995 season. Velarde wore No. 29 his first two Yankees seasons of 1987–88, then switched to No. 18 and settled in as a utility infielder who occasionally took a turn in the outfield. Velarde played more than 100 games twice, was a consistent hitter, usually in the .270s range, with a bit of pop. In 1995, he played 111 games, hitting .278 with seven homers and 46 RBIs. Even though the Yanks finally made the playoffs and were again becoming a top team, Velarde at age 32 decided to test the free agent market and signed with the Angels.

Infielders **Mariano Duncan** in 1996 and '97, and **Andy Fox** in 1997, both wore No. 18 for a short term. Then in November 1997, the Yanks sent pitcher Kenny Rogers and cash to Oakland for a player to be named later and that turned out to be third baseman **Scott Brosius**. This was really a case of right place, right time, and Brosius, in truth a mediocre player, would carve out a place in Yankees lore wearing No. 18. He joined the Yanks the year the team won an AL record 114 regular season games. Brosius picked the right time to have his biggest year, hitting .300 with 19 homers and a career best 98 runs batted in. He also played

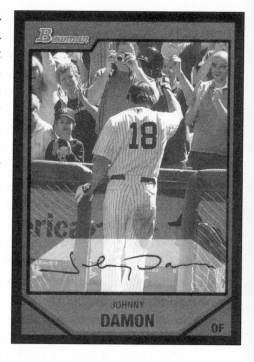

JOHNNY
DAMON
OF

a solid third base. Brosius went on a tear in the World Series, batting .471 with two homers and six RBIs, and was named MVP as the Yanks swept the San Diego Padres in four games.

So Brosius had joined a dynasty. The Yanks would win the World Series the next two years so people hardly noticed that the third sacker's numbers were going down. And while he was a good third sacker, he certainly wasn't great. Then came 2001. That year, Brosius rebounded to .287, but he power numbers continued downward. He had just 13 homers and 49 ribbies, not the kind of numbers teams like from their third baseman. He also made 22 errors, most in the league for a third sacker. The Yanks lost the World Series in seven games, and shortly after it ended, Brosius announced his retirement at the age of 34.

Young **Marcus Thames** was No. 18 for just seven games in 2002. He would later have some good years with Detroit. Then came pitcher **Jeff Weaver** in July 2002, a lanky righthander who was acquired from Detroit with some big expectations. Instead, the Yankees got a petulant pitcher who had a hard time dealing with jeers from the fans, a pitcher who would throw his arms up in disgust if one of his teammates made an error behind him, and one who ultimately couldn't win in New York. In December of 2003, he was part of a trade with the Dodgers that brought the Yanks veteran Kevin Brown.

Utility infielder **Homer Bush** and veteran first sacker **John Olerud** both wore No. 18 in 2004, while infielder **Andy Phillips** and outfielder **Bubba Crosby** split time with it in 2005. Then, in 2006, the Yanks signed free agent centerfielder **Johnny Damon**, and No. 18 had a top player once more.

Damon came up with the Royals in 1995 and stayed in Kansas City through the 2000 season, during which time he became a star. Speedy centerfielder and leadoff man, Damon had multiple skills. At age 26 in 2000, he hit .327, had 16 home runs and 88 RBIs. In addition, he led the American League with 136 runs scored and 46 stolen bases. Two years later he signed with Boston and continued to star.

He was one of the leaders of Boston's World Series title team of 2004 and in 2006 the Yankees outbid the Red Sox for his services by offering him a four-year deal as opposed to Boston's three. So he moved on to New York, where he cut his long hair, shaved his beard, and became a Yankee with the No. 18 on his back.

Damon was 32-years old then but still a force at the plate. He began to break down in center field a bit and the Yanks started using him more in left, but he helped the Yanks into the playoffs his first two seasons. The team missed in 2008, but Damon had another fine year in 2009. Switched to number two in the batting order behind Derek Jeter, he found the new Yankee Stadium to his liking, tying his career high with 24 homers while hitting .282 and driving in 82 runs. Plus he got a ton of clutch hits and was an offensive force once more. A free agent once more, the Yanks did not seem inclined to bring him back since they didn't want to give him the multiple-year deal he was seeking. But his New York legacy is secure.

#19: FROM MURPHY TO RAGS, A COUPLE OF STOPPERS

No. 19 with the Yankees has been pretty much dominated by pitchers, especially through 1995. Of those who wore the number until it became their own, two relievers stand out. One is often considered the first ever "closer," though that term wasn't part of the baseball lexicon when he pitched. The other was a starter who seemed poised for a possibly great career when bullpen duty called. The Yanks needed a closer after the departure of Goose Gossage in 1983, and that's when **Dave Righetti** stepped into the breach, continuing a tradition that began with **Johnny Murphy** nearly half a century before.

Johnny Murphy was called "Grandma" by his teammates, but it wasn't because of the way he pitched. Teammate Pat Malone gave him the nickname because Murphy was a complainer, always carping about meals, accommodations, and anything else that bugged him. On the mound he was essentially a curveball pitcher who was signed by scout Paul Krichell after he graduated from Fordham University in 1929. He had a cup of coffee in 1932, appearing in two games at the age of 23 wearing No. 20. When he returned for good two years later, he was wearing No. 19 and would keep it for the remainder of his Yankees career.

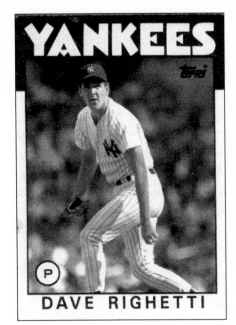

DAVE RIGHETTI

Murphy was a workhorse in '34, doing what so many pitchers did in those days, both starting and relieving. He appeared in 40 games, half of them starts, and had a 14–10 record with a 3.12 ERA. He threw 207 2/3 innings, had 10 complete games, and four saves. But the following year the Yanks began thinking that he was too valuable pitching out of the pen . In an age where there really weren't any relief specialists, Johnny Murphy became one.

Murphy made just 17 starts in 106 appearances over the next three years, and just three more after that. He was too valuable closing games before the concept of a "closer" was even conceived. While he wasn't limited to one inning like so many of today's closers, the Yanks usually waited until late in the game to bring him and his wicked curve to the mound. He had a winning record in all but two seasons and led the league in saves four times (though the stat wasn't kept then, rather recreated from box scores in later years), with a high of 19 in 1939. He was great during the Yanks' four straight World Series wins from 1936–39, and in six Fall Classics had a 2–0 record and 1.10 ERA.

Murphy departed in 1943 so he could perform war work for two years, rejoined the Yanks in 1946 at the age of 37, had another good year, and was then released. He pitched one more season for Boston before retiring for good.

By the time Dave Righetti became the Yanks' top reliever, the bullpen had evolved. Every team had relief specialists and one guy they wanted on the mound to close the game. The fine Yankees teams of the mid to late 70s had two outstanding relief specialists, Sparky

Lyle and Goose Gossage. Lyle was finally traded to Texas in 1978, and the player the Yanks wanted was the 20-year-old southpaw Righetti.

The man who would become known as "Rags" had his three-game cup of coffee in 1979, wearing No. 56. But when he returned two years later and was inserted into the rotation, he was given No. 19. Righetti started 15 times that season and went 8–4 with a 2.05 earned run average, good enough for him to be named Rookie of the Year. Control problems led him to go just 11–10 the following year, but he began to right the ship the next year with a 14–8 mark, throwing a July 4th no-hitter against the Boston Red Sox, the first Yankees' no-no since Don Larsen's perfect game in the 1956 World Series.

Then at the end of the season, fate took a hand. Rich Gossage left via free agency, signing with San Diego, and the Yanks were left without a closer. It was manager Yogi Berra who made the decision to move Righetti to the pen in 1984. Rags took to his new role easily, and a year after winning 14 as a starter, he saved 31 as a reliever, making 64 appearances. Two years later, he set a major league mark (since broken) by saving 46 games with another 74 appearances. Mixing essentially a fastball and curve, he had become one of the best.

It's unfortunate that the Yankee teams during Righetti's tenure weren't up to those of the past. His only taste of the postseason came early, in 1981, his rookie year. He continued to close for the Bombers through 1990, sometimes getting in trouble with his control, but more often than not getting out of it by making a clutch pitch. Then, after the 1990 season, the California native decided he wanted to be closer to home and he signed as a free agent with the Giants. He closed one year for the Giants, then became a situational reliever for a couple of years. Rags finished his career with the White Sox in 1995. At the age of 36, he started nine games and went 3–2, to end it the way it began.

Righetti's 224 saves as a Yankee were a team record pre-Mariano Rivera, and he finished with an 82–79 record and 252 career saves. He would later return to San Francisco as the Giants' pitching coach, a position he continues to hold as of 2009.

SAVING THE DAY

Today's closers are used much more often and more differently than those of the past. There wasn't even a "save" statistic years back, though statisticians have gone back over thousands of box scores so that they could count the saves of early relief pitchers. The Yanks have had a handful of outstanding closers, including the guy considered the best ever, Mariano Rivera. Here are the top five Yankee save artists. A couple of top guys—John Wetteland, Luis Arroyo, and Joe Page—aren't on the list because they weren't in pinstripes long enough. The top five.

Mariano Rivera....................... 526 saves (and counting)

Dave Righetti................................. 224 saves

Goose Gossage .... 151 saves

Sparky Lyle .... 141 saves

Johhny Murphy .... 104 saves

Remember, these are only saves with the Yankees. Gossage, for example, had 310 for his career, but in the modern game, many players don't stay with one team that long.

At the beginning, No. 19 was like a lost soul, shuffling between some forgettable players. Lefty pitcher **Ed Wells** was the first in 1929, but he quickly switched to No. 17 the next two years and then finished his Yankees career in 1932 as No. 14. Pitcher **Gordon Rhodes** was No. 21 in 1929, then No. 19 for three games the following year. He continued the game of musical numbers by pitching again as No. 21 in 1931 and then as No. 16 in 1932. Then he was traded to Boston for Wilcy Moore.

Utilityman **Harry Rice** came to the Yanks in 1930, wore No. 19, and played 100 games with a .298 batting average, seven homers, and 74 RBIs. His reward? He was placed on waivers and picked up by the Washington Senators. **Lefty Weinert** threw 17 games as No. 19 in 1931, going 2–2 with an elevated 6.20 earned run average. Mammoth **Jumbo Brown** wore No. 19 in 1932 and '33, then No. 17 the next two years. Then along came Johnny Murphy and the number received stability for the first time.

When Murphy left in 1943 to aid in the war effort, both **Larry Rosenthal** and **Hersh Martin** wore No. 19 in 1944. Outfielder

Rosenthal played just 36 games and hit .198. Martin, another wartime player, hadn't been in the majors since 1940, when the Yanks picked him up from Milwaukee of the American Association. He was soon gone. Pitcher **Ken Holcombe** wore No. 19 in 1945, pitching in just 23 games, and was grabbed by the Pirates in the Rule 5 draft.

Johnny Murphy reclaimed his old number when he rejoined the team for a year in 1946. A year later young Vic Raschi wore it for part of the year. He would, of course, switch to No. 17 and become a star. Pitcher **Karl Drews** wore No. 19 as well as No. 38 in 1947 and then just No. 19 in '48 after wearing No. 18 in 1946. If you look at the years between 1948 and 1955, you'll see seven different players wearing No. 19, a different player each year

It started with **Dick Starr**, who had more numbers than years with the team. He pitched in four games with a 1–0 record in 1947, wearing No. 30. The next year he was up twice, wearing No. 19 and then No. 36, but got into just one game. Then it was bye-bye. He was followed by **Clarence Westly Marshall**, called "Cuddles" by his teammates. Marshall was another marginal pitcher who had four numbers in three years with the team. He wore both No. 14 and No. 20 in 1946, No. 21 for a game in 1948, and No. 19 in '49, when he pitched in 21 games before being shipped to the Browns.

In 1950, **Whitey Ford** wore No. 19 when he recorded a 9–1 record in just half a season. Next came **Spec Shea**, who was signed by the Yankees before the 1940 season but thanks to WWII, didn't get to the majors until 1947. He may have been the best rookie in the American League that year, sporting a 14–5 record despite missing seven weeks with a pulled muscle in his neck. Shea wore No. 20 that year and would keep the number through 1949.

His neck injury bothered him the next year, when he was 9–10, then seriously curtailed him in 1949 and '50. The team thought he had arm trouble but it was a chiropractor who found the neck problem and fixed it almost immediately. In 1951 he switched to No. 19 and went 5–5 before being traded to Washington. And by the way, the nickname of Spec had nothing to do with him wearing glasses—he got the name because of the many freckles on his face.

Three more pitchers wore No. 19 between 1952–54: **Jim McDonald**, **Ray Scarborough**, and **Harry Byrd**. None made much of a mark, but Byrd was including in the big trade with Baltimore that brought both Don Larsen and Bob Turley to the Bombers.

Larsen, of course, became famous for his perfect game in the 1956 World Series, but "Bullet" Bob Turley turned out to be the better acquisition. A burly, 6'2", 215-pound righthander, Turley could throw in the mid-90s, but like many fastball pitchers, his big issue was control. He had his first big league taste with the St. Louis Browns in 1951 and '53. When he became part of the rotation the next year the team had moved to Baltimore. The 23-year-old Turley went 14–15 with a 3.46 ERA for a bad team. He led the league with 185 strikeouts, but also led the league with 181 walks. His raw potential prompted the Yanks to act and the next year Turley was in New York. Pitching for the pennant-winning 1955 Yanks, Turley started to shine. He went 17–13, with a 3.06 ERA, 13 complete games and six shutouts. He also fanned 210 hitters, but again led the league with 177 walks. He looked like a coming star.

He was injured for part of 1956, but began coming into his own when he went to a no-windup style that improved his control. He was 13–6 in '57, then had a Cy Young season in '58 when he went 21–7 with a 2.97 ERA and 168 strikeouts before starring in the World Series. After being knocked out in the first inning of Game Two, he came back to win Game Five, then picked up a save in Game Six and finally won Game Seven with 6 2/3 innings of sparkling relief. Not surprisingly, he was the Series MVP.

After that, however, it began going downhill. Had a losing record (8–11) in '59 with a diminished fastball and then a problem with bone chips the next year that required surgery. He would never win more than nine games again. The Yanks sent him to the Angels in October 1962 and he retired the following season.

In November 1962, the Yankees sent veteran first baseman Moose Skowron to the pitching-rich Dodgers in return to 6'5", 230-pound righthander, **Stan Williams**. Williams has a reputation as one mean dude on the mound, a guy who not only wouldn't hesitate to pitch inside, but would also drill a hitter with little provocation. It didn't hurt that he had control problems as well. After Williams won 14, 15, and 14 games from 1960–62 the Yanks thought they had a coming star. It didn't work out that way. The latest No. 19 was 9–8 in 1963 and then a pitiful 1–5 in 21 games the next year. The Yanks sold Williams to the Indians in the off-season and he finished his career mainly as a reliever for several teams.

Veteran **Bob Friend** came to the Yanks from Pittsburgh in December 1965 at the age of 35 in exchange for reliever Pete Mikkelsen. Friend had pitched his heart out for terrible Pirates teams a good part of his career, though he was 22–14 in 1958 and 18–12 in the World Series winning year of 1960. He would wear No. 19 in 1966 and was used sparingly (12 games) until the Yanks sold him to the Mets on June 15, in what would be the last year of his career. The very next year the team got another longterm tenant for No. 19. Lefthander **Fred "Fritz" Peterson** would wear the number from 1967 to early in the 1974 season.

Unfortunately, Peterson is often remembered as the guy who switched families with teammate Mike Kekich in one of the Yankees' rare headline-making scandals. But he had his moments on the mound, as well. Peterson didn't have great stuff—an average fastball and curve—but he had control, smarts, and finesse. For a few years he made it work even without the luxury of playing on great Yankees teams. He was 12–11 his rookie year of 1966 to show he belonged, then three years later began a run in which he won 17, 20, 15, and 17 again. In 1973 he slumped to 8–15, and the story about the swap of families with Kekich' broke. Kekich was dealt immediately, and in late April of the following season Peterson was traded to Cleveland in a seven-player deal that brought first sacker Chris Chambliss and pitcher **Dick Tidrow** to the Yanks.

The trade of Peterson and arrival of pitcher Tidrow made it easy for the Yanks to get a new No. 19. A spot starter and reliever, the righthander would be a big contributor to the Yanks' title teams of 1976–78. What made the 6'4", 215-pound righthander so valuable was his ability to swing effortlessly between the bullpen and a starting role.

In the pennant-winning year of 1976, he was 4–5, relieved in 47 games and had 10 saves, even though Sparky Lyle was considered

DICK TIDROW
PITCHER YANKEES

the closer. The next year, as the Yanks won their first World Series since 1962 Tidrow was 11–4, relieving 42 times and starting seven games. But after that his performance fell off, and early in the 1979 season Tidrow was shipped to the Cubs for righthander Ray Burris.

Pitcher **Rick Anderson** took No. 19 when Tidrow left in '79, but he was around only long enough to pitch in just a single game. In 1980, backup catcher **Brad Gulden** wore the number, but only long enough to play in two games. Gulden had played in 40 games the year before as No. 27, but hit just .163, the tipoff that his Yankees days were numbered. Then in 1982, Dave Righetti arrived and kept the uniform occupied until 1990. In the two decades since Righetti moved on, no one has stepped forth to claim the number big time, but there certainly have been some big moments involving No. 19.

Between 1992 and 1995 the uniform was worn by a guy trying to live up to his potential, a pair of former Mets stars, and a two time 20-game winner. But **Dion** James, **Bobby Ojeda**, **Kevin Elster**, and **Jack McDowell** didn't remain Yankees for long. Outfielder **James** signed with the Yanks as a free agent in April 1992 and inherited No. 19. With the Yanks he played all three outfield positions, hit .262 in '92 and then teased again with a .332 average in 115 games in '93. He promptly left as a free agent, wasn't in the majors in '94, returned in '95, now wearing No. 39, and hit .287. He left after just six games in '96.

Both Bobby Ojeda and Kevin Elster wore No. 19 in 1994. Ojeda was 36, a veteran southpaw who had gone 18–5 in the Mets' World

Series year of 1986. The Yanks took a chance in '94 and it backfired. Just two games showed them Ojeda was done and he was released in May. It was very similar with Elster. He had become the Mets' starting shortstop in 1988 with a rep as a fine fielder and a question about his hitting. Elster never did hit and then had shoulder problems that hampered his throwing. The Yanks took a chance by signing him in May 1994. He played seven games, went 0-for-20 at the plate, and was sent down. He got another brief shot the next year, switching to No. 26, but when he went just 2-for-17 in 10 games he was released. So much for the Mets' retreads.

Jack McDowell was another story. Drafted by the White Sox in 1987 he soon became a star. The 6'5", 180 pound righty had good stuff and good control. Beginning in 1990, he won 14, then 17, then was 20–10 in 1992 and 22–10 a year later, winning the Cy Young Award for his efforts. He was just 10–9 in the strike year of 1994 and when the strike ended early in '95, was dealt to the Yankees for two minor leaguers. With the Yanks looking like a potential playoff team, "Black Jack" was expected to make a major contribution. He did, going 15–10 with a 3.93 ERA and a league best eight complete games. But there were complications.

That August he was booed off the mound after a bad performance and made an obscene gesture toward the crowd. The team fined him and after that he didn't pitch as well. He left the Yanks after the season as a free agent and signed with Cleveland, a case of another talented player not finding New York to his liking.

Utility infielder **Luis Sojo** was No. 19 from 1996–2001 and proved a very valuable player during the Yanks' dynasty years. He was so valuable that when he signed with Pittsburgh as a free agent in 2000, the Yankees traded to get him back that August. Originally coming off the waiver wire from Seattle in August of '96, Sojo played all four infield positions. He was a solid fielder with the ability to get a clutch hit, almost the perfect utility player. His reward was to be in five World Series and on the winning side four times. He left the Yanks after 2001 but returned to play three games at the age of 38 in 2003, wearing No. 27. Luis has remained with the organization since his retirement.

During the short period when Sojo was at Pittsburgh in 2000, outfielder Luis Polonia briefly wore No. 19.

Robin Ventura was one of the best third basemen of his era, joining the Chicago White Sox in 1989 and soon becoming a star. He was right out of the Graig Nettles mold, an excellent fielder who hit with power, if not always for average. His best year may have been 1999, when he came to the Mets and hit .301 with 32 homers and 120 RBIs. Three years later the Yanks got him in a trade for David Justice and he took over third base wearing No. 19. Ventura hit just .247, but slammed 27 homers and drove home 93 in 141 games for the Bombers at the age of 34. The next year he played in 89 games and hit .251 before being dealt to the Dodgers on July 31 for outfielder Bubba Crosby and relief pitcher Scott Proctor. The same day the Yanks brought in his replacement, making a deal with Cincinnati for third sacker **Aaron Boone** in return for two minor leaguers and cash.

Boone's Yankees career would last just 54 regular season games and another handful in the playoffs in 2003. Aside from taking over No. 19, he took over a key position, third base, that had really been in a state of flux since the retirement of Scott Brosius.

Boone finished the year by hitting .254 for the Yanks with six homers and 31 RBIs, giving him season totals of .267, 24 HRs, and a career best 96 RBIs. He looked as if he had a future in New York. Then in the ALCS against Boston, Aaron Boone cemented his New York legacy forever. The two archrivals battled for seven games, and the final contest went to nail-biting extra innings. Boone led off the bottom of the 11th. Facing knuckleballer Tim Wakefield, he promptly blasted the ball into the left field stands for a pennant-winning home run.

Though the Yanks lost the World Series to the Marlins that year, Boone's future with the team seemed safe. But on February 27, 2004, he was suddenly cut from the team shortly after tearing a knee ligament in an off-season pickup basketball game, which was a violation of his contract.

Since Boone, No. 19 has been one-stop shopping for a number of players. Reserve outfielder **Bubba Crosby** had the number for parts of 2004, '05, and '06. Veteran hurler **Al Leiter** finished his career with the

Yanks in 2005, wearing No. 19 when Crosby went back to the minors. Leiter, 39, had started his career with the Yankees as a 21-year-old in 1987 wearing No. 56, then pitched parts of the next two years as No. 28 before moving on. He got the bulk of his 162 wins in other uniforms. He's now a Yankees broadcaster. Utility infielder **Chris Basak** and pitcher **Tyler Clippard** both wore No. 19 in 2007, as did outfielder **Kevin Thompson**. And in 2009, infielder **Ramiro Pena** became the latest to wear a number that is still distinguished by two outstanding relievers, Johnny Murphy and Dave Righetti.

#20: HIP HIP JORGE

Great catchers are few and far between. Sure, there have been a lot of quality backstops who know how to call a game and have the ability to throw runners out. They are valuable commodities, to be sure. But when you get a guy like that who can also hit, then you've got a real diamond in the rough. The Yankees have had four such catchers—Bill Dickey, Yogi Berra, Thurman Munson, and the most recent, **Jorge Posada**. Posada has been a lifelong Yankee, from his cup of coffee in 1995 through 2009, and is considered one of the core group from the latest Yankee dynasty that began in 1996. He's been a leader, a very solid defensive catcher, a switch hitter who has power from both sides of the plate. And he's a competitor who, like his coremates Derek Jeter, Mariano Rivera, and Andy Pettitte, hates to lose.

The Puerto Rican-born Posada was drafted by the Yanks in the 24th round in 1990 and eventually converted to catcher because he lacked the speed to be an infielder. He got his first cup of coffee with the big club, a one-game stay at No. 62 in 1995. The next year the Yanks won their first World Series since 1978 as Posada had an eight-game trial, this time wearing No. 55. Then in 1997, the Yanks began working him into the lineup. He played in 60 games and hit .250 with six homers and 24 runs batted in. He wore No. 22 at first, but before the year ended switched to No. 20, and he would proceed to make it his own.

Jorge Posada

Joe Girardi was the main receiver in 1996, having come over from Colorado. Girardi, who would someday be Posada's manager, was an excellent defensive catcher and handler of pitchers, but by 1998 Posada began assuming the number one role. It was his hitting that made the difference. He caught 111 games that year, batting .268 with 17 homers and 63 RBIs. His real breakout year came in 2000, the year the Yanks won their third consecutive World Series and fourth in five years. Posada was in 151 games that year, hit .287 with 28 homers and 86 RBIs. He had become one of the top hitting catchers in the majors.

Posada has continued to be an extremely consistent player and one of the most respected of the Yankees. In 2007, at the age of 35, he was in 144 games, hitting a career best .338 with 20 home runs and 90 RBIs. That year he became the only major league catcher ever to hit .330 or better and to also have 40 or more doubles (he had 42), 20 or more homers, and 90 or more RBIs. A bad shoulder that curtailed his throwing and eventually his hitting slowed him in 2008, but after off-season surgery he was ready to go again in 2009 and once more became a major contributor to the Yankees as they compiled the best record in baseball and won yet another World Series.

Posada's career is not yet complete. He has a solid .277 career batting average and has hit 243 home runs while driving in nearly 1000 runs. It isn't a stretch to say that his No. 20, which he has worn for 13 seasons through 2009, may someday hang in Monument Park at Yankee

Stadium, and that the latest in the line of great Yankees catchers may also join Dickey and Berra as a resident of the Hall of Fame at Cooperstown.

There's no doubt that Jorge Posada is the best Yankees player ever to wear No. 20, not counting some of the early stars who might have had it for one year during the days when numbers were changed like T-shirts. Unlike the previous few numbers, this one was not dominated by pitchers, but moreso by infielders and then a couple of catchers.

The first three Yankees to wear No. 20 were **Julie Wera**, **Myles Thomas**, and **Billy Werber**. Quite an inauspicious debut for a number. They wore the number between 1929 and '30. Then in 1931, Lefty Gomez wore No. 20 in his second season and first as a 20-game winner. The next year he switched to No. 11, for which he is remembered.

Pitcher **Charlie Devens** was a Harvard man. He lasted with the Yanks for parts of three years, pitching one game as No. 20 in 1932, then wearing No. 33 for parts of 1933 and '34. **Johnny Murphy**, the great relief pitcher, wore No. 20 in 1932 to a two-game debut, then returned two years later as No. 19, which he kept the remainder of his Yankees career. Righthander **Don Brennan** wore No. 20 in 1933, went 5–1 in 18 games and was sold to Cincinnati. A year later pitcher **Floyd Newkirk** inherited the number for a single game and was gone from the majors forever. Another hurler, **Harry Smythe,** was No. 20 for just eight games in 1934. He went 0–2, then found himself on waivers and picked up by the Dodgers.

Hurler **Johnny Broaca,** was quite another story. A graduate of Yale, Broaca wore glasses befitting an Ivy League intellectual, but his mentality was pure baseball flake. A flake with talent. He joined the Yanks in June 1934 and promptly went 12–9 the rest of the way wearing No. 26. A year later Broaca returned wearing No. 20 and put together a 15–7 season for a team getting close to championship level. He was 12–7 in '36 when the Yanks the pennant, but didn't pitch in the World Series that year. It seems the former Eli had a restless soul and decided to bolt the team, announcing that he would become a professional boxer, thus missing the Series. He came back the next year, went just 1–4 and bolted again. This time the Yanks had enough, selling him to Cleveland.

Two other pitchers, **Kemp Wicker** and **Oral Hildebrand** split time with No. 20 between 1936 and '40. Southpaw Wicker started as No. 25 in '36, then switched to No. 20 the next two years. The righty Hildebrand came to the Yanks at age 32 and went 10–4 in 21 games in 1939, pitching four innings in the World Series that year. In 1940, he was just 1–1 in 13 games and was gone.

Then there was the sad story of **Ernest "Tiny" Bonham**. Like other players nicknamed Tiny, Bonham was a big guy. He joined the Yanks in 1940 and would be an effective wartime pitcher for them. Tiny was considered one of the first pitchers to successfully throw the forkball and he combined that with excellent control, going 9–3 as a rookie and leading the league with a 1.90 ERA. He would go 21-5 in 1942 and win 27 more the next two years. In 1946 with the vets returning and Tiny at 5-8, the Yanks dealt him to Pittsburgh at season's end.

Why a sad story? Tiny pitched three years for the Pirates, going a combined 24–22. Then on September 15, 1949, just two weeks after pitching his final game of the 1949 season, Tiny Bonham died from complications after having his appendix removed.

One other pitcher donned uniform No. 20 during this era. On May 28, 1934, the Yanks signed 40-year-old righthander **Burleigh Grimes**, who had been released by the Cards two weeks early. They kept him until July 31, when they, too, released him, and he'd finish the season and his career with Pittsburgh. Grimes won just one game for the Yanks and a final game for the Bucs. That gave him 270 victories in a Hall of Fame career that began in 1916, though few remember Grimes as a Yankee.

At 6'3" and 200 pounds, **Cuddles Marshall** didn't seem like the cuddly type, and he couldn't really hang on with the Yanks. The big righthander was with the team parts of three seasons, wearing Nos. 20, 21, and 19 in 1946, '48 and '49, respectively. Pitcher **Spec Shea** was detailed in Chapter 19 though he wore No. 20 from 1947–49, and then No. 19 in 1951. Two players wore No. 20 in 1951, yet another pennant-winning year for the team. Marginal lefty **Art Schallock** was another yo-yo, bouncing between the Yanks and their minor league clubs from 1951 until May of 1955, when he was waived. Schallock pitched in a total of 28 games in four plus years, wearing No. 20 for the first three and No. 38 for the final two. Catcher **Clint Courtney** had a one-game call-up for the Yanks in 1951 wearing No. 20 for his first few hours in the majors. At the end of the season he was traded to the Browns for Jim McDonald.

Once pitcher Schallock gave up the uniform in 1953, No. 20 became almost exclusively the domain of infielders for almost four decades. It began with utilityman **Willie Miranda** in 1953 and '54, continued with **Billy Hunter** for the next two years. Both could be described as good-field, no-hit players, of which there were many back then. Both eventually left in trades, with Cleve Boyer coming over in the Hunter deal.

The next player to wear No. 20 was a first baseman who would later become an odd kind of folk hero in New York. But when **Marv Throneberry** had a one-game cup of coffee wearing No. 41 in 1955, no one knew anything about him. He did go two-for-two that day and left with a batting average of 1.000, not returning until 1958, when he was given No. 20. That year he played in 60 games and hit just .227 with seven homers and 19 RBIs. Throneberry wasn't a very good fielder and after another season in which he hit just .240 with eight homers in 80 games he was dealt to Kansas City.

How, then, did he become a folk hero? Simple. He was a charter member of the 1962 expansionist New York Mets. "Marvelous" Marv soon became a symbol of that team's futility. He still had enough pop to hit 16 homers for a team that would lose a record 120 games, but was a butcher in the field and a guy who couldn't seem to do anything right.

When the Yanks dealt Marvelous Marv they gave No. 20 to another infielder, **Joe DeMaesti**, who played the last two seasons of his career in New York. Bill Kunkel, a relief pitcher who was No. 20 in 1963 threw in 22 games for the Yanks that year, spent two seasons in Kansas City, and decided to become an umpire.

Some older Yankees fans feel that second sacker **Horace Clarke** never really got a fair shake. Clarke, who joined the Yankees in 1965 and replaced the popular Bobby Richardson two years later, had the misfortune to play for the Bombers at a time when they just bombed. He left the team in 1974, two years before they would begin reeling off another three pennants and two World Series. A pesky switch hitter, Clarke had virtually no power like so many second baseman of the time, and had a lifetime average of just .256. But he was good enough to set an American League record by leading the junior circuit in assists at second for six consecutive seasons. He also led the league in putouts from 1968 to '71 and was rarely injured. Clarke was sold to the Padres in May of 1974 and retired at the end of the year.

Three more infielders split time as No. 20 in 1975 and '76. Shortstop **Eddie Brinkman** played the final 44 games of a 15-year career with the Yanks in 1975, while **Eddie Leon** the same year played just one game at the

NEW YORK 2nd BASE

HORACE CLARKE YANKEES

end of an eight-year big league tenure. Then in 1976, young **Mickey Klutts** played two games in jersey No. 20. He would be there for parts of the next two seasons wearing Nos. 39 and 24 before being traded and ending an eight-game Yankee career. But this was just a prelude to the next main event . . . one **Russell Earl Dent**.

Call him "Bucky." The Yanks had won a pennant in 1976 before being swept by the Big Red Machine of Cincinnati in the World Series. One improvement they wanted to make before 1977 was at shortstop. On April 5, they pulled the trigger on a deal that would bring them shortstop Dent from the White Sox for two minor leaguers, outfielder Oscar Gamble, and $200,000. Dent would be just 25 years old in 1977 and had been the Sox' regular shortstop for three years. He was a very steady performer in the field if not a spectacular one, and while he had hit .274 his first year as a regular, he was coming off a .246 season with just two homers and 52 RBIs.

What you saw was what you got with Bucky Dent. The latest No. 20 was basically a .250 hitter with limited power, but a very good short-stop who made all the necessary plays and didn't let you down in a big spot. Sure-handed and with an accurate throwing arm, he led American League shortstops in fielding three times and joined with second sacker Willie Randolph to form one of the league's best double-play combinations. Sure enough, the Yanks won the World Series in 1977 and the next year were in a pennant fight with the rival Red Sox. The Yankees caught the Sox late and the two teams met in a one-game, do-or-die playoff at Fenway Park.

By the seventh inning the Sox, behind Mike Torrez, had a 2–0 lead over Yankee ace Ron Guidry when Dent came up with two men on base. He was just a .243 hitter with five homers in the regular season, but this time he hit one over the Green Monster in left for a three-run shot that gave the Yanks the lead, and ultimately a 5–4, pennant-clinching win. They went on to win a second straight World Series with Dent being named the MVP after going 6-for-9 with four RBIs in the final two games.

Dent remained the Yankees' shortstop until August of 1982. He missed the '81 World Series with an injury and his hitting really started to go downhill. He was hitting just .169 in 59 games in '82 when the Yankees traded him to Texas for veteran outfielder Lee Mazzilli. He later managed in the Yankees system and was picked to skipper the Bombers late in the 1989 season. But he was fired early the next year when a bad Yankees team got off to an 18–31 start.

After Dent, another group of utility infielders and regular

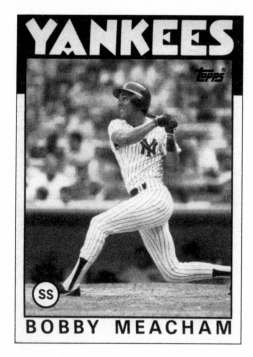

BOBBY MEACHAM

wannabes climbed into No. 20, staring with **Edwin Rodriguez** in 1982, who took it over for just three games late in the season. Outfielder **Rowland Office** played just two games as No. 20 in 1983, his last major league stop, and shortstop **Keith Smith** played two games as No. 20 in 1984 and another four as No. 13 in 1985. Shortstop **Bobby Meacham** was No. 20 from 1983–1988, though he only played regularly for one year, 1985, and batted just .218. Finally, there was **Alvaro Espinosa**, who was signed as a free agent for three games in 1988, wearing No. 47. When Meacham left he became the regular shortstop from 1989 through '91, wearing No. 20, and then was abruptly released.

With the exception of Netherlands-born infielder **Robert Eenhoorn**, who wore No. 20 for 12 games in 1996 after appearing with No. 50 for a handful of games in '94 and '95, and veteran outfielder/first baseman **Mike Aldrete**, who wore No. 20 for the final 32 games of his career in 1996, it was catchers **Mike Stanley** and Jorge Posada who made No. 20 a backstop's number from 1992 through 2009 and beyond.

Stanley was a part time catcher with Texas from 1986–91. He wasn't a top flight receiver and didn't show much power at the plate, never hitting more than six homers in a season. Then, prior to the 1992 season, he signed with the Yankees and was given No. 20. That year he backed up veteran Matt Nokes, but did hit eight homers in 69 games. A year later he took over the regular job and emerged, hitting .305 with 26 homers and 84 RBIs. His production was a pleasant surprise. It would be his best year with the Yanks. He caught the majority of games the next two years, hitting 17 and then 18 homers. The Yanks made the playoffs in 1995 and Stanley hit .313 with a homer in the five-game loss to Seattle.

After the season, the free agent Stanley signed with Boston. That's when the Yanks went out and got Joe Girardi, but they brought Stanley back in an August 13, 1997 trade with the Red Sox and he played 28 games down the stretch, hitting .287 with three homers. After the season, however, he left again as a free agent, signing with Toronto. The Yanks already had Jorge Posada waiting in the wings and Stanley saw the handwriting behind home plate. It was almost Posada's time, and has been ever since.

HOW ABOUT SOME NAMES?

In this past chapter there's been a couple Yanks called Cuddles and Kemp. How about a quick look at some of the names, given or otherwise, that are out of the realm of Lou, Billy, Derek, Paul, Joe, Ron, and others like that?

Snuffy, Tuck, Bubbles, Myril, Ownie, Monk, Cuddles, Wilcy, Tippy, Jumbo, Fritz, Julie, Kemp, Tiny, Spec, Spud, Ivy, Homer, Fenton, Zeke, Liz, Atley, Bots, Hensley, Foster, Bobo, Sterling, Dooley, Donzell, Stubby, Rip, Dixie, Moose, Doc, Dock, Ewell, Buster, Frenchy, Sparky, Goose, Marlin, Catfish, Bucky, Blondy, Sherm, Rocky, Chili, and Colter.

This is in no way making fun of these names, just another way of showing the wide variety of players who passed through the doors at Yankee Stadium.

#21: PAUL O'NEILL: THE WARRIOR

In many ways, **Paul O'Neill** was the perfect Yankee, and the right player in the right place at the right time. The Yankees' right fielder from 1993 to 2001, he was one of the guys who spearheaded the Yankees' rising to another dynasty and winning four World Series in five years. The man owner George Steinbrenner dubbed the "warrior" was an excellent outfielder with an outstanding throwing arm. At the plate he hit for both average and power, came through in the clutch, and competed to the hilt every game. Paul O'Neill hated to lose and hated when he played at any level less than his best. He wore No. 21 proudly and put his stamp on it like no player before him. It hasn't been retired yet, but many think it will be, and soon.

O'Neill spent the first eight years of his career with his hometown Cincinnati Reds, five of them as a regular. He never hit higher than .270, though he did club 28 homers and drive in 91 runs during a .256 1991 season. He was also part of the 1990 Reds World Series winners. Then, in 1992, he batted just .246 with 14 homers and 66 RBIs, almost looking like a player in decline at the age of 29. On November 3, 1992, O'Neill learned he had been traded to the Yankees with a minor leaguer in return for centerfielder Roberto Kelly.

It was a time when the Yanks were looking to recapture lost glory and they tabbed O'Neill as their new right fielder.

From a guy who never hit .300 once, O'Neill would bat .311 in his first Yankees season and then hit .300 or better for the next five years. In the strike-shortened 1994 season, the 6'4", 215-pound outfielder became a superstar. In just 103 games before play stopped, Paul O'Neill batted a league best .359, adding 21 home runs and 83 RBIs. Three years later, he began a streak of four straight seasons with 100 or more RBIs, despite never hitting more than 24 homers in a single season during that span. The intense southpaw swinger had become tough in the clutch, a guy who demanded perfection of himself. Fans at Yankee Stadium were used to the sight of O'Neill, after making an out, throwing his batting helmet, slamming his bat into the rack and maybe kicking the water cooler for good measure.

When O'Neill announced that he would retire after the 2001 season at the age of 38, the fans at Yankee Stadium began chanting his name during Game 5 of the World Series against Arizona, the last game of the season in the Bronx. He would retire with a .288 lifetime average, 281 homers, and 1,269 RBIs, not quite Hall of Fame numbers, though during his tenure with Yanks, O'Neill certainly performed at a Hall of Fame level.

In 2008, the Yanks acquired relief pitcher **LaTroy Hawkins** who started the season wearing No. 21. He was the first to wear it since O'Neill had retired seven years earlier. The fan outcry was so great that in a matter of weeks, Hawkins switched to No. 22. Someday soon, the Yanks may well make it official and retire it for good.

Aside from O'Neill, Yankees fans may be hard-pressed to name other players who have worn No. 21. Righthanded pitcher **Gordon Rhodes** was the first to wear No. 21 in 1929. Rhodes switched to No. 19 the next year, then in 1931 wore both No. 19 and No. 21, before finishing his Yankees career wearing No. 16 in 1932. Also wearing No. 21 for just nine games in 1929 was a 36-year-old first baseman named **George Burns**, who was finishing up a 16-year big league career with six teams.

Hall of Famer **Red Ruffing** began his Yankees career as No. 21 in 1930. He switched to No. 18 the following year, then to No. 15 in 1932, which remained his number for the remainder of his outstanding days with the Bombers. Veteran infielder and future Hall of Famer **Joe Sewell** played the last three years of a 14-season career with the Yanks, signed in January 1931 after Cleveland released him. Though he had been a shortstop with the Indians since 1920, the 5'6", 155-pound Sewell played third for the Yanks, wearing No. 27 in 1931 before switching to No. 21 his final two seasons. Though Sewell was still good enough to hit .302, .272, and .273 as a Yank, he had really made his mark at Cleveland.

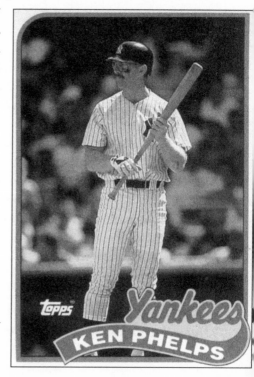

His most remarkable achievement was that he was the toughest man in the history of baseball to strike out. He fanned just 114 times in 7,131 at bats, an average of one strikeout every 62.6 at bats.

Pitcher **Johnny Broaca** wore No. 21 in his first Yankees season of 1934, switching to No. 20 for the next three. After Broaca made the switch, southpaw hurler **Pat**

Malone took over No. 21 from 1935–37. Malone had won 18 games as a rookie with the Cubs in 1928, then had records of 22–10 and 20–9 the next two seasons, but his love of fast living and the nightlife helped curtail his career. As a Yankee, Malone pitched well out of the bullpen, leading the league in relief wins (12) and saves (9) in 1936. He spent one more season with the Yanks before spending his final baseball years in the minor leagues.

Had **Spud Chandler** gotten an earlier start he might have been a legitimate Hall of Fame candidate. As it was, he didn't reach the majors until the age of 29 and then had several seasons shortened by injury and later lost time to military service. Yet when he hung them up in 1947, just after his 40th birthday, he had a 109–43 record, which translates to a .717 winning percentage, the highest ever for a pitcher with 100 or more victories.

Chandler, whose given name was Spurgeon, spent five years in the minors before getting his chance in 1937. He wore No. 24 that year and went 7–4. A year later he switched to No. 21, which he wore the remainder of his career. He was 14–5 that second year, then had some arm problems that relegated him to 3–0 and 8–7 records the next two seasons. Always a control pitcher, he added a slider to his repertoire in 1941 and went 10–4 and 16–5. Then in 1943, he fully emerged as an ace, compiling a 20–4 record, leading the league in winning percentage (.833), complete games (20), earned run average (1.64), and shutouts (5).

Chandler threw just one game before joining the military in 1944 and four games after returning in 1945. Then in 1946, at the age of 38 he went 20–8 with a 2.10 ERA. He was back on top. He had nine quick wins in 1947 before arm trouble returned. He finished at 9–5 with a 2.46 ERA and retired. How good was Spud Chandler? The great Ted Williams said he was one of the three toughest pitchers he ever faced, while his own catcher, Bill Dickey, said he was the best he ever caught. Proof enough?

During Chandler's time in the military, outfielder **Johnny Cooney** (1944) played the final 10 games of a 20-year career and pitcher **Bill Bevens** also wore No. 21 briefly in 1944 and '45. **Cuddles Marshall,** who like Bevens was mentioned before, wore the number for a single game in 1948, his second of three years with the team. Then in 1949, the Yankees made a mistake. They decided to send three players and $100,000 to the St. Louis Browns for righthander **Fred Sanford**, who had lost a league high 21 games in 1948. Sanford won just 12 games in two and a half years (1949–51) and the New York press referred to him as the "$100,000 Lemon." He was eventually traded away to Washington.

For the next six years, 1951–1956, No. 21 would be the property of two valuable relief pitchers, lefthander **Bob Kuzava** and righty **Jim Konstanty**. Kuzava's career began after the war with his offical rookie in year 1949. In June 1951, he was shipped to the Yanks from Washington in return for three pitchers and became a spot starter and long reliever right in the midst of five straight World Series wins. Kuzava showed his value immediately. In a little more than half a season he was 8–4 with a 2.40 ERA. He appeared in 23 games with eight starts, had four complete games, and recorded five saves. That's how valuable he was. Then he came into the sixth and final game of the 1951 World Series in the ninth inning with the bases loaded, two runs in, none out, and the Yanks leading the Giants, 4–3. He closed them out without another run scoring to give the Bombers their third straight championship.

Kuzava continued in a similar role the next two years as the Yanks won another pair of titles, making it five straight. He seemed to slip in 1954, and that August the Yanks put him on waivers. He was taken by the Baltimore Orioles and pitched for several other teams through 1957. Bob Kuzava was far from a great Yankee, but he was one of those guys the Bombers always seemed to find in those days who made major contributions to a team that always seemed to be in the World Series.

Jim Konstanty was another case entirely. The Yanks didn't pick him up until August of 1954 when he was 37 years old. But just four years before that, Konstanty changed the face of relief pitching while compiling one of the greatest seasons ever. Casimir James Konstanty didn't get a real shot at the majors until 1949, when he was already 32 years old. The Phils picked him up before the 1948 season. The next year, he relieved in 53 games, using an improved forkball and slider, and he went 9–5. Then came 1950.

That was the year of the Phillies' famed "Whiz Kids" team that won the National League pennant, and that year Jim Konstanty showed the baseball world just what a dominant relief pitcher could do. He got the call from the pen 74 times, pitched 152 innings, compiled a 16–7 record, a 2.66 earned run average, and 22 saves. He was the last pitcher on the mound for the Phils 62 times. He made his only start in the World Series that year and lost, 1–0, to the Yanks' Vic Raschi. For his efforts, he was the first reliever to be named the National League Most Valuable Player.

The Phillies waived him in August of 1954 and the Yanks picked him up. Wearing No. 21 he appeared in just nine games, but the following year helped the Yanks to another pennant by answering the call 45 times and going 7–2 with a 2.32 ERA and 11 saves. The next year, the Yanks released him in May, the Cards picked him up to finish the season and then he retired.

From 1956 to 1980, No. 21 was the home of a variety of veterans and youngsters, players remembered for other number, and a few passing through so quickly not to be much more than a dot on the Yankees map. Oddly enough, the number saw five players during this period who played their final major league season in pinstripes. Righthander **Sonny Dixon** appeared in just three games in 1956 wearing No. 21 before he was gone.

On September 1, 1957, the Yankees picked up 40-year-old right-hander **Sal Maglie** off the waiver wire from the Dodgers. The year before, Maglie, a longtime New York Giants star, helped the archrival Dodgers win the pennant with a 13–5 record and was then the losing pitcher when Don Larsen threw his perfect game in the World Series. Wearing No. 21, Maglie pitched in just six games down the stretch and went 2–0 with a 1.73 ERA. The next year, he was 1–1 in seven games before the Yanks sold him to St. Louis in June, where he finished his career.

In June 1958, the Yanks made yet another trade with Kansas City. This one produced 41-year-old righthander, **Virgil "Fire" Trucks**. The aging fireballer pitched in 25 games for the Yanks before the end of the season, going 2–1 with a 4.54 ERA before hanging up his spikes. He wore No. 21 for his swan song, getting the last of his 177 major league victories.

Righthander **Tex Clevenger** and third sacker **Eric Soderholm** were the other two players who ended careers with the Yanks during this period. Clevenger came over in a trade with the Angels in May of 1961, going 1–1 in 21 games wearing No. 16. The next year, he was 2–0 in 21 games wearing No. 26 and switching to No. 21 before the year and his career ended. Soderholm was a good player with bad knees. He played 95 games for the 1980 Yanks and hit a respectable .287. But his knees were shot by then and he couldn't continue, hanging them up at the tender age of 31.

Young righthander **Ralph Terry** wore No. 21 for three games in 1956 and seven more in '57. He was then traded to Kansas City, only to return in 1959 and become a 20-game winner in 1962. He would make his Yankees mark with No. 23 on his back. Outfielder **Roy White** wore No. 48 his first three years with the team (1965–67), then wore both No. 48 and No. 21 in 1968. By 1969, as he became a Yankees fixture, he switched to No. 6, for which he is remembered. **Nate "Pee Wee" Oliver** had a Yankee tenure of one game in 1969. By April 19 he was gone, traded to the Cubs for Lee Elia. Uniform No. 21 barely had time to get warm on his back. Outfielder **Jim Lyttle** also wore No. 21 in 1969, 28 games worth. He hit .181. A year later he switched to No. 27, showed some potential by hitting .310 in 87 games, but in 1971 he dipped back below the Mendoza Line at .198 and was traded away.

Frank Tepedino, Danny Walton, and **Rusty Torres** all wore No. 21 at times between 1969 and 1972. When the Yanks got southpaw-swinging outfielder **Steve Kemp** as a free agent in December 1982, they were hoping to get the Steve Kemp who hit .318 with 26 homers and 105 RBIs for the Tigers in 1979, or the Kemp who went to the White Sox in 1982 and batted .286 with 19 homers and 98 RBIs. Instead they got a guy who struggled to hit .241 in 1983 with just 12 homers and 49 RBIs. The next year he improved to .291, but the power was all but gone as he hit just seven homers despite the short right field porch at the Stadium. Kemp was quickly exiled to Pittsburgh after the season, where he continued to struggle as vision problems ended his career prematurely.

The team continued to search for a power hitter to fill uniform No. 21. The first after Kemp was outfielder **Dan Pasqua**, taken in the third round of the 1982 Amateur Draft. The powerful lefty swinging native New Yorker hit his way through the minors, becoming the Triple-A International League's Rookie of the Year and Most Valuable Player in 1985. So the Yankees brought him up for a 60-game audition, in which he hit just .209 and banged nine homers, the first of which came on just his second big league at bat. In 1986, he got a more thorough look and showed his potential with a .293 average, 16 homers, and 45 RBIs. But when he slipped back to .233 the following year with 17 homers and just 42 ribbies, the Yanks send him packing to the White Sox. His star would never fully emerge.

There was no doubting the ability of slugger **Jack Clark**. He had proved his mettle during 13 National League seasons with the Giants and Cardinals, beginning when he was 19 years old. But he was also hurt often and never the most popular guy in the clubhouse. In1987, Clark put together a great year that saw him hit .286 with 35 homers and 106 RBIs. He also led the league with 136 walks. He became a free agent after a salary dispute and the Yanks, looking for a big banger to help them recapture past glory, signed him. Clark was given No. 21 and turned loose. Later in the season he changed to No. 33, so he didn't even have a real identity in what would be his only New York season.

Though he played 150 games and hit 27 homers with 93 RBIs, his batting average dipped to .242 and he didn't endear himself to anyone. After the season, he was shipped to San Diego for three prospects, hardly a king's ransom for one of the game's premier sluggers. Some called it a salary dump, but the Yanks apparently didn't see him as a longterm answer. So it was one and gone.

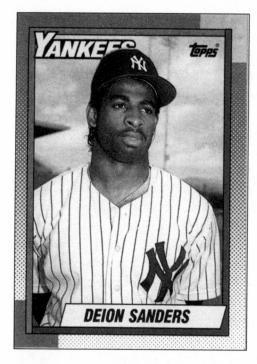

DEION SANDERS

The habit of taking a chance on aging veterans continued with **Jose Cruz**, signed as a free agent before the 1988 season. The latest No. 21 was already an 18-year veteran, having been an All-Star with Houston and a very good player. But with the Yanks all he could do was hit .200 in 38 games before calling it a career. Another vet, first baseman/DH **Kenny Phelps**, came in a July 1988 trade with Seattle. The southpaw swinger had hit 51 homers the past two seasons. With the Yanks he was a .224 hitter who hit 10 over the fence in 45 games. But after playing just 86 games the following year with just seven homers, he was shipped off to Oakland.

First sacker **Hal Morris** played his first two seasons in New York, wearing No. 62 for 15 games in 1988 and switching to No. 21 for another 15 games the following year. There was just no room for him and he was shipped to Cincinnati, where he played most of his career before retiring as a .304 lifetime hitter and solid player. No one, however, could call **Deion Sanders** an ordinary player. Sanders was a football star who decided to also play baseball, à la Bo Jackson. But unlike Jackson, who looked as if he could have been a superstar in both sports, Neon Deion was definitely more suited to the gridrion. He never quite cut it on the diamond despite his great speed. Part of the problem was that he'd leave the team early to play football, so the Yanks shipped him to Atlanta. He hung around with Cincy, the Giants, and Cincinnati again until 2001. In the NFL, however, he was one of the greatest cornerbacks ever.

Infielder **Mike Blowers** played parts of three years and wore three different numbers, the result of his numerous call-ups from the minors. He was No. 13 in 1989, No. 21 a year later, and finally No. 14 in 1991. He didn't help his case by hitting .188 and .200 his last two seasons and was shipped to Seattle in a minor deal. Righthander **Scott Sanderson** was purchased by the Yanks from Oakland prior to the 1991 season, the first pitcher to be given No. 21 in quite some time. The 6'5" Sanderson was a winner and coming off a 17–11 season with the A's, he went 16–10 with the Yanks in '91. But the next year saw the return of his old bugaboo—injuries, of which he had many. He pitched in pain all year to the tune of a 12–11 record and, at the end of the year, the Yanks let him go via free agency. Sanderson would pitch for 19 seasons and win up with a 163–143 record.

The year after Scott Sanderson left, Paul O'Neill arrived and No. 21 finally had a real home, and maybe someday a permanent one.

BATTING CHAMPS

When Paul O'Neill hit .359 in 1994 he joined a small but elite group of Yankees batting champs. Over the years the Bombers have had just eight league batting champions, four less than Ty Cobb won all by himself. But with a single exception, all the batting champs were top players who had great careers, all of mostly with the Yankees.

Player	Year	Average
Babe Ruth	1924	.378
Lou Gehrig	1934	.363
Joe DiMaggio	1939	.381
Joe DiMaggio	1940	.352
Snuffy Stirnweiss	1945	.309
Mickey Mantle	1956	.353
Don Mattingly	1984	.343
Paul O'Neill	1994	.359
Bernie Williams	1998	.339

The exception, of course, was Snuffy Stirnweiss, who won it in the last of the war years, 1945, when many of the top hitters were in the service. His .309 was one of the lowest averages ever to be the best in the league.

#22: THE SUPER CHIEF AND THE ROCKET

In the long annals of uniform No.22, two pitchers stand out, two very different kinds of pitchers. The first was nearly the perfect combination of starter and reliever, a guy who be counted on for both the complete game and to come in late to close and tight one. He was at his best when the chips were down and rarely failed in a clutch spot. The second was perhaps the most dominant pitcher of his generation, winner of 354 games, ninth best of all time, and a guy who won a record seven Cy Young awards. Neither pitcher was with the Yankees his entire career, but while one is considered a true Yankee, the other is sometimes looked upon as something of a mercenary, a right arm for hire. The two pitchers are **Allie Reynolds** and **Roger Clemens**, who wore No. 22 some 45 years apart, each staking their individual Yankees legacy.

Allie Reynolds was of Native American heritage, thus his nickname of "The Chief," later expanded to "The Super Chief." He was both a track star and running back at Oklahoma A&M, but it turned out that baseball was his best sport. Though the NFL's New York Giants offered him the grand fee of $100 a game after he graduated, he signed with the Indians instead, getting a $1000 bonus in 1939.

Reynolds made the majors in 1943, his repertoire featuring a good fastball and sharp curve . . . and control issues. He was 11–12 that year, leading the league with 151 strikeouts but also walking 109 batters in 199 innings. The next two years he was 18-12 and 11-15, so no one was yet sure just what kind of pitcher Allie Reynolds would be. Then fate took a hand. The Indians needed a second baseman and the Yanks had no qualms about parting with veteran Joe Gordon. In return, they asked for Allie Reynolds. The deal was done and the 30-year-old pitcher with a mediocre 51–47 record became a New York Yankee.

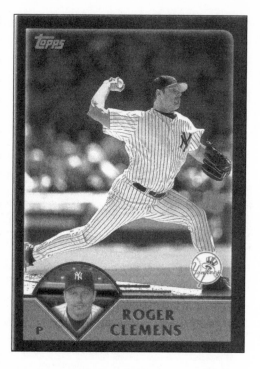

When he joined the team, Reynolds received some advice from veteran Spud Chandler, who was in his last season at the age of 40. He told his protege not to just throw, but to think on the mound and set hitters up by changing speeds. Reynolds listened, put the suggestions into practice, and went 19–8 for a league-leading .704 winning percentage. That started a great run in which No. 22 won 66 games over the next four years, then topped it with a 20–8 season with a 2.06 ERA in 1952.

Manager Casey Stengel also began using him in relief between starts and found that Reynolds could slip from one role to another seamlessly. In 1951, he pitched in 40 games, just 26 of them starts. Yet he was 17–8 with seven shutouts and seven saves. In his 20-game season of 1952, he had 24 complete games, six shutouts and six saves.

And, of course, he teamed with Vic Raschi and Eddie Lopat to give the Yanks a "big three" during their five straight pennants and World Series from 1949–1953.

In 1953, the Yankees team was in a bus accident and Reynolds hurt his back. Though he was a combined 26–11 in 1953 and '54, including 13 saves in '53, the back grew worse. And at the end of the '54 season, when he was still good enough to go 13–4 with four shutouts and seven saves, he decided to retire. But the Super Chief had done the Yankees and No. 22 proud.

By the time Roger Clemens became a Yankee and took over No. 22 in 1999 he was already a legend, a pitcher who had won 20 or more games five times, had a record five Cy Young award and a guy who had struck out 20 batters in a game twice. At 6'4", 220 pounds, he was an imposing figure on the mound, a guy who wasn't afraid to pitch inside. Old-school in so many ways. He had just come off two straight 20-win seasons and Cy Young prizes with mediocre Toronto Blue Jays teams after his storied career in Boston ended. The Jays sent him to New York for lefty David Wells, and two lesser players. The reason "The Rocket," as he was called, wanted to pitch for his old arch enemies was simple. He had never pitched for a World Series winner and the Yanks were in the midst of another big run, having won in 1996 and '98, and had the kind of team that was poised to win more.

The Rocket was 14–10 and 13–8 in his first two Yankees seasons, but got his wish. The Bombers won another pair of World Series in 1999 and 2000, and Clemens was 1–0 in both fall classics against the Braves and Mets. The following year came another super season, a dominant 20–3 record and sixth Cy Young, though the Yanks lost the Series to the Arizona Diamondbacks.

Clemens would pitch two more years for the Yanks before returning to his home state of Texas to pitch for the Astros, where he went 18–4 in 2004 to win a seventh Cy Young. The next year he pitched in tough luck, his 13–8 record not doing justice to a sparkling, 1.87 ERA. After a 7–6 year in 2006, he opted not to sign in the spring of 2007, but made a dramatic return to the Yankees at mid-season. This time he wasn't a savior, going just 6–6 in 17 starts. But he was also 44 years old and had pitched so well for so long.

Then, after the season, it all started to crumble with allegations of steroid use from a former trainer, and then a Congressional investigation into possible perjury. The bloom had come off the rose, and while Clemens steadfastly denied using performance enhancing drugs, he was performing in the so-called "steroid era" and many people suddenly saw him differently. Even his slam-dunk Hall of Fame induction was suddenly in doubt, as the baseball writers were showing a propensity toward ignoring admitted and perceived steroid users when it came to the Hall vote.

As of 2009, the future of this very great pitcher remains in limbo. It's apparent he won't pitch anymore with age and the allegations finally derailing a guy who looked like he could win forever. But Roger Clemens at his best was something to see. His 4,672 strikeouts have been topped only by Nolan Ryan and Randy Johnson and baseball may not see a 350-game winner ever again. And the Yankees may never see another pitcher wear No. 22 and perform the way the Rocket did.

Once past Reynolds and Clemens, there weren't too many real stars adorning No. 22. Perhaps the best of the rest was southpaw hurler **Jimmy Key**, who pitched just four years for the Bombers. There were a couple of stars who wore the number briefly before making their marks with another, and then the usual collection of players who were in and out quickly. Infielder **Gene Robertson** set the tone, being the first to wear No. 22 for 90 games in 1929, his second and last year with the club. Hall of Famer **Lefty Gomez** wore it in 1930, his first year with the Yanks, but is best remembered for wearing No. 11. And in 1931, the number was passed on to righthander **Ivy Andrews**, who threw just seven games, then four the next wearing No. 28. His nickname: Poison. Get it?

During the 1930s and through the war years there was the usual variety of players wearing No. 22, some recognizable to fans, others long forgotten, and one or two surprises. Few, if any, probably recall **Doc Farrell**, an infielder who played sparingly for two seasons in 1932 and '33. Pitcher **Johnny Broaca** wore both Nos. 22 and 21 in 1934 before settling on No. 20 his next four Yankees seasons, while infielder **Lyn Lary** had No 22 in 1934, his final year with the team. **Vito Tamulis**, a little junkballing lefthander, got a late September start in 1934 against the A's and threw a complete game shutout in his Yankees debut. A year later, he went 10–5 in 19 games, then was out of the majors until resurfacing with the St. Louis Browns in 1938.

Then there was **Bob Seeds**, "Suitcase Bob" to those who knew how much he moved around. He was an outfielder who played 13 games with the Yanks in 1936 as No. 22. Seeds would play with five big league teams (the Indians twice) in a nine-year career and many more in the minors. Old Reliable **Tommy Henrich** wore No. 22 for 67 games in his rookie year of 1937, but is remembered by fans for wearing both No. 7 and No. 15. Outfielder **Roy Johnson** appeared as No. 1 in 1936, then wore No. 22 for 12 games in '37. The comings and goings continued with **"Fireman" Joe Beggs**, who was No. 22 for the Yanks in 14 games in 1938. Then the number got a taste of stability when pitcher **Marius Russo** appeared on the scene in 1939. Russo would wear No. 22 right through 1943.

The Queens native was a southpaw who threw a sinking fastball, was 8–3 his first season of 1939, then won 14 the next two seasons and looked like a coming star. But arm problems limited him to just nine games and a 4–1 record in '42, and a diminished fastball led to a 5–10 record the following season. He went into the Army after the 1943 seasons and returned just briefly (eight games) in 1946, wearing No. 26, and then retired.

Two more largely forgotten names followed. Catcher **Bill Drescher** wore No. 22 for just four games in 1944, returned for 48 games the next year as No. 29 and finished his Yankees days in 1946 by wearing No. 26 for just five games. Outfielder **Russ Derry** also wore the double-deuce in 1944, playing in 38 games and hitting .254. A year later he was No. 27 and got in 78 games. He was sold to the A's after the season.

Paul Waner signed with the Yanks as a free agent on September 1, 1944, and played in nine games before the season ended. That year he wore No. 24. A year later he played just a single game as No. 22 before being released on May 1, ending his career at the age of 42. It was a career spent mainly in the National League with the Pittsburgh Pirates. Waner, known as "Big Poison," was a three-time batting champion with averages of .380, .362, and .373, and the author of 3,152 career hits. When he retired he had a .333 lifetime average and was soon elected to the Hall of Fame.

The great righthander **Red Ruffing** wore No. 22 in 1945 and '46 after returning from the military. Ruffing, of course, made his Yankees mark wearing No. 15. Then came Reynolds, who occupied the uniform through 1954. Lefthander **Mickey McDermott**, who had won 18 games for Boston in 1953, came over in a trade before the 1956 season. The latest No. 22 went just 2–6 in 23 games and was sent packing to Kansas City. The number then went to little-used backup catcher **Darrell Johnson**, who started with No. 39 for 21 games in 1957, then switched to No. 22 for his final five games as a Yankee in '58. He was off to St. Louis via the Rule 5 draft. Young righthander **Jim Bronstad** was next in 1959, going 0–3 in just 16 games. He would pitch two years for Washington and then see his career end. Pitcher **Gary Blaylock** was picked off waiver in July of '59 and was 0–1 in just 15 games. It would be his only year in the majors.

In 1960, the Yanks brought up 20-year-old righthander **Bill Stafford** and planted No. 22 on his back. Stafford had some big league success before being derailed by arm problems. After going 3–1 his first season, he won 14 games in both 1961 and '62, helping the Yanks to a pair of pennants and World Series triumphs. Stafford made his first start of the 1963 season on an unusually cold night in April and the result was an arm injury that would lead to a 4–8 season and 6.02 ERA. His career would end two years later. He never won another big league game.

When the Yanks shipped Stafford to the A's, they received righthander **Fred Talbot** in return. He took Stafford's number and went 7–7 the rest of the year, mostly starting. It was pretty much the same until May 1969, when he was shipped to the Seattle Pilots in return for reliever Jack Aker, and No. 22 was passed on to yet another pitcher.

Aker was no slouch. He was a sidearming righthander with a nasty sinker. Just three years earlier, in 1966, Aker had gone 8–4 with Kansas

City, appearing in 66 games with a 1.99 ERA and 32 saves. For his efforts he was named Fireman of the Year. Though the Yanks struggled, Aker was good. After coming to the Yanks on May 20, Aker went 8–4 with a 2.06 ERA and 11 saves. That winter he underwent career-threatening spinal surgery, yet recovered to get another 16 saves in 1970. But Aker was now pitching in pain and wasn't as effective. When the Yanks acquired reliever Sparky Lyle in 1972, Aker became expendable. He was sent to the Cubs and would finish his career with the Mets in 1974.

More short termers followed. Pitcher **Ron Klimkowski** threw three games as No. 51 in 1969, had a pretty good 1970 as No. 24, going 6–7 in 45 games out of the pen. Then he was dealt to Oakland, released at the end of 1971, and returned to the Yankees to go 0–3 in just 16 games wearing No. 22. Infielder **Hal Lanier** played the final two years of his career with the Yanks in 1972 and '73 wearing No. 36 the first year, No. 22 the second. Infielder **Jim Mason** saw action at short from 1974–76, but had problems with the Mendoza Line his last two years, hitting just .152 and .180. Righthander **Gil Patterson** pitched one year in the majors, for the 1977 Yanks, going 1–2 with a 5.40 in 10 games. No. 22 was on and off his back in a whisker.

Next came the game of musical outfielders who kept getting traded for one another and all wearing No. 22. It began with **Ruppert Jones** in 1980. He hit just nine homers and batted .223 in 83 games, then went to San Diego in return for **Jerry Mumphrey**, an outfielder who could hit but couldn't field. In three years (1981–83), Mumphrey hit .307, .300, and .262 without a lot of power and made his share of errors. So off he went to Houston in August 1983 in return for centerfielder **Omar Moreno**.

Moreno had been a force with Pittsburgh as a leadoff man, flychaser, and base thief. From 1978–1980 he had 71, 77, and 96 steals and was on the Pirates' 1979 title team. In New York, Moreno was something else. He hit just .250 in 48 games to finish the 1982 season. The next year, he played in 117 games and hit just .259 with only 20 steals. By early August of 1985 he had fallen below the Mendoza Line at .197 and was released. Infielder **Mike Fischlin** broke the string of outfielders wearing No. 22 in 1986, but hit just .206 in 71 games, assuring him of no future with team. One and out.

Outfielder **Gary Ward** signed as a free agent before the 1987 season. He had a couple of fine seasons in Minnesota, but never quite duplicated that success in New York. After eight games in 1989, the latest No. 22 was unceremoniously released. **Luis Polonia** took over Ward's spot and his number for the balance of 1989, hitting .313 in 66 games, but he played just 11 games the following year before getting his ticket out of town. Polonia would return as a part-time player in 1994 and '95, as well as in 2000.

Lanky 6'7" pitcher **Mike Witt** came over the Angels in May 1990 as the Yankees sent future Hall of Famer Dave Winfield west. Between 1984 and '87 Witt had won 15, 15, 18, and 16 games and the Yanks felt he could help. In truth, Witt had begun to lose some of his stuff midway through the 1987 season and though just 29 years old when he came to New York, he was struggling. Witt was 5–6, 0–1, and 3–2 in his three New York seasons as No. 22. He was granted free agency but never pitched in the majors again.

Righthander **Scott Kamieniecki** was with the team from 1991 to 1996, but never really made a mark. He was one of those multiple number guys, starting out as No. 40 his first year, going to No. 22 in 1992, then wearing No. 28 his final four seasons. He had some moments, but after posting a 1–2 record and an inflated 11.12 ERA in just seven games in 1976, he was returned to the minors and then shipped to Baltimore.

So No. 22 had pretty much a nomadic existence for 30 some odd year since Bill Stafford donned it five straight seasons in the 1960s. Then, in 1993, along came lefthander Jimmy Key, who signed as a free agent after nine successful seasons in Toronto. Key was just 32 years old and seemed to have a lot of pitching left in him . . . if he could stay healthy. Key was a control pitcher with a sinking fastball, curve, and backdoor slider. He emerged in just his second season, going 14–6 in 1985. He continued to be a solid winner and won a pair of games for the Blue Jays in the 1992 World Series. The Yanks were building toward the great late '90s ballclubs and Jimmy Key gave them a boost. He was 18–6 in 1993 and a major league leading 17–4 in the strike-shortened

'94 season. You couldn't ask for more. Then the injury jinx hit again and he missed almost the entire year following serious rotator cuff surgery, as the Yanks finally made the playoffs. He returned to make 30 starts in '96, going 12–11 as the Yanks won the pennant, and was the winning pitcher in the sixth and final game of the World Series.

After the season, the Yanks signed free agent lefty David Wells away from the Orioles, and Key did a turnabout-fair-play and signed with Baltimore. He pitched two more years before shoulder problems resurfaced and was forced to retire. But Jimmy Key was a winner with a 186–117 career record. In four years with the Yanks, he was 48–23, a real winner.

Jorge Posada wore No. 22 for 60 games in his third season of 1997, after wearing Nos. 62 and 55 his first two cup-of-coffee seasons. A year later, he switched to No. 20 and the rest is history. Big **Mark Whiten** signed as a free agent in January 1997. He was a guy with home run power and one of the best outfield arms in the game. But he also changed teams eight times between 1991 and '98. The reason was simple—Whiten couldn't hit a breaking ball. As a Yankee he played just 69 games as No. 22 and hit .265 with just five homers. After the season, he continued his team tour, heading on to Cleveland where he would finish up.

Utility infielder **Homer Bush** was the spark plug type, but could never crack the Yankee lineup. He played just 10 games as No. 38 in 1997, then 45 games as No. 22 the next year before moving on to Toronto. By 2004 he was back for nine games with the Yanks, wearing No. 18, then retiring. Outfielder **Tony Tarasco** had a 14-game shot in 1999. It didn't work out as he hit just .161 and never got a second chance. Before that year was out, Roger Clemens switched from No. 12 to 22 and made it his own.

Pitcher **Jon Lieber** was signed as a free agent in February 2003, the Yankees knowing he had undergone Tommy John surgery and couldn't pitch that season. The 6'3" righthander with the natural sinker returned in 2004 to go 14–8 with a 4.33 ERA. The Yanks, however, let him go to the Phils as a free agent and he promptly went 17–13. Second sacker **Robinson Cano** wore No. 22 in both 2005 and 2006. Cano, a coming superstar, switched to No. 24 in 2007 in tribute to the man he was named for, Jackie Robinson. Since Jackie's No. 42 is permanently retired by baseball, Cano reversed it and is making his own Yankee legacy with that number.

Pitcher **LaTroy Hawkins** started the 2008 season as No. 21. But when fans protested that no one should be wearing Paul O'Neill's old number, Hawkins switched to No. 22. It didn't help. He pitched in just 33 games and was shipped to Houston on July 30. Four days earlier the Yanks had made a deal with Pittsburgh, sending three young pitchers to the Pirates for outfielder **Xavier Nady** and relief pitcher Damaso Marte. Nady donned No. 22 and played very well, getting big clutch hits and driving home runs. In 59 games, he hit .268 with 12 homers and 40 RBIs, and for the entire season he was at .305 with 25 homers and 97 RBIs. He was penciled in as the rightfielder in 2009, but played in just seven games before throwing his elbow out and learning that he needed Tommy John surgery for a second time.

#23: DONNIE BASEBALL

When a guy has nicknames like "Donnie Baseball" and "the Hit Man," you've got to assume he's good. For a period of six seasons, first baseman **Don Mattingly** was as good or better than any player in the game, both at the bat and in the field. In fact, the *New York Times* took a poll of every major leaguer in 1986, asking them to name the best player in the game: Don Mattingly was the overwhelming choice. The Yankees' No. 23 was coming off an MVP season in 1985 in which he had hit .325, slammed 35 home runs, and drove home a league best 145 runs. He also led the AL in doubles (48) and fielding percentage while winning the second of his nine Gold Gloves.

Picked by the Yankees in the 19th round of the 1979 draft, Mattingly wasn't projected to be a superstar, wasn't projected to hit with significant power, and wasn't even projected as a Gold Glove first baseman. He was simply another prospect. He finally got a seven-game cup of coffee in 1982 and then a 91-game trial the following year, wearing No. 46 both times. In 1983, he played as much outfield as first base and hit .283 but with just four homers and 32 RBIs. The following year, he won the first base job in spring training, cut his uniform number in half to 23, and proceeded to announce his presence to the baseball world.

All Don Mattingly did his first full season was win the American League batting title with a .343 average, surprise with 23 home runs while driving in 110, and lead the league with 44 doubles. He followed

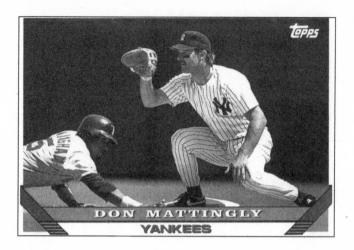

his MVP season of 1985 by hitting a career-best .352 the next year while leading the league with 53 doubles and 238 hits. And the year after that, 1987, he tied one great record and set another.

The first was a record-tying eight home runs in eight consecutive games. Then on September 29, Mattingly came up with the bases loaded in a game against Boston and slammed a home run off southpaw Bruce Hurst. It was his record-setting sixth grand slam of the year. It was a typical Mattingly season: .327 avg., 30 HRs, 115 RBIs. At the age of 26, he was at the absolute top of his game.

Mattingly wasn't a big man, but he generated tremendous power with his legs and hips and he practiced his swing incessantly. He continued his great play until it all came to a screeching halt in 1990, when Donnie Baseball hurt his back. He still played in 102 games that year and would bounce back to play full seasons the next two years. But he wasn't the same hitter, especially in the power department.

He played through the pain in '90, hitting just .245 with five homers and 42 RBIs. Despite that, the following February he received the high ultimate honor of being named captain of the Yankees, a title only a few special players have held. It was hoped then that the real Don Mattingly would again stand up. Unfortunately, the expected comeback never materialized. He did get back to 14 and 17 homers in '92 and

'93, driving in 86 runs in both years while hitting .288 and .291. Those would be considered very good seasons for a lot of players, but not for a guy who had scaled the heights of superstardom just a few years earlier. He reached .300 for the last time in the strike-shortened 1994 season, but had just six homers and 51 RBIs. And the next year, Mattingly batted .288 but with just seven jacks and 49 ribbies.

Sadly, his career was ending just as the Yanks were getting better. In 1995, the team made it to the playoffs as the wild card for the first time since Mattingly started. In his only playoff action against the Seattle Mariners, Mattingly went 10-for-23 with a homer and six RBIs, good for a .417 average as the Yanks were beaten in five games. A year later, the team would begin its run of four World Championship in five years, but Mattingly was gone. His back pain had become chronic, and while he didn't officially announce his retirement until January 1997, he could no longer play up to his own high standards.

Don Mattingly retired with a .307 lifetime batting average, 222 home runs, and 1099 runs batted in. He had 2,153 hits. Because his peak years were so limited, he has never been a serious candidate for the Hall of Fame. He returned to coach for the Yankees and wound up as manager Joe Torre's bench coach. When Torre left after the 2007 season, Mattingly interviewed for the vacant job, but the team picked Joe Girardi. Mattingly then followed Torre to LA where he became the Dodgers' bench coach.

But Mattingly will forever be a Yankee. His No. 23 was retired in 1997 and he has always received huge ovations when he's returned to Yankee Stadium. There's also a plaque dedicated to him in Monument Park at the Stadium that reads, "A humble man of grace and dignity, a captain who led by example, proud of the pinstripe tradition and dedicated to the pursuit of excellence, a Yankee forever."

If you go back to the beginning, No. 23 almost looks like an orphan, a number nobody wanted. It didn't appear at all until. The Yanks great second sacker, **Tony Lazzeri** decided to wear it in 1932, the first Bomber to do so. The strange part is that Lazzeri began as No. 6 (corresponding with the batting order), then wore No. 5 for a couple of seasons. After wearing No. 23 for one year, he went back to No. 7 and then No. 6 for the last four years of his Yankees career. But after Poosh 'Em Up Tony donned the number, no one wore it until pitcher **Frank Makosky** turned up wearing it for 26 games in 1937. Makosky went 5–2, then disappeared from the Majors and the number went back into mothballs.

It didn't reappear until pitcher **Tiny Bonham**, who had a nice Yankees career, showed up with it on his back in 1946. That was a surprise since Bonham had worn No. 20 from 1940–1945, and was identified with that number. He just had No. 23 for part of the season, then switched back No. 20 for the rest of the year, his last with the Yankees. Another three years passed until first sacker **Dick Kryhoski** was given No. 23 during his rookie year of 1949. Kryhoski hit .294, but with just a single home run in 54 games, not good enough for a Yankees first sacker. He was traded to Detroit at season's end. That same year, the one and only **Fenton Mol**e also wore No. 23. Mole played just 10 games, hit .185, but found time enough to also wear No. 18.

Pitcher **Bob Porterfield** wore No. 23 for just two games in 1951 after wearing No. 18 the previous three seasons. Outfielder **Artie Wilson** wore No. 23 for four games in 1951, then switched to No. 15 for another three in '52. He went to Washington, then Boston in that same 1952 season. Lefty **Bill Miller** (1952–54), known to some as "Hooks," was another three-year marginal pitcher. He was No. 23 during his 36-game tenure that produced a 6–8 record.

The **Tommy Byrne** saga is an interesting one. The fastballing, sometimes control-challenged lefty had two tenures in the Bronx, the first beginning in 1943 and continuing after the war from 1946 to June of 1951. The second came from 1954 through 1957. Byrne wore three different numbers, 11 and 28 before and after the war and his 1951 trade to the Browns, and then 28 and 23 when he returned prior to the 1954 season. But because Byrne's biggest historical stage came when he was wearing No. 23 in his final three Yankees seasons, this is where he belongs.

Byrne was a hard-throwing lefty who had no fear of pitching inside. That, coupled with his erratic control, often made hitters think twice before digging in at the plate. It took Byrne a couple of years to get his legs back after returning from the war, but he went from an 8–5 mark in 1948 to a pair of 15-win seasons the following two years as the Yanks won a pair of World Series. Then on June 15, 1951, he was dealt to St. Louis after going just 2–1 in nine games.

The Yanks brought him back on September 3, 1954. He went 3–2 in five games before the end of the season, wearing the same No. 28 he had worn with the Yanks beginning in 1946. But when he returned for 1955, he suddenly switched to No. 23 and soon became the team's number two pitcher behind Whitey Ford. Byrne would go 16–5 as the Yanks drove to another American League pennant. He had a league best .762 winning percentage, and even saved a pair of games.

Byrne would win Game Two of the World Series against Brooklyn, going the distance in a 4–2 Yankees victory and giving his team a 2–0 lead. The Dodgers stormed back to win three straight at Ebbets Field. Back at the Stadium, Whitey Ford won Game Six and Byrne then took the mound against young Johnny Podres in Game Seven. Podres threw an eight-hit shutout and Brooklyn won, 2–0. But Tommy Byrne had done his job again, throwing 5 1/3 innings and giving up just one earned run. He had a 1.88 ERA for the series.

In his final two Yankees seasons, Byrne would throw more out of the pen, going 7–3 in 1956 and 4–6 in '57. He did get to pitch in two more World Series before retiring at 37. But he was 30–16 in his second Yankees tour, giving him a 72–40 record as a Yankee. After retirement, he went home to Wake Forest, North Carolina, and became that town's mayor from 1973–1987.

Veteran righty **Murry Dickson** came to the Yanks at the age of 41 in 1958 to pitch in just six games. He was No. 23, but not many people remember him with it. Dickson, however, had been a good pitcher with some very bad teams throughout his career.

Righthander **Ralph Terry** would stabilize No. 23, but not right away. Like Tommy Byrne, Terry had two separate tenures with the Yanks. He had cups of coffee in both 1956 and '57, pitching in a total of 10 games while wearing No. 21. Then in June of '57, he was dealt to Kansas City before being traded back to the Yanks in late May 1959. The 6'3" righty donned No. 23 this time, went 3–7, and a year later started to emerge.

As the Yanks' fourth starter he was 10–8 with a 3.40 ERA in 1960, then had the misfortune of being the pitcher who threw the World Series-ending home run to Pittsburgh's Bill Mazeroski. Yet Terry rebounded to go 16–3 season in 1961, and then put it all together with a 23–12 slate the following year. He became the World Series MVP by winning two games, including a 1–0 victory over the Giants in Game 7.

After 17-15 and 7-11 records the next two years, Terry was dealt to Cleveland, where he rebounded to go 11–6 for the Indians in 1965. But he would win just two more games and was gone after the 1967 season at the age of 31. Terry would soon choose a second sport and ultimately become a golf pro.

Terry's departure sent No. 23 back into journeyman limbo, with revolving door comings and goings for some two decades leading up to the ascension of Don Mattingly. Pitcher **Rich Beck** was the first, his Yankees career and his MLB career lasting just two weeks in 1965. That same year pitcher **Jim Brenneman** took over No. 23. His three-game audition led to an 18.00 ERA. Gone.

Catcher/first baseman **Billy Bryan** lasted parts of two seasons, 1966 as No. 23 and 1967 as No. 50. He played just 43 games those two years before going to Washington as a Rule 5 draft pick. Veteran catcher **Bob Tillman** was purchased from the Red Sox on August 8, 1967, and was a backup in just 22 games before being traded to Atlanta at the end of the season. Young catcher **Ellie Rodriguez** got his first big league experience in 1968, playing just nine games

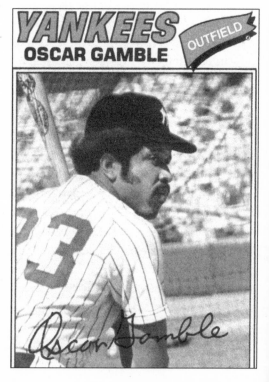

as No. 23 and hitting .208. He went to the Royals at year's end in the 1968 expansion draft.

Righthander **Don Nottebart** pitched for the Yanks as No. 23 in 1969, but was all but done. The Yanks purchased him from the Reds before the season, watched him pitch just four games, and returned him to Cincy. After Nottebart left, No. 23 was given to a big, strong 20-year-old from Connecticut who seemed to have big time potential as a hitter.

At 6'2", 225-pounds, **John Ellis** was a catcher/first baseman with a big bat. He wasn't very graceful in the field but hit. 290 in 22 games in 1969. Ellis never lived up to his potential and was finally dealt to the Indians in November 1972. Career backup catcher **Jerry Moses** came over from Cleveland in the Ellis deal and played 21 games in 1973. The latest No. 23 was shipped to Detroit the following March and then along came the enigmatic outfielder, **Alex Johnson**, a solid hitter and outfielder who had won a batting title with the Angels in 1970,

hitting .329. But Johnson was also surly and often didn't hustle in the field—which he admitted—despite having a great throwing arm. The Yanks bought his contract on September 9, 1974, but he hit just .214 in 10 games. A year later, he played in 52 games, hit just .261 with one homer, and was released on September 4.

Outfielder **Oscar Gamble** wore No. 23 in his first stint with the Yanks in 1976. He came over from Cleveland, hit .232 with 17 homers, and was dealt to the White Sox the following April for Bucky Dent. Gamble would return in 1979 and stay until August 1984, wearing No. 17, the number most Yankee fans remember him by. Infielder **Damaso Garcia** had an 18-game trial in 1978 as No. 23 and an 11-game fill-in stint in '79 as No. 59, then was shipped to Toronto along with 1976 hero Chris Chambliss.

Then, prior to the 1979 season, the Yanks made a surprise free agent signing, inking 38-year-old righthander **Luis Tiant**. The Cuban-born, cigar-smoking "El Tiante" was a four-time 20-game winner and a huge hero in Boston where he went 2–0 in the 1975 World Series. Known for his funky delivery, where he momentarily turned his back to home plate, Tiant was a competitor who still had enough guile to go 13–8 with a 3.91 ERA for the Yanks in '79. Unfortunately, he began losing it the next season, dropping to 8–9 with a 4.89 ERA and the Yanks let him go via free agency. He would pitch two more years before retiring.

Backup catcher **Barry Foote** was the last player before Don Mattingly to wear No. 23. He came over from the Cubs, where he had a 16-home run season in 1979. He played in just 57 games for the Yanks over two years, didn't hit a lick, and then retired at the age of 30. Two years later, Mattingly took the field with No. 23 on his back and no Yankee has worn it since.

THE MOST VALUABLE PLAYERS

When Don Mattingly was named the American League's Most Valuable Player in 1985, he joined an elite group of Yankees to win that coveted prize. Here's a list of Yankees MVPs down through the years. As with so many other things, it starts with the Babe.

Babe Ruth	1923		Yogi Berra	1955
Lou Gehrig	1927		Mickey Mantle	1956
Lou Gehrig	1936		Mickey Mantle	1957
Joe DiMaggio	1939		Roger Maris	1960
Joe DiMaggio	1941		Roger Maris	1961
Joe Gordon	1942		Mickey Mantle	1962
Spud Chandler	1943		Elston Howard	1963
Joe DiMaggio	1947		Thurman Munson	1976
Phil Rizzuto	1950		Don Mattingly	1985
Yogi Berra	1951		Alex Rodriguez	2005
Yogi Berra	1954		Alex Rodriguez	2007

It's no coincidence that most of the MVPs are also associated with championship teams during their careers. There's no substitute for winning, and that usually gives the Yankees' stars a leg up on the MVP.

#24: RICKEY, TINO AND ON TO CANO

Number 24 has always been a popular one, maybe moreso after the great Willie Mays wore it for all those years with the Giants. With the Yanks, there have been a number of players who have worn it for multiple seasons, with only two periods when it seemed to be passed on from one player to another season to season. Three players stand out, with the latest just now establishing himself as one of the game's big stars. They are **Rickey Henderson**, **Tino Martinez**, and **Robinson Cano**. The first two came to the Yankees after making reputations elsewhere, but continued to shine in the Big Apple. The latter has been a Yankee since the beginning, and as of 2009 was en route to becoming one of the best all-around second basemen of his era.

Rickey Henderson was a guy who never wanted to quit. He played for 25 seasons, until he was 44 years old, and insisted for the next four years or so that he could still help a team. Henderson performed for nine different teams, including four stops with Oakland, his first ballclub. He was a Yankee for just four and a half seasons, coming over in a trade before the 1985 campaign. By that time, he had already set the single-season record for stolen bases with 130 in 1982, his third full

RICKEY HENDERSON

season in the league, and had proven himself a devastating leadoff hitter with a penchant for the leadoff home run or leadoff walk. And with Rickey Henderson, a bases empty walk was almost as good as a double. Like others, he chose to wear number 24 because his idol was Willie Mays.

In his first year in pinstripes, Henderson hit .314 with 24 homers and 72 RBIs. He led the league with 80 steals and 146 runs scored. He also became the first player ever to have 20 or more homers and 50 or more steals in a single season. That year, Don Mattingly had a career-high 145 RBIs and he knocked in Henderson 56 times. A year later, Rickey had 28 homers and 87 steals before problems arose in 1987 when he played in just 95 games. His numbers were good, not great. However, by then he wasn't getting along with manager Lou Piniella, an old school tough guy, and owner George Steinbrenner voiced his displeasure. He had a bounce-back season in '88, hitting .305 with a league-best 93 steals, only his home run output dropped to just six. A year later he really floundered. After 65 games, he was hitting just .247 with just three homers when the Yanks pulled the trigger on a trade.

On June 21, he was returned to Oakland for pitchers Greg Caderet, Eric Plunk, and outfielder Luis Polonia. The Henderson era in New York was over, but not Rickey's career. He may not have created a real legacy in New York, but he was far from done. He had a great postseason with the A's in '89, hitting over .400 in both the ALCS and World Series. A year later, he was the AL's Most Valuable Player when he hit .325 with 28 homers and 61 RBIs, a league best 65 steals and 119 runs scored. It was a typical Rickey Henderson great all-around season.

He finally retired after the 2003 season as baseball's all-time steals leader with 1,406. Though Barry Bonds eventually passed him in walks, he has the most unintentional bases on balls with 2,129. He also walked to lead off an inning 796 times and had a record 81 home runs to lead off a ballgame. In addition, he led the league in stolen bases 12 times and retired with 3,055 hits. In 2009, he was elected to the Hall of Fame in his first year of eligibility. For a guy who once called himself the greatest, he gave a humble and appreciative acceptance speech. No matter what you thought of him, Rickey Henderson absolutely loved playing the game of baseball.

When Don Mattingly retired after the 1995 season, the Yankees needed a first baseman. Enter Tino Martinez, who had been the Seattle's starting first sacker since 1992. Martinez had a breakout season in '95 with 31 homers and 111 RBIs to go with a .293 average. That Seattle would deal him was surprising, but in December the Mariners sent him to the Yanks with pitchers Jim Mecir and Jeff Nelson in return for infielder Russ Davis and pitcher Sterling Hitchcock. The Yankees wouldn't regret making the deal.

Replacing a legend is never easy, but Martinez eased into his position. He never tried to be Don Mattingly, but slowly went about proving he belonged in the Bronx. Wearing No. 24, Martinez debuted with a .292, 25, 117 season. What's more, he helped the Yankees to their first World Championship since 1978. From there, the Yankees went on a run and so did Tino. He was an All-Star in 1997 as he hit .296 with career highs of 44 homers and 141 RBIs, a season that elevated him to star status.

His consistency continued as the Yanks won two more titles in '98 and '99. In the '98 World Series, he belted a grand slam home run off Mark Langston of San Diego in Game One to break a 3–3 tie and start the Bronx Bombers on the road to a sweep. Tino tailed off a bit in 2000, hitting just .258 with 16 homers and 91 RBIs, but the Yanks won their fourth World Series in five years since he joined the team. A year later, he rebounded to .280, 34, 113, and hit another dramatic, clutch home run in the World Series against Arizona.

That season would be a last hurrah. In the off-season, the Yankees signed Oakland first baseman Jason Giambi to a huge free agent contract and let Tino become a free agent. He signed with the Cardinals, then played the 2004 season in his hometown of Tampa for the Devil Rays before signing with the Yankees again before the 2005 season. He took his old No. 24 once again and played a lot of first base while Giambi, the weaker fielder, was the DH. Tino got hot early and carried the Yanks in May, at one point hitting five home runs in five games, and thanks to a two-homer day, eight over eight games, treating his many fans to one final display of his talents. He finished the season at .241 with 17 homer and 49 RBIs, then he retired.

A true Yankee, Tino is welcomed with warm cheers on Old Timers' Days and other special occasions. He's a part-time instructor for the team and part-time commentator. He finished his career with a .271 average, 339 home runs and 1,271 RBIs, not a Hall of Famer, but a fine ballplayer who could always be counted on to give his best, which was plenty.

At the beginning, there was the usual helter-skelter effect, with players who wore different numbers almost every year. Infielder **Lyn Lary** was the first to wear No. 24 in 1929 and '30, but he's been heard from before since he wore No. 2 for three seasons and No. 22 his final Yankees season of 1934. **Big Jim Weaver** was No. 24 for 17 games in 1931. At 6'6", 230 pounds, he was exceptionally large for a pitcher back then, but he didn't impress the Yanks. He disappeared from the majors until 1934 and became a two-time 14-game winner with the Pirates in the mid-1930s.

Outfielder **Sammy Byrd** had an unusual nickname. They called him "Babe Ruth's Legs." He was with the Yanks from 1929–1934 and often spelled the aging Ruth in right field during the late innings of games. Byrd was also one of those guys that was introduced to a new uniform almost every year. Starting in '29 he wore Nos. 27, 36, 29, 24, 25, and

25 again. This was a case where the player needed a scorecard to find himself.

Infielder **Billy Werber** played three games for the Yanks as No. 20 in 1930, then four more as No. 24 in 1933. From there he went to Boston, where he led the league in steals three times during the 1930s. Right-hander **Charlie Devens** was another multi-number guy wearing Nos. 20, 33, and 24 between 1932 and '34, but pitched a total of just 16 games those three years. Southpaw **Vito Tamulis** wore both No. 24 and 22 in 1934, then No. 22 the next year, when he went 10–5. He resurfaced with both the St. Louis Browns and Brooklyn Dodgers in 1938. Righty **Steve "Smokey" Sundra** was No. 24 for a single game in 1936, then returned as No. 32 in '38 and '39, finishing up as No. 25 in 1940 before moving on to Washington. In 1939, Sundra won his first 11 decisions before losing in his final start of the season. Three of his wins were out of the pen and he was 11–1 for the year, which earned him a couple of innings in the 1939 World Series. But the next year he dropped to 4–6 and was moved out.

Hurler **Ivy Andrews** was another two-tenure guy. The righthander pitched in just 11 games in 1931 and '32, wearing Nos. 22 and 28. He returned in 1937 and '38 wearing No. 24, but the results weren't much better and he was out of baseball. The effective **Spud Chandler** made his Yankee rep as No. 21. But in his rookie year of 1937, he was a three-number guy. At various stages of the season, he appeared as No. 24, No. 13, and No. 35. That could be a record. **Marv "Baby Face" Breuer** finally gave the number of bit of stability when he wore No. 24 from 1940–43. The righty was a 25–26 pitcher for the Yanks after starring in the minor leagues at Newark. Like so many others, he couldn't make the minor-major transition.

Hall of Famer **Paul "Big Poison" Waner** played the last two seasons of his career with the Yanks during the war years of 1944 and '45, wearing No. 24, then 22. Righthander **Al Lyons** also wore No. 24 for 11 games in 1944, then came back as No. 36 in 1946 and No. 38 in 1947 before going to Pittsburgh after a Yankees career of just 20 games. Another righty, **Steve Roser**, didn't have much better luck. He started as No. 26 in 1944, when he went 4–3, then switched to No. 24 the next year for 11 games, and back to No. 26 in 1946 when he appeared just four times. He went to the Braves before the year was out and was finished in the majors at season's end.

Catcher **Gus Niarhos** didn't fit the mold. At a time when catchers were generally short and squat, tough little fireplugs, Niarhos was six feet tall and rather thin at 160 pounds. He wore both Nos. 24 and 37 for 37 games in 1946. Two years later, he returned from the minors wearing No. 38 and that year platooned with Yogi Berra, hitting .268 in 83 games. But his playing time diminished in 1949 and, after playing just one game in 1950, he was shipped off to the White Sox.

Then, in 1946, No. 24 finally got a kind of permanent home, on the back of third baseman **Billy Johnson**. The Jersey-born Johnson was signed by the Yanks in 1936 when he was just 18, but wasn't given a full shot until the spring of 1943 when he won the third base job from aging veteran Red Rolfe. And what a rookie season it was. Johnson led the league by playing in 155 games, hit a solid .280 and had 94 RBIs (third best in the league) to go with just five home runs. He also led AL third baseman in putouts, assists, and double plays. And he did it wearing No. 7, a number that would be worn by Mickey Mantle less than a decade later.

Then he went into the military for two full years, returning to play just 85 games in 1946, hitting just .260. But now he had No. 24 on his back. A year later, he had his baseball legs again and had a .285 season with 10 homers and 95 RBIs, once again one of the best third sackers in the league.

While he had career bests with a .294 average and 12 homers in 1948, a year later his career path changed. Casey Stengel took over as manager and began platooning Johnson with Bobby Brown, and sometimes playing him at first. By 1951, infielder Gil McDougald had joined the team and was on his way to becoming Rookie of the Year. That made Johnson expendable. On May 14, he was traded to the Cardinals for first sacker Don Bollweg.

When Johnson departed, his number didn't stay lonely for long. A June 15 trade with the St. Louis Browns brought pitcher **Frank "Stubby" Overmire** to New York in return for Tommy Byrne. Overmire was 5'7" and 170 pounds, thus the nickname. He was 32 years old when the Yanks got him and was used sparingly, pitching in just 15 games as No. 24 in 1951, then waived to the Browns the following May. Reliever and spot starter **Tom Gorman** was No. 24 from 1952–54, didn't really make much of a splash, and moved on to Kansas City.

On July 22, 1954 the Yankees signed righthander **Ralph Branca** as a free agent, the same Ralph Branca who had been on the mound for the Dodgers when the Giants Bobby Thomson hit his epic Shot-Heard-Round-the-World home run to win the 1951 pennant. As No. 24 with the Yanks, he pitched in just five games and won the final game of his career.

Another veteran righty, **Gerry Staley**, wore No. 24 for two games in 1955 and one more in '56 before being waived. Rookie righthander **Al Cicotte** then took over the number in 1957, but not for long. He pitched in 20 games that year, then was sold to the Senators the following May. In June of 1958, the Yanks reopened the Kansas City shuttle and received pitchers **Duke Maas** and Virgil Trucks.

Duane "Duke" Maas was a 29-year-old righthander who had won 10 games for Detroit the season before and was 4–5 for a weak Athletics team before the trade. He pitched in 22 games the rest of the year, 13 of them starts, and finished with a 7–3 record as the Yanks won the pennant. Maas was 14–9 in 1959, but after the 1960 season went to the Angels in the expansion draft, came back briefly as No. 29 the following April, threw one game, and was released.

Lefty **Danny McDevitt** went 10–8 for the Dodgers in 1959, but with the Yankees in 1961, he was just 1–2 in eight games before being traded to the Twins in June. He had worn No. 24 for a scant three months. The next player to wear it would keep it on his back for nine long years. He was lefthander **Al Downing,** whom the Yanks signed out of Rider College in 1961. By 1963 he was a fixture in the rotation and a pitcher who appeared to have a bright future.

Possessor of a lively fastball ball and electric curve, Downing was the first African-American pitcher to crack the Yankees rotation. And he cracked it to the tune of a 13–5 record with a 2.56 ERA and 171 strikeouts in 175 2/3 innings after being recalled from the minors in June. A year later he was 13–8 with a 3.47 ERA and led the AL with 217 strikeouts.

Unfortunately for Downing, after the 1964 season the Yankees dynasty began to crumble, and the next two seasons he was 12–14 and 10–11. In 1967, he seemed to put it all together, but in early 1968, he heard something "snap" in his elbow and his lost his effectiveness, going 3–3 and 7–5 in 1968 and '69. The Yanks gave up, trading Downing to Oakland that December. He wound up with the Dodgers in 1971, found the magic again and went 20–9 with five shutouts.

For the last six years of his career with the Dodgers, Downing was essentially a .500 pitcher. But in 1974 he unwittingly became the answer to a trivia question. He was the guy who served up Henry Aaron's record-breaking 715th home run. His lifetime mark was a serviceable 123-107.

Downing's departure opened up No. 24 for pitcher **Ron Klimkowski**, who had three uneventful years in New York. When Klimkowski was traded to Oakland in April 1971, the Yanks received 36-year-old outfield veteran **Felipe Alou** in return. The oldest of three Alou brothers to star in the majors, Felipe became the first native of the Dominican Republic to play regularly in the major leagues when he earned a starting outfield job with the Giants in 1961, his fourth year in the bigs.

Alou had a fine career, a cut below big star level. With the Yanks in 1971, he played 131 games and had a solid .289 year with eight homers and 69 ribbies. He fell off a bit the next year and by 1973 was waived to Montreal in early September. But he gave the Yanks two good years, then moved on to a long and successful managerial career with Montreal and the Giants.

In young **Otto Velez**, the Yanks thought they might have an up-and-coming power hitting outfielder/first baseman. He came up in 1973 wearing No. 53, but changed to No. 24 on his second call-up. In 23 games, he hit just .195. He hit .209 in 27 games the next year and played just six games as No. 52 in 1975. His final chance came in 1976 as No. 24 again. But the power never came and he went to Toronto in the expansion draft. Outfielder **Rick Bladt** was the reason Velez wore No. 52 in 1975, as he had No. 24. Bladt played in 52 games, hit just .222, and after the season was part of the trade that sent Elliott Maddox to Baltimore in return for Paul Blair.

When 35-year-old **Jimmy Wynn** joined the Yanks in 1977, he asked for, and received, his old number 24 which he had worn during his All-Star years in Houston. Known as "The Toy Cannon," the 5'9", 170-pound Wynn had been a good home run hitter in his prime, but he was pretty much done when he donned the pinstripes. He hit a paltry .143 in 30 games with a single homer and was released in June. When Wynn was released, pitcher **Mike Torrez** switched uniforms, going from No. 48, in which he started the year, to his familiar No. 24. Torrez had come to the Yanks in a late April trade for pitcher Dock Ellis, and with injuries to Catfish Hunter and Don Gullett, became an important piece in the Yanks' pennant run.

Torrez was a baseball nomad who would win up playing for seven teams, and the big, 6'5", 220-pound righthander always won. Just two years earlier, he was 20–9 for the Orioles. With the Yanks he would go 14–12 with a 3.82 ERA in 31 starts, winning some big games, including two complete game victories in the World Series against the Dodgers. It was Torrez who was on the mound in Game Six when Reggie Jackson hit his epic three home runs. But after the season Torrez decided to test the free agent market and moved on to Boston, where he would give up Bucky Dent's huge home run a year later. He retired with a 185-160 record.

Then No. 24 was passed around again. Infielder **Mickey Klutts** wore it for part of 1978, outfielder **Gary Thomasson** for another portion of the same season. Next came outfielder/first baseman **Dennis Werth**, who wore it for part of three seasons (1978–81). **Butch Hobson**, a third sacker who once hit 31 homers and drove in 112 runs for the Red Sox, wore Nos. 24 and 35 for just 30 games in 1982. Hobson hit just .172 in what would be his last year in the majors. Outfielder **Lee Mazzilli**, who had once been a matinee idol with the Mets, wore No. 24 for 37 games in 1982. He hit .266 with six homers but was traded at the end of the season. Mazzilli would subsequently become a Yankees coach and manage for a year in Baltimore.

Then in 1983, along came "the Count of Montefusco." Righthander **John Montefusco**, nicknamed for the literary character, the Count of Monte Cristo, was a bombastic, outspoken pitcher who backed up his bragging in his early years with the Giants, when he won 15, then 16 games in 1975 and '76. But arm and hip injuries limited his effectiveness. He was 33 years old when he reached the Yankees but impressed by going 5–0 with a 3.32 ERA in six starts in 1983, when he wore No. 24. He was 5–3 in 11 games the next year as injuries continued to plague him. In 1985, he switched to No. 26 in deference to Rickey Henderson—who had joined the team—but could pitch in just three games. In 1986, he was healthy enough for just four games and his career was over. **Deion Sanders** wore No. 24 in 1989 before switching to No. 21 the following year, and outfielder **Marcus Lawton** also donned the uniform for 10 games in 1989 before Sanders arrived. That was the total length of his big league career.

In 1990, the Yankees thought they might have a coming star in 6'3" first baseman/DH **Kevin Maas**. Called up the same year that All-Star first sacker Don Mattingly suffered a back injury that would curtail his career, he showed some power, hitting 21 and 23 homers in 1990 and '91, but his average was low, and when his power dipped by '93, he was released after the season and was out of baseball by 1995 at the age of 30.

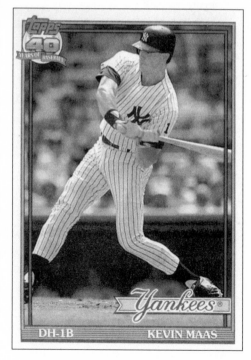

DH-1B   KEVIN MAAS

Russ Davis was the next prospect, a third sacker, who seemed to have some pop in his bat. He didn't pass muster with the Yanks in 1994 and '95 and was sent to Seattle, where he did have three straight 20-home run seasons from 1997–99. After Davis, Tino Martinez took over through the 2001 season and reclaimed his No. 24 when he returned for a year in 2005.

Enigmatic switch-hitting slugger **Ruben Sierra** returned as a free agent in 2003 and took on No. 24. Sierra had been with the Yanks for half seasons in 1995 and '96, wearing Nos. 25 and 28, and failing to deliver the goods both times. In 2003, the Yanks were headed to another World Series and Sierra hit .276 in 63 games, with six homers and 31 RBIs. He was 37 years old then and a serviceable part-time player. Though he got some big hits, by the age of 39 he was all but done.

In 2006, righthander **Sidney Ponson** wore No. 24 for just five games when the team needed a pitcher. He was signed in mid-June and released in late August. Ponson returned for 16 games during the second half of the 2008 season, going 4–4.

Finally, No. 24 found another steady home, and with a player who has the ability to retire it some day. Second baseman Robinson Cano is a native of the Dominican Republic. He was signed by the Yanks as an amateur free agent in 2001 and was called up to the big club in 2005, quickly winning the second base job. He started off as No. 14 his rookie year, but switched to No. 22 before the year was out. In 132 games, Cano hit .297 with 14 homers and 62 RBIs.

Though he wasn't considered a top prospect when he was signed, the southpaw swinging Cano surprised everyone. In his second year, he batted .342 despite missing 40 games with a hamstring injury. He finished third in batting behind the Twins' Joe Mauer and teammate Derek Jeter. In 2007 he switched his uniform number to 24, the reverse numbers of his idol and namesake, Jackie Robinson. When he batted .306 with 19 home runs and 97 runs batted in, he firmly established himself as one of the game's bright young stars.

There were some hiccups in 2008. Cano hit just .271 with 14 homers and 72 RBIs for a Yankees team that missed the playoffs for the first time since 1994. But he rededicated himself during the off-season and, in 2009, emerged as a full-fledged star, both at the bat and in the field. He hit .320 with more than 200 hits, a career best 25 home runs and 85 RBIs. He was often spectacular in the field, with a throwing arm second to none at his position. Cano didn't turn 27 until October 22, 2009, and right now there's no telling how good he can be.

#25: TOMMY JOHN: PITCHER, SURGERY

Tommy John is the only professional athlete ever to have a surgical procedure named after him. The sinker-balling lefthander was the first pitcher to have ligament replacement surgery on his pitching elbow and return to top form. The surgery, which is a common procedure today with pitchers as young as high school age and sometimes even younger, is now almost always successful, with some hurlers coming back even stronger than they were before. John had two tenures as a Yankee after the surgery, and pitched well both times, including a pair of 20-win seasons. He would ultimately pitch for 26 seasons, a record until Nolan Ryan broke it, and would win 288 games.

John began his career with the Indians at the age of 20 in 1963. Two years later, he was dealt to the White Sox where he won 14 games in both 1965 and '66. He was with the Sox until 1972, when he was dealt to the Dodgers, where he went 11–5 and 16–7 his first seasons on the coast. In 1974 he was 13–3 on July 17, the top winner in the league and a definite Cy Young Award candidate when he heard a crunch in his left elbow while pitching against the Expos. He shut down for three weeks, then found he still couldn't throw. Dr. Frank Jobe performed the surgery, which entailed transplanting a ligament

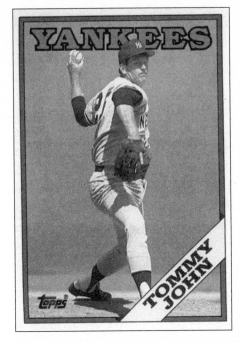

from his right wrist into his left elbow. It was the first time that type of surgery had been done and the odds of John returning to form were set at 100–1. Besides transplanting the ligament, doctors also had to repair muscle and nerve damage.

Slowly, he began to rehab, throwing a ball up against a wall and doing rudimentary exercises like squeezing a rubber ball and golf club grips. He sat out the entire 1975 season, and then there was a lockout in the spring of 1976 so he didn't have much chance to get into pitching shape. The Dodgers saw that he couldn't throw more than 85 mph, and at one point the team was planning to release him. Then, in his second start he threw seven shutout innings. He wound up going 10–10, with a 3.09 ERA, pitching 207 innings. The surgery had been a success. The man they called "T. J." was back. He proved it for real a year later by going 20–7 and winning 14 of his final 17 decisions. After winning 17 the next year, he became a free agent and signed with the Yankees.

Wearing his familiar No. 25 with the Yanks, T. J. went 21–9 and 22–9 for the Bombers and quickly became a fan favorite, as well as a marvel of modern surgery. He fell off the next two seasons, going 9–8 and 10–10, and the Yanks dealt him to the Angels on August 31, 1982. After splitting the 1985 season between the Angels and Oakland, he returned to the Yankees in 1986 as a free agent. He was just 5–3 in 13 games that year, but in 1987 at the age of 44, he produced a 13–6 year. His final two seasons he was 9–8 and then 2–7 before the Yanks released him on May 30. But by then Tommy John was 46 years old and had pitched for 25 full seasons.

With a 288–231 record, many feel Tommy John should be in the Hall of Fame, but he still hasn't gotten the call. It seems like the voters are splitting hairs. Every pitcher who has won 300 games has been voted in, and TJ was just 12 short.

No. 25 was up in the stratosphere in the early years and the better players didn't begin wearing it until the late 1940s. How many Yankees fans, for instance, remember **Ben Paschal**? He was a reserve outfielder who had been with the Yanks since 1924 and was the first to wear No. 25 in 1929, his last year in the majors.

Paschal set the tone for those early years. Second sacker **Jimmie Reese** was next, wearing No. 25 in 1931 and switching to No. 26 the next year for no apparent reason. Reese went to St. Louis a year later, his final season in the majors.

THE REAL JIMMIE REESE

There are a number of little known pieces of information about Jimmie Reese. His real name was Hyam Soloman, which he changed due to the open prejudice against Jewish ballplayers in the early days. Yes, prejudice in baseball existed long before Jackie Robinson became the first African-American to play in the bigs in 1947. Just ask Hank Greenberg. Reese was also a roommate of Babe Ruth during his Yankee days and became one of the last surviving players to have known the Babe personally during his playing career. And when he joined the Angels as a coach in 1972, he was still one of the most skilled men at hitting fungoes in the game, another of baseball's lost arts.

Outfielder **Sammy Byrd,** he of the musical numbers, wore No. 25 in 1933 and '34, but between 1929 and '32 he donned Nos. 27, 26, 29 and 24, a different number each year. Rookie outfielder **Jesse Hill** played 107 games as No. 25 in 1935, hitting .293. Next came left **Ted Kleinhans**, who pitched in 10 games in 1936 and was 1–1 in his Yankee career.

Say hello next to lefty **Kemp Wicker**, who lasted parts of three seasons (1936–38) and pitched a total of 25 games. He wore No. 25 the first two years, then No. 20 for a single game in 1938. **Joe Vance** was a righthanded pitcher who wore No. 25 for five games in 1937 and '38. Then he was gone for good. But when another righty, **Wes Ferrell**, took over the uniform in 1938, he was a guy with a track record. Unfortunately, he also had a bad arm.

Ferrell was a junkballer who pitched in just five games the remainder of the year, then three more in 1939 before he was released on May 28. Two years later, he retired at the age of 33 with a 193–128 lifetime mark, almost all of which came before his Yankee days.

Pitcher **Steve Sundra** wore No. 25 in 1940, his last year with the Yanks, after wearing No. 24 in 1936, and No. 32 in 1938 and '40. **Eddie Kearse**, a catcher, continued the one-year-and-out tradition by appearing in 11 games as No. 25 in 1942, his only 11 games as a big leaguer. He was followed by catcher **Aaron Robinson**, who played a single game as No. 25 in 1943, then returned from 1945–47 as No. 8, 7, and 8 again, before losing his job to young Yogi Berra. The parade continued with outfielder **Larry Rosenthal**, who donned No. 25 for 36 games in 1944 before he and his .198 batting average were sold to the A's on July 6. Righthander **Al Gettel** pitched his first two years with the Yanks in 1945 and '46, going a combined 15–15 before being shipped to Cleveland.

Second baseman **Ray Mark** was the latest No. 25 not to make a mark as he threw in just one game in 1947, finished the year with the Cubs, and was gone. Righty **Butch Wensloff** appeared on the scene as No. 14 in 1943 and showed promise with a 13–11 record. Then he went to work in a war plant and eventually joined the Army. When he returned in 1947 as No. 25 he quickly found his arm was dead. Finally, in 1948, a tough young outfielder named **Hank Bauer** took over the number and stayed. Bauer wore No. 25 his first four seasons with the Yanks, then in 1952 switched to No. 9, the number for which he is most remembered. But it was a start.

The next guy to wear the number came with the same kind of predicted star power as Mickey Mantle. When **Jackie Jensen** ran for 1,080 yards as the University of California's All-American fullback in 1948, he acquired the nickname of "The Golden Boy." It followed him to the Yankees in 1950, where he was predicted to be Joe DiMaggio's successor in centerfield. He looked like a five-tool player, yet hit just .171

in 45 games as No. 40 in 1950. A year later, he was in 56 games and began showing potential, hitting .298 this time with eight homers and 25 RBIs. In 1952, he donned No. 25 but it was anything but a breakout year. On May 3, the Yankees shipped him to Washington with three other players in return for outfielder Irv Noren and a minor leaguer.

But the Jensen story wasn't over. The Yanks gave up on him and so did the Senators, sending him to Boston before the 1954 season. Jensen then proceeded to drive in more than 100 runs five times in the next six years, leading the AL in that department three times. There was one problem. Jackie Jensen had a real fear of flying, to the point of having panic attacks at the airports. Even a hypnotist couldn't cure his problem and he called it quits after the 1959 season, a year in which he hit 28 homers and led the league with 112 RBIs. He changed his mind two years later, but after hitting just .263 with 13 homers and 66 RBIs, he packed it in for good at the age of 34.

Outfielder **Irv Noren** wore No. 25 between 1952 and 1956, the southpaw swinger often platooning with Hank Bauer or playing the corner opposite him with Mantle in the middle. Noren was more of a contact hitter than a slugger, and a good outfielder with a strong arm. His best year was 1954, when he hit .319 with 12 homers and 66 RBIs. After hitting just .216 in 26 games in 1956, he was shipped to Kansas City.

One of baseball's few Zekes, **Zeke Bella** played five games for the Yanks in 1957, hitting just .182, and was in and out of uniform No. 25 before you could look him up. He gave way to tall (6'3"), rangy **Norm Siebern**, who debuted as No. 36 in 1956, hitting .204 in 56 games. After another year in the minors, Siebern returned as No. 25 in 1958 and this time had a .300 season with 14 homers and 55 RBIs. He also won a Gold Glove for his play in left field.

A year later, Siebern hit .271 in 120 games, but the Yankees suddenly had a deal they couldn't pass up. After the season, he was shipped to —guess where?—Kansas City in a swap that brought Roger Maris to New York. But he proved himself a good player. In 1962, he hit .308 with 25 homers and 117 RBIs for KC.

For the next couple of years No. 25 was passed around again. Veteran first sacker **Dale Long** wore it for 26 games in 1960 after being purchased from the Giants on August 21. For the Yanks he did a nice job, hitting .366 with three homers as they won the pennant. But after the season, he was taken in the expansion draft by the new Washington Senators. He would return briefly in 1962 and '63, wearing No. 26 before retiring. Earlier in 1960, first sacker **Kent Hadley** wore No. 25 for 55 games. But he didn't do nearly as well as Long, hitting just .203 in what would be his last year. Catcher **Jesse Gonder** wore No. 27 for seven games in 1960, then No. 25 for 15 more in 1961 before being traded to the Reds for pitcher Marshall Bridges.

Then in 1962 came the often frustrating, sometimes enigmatic **Joe Pepitone**. The Brooklyn-born, lefty-swinging first sacker was signed by the Yankees in 1958 and made the big club in 1962 at the age of 21. He was issued No. 25 and would wear that number throughout his Yankees career, which lasted through 1969. When they brought him up, the Yanks envisioned him as a player who would fit in beautifully and eventually help perpetuate the dynasty, which was still in full swing. He had power, fielded his position well, and looked like a Yankee. The Yanks thought so much of him that before the 1963 season they traded long-time first baseman Moose Skowron to the Dodgers. Pepitone responded by hitting .271 with 27 homers and 89 RBIs. Soon the Yanks even began using him in centerfield to spell the aging Mantle, whose legs had robbed him of speed and mobility.

But "Pepi" never quite became the star the Yankees envisioned. He was soon associated more with the crumbling dynasty than a continuing one. He won a Gold Glove in 1965 but hit just .247. In fact, in his last six years with the Yanks, he wouldn't hit above .255. In 1967 and '68 he hit just 13 and 15 home runs, injuries now robbing him of playing time. Finally, the Yanks had enough. In December 1969, they shipped him to Houston in return for Curt Blefary.

After that, No. 25 fell into old habits. It started with **Pete Ward** in 1970. Ward was a third sacker who hit 45 home runs and drove home 178 runs his first two years with the White Sox in 1963 and '64. With the Yanks he played 66 games, hit .260 with one home run and 18 RBIs, then retired. Infielder **Len Boehmer** was in 45 games in 1969 as No. 38 and hit .176. He returned for just three games the next year, wearing

No. 25, and was out of baseball. Next came outfielder **Johnny Callison**, who had been all All-Star with the Phils in the 1960s. But with the Yanks he hit just .258 with nine homers in 92 games in 1972, then sunk below the Mendoza Line at .176 in 45 games in '73. Like the others, he promptly retired.

In 1974, the number was fallow. Then in 1975 it looked like it might have a solid home for a number of years. The Yanks made a trade before the season sending longtime favorite Bobby Murcer to San Francisco in return for outfielder **Bobby Bonds**. The elder Bonds, a fine ballplayer who spent the first seven years of his career with the Giants, hit for power and used his great speed to become one of the better basestealers in the National League. Two years before the trade, in 1973, Bonds hit .283 with 39 home runs, 96 RBIs and 41 steals. The Yanks pretty much knew what they were getting.

The great Bonds experiment, however, lasted just one season. He did his job, hitting .270 with 32 home runs, 85 RBIs, and 30 steals, and he made the All-Star team. But that December, the Yanks traded Bonds to the Angels in return for speedy centerfielder Mickey Rivers and righthander Ed Figueroa.

The merry-go-round continued. Lefty **Grant Jackson** came to the Yanks in June 1976 from the Orioles and went 6–0 down the stretch with a 1.69 ERA in 21 games, helping the Yanks win the pennant. But after the season, he was taken by the Seattle Mariners in the expansion draft. Infielder **George Zeber** wore No. 25 his only two years in the majors, 1977 and '78. Another infielder, **Brian Doyle**, wore the number for 39 games in 1978, hitting just .192, and only saving his job by filling in for the injured Willie Randolph in the World Series and hitting .438. He wore No. 18 the next two years and couldn't clear the Mendoza Line, hitting just .125 and 173. Then came Tommy John, who wore it from 1979–82. After John was traded to the Angels at the end of August, righty **Stefan Wever** had his game in the sun. Just one.

In 1983, No. 25 passed on to **Don Baylor**, an outstanding ballplayer, leader, and one of the toughest individuals ever to step on a major league diamond. Baylor started out as an outfielder, played some first base, but really was a quintessential designated hitter. In 19 seasons,

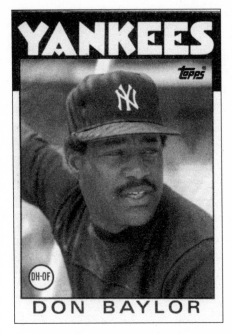

YANKEES Topps

DON BAYLOR

DH-OF

he hit 338 homers, had 285 stolen bases, and set a major league record by being hit by pitches 267 times.

Baylor didn't have a long Yankees career. He was 34 when he joined the Yanks and the team from 1983–85 wasn't the best, but Baylor played well. His batting average went down each year (.303, .262, .231), but his RBIs went up (85, 89, 91). In his final year with the Yankees, he was named the league's outstanding designated hitter and also received the Roberto Clemente Award for humanitarian service.

Nevertheless, the Yanks traded him to the Red Sox for Mike Easler before the 1986 season.

Tommy John returned to the Yanks in 1986 and took his old No. 25 for two plus years. He was released in late May 1989, and that June the Bombers traded Rickey Henderson to Oakland in return for pitchers Eric Plunk, **Greg Cadaret** and outfielder Luis Polonia, with southpaw Cadaret taking over No. 25. Though he had both started and relieved during his career, Cadaret mostly came out of the pen for the Yanks and stayed for four years, through 1992. His best year was 1991 when he went 8–6 with a 2.62 ERA in 68 games, all but five in relief.

Then along came **Jim Abbott**, who authored one of the most heartwarming success stories in baseball. Abbott was born without a right hand, yet he wanted to pitch. He became adept at holding his glove with his right arm while he delivered his pitch, then immediately putting it on his left hand so he'd be ready to field the ball. If he got a comebacker, he'd glove it and in a quick motion remove the glove, take the ball out and make his throw. He did all this so effortlessly that fans hardly noticed. After pitching the United States Olympic baseball team to a gold medal in 1988, Abbott joined the California Angels.

The fact that he made it to the majors with just one hand was amazing in itself. Then he more than held his own, going 12–12 in his rookie season of 1989, followed by a 10–14 sophomore season and then a breakout, 18–11, 2.89 year in 1991. That season, Jim Abbott was one of the best pitchers in the American League. A year later, the Angels traded Abbott to the Yanks in the offseason in return for three players.

Wearing No. 25, Abbott quickly became a fan favorite. The Yanks were an improving team and it seemed as if the 25-year-old Abbott could be with them for years. He went 11–14 his first Yankees season with a 4.37 ERA, somewhat disappointing. But he made everyone forget that on September 4, when he spun a no-hitter against the Indians to highlight the season. Then in '94, he went just 9–8 with a 4.55 ERA and the Yanks granted him free agency and he signed with the White Sox before going back to the Angels in July. In 1996, Abbott lost velocity and wound up with an atrocious 2–18 season with a bloated 7.48 ERA. He would never regain his form and would retire after the 1999 season at the age of 31 with an 87–108 lifetime record.

Righthander **Scott Bankhead** wore No. 25 in 1995. He pitched in 20 games to a 6.00 ERA and was released in July. Outfielder **Ruben Sierra** took on No. 25 in his first tour with the Yanks in 1995 and '96. When he returned from 2003–2005, he wore Nos. 24 and 28. As the Yanks looked to return to championship form in 1996, they felt they needed a stronger defensive catcher. They made a deal with the Colorado Rockies in December and acquired veteran **Joe Girardi**. He was then 31 years old and gave the New Yorkers just what they needed.

A smart and wily defender, Girardi called a strong game and knew how to handle his pitchers. As the Yanks moved to their first World Series triumph since 1978, he also gave them a .294 bat, though he had little power. He was the catcher when an aging Dwight Gooden spun a no-hitter that year and he had a game-changing triple in the World Series against Atlanta. Girardi hit .264 and .276 over the next two seasons but by 1998 was splitting the catching chores with young Jorge Posada, who was a better hitter with more power.

In 1999, Girardi was behind the plate when David Cone threw his perfect game, but he hit just .239 in 65 games that season as the Yanks won their third World Series in four years. After the season, the New Yorkers didn't offer him a contract and he was signed as a free agent by the Cubs. Girardi would later become a Yankees coach and was named the manager of the Yankees prior to the 2008 season. As a manager, he wore No. 27, symbolic of the 27th World Championship he hoped to see his team win. And the Yankees did so in 2009.

After Girardi left, catcher **Chris Turner** took over No. 25 for just 37 games in 2000. He was released on August 31. Infielder **Randy Velarde** then borrowed No. 25 for just 15 games in 2001. Velarde was 38 years old by then but had previously been with the team from 1987 to '95. He is much better remembered as No. 18. Then a year later, along came **Jason Giambi**, a slugging first baseman who had been with Oakland since 1995. Giambi was coming off two monster years. In 2000 he hit .333 with 43 homers and 137 RBIs to become the American League's Most Valuable Player. He followed that with a .342 season in which he hit 38 dingers and drove home 120. That production earned him a seven-year, $120 million free agent contract from the Yanks.

The Yanks tabbed Giambi to replace long-time first sacker Tino Martinez. Giambi wasn't the fielder that Martinez was, but his history showed he was a somewhat better run producer. And when he hit .314 with 41 homers and 122 RBIs in 2002, he appeared to be worth the money. The following year he hit another 41 and drove home 107, but his average dipped to .250. After that, Giambi's Yankees career became checkered.

In 2003, Giambi's name leaked out as a player who received performance enhancing drugs during the infamous BALCO investigation, and he had to testify before a grand jury. He also had his 2004 season shortened to 80 games by a "benign tumor," which was never fully discussed, and he hit just .208. In 2005, he hit 32 homers and drove home 87 to win the Comeback Player of the Year award. He followed that with a 37-homer season in 2006, driving home 113.

Giambi was also proving to be a defensive liability at first base. He had little mobility and often made bad throws. A wrist injury limited him to 83 games in 2007 and while he rebounded to hit 32 homers in 2008, the final year of his mammoth contract, the Yankees had seen enough. Giambi was 37 and the team was retooling. They signed free agent first sacker **Mark Teixeira** and another No. 25 was sent packing.

As for Teixeira, he came with a great pedigree and signed a multi-year, $180-million contract, taking over No. 25 and threatening to make it more memorable than ever. The switch-hitting slugger started with Texas in 2003 and has now driven in 100 or more runs in six straight years. His top season was 2005, when he had 43 home runs and 144 RBIs. In his first year with the Yanks, Teixeira was brilliant. He won a Gold Glove for his stellar play at first base, batted .292, tied for the league lead in home runs with 39 and led in RBIs with 122. The big guy looked like a natural in pinstripes and should remain for a long time.

A SECOND CHANCE AT FIRSTS

Here are some more firsts, these from the second incarnation of the Stadium after it was refurbished and reopened in 1976:

First Yankee winning pitcher at refurbished stadium: Dick Tidrow, April 15, 1976.

First Yankee home run at refurbished stadium: Thurman Munson, April 17, 1976.

First night World Series game: October 19, 1976, a 6–2 loss to Cincinnati.

First team to host both the All-Star Game and World Series in the same season: New York Yankees in 1977.

First pitcher to throw a regular-season perfect game at Yankee Stadium: David Wells, May 17, 1998.

First U.S. President to visit Yankee Stadium during the World Series: George W. Bush, throwing out the first ball at Game 3, October 30, 2001.

#26: THE MAGIC THAT WAS EL DUQUE

No one has ever been sure of his real age, but baseball fans know his story and they also know how well he could pitch. **Orlando "El Duque" Hernandez** was an artist on the mound, a pure pitcher in every sense of the word. His birthdate is now listed as October 11, 1965, which would have made El Duque a 32-year-old rookie when he joined the Yankees in 1998. How he joined them is a story in itself, for Orlando Hernandez was one of the greatest pitchers in Cuban baseball history, and in the 1990s, Cuban baseball players were prevented by the Fidel Castro regime from coming to the major leagues . . . unless they defected and escaped.

Hernandez starred for the Cuban National Team for years. He had a 126–47 record in league play and led the National team to a gold medal at the 1992 Olympic Games in Barcelona. For years, however, the best Cuban players longed to test their skills against the best of the rest, and that meant the majors. Then in 1995, El Duque's half brother, Livan Hernandez, defected and eventually went on to pitch in the bigs. Fearful that El Duque would follow, he was banned from Cuban baseball in 1996. Finally, on Christmas Day of 1997, he escaped by boat. The US Coast Guard intercepted the craft he was on in

Orlando Hernandez

Bahamian waters. For a while, it looked as if he'd be sent back, but a sports agent and ultimately Attorney General Janet Reno worked to get him to the U.S. on "humanitarian parole."

But El Duque was shrewd. Instead of coming to the United States, he accepted an offer of asylum from Costa Rica. In the States, he would have been subject to the regular baseball draft and not have a say about which team picked him; in Costa Rica, he could negotiate as a free agent, and that's what he did, ultimately signing a four-year deal with the Yankees worth $6.6 million. He wanted to play with the best and that meant proving himself. So he donned uniform No. 26 and went to work.

After a stint in the minors the Yanks brought him up for a June 3rd debut. The 6'2", 220 pound righty was close to amazing. Using a high leg kick and a variety of arm angles, he changed speeds brilliantly, offsetting a good fastball with a tantalizingly slow curve. He simply out-thought the hitters and by the time the season ended he was 12–4 with a 3.13 ERA. The Yankees not only had themselves a star, but a guy who pitched even better in big games. He was the real deal. He proved it in the ALCS that year when, with the Yanks down two games to the Indians, El Duque threw seven innings of three-hit, shutout ball to get his team back in the series, one that they ultimately won.

When he followed that with a 17–9 season, he had really established himself. He did slip a bit to 12–13 the following season and after that he fell victim to injuries that restricted his time on the mound. He went 4–7 and 8–5 the next two years, sat out the 2003 season while rehabbing from surgery, and then went 8–2 in just 15 games in 2004. When healthy and in a big game, he was still one of the best. His post-season record with the Yanks was 9–3 with a 2.55 ERA. But by the end of the 2004 season he was almost 39 years old, and with his history of injuries, the Yanks decided not to offer him a new contract. He then signed with the White Sox and would eventually finish his career with the Mets. When right, he was as good as anyone.

The early years of No. 26 were like the other numbers in the mid and upper twenties, seemingly handed out arbitrarily and exchanged from year to year. That's why a number of players who wore No. 26 have appeared before and will likely be mentioned again. Some seemingly had a different number each year or were given a new number as they bounced on and off the roster. It all began with outfielder/first baseman **Cedric Durst**, essentially a part-timer who joined the club in the epic year of 1927 and even appeared briefly in two World Series (1927 and '28). A year after his debut, he wore No. 26 as the team donned numbers for the first time, then appeared with No. 27 before perhaps his biggest Yankees contribution. He was traded to Boston for pitcher Red Ruffing.

After that, the parade began. **Sammy Byrd**, the Babe's caddy in the outfield, was No. 26 in 1930 but wore four other numbers between 1929–34. Infielder **Jimmie Reese** was assigned No. 26 in 1931, moving up from No. 25 a year earlier in his only two Yankees seasons. Catcher **Joe Glenn**, called "Gabby" by his teammates, was a backup from 1932–38 (he didn't play in 1934) and wore No. 26 in 1932 and from 1936–38. In 1933 and '35, he was No. 28. Then came **George Uhle**, a righthanded pitcher who few remember as a Yankee and fewer remember as a 200-game winner.

Uhle only pitched for the Bombers for two years (1933–34) and wore No. 26. He was 33 years old when the Yanks signed him and he threw just 22 games over two seasons, going a combined 8–5. He was one of the first to throw the slider and is considered an innovator with that pitch. He also set a record for pitchers when he banged out 52 hits during the 1923 season and hit .289 for his career. Uhle finished with a 200–166 record and certainly could have helped the Yankees more had he pitched for them in the 1920s.

Johnny Broaca, who wore No. 20 from 1935–37, was No. 26 in his first Yankees season of 1934. Backup catcher **Buddy Rosar** had the number his first two New York seasons of 1939–40, then wore No. 12 his final two years in the Bronx. Catcher **Ken Silvestri** came from the White Sox in 1941 and caught 17 games as No. 26. He returned in 1946 and '47 and this time was No. 34. Another catcher, **Kenny Sears**, called "Ziggy" by his friends, caught 60 games as No. 26 in 1943, as players came and went due to the war. Big **Steve Roser** was a wartime pitcher who saw limited action from 1944–46, wearing No. 26 his first and last years, and No. 24 in between. Righthander **Karl Drews** had Nos. 18 and 26 in 1946, when he pitched in just three games, then was No. 19 his final two Yankees seasons before departing to the Browns. Lefty **Marius Russo** was No. 22 between 1939 and '43, then returned from the war in 1946 and was given No. 26 in his last Yankees season.

The parade of players continued. Catcher **Bill "Dutch" Drescher** was No. 22 for four games in 1944, wore No. 29 in 1945 and then was given No. 26 for his last five games in 1946. He passed the number on to righty **Don Johnson**, a rookie who went 4–3 in 1947, went back to the minors, then pitched for eight games in 1950 before being shipped to the Browns at mid-season. In 1949, veteran reliever **Hugh Casey** wore No. 26 for four games during his final season in the majors. Reliever **Tom Ferrick**, another righthander, came from the Browns in June of 1950 and went 9–7 in 46 games, then was sent to Washington the following June. **Ernie Nevel** was the next righty to make a cameo, starting out as No. 16 for a single game in 1950, then switching to No. 26 for three more in '51 before making his exit.

Gus Triandos was a big, powerful, but slow-footed catcher who joined the Yanks in 1953, pulled on No. 26, and proceeded to hit just .157 in 18 games with a single home run. The next year he was up for a single game before going in the big trade to Baltimore. Triandos, however, went on to a very solid career, retiring with 167 homers.

When the Yankees obtained relief pitcher **Ryne Duren** from Kansas City in June 1957, they didn't realize they had just acquired an intimidator. For openers, Duren had a 95-mph fastball at a time when not many pitchers threw that hard. Then there was his vision: 20/70 in one eye, 20/200 in the other. No wonder they called him "Blind Ryne." He always wore very thick glasses, the classic Coke bottles, and had a habit of throwing his first warmup pitch back to the screen. Hitters went up there wondering if he could even see them.

But Duren wasn't as wild as he appeared and he knew how to close games. He became the closer in 1958 and in 44 games, had a league best 20 saves with a 6–4 record and 2.02 earned run average, followed by an outstanding World Series. The next year, he had 14 saves in 41 games and a 1.88 ERA. In those two seasons, he struck out 183 batters in just 151 innings of work and gave up only 89 hits. But by 1960 he was starting to fade. His ERA skyrocketed to 4.96 and he had just nine saves. Ryne Duren had a problem. He was an alcoholic and close to out of control. By May of 1961, the Yanks had seen enough. They swapped him to the Angels with two other players for outfielder Bob Cerv and pitcher **Tex Clevenger.**

Duren never regained any semblance of his dominance. Instead, he sunk deeper into his disease, which included a couple of suicide attempts. "I realized that as a human being I was one big mess," he once said, "but I felt powerless to do anything about it." Fortunately, Duren managed to recover and chronicled his fall and rise in an auto-biography called *The Comeback.*

When Duren went to KC in '61, **Tex Clevenger**, who came over in the trade, took over No. 26. The righthanded reliever pitched in 21 games in both 1961 and '62, his final years in the majors, and had just a 3–1 combined record. Veteran first sacker **Dale Long** returned to the Yanks in July of 1962 and played as No. 26 until his release on August 2, 1963 at the age of 37. He had also been there in 1960 when he wore No. 25. Next came a couple of familiar names, only just the name was the same. Outfielder/first baseman **Archie Moore** wasn't the light heavyweight boxing champion and infielder **John Kennedy** certainly wasn't President of the United States. Moore wore No. 26 in 1964 and '65, playing just a total of 40 games, while Kennedy had a 78-game stay in 1967. He was a typical good-field, no-hit infielder who batted just .196 in his year with the Yanks and .225 for his career.

Third sacker **Mike Ferraro** played his first two seasons in New York, there for 10 games as No. 45 in 1966 and then playing 23 games as No. 26 two years later. He then went off to Seattle in the expansion draft, retiring after 1972. He would later become a Yankees coach. The Yanks brought outfielder **Jimmie Hall**'s contract from Cleveland in April 1969. Hall had a .260, 33, 80 rookie year with the Twins in 1963, but went into decline early, and as No. 26 with the Yankees, hit just .236 in 80 games with only three homers and was traded to the Cubs on September 11. Shortstop **Frank Baker**, no relation to Frank "Home Run" Baker from baseball's early days, played sparingly for the Bombers in 1970 and '71.

The comings and goings continued. Infielder **Fernando Gonzalez** was No. 26 in 1974, hitting just .215 in 51 games. He didn't reappear in the majors again until three years later with Pittsburgh. Outfielder **Rich Coggins** didn't fare much better. He wore No. 26 in 1975 after being purchased from Montreal and hit just .224 in 51 games. The next year, he played just seven games before being traded to the White Sox for Carlos May. The versatile **Cesar Tovar** was signed as a free agent on September 1, 1976. But the Yanks got him at the tail end of his career and he hit just .154 in 13 games before calling it a career.

Infielder/outfielder **Juan Bernhardt** played just 10 games in 1976 and hit .190. Two years later, rookie infielder **Domingo Ramos** wore it for a single game as a Yankee. Veteran **Juan Beniquez** was the choice for 62 games in 1979. He hit just .254 in New York. Then veteran catcher **Johnny Oates** became the next No. 26 when he played the final two seasons of his career as a Yankees backup in 1980 and '81. He later became a successful manager.

When the Yankees gave No. 26 to southpaw **Shane Rawley** in 1982, they finally got a little more bang for their bucks. Rawley started his career as a short reliever, but by the time he came to the Yankees he was a swing man. He went 11–10 for the Bombers in 1982, starting 17 times in 47 games, and then going 14-14 pitching in the rotation the following season. A year later, he was just 2–3 with some injury problems when he was dealt to the Phillies on June 30. Rawley retired with a 111–110 record, pretty much even-steven.

Pitcher John Montefusco, who wore No. 24 his first Yankee seasons of 1983 and '84, switched to No. 26 his final two years before retiring with injuries. The Yanks took a flyer on short reliever **Neil Allen** in 1985, purchasing his contract from the Cards on July 16. Allen had been the Mets' closer from 1979 to '82 and was with the Yanks parts of three seasons. He wore both Nos. 53 and 26 in '85, and Nos. 48 and 27 when he returned in 1987 and '88.

Then once again the number was passed around like it was dealt from a deck of cards. Infielder **Paul Zuvella** wore it for 21 games in 1986 before going to Nos. 17 and 29 the following year as he jumped back and forth between the majors and minors. Infielder **Bryan Little** lasted just 14 games in 1986 and veteran infielder **Ivan DeJesus** also had it in 1986, for just seven games. Finally, in 1987, the number went back to a real pro, but he only stayed for two years.

Righthander **Rick Rhoden** came over in a trade with Pittsburgh and proceeded to go 16–10 in 1987, tying a career high for victories, a good start for the latest No. 26. Rhoden had been a dependable fastball/slider pitcher with several teams. He was 34 when he came to the Yanks and a bit past his prime, so when he went just 12–12 in 1988, the New Yorkers decided to cut bait and dealt him to Houston. Rhoden finished his career with a 151–125 record and was also one of the best golfers among major league players.

Righthander **Jimmy Jones** pitched in 28 games in 1989 and '90 wearing No. 26, went 3–3, and was granted free agency. Outfielder **Stan Jefferson** also wore the number for ten games in 1989, his exile hastened by an anemic .083 batting average. Then along came another veteran reliever, **Steve Farr**, who stayed in pinstripes from 1991–93 and made No. 26 somewhat recognizable and appreciated once more. Farr was 34 years old when he signed with the Bombers. But he pitched in 60 games in '91, going 5–5 with a 2.19 ERA and 23 saves. He was even better the next year, putting up a 1.56 ERA in 50 games and saving 30. He had another 25 saves in 1993, but because his ERA rose to 4.21 the Yanks decided to go in another direction and granted the slider/curveballer free agency.

Next came a Daryl, a Kevin, and a Darryl. Veteran outfielder **Daryl Boston** became the latest to wear No. 26 in what would be his final season. He played 52 games in 1994 after being signed as a free agent and hit just .182. Shortstop **Kevin Elster** played seven games in 1994 as No. 19 and 10 more in '95 as No. 26 before moving on to Texas. Then came **Darryl Strawberry,** "the Straw Man," who wore No. 26 in his first Yankees season of 1995. Straw, of course, was a big story in New York beginning with his days as a Met. He would stay with the Yankees through 1999, writing the last chapter of his baseball career. But since he wore No. 39 from 1996 to 1999, he will be discussed more fully there.

Utility infielder **Andy Fox** came up in 1996 with a chance to be a part of something special. Donning No. 26, he got to play in 113 games but hit just .196, and that performance limited him to just 22 games the next season. As the latest Yankees dynasty began moving into full swing, Fox was exiled to Arizona. Veteran infielder **Rey Sanchez** wore No. 26 in a pair of Yankees stints, first in 1997, when he hit .312 in 38 games before leaving as a free agent, then in 2005 when he hit .279 in 23 games.

Another infielder, **Mark Bellhorn,** was released by the rival Red Sox on August 19, 2005, and signed with the Yanks 11 days later. But in nine games Bellhorn could only manage a .118 average with the Yanks and was granted free agency at season's end. Then came another career finale, as outfielder **Terrence Long** played 12 games with the Bombers in 2006, hit .167 and bid adieu to the majors. Catcher **Sal Fasano** was another of Jorge Posada's infrequently used backups, playing in 28 games and hitting .143 in 2006 before being traded to the Phils at the end of July. **Wil Nieves** was another catcher who had three brief trials, playing three games in 2005 as No. 60, six more in 2006 as No. 60, and then No. 26, and finally 26 games as No. 26 in 2007. But Nieves hit just .164 in his most extended shot and was off to Washington.

Finally, **Jose Molina** settled in as Posada's backup and gave No. 26 a strong presence, which continued through 2009. One of three catching brothers in the majors, Jose is an outstanding defensive catcher who played behind brother Bengie with the Angels. In July 2007, he was dealt to the Yankees for a minor leaguer and immediately showed his catching and throwing skills, and his ability to handle pitchers. He even hit over his head that first year, batting .318 in 29 games, but in reality it has always been his weak stick that has kept him from being a regular.

In 2008, when Posada went down with a shoulder injury, Molina caught 100 games and did his usual yeoman work behind the plate, but hit just .216 with three homers and just 18 RBIs. As the retooled Yankees drove toward a 103-win season in 2009, Molina again proved invaluable behind the plate, especially in handling the new Yankees pitchers, CC Sabathia and A. J. Burnett. Molina caught just 52 games and hit .217, but again caught extremely well. At age 34, he should still be able to find a job behind the dish somewhere, even if the Yanks choose not to bring him back in 2010.

#27: A REAL MIX WITH A MANAGER LEADING THE WAY

When Joe Girardi was named the team's manager in 2008, he requested No. 27, and for a good reason. The Bronx Bombers had already won a record 26 World Series, but hadn't won since beating the Mets in 2000, their fourth in five years under Joe Torre. For Girardi, the No. 27 represented his immediate goal, to lead the Yanks to that 27th world title.

In the 80-odd years since numbers were worn, not one big star has worn No. 27 while he was in his prime. Still, there were some interesting players putting the jersey onto their backs.

At first it was round up the usual suspects. **Sammy Byrd**, he of many different numbers, and **Cedric Durst** simply flip-flopped numbers. Durst was No. 26 in 1929 and No. 27 in 1930. Byrd started as No. 27 in '29 and was down to No. 26 in 1930. Outfielder **Myril Hoag** had two tenures with the Yanks (1931–32, 1934–38). He wore No. 27 in 1932, but also spent four seasons wearing No. 28 and his final two seasons in No. 9. And then there was a guy who did become a star, but not with the Yankees. In fact, many fans don't remember him as a Yankee because his days in pinstripes were injury-filled and disappointing. His name: **Dixie Walker**.

Walker, an outfielder who would later become a beloved and productive player

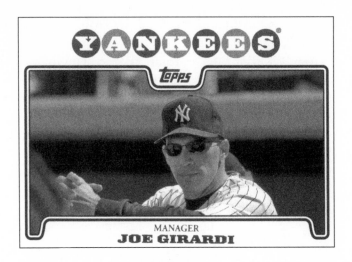

MANAGER
JOE GIRARDI

with the Brooklyn Dodgers (and known in Brooklynese as "The Peoples Cherce"), came up to the Yanks in 1931 for a two-game cup of coffee. He wore No. 35 for his cameo. Two years later he returned and took No. 27, which he would wear through 1936. Walker began showing his potential in 1933 but sustained a severe shoulder injury the next year. In his last three Yankees season, he barely played and the Yanks couldn't wait any longer, waiving him on May 1, 1936. He was picked up by the White Sox, then went to the Tigers and was finally picked up by the Dodgers off waivers on July 24, 1939.

That's when Walker finally became a star. By 1944 he led the National League with a .357 batting average, and a year later led the senior circuit in RBIs with 145. But after the 1947 season he was traded to Pittsburgh in return for Preacher Roe and Billy Cox, two players who played large roles in the Brooklyn dynasty of the late 1940s and 1950s.

James "Zack" Taylor was a catcher who came to the Yanks when he was almost at the end of a 16-year career. He played just four games in 1934 after joining the team in late August. Wearing No. 27, he got one hit and finished his career the next season in Brooklyn. Infielder **Blondy Ryan** didn't do much better in New York. The Yanks got him from the Phils on August 6, 1935, and he played 35 games as No. 27, hitting just .238 before he was sold to Cleveland at season's end. Righty

Spud Chandler was given uniform No. 27 in 1939, after wearing Nos. 13 and 24 in 1937 and No. 21 in 1938. From 1940 to 1947, he wore No. 21, the number for which he is remembered. Outfielder **Joe Gallagher**, pitcher **Lee Grissom**, and outfielder **Buster Mills** were three in-and-out guys in 1939 and '40 who all wore No. 27

Stanley George Bordagaray, known as "Frenchy," had a great nickname but a short New York career. The utilityman was in 36 games in 1941 after coming over from Cincinnati, then was sent packing to the Dodgers. Catcher **Rollie Hemsley** fared somewhat better, staying in pinstripes as a part timer from 1942–1944. Hemsley hit .294, .239, and .268 in his three Yankee seasons after signing as a free agent at the age of 35.

Russ Derry had two years in pinstripes, wearing No. 22 in 1944 and No. 27 a year later. Outfielder **Johnny Lindell** played for 10 seasons and had a .303 lifetime average. Lindell wore Nos. 16, 18, and 8 in his early Yankees years and then No. 27, from 1946–50. In 1950, the Yanks brought up a young righthander named **Selva Lewis Burdette**, gave him No. 27, and let him pitch in two games. In August 1951, they shipped him, along with $50,000, to the Boston Braves for veteran righthander Johnny Sain, who would help them win a couple of pennants and World Series. But Burdette didn't exactly fade away. He went on to a great career with the Braves, becoming a two-time 20-game winner and a guy who would come back to haunt the Yanks by winning three games against them in the 1957 World Series.

Golden Boy **Jackie Jensen** wore both No. 40 and No. 27 in 1951, had worn No. 40 the year before, and then No. 25 in 1952 before he was traded. Three infielders, **Jim Brideweser**, **Woodie Held**, and veteran **Bobby Brown,** wore No. 27 at various times between 1952 and 1957. Pitcher **Marlin Stuart** went 3–0 with a save as No. 27 in a 10-game Yankees career in 1954, his final season in the bigs.

From the 1950s right into the 1970s, No. 27 continued to be passed around to a variety of players who didn't stay with the team long. Veteran outfielder **Bobby Del Greco** wore it for a total of just 20 games in 1957 and '58. Righthander **Johnny James** lasted three seasons with the Yanks, if you count one game in 1958 and one game in 1961. In 1960 he wasn't on the club, but in '59 he pitched in 28 games and was 5-1 with a 4.36 ERA in relief. He wore No. 27 in '58 and No. 53 in the final two seasons.

Good-hit, no-catch catcher **Jesse Gonder** was No. 27 in 1960 and No. 25 in '61, while outfielder **Jack Reed**, mainly a defensive replacement, was No. 15 in 1961 and No. 27 the next two years. Another outfielder wearing No. 27 in 1965 was **Duke Carmel**. He bore no resemblance to Duke Snider and lasted just six games. Utility infielder **Dick "Ducky" Schofield** would play 19 years for a number of teams, but his 1966 Yankees career lasted just 25 games due to his anemic .155 batting average. Young **Tom Shopay** auditioned in the Yankees' outfield for eight games in 1967 and then played his way off the field with an .083 average in 1968. Outfielder **Jim Lyttle** batted .181 in 28 games in 1969 wearing No. 21. He switched to No. 27, showed promised with a .310 mark the next year, then dropped back to .198 in '71 and was shipped to the White Sox. **Rich McKinney**'s infield audition lasted just 37 games in 1972. His .215 average was as good a reason as any to dump him on the A's.

One player who looked as if he might have a bright Yankees future at an opportune time was center fielder **Elliott Maddox**. Maddox was purchased from the Rangers in March 1974 and immediately took over the center field job. The newest No. 27 was an outstanding outfielder with good instincts to the ball and a strong and accurate throwing arm. The big question was could he hit enough?

In 1974, he played 137 games and hit .303. In addition, his play in center was close to brilliant. He chased down all kinds of fly balls and his strong arm provided 14 assists, a high number for a center fielder. In 1975, a knee injury limited him to just 55 games, though he hit .307.

But the knee injury cost him some mobility. Concerned because they knew they had a good shot at the playoffs or more in 1976, the Yankees went out and traded for the speedy Mickey Rivers, who began playing up a storm. That made Maddox expendable. In January of 1977, he was traded to the Orioles for veteran centerfielder Paul Blair.

Even as the Yanks returned to winning pennants and World Series, No. 27 didn't have much of a shelf life. Case in point. Infielder **Marty**

Perez was given No. 27 for a single game in 1977. He had been dealt to the Yanks from the Mariners before the season and was traded to Oakland on April 27. Outfielder **Dell Alston** hit .325 in 22 games after a 1977 callup, but lasted just three games in 1978 before being dealt to Oakland. **Jay Johnstone** came to the Yanks in June 1978 and hit just .179 in 35 games. He got another shot wearing No. 27 the following year and managed a .208 average in 23 games before being dealt to San Diego that June.

Outfielder **Darryl Jones**, who played 18 games for the Yanks in 1979, quickly proved he was no Darryl Strawberry and never appeared in the majors again. Catcher **Brad Gulden** didn't fare much better. He wore No. 27 for 40 games in 1979 and hit an underwater .163. He had a two-game callup as No. 19 the next year before being traded to Seattle. Veteran **Paul Blair** was a major contributor to the Yanks' pennant and World Series efforts from 1977–80, but he is better remembered as No. 2. He wore No. 27 only for his final 12 games with the club in 1980.

The Yanks picked up veteran third baseman **Aurelio Rodriguez** from the Padres in August 1980, but he was only able to hit .220 in 52 games that year. A year later, he was traded to the Blue Jays for a minor leaguer. Finally, in May 1983, the Yanks made a trade with Minnesota and picked up switch-hitting catcher **Butch Wynegar**, who would stay with them through the 1986 season and give No. 27 some solid moments for mediocre Yankees teams. Wynegar was a solid defensive catcher, though slow of foot.

He also hit over .290 his first two Yankees seasons, caught Dave Righetti's no-hitter in 1983, and became the full-time catcher in '84. Injuries limited him to 102 games and a .223 average in '85 and the next year he began suffering from what was called physical and mental fatigue. Worse yet, he hit just .206 in 61 games and that wouldn't do. After the season he was traded to the Angels, and another No. 27 was gone.

Two players shared the number in 1987. Outfielder **Keith Hughes** arrived in 1984 , but stayed in the minors until appearing in four games with the big club in 1987. That June, he was shipped back to Philly in a trade that brought Mike Easler to New York. Catcher **Mark Salas** hit just .200 in 50 games after arriving in New York from Minnesota on June 7. He went to the White Sox after the season. Reliever **Neil Allen** wore No. 27 in his final Yankees season of 1988 after wearing Nos. 53 and 26 in 1985 and No. 48 in his return in 1987.

When the Yankees learned that star outfielder Dave Winfield would miss the 1989 season due to back surgery, they quickly looked to replace him. On March 19, they acquired lefty swinging **Mel Hall** from the Indians in return for catcher Joel Skinner. Hall was a solid hitter who had a pair of 18-home run seasons for the Indians in 1986 and '87 while hitting .296 and .280. He wasn't fast, which limited his range in the outfield, but he had no fear of diving for the baseball and putting his body on the line to make a catch. With the Yanks he donned No. 27 and proceeded to play well from 1989 to '92, with his final two seasons being his best. He had a total of 34 home runs and 161 RBIs in those years, hitting close to .290. Hall became a free agent after the 1992 season and made a decision to play in Japan, ending his Yankees career.

Hall's departure for Japan made way for another player to wear No. 27 for several years. Burly righthander **Bob Wickman** joined the team in 1992, wearing No. 31, and went 6–1 with a 4.11 ERA in eight starts. A year later, he switched to No. 27 and the Yankees began switching him to the bullpen. He still made 19 starts in 41 games, had a 14–4 record and 4.63 ERA, along with four saves. After that he was strictly a reliever.

Wickman threw a natural sinker, crediting a childhood farming accident that cost him part of the index finger on his right hand as the reason his ball dipped so sharply. Over the next three years with the Yankees, he did a nice job, relieving in 53, 63, and 58 games. Unfortunately, Wickman didn't get to enjoy the Yanks' upcoming dynasty years. On August 23, 1996, he was traded to Milwaukee in a five-player deal that brought the Yanks lefty reliever **Graeme Lloyd**.

Lloyd was a 6'7", 234-pound lefthander and one of just a few major league players born in Australia. He threw a sinking fastball and later added a palm ball to his repertoire. Strictly a situational lefty, the latest No. 27 often came in to get just one batter out. He appeared in 568 games over a 10-year career and never started a single one, and he pitched fewer total innings than the number of appearances.

With the Yanks, Lloyd proved a valuable piece from 1996 to 1998. He pitched in four games of the 1996 World Series and had a 1.67 ERA in 1998. As it turned out, his Yankees career ended abruptly when he was included in the February 1999 deal with the Blue Jays that brought Roger Clemens to New York.

While Hall, Wickman, and Lloyd remained in pinstripes long enough to wear No. 27 for several seasons, **Allen Watson, Tony Fossas, Rondell White,** and **Todd Zeile** did not. Lefthander Watson pitched for parts of the 1999 and 2000 seasons, his final two years in the majors. Fossas, another southpaw, appeared in just five games in 1999 and pitched a total of one inning, giving up four runs. Outfielder White was signed as a free agent before the 2002 season with big expectations, but hit just .240 with 14 homers, far below his career best. He was shipped to San Diego before the next season.

Todd Zeile, on the other hand, was pretty good wherever he played, a trait which came in handy since he was on 11 teams in 16 years. He caught, played first and third, and did some duty in the outfield. He hit 253 home runs during his long career, including 31 with the Dodgers in 1997, but when he signed with the Yankees as a free agent prior to the 2002 season he was 37 years old and close to the end. In 66 games, he hit just .210 with six homers and 23 RBIs. His bat was so weak that the Yankees released him in mid-August.

Utilityman Luis Sojo wore No. 27 when brought back for the final three games of his career in 2003. In his previous six Yankees seasons (1996–2001), the valuable Sojo wore No. 19. When pitcher **Kevin Brown** appeared on the scene in 2004, the Yanks felt they might have a pitcher who would help them back to the World Series. Brown was a talented pitcher with a live arm who threw a naturally sinking fastball in the mid-90s, and had a sharp slider and split-finger fastball. He had a 21–11 season with the Rangers in '92, and then a pair of 18-win seasons with the Padres and Dodgers in 1998 and '99. But he also had a balky back and a tendency to get hurt in addition to being a rather surly individual who rarely made friends on his various teams. Plus the Dodgers had given him a seven-year pact worth $105 million.

But his 14–9 record with 2.39 ERA in 2003 prompted the Yanks to deal for Brown, sending the Dodgers three players and $2.6 million in cash. They assumed the remainder of the contract and it was not money well spent. Brown was 10–6 with a 4.09 ERA in 2004, but only made 22 starts because, in one of his patented temper tantrums, he punched a wall and broke his left hand. He was back by the playoffs and flopped in Game Seven of the ALCS against Boston. Brown tried again the next year but was just 4–7 with a 6.50 ERA and a bad back. His contract, his Yankees days, and his career ended after the season.

After Brown, No. 27 went into limbo again. Outfielders **Kevin Thompson** and **Kevin Reese** wore it for short stints in 2006, making it three straight Kevins with the number. Thompson also wore Nos. 12, 14, and 19 in 2007, all for a total of 13 games, while Reese was No. 39 for two games in 2005. Pitcher **Darrell Rasner** wore it for six games in 2007 after wearing Nos. 58 and 61 during short callups in 2006, and No. 43 in 2008 when he went 5–10 with a 5.40 before going to pitch in Japan. Finally, it was the manager who took the number. But Joe Girardi may also play musical numbers. After the Yanks won their 27th championship, he indicated he might switch to No. 28 in 2010 with the hope it would help lead to yet another title. Good luck.

#28: SPARKY: FUN GUY WITH A KILLER SLIDER

If they'd just called him **Albert Lyle** he still would have been one helluva relief pitcher, a guy with a big mustache, an impish grin, and the ability to shut down any team. Add the nickname "Sparky" and he became even more of a distinct individual. Either way, he was one of the best closers of the 1970s. Only they didn't call them closers then. They were more akin to being known as late-inning relievers and would often pitch two, three, or more innings when a big game was on the line and someone had to get the job done. Lyle did it primarily with a devastating slider, mixed with an occasional fastball and curve. He never looked like superman, often carrying some extra pounds around the middle. But when he stood 60 feet, 6 inches from a batter, any batter, he was all business.

Sparky reached the majors with the Red Sox in 1967 when he was 22. He would pitch for five years in Boston, his one complaint being not enough work. Then, on March 22, 1972, everything changed. The Red Sox dealt Sparky to the Yanks for journeyman infielder Danny Cater.

Sparky's 1972 season was his first in pinstripes and his best yet. That year, he was in 59 games, but threw 107 2/3 innings with a record of 9–5 and an earned run

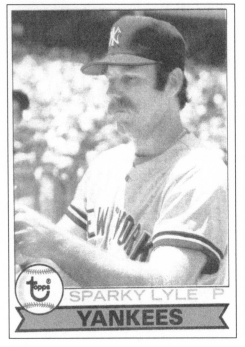

average of 1.92. He led the league in games finished with 56 and in saves with 35. Sparky Lyle had arrived. In the coming years his reputation as a clutch pitcher grew, and he also became known as one of baseball's great flakes. One never interfered with the other.

By 1974 he was looking like baseball's best, compiling a 9–3 record with a microscopic 1.66 ERA. He finished off 59 games and had 15 saves. He continued to pitch at a high level and then his career crested in 1977. The Yankees would win the World Series that year, and it may not have happened at all had it not been for the heroics of Sparky Lyle. In the regular season, he had a 13–5 record in a league-high 72 games, finishing off an AL best 60 with 26 of them saves. His ERA was just 2.17. For his efforts he would become the first American League reliever to win the coveted Cy Young Award. He also starred in the ALCS and World Series that year, doing the job for multiple innings whenever he was called upon.

Things began unraveling in 1978, but not because Sparky's talent level dropped off. Seeing the value of a top relief pitcher, the Yanks went out and signed the imposing Goose Gossage. Sparky at once let it be known he wasn't happy. He just felt he wouldn't get the kind of work he needed to thrive. Future Hall of Famer Gossage was the real deal, and while Sparky saw a lot of duty, it was Gossage who began getting the crucial innings. Sparky finished the year with a 9–3 record in 59 games, but he had just nine saves in 111 2/3 innings of work and his ERA rose to 3.47. Gossage, by contrast, was in 63 games, leading the league by finishing 55 games with 27 saves. And his ERA was 2.01. That November, the Yanks decided to cut bait. They didn't have room for two relief stars, so Sparky was sent to Texas in a 10-player deal that brought future closer Dave Righetti to the Bronx.

Sparky Lyle would retire after the 1982 season. In 16 seasons, he had a record of 99–76, more decisions than today's relievers ever have, yet he still had time for 238 saves and a fine 2.88 ERA.

The first player wearing No. 28 played just one game as a New York Yankee. But what a name he had. **Elias Calvin Funk** was known as "Liz." The multi-numbered **Art Jorgens** came next in 1930. But to follow Art's Yankees career you really need a scorecard, since he wore five different numbers between 1929 and 1939, the lowest being No. 9 and the highest No. 32. It was the same for **Myril Hoag,** who wore No. 28 in 1931 before going to No. 27 and No. 9. It was almost like the subs drew straws for their numbers in spring training every year.

Next came the guy who took over first base in 1939 when Lou Gehrig's consecutive game streak finally ended. **Babe Dahlgren** was no Babe like Ruth and no first sacker like Gehrig. He wore No. 28 for one game in 1937, then No. 12 his last three years with the club. Reliever **Frank Makosky** wore No. 28 for just 26 games in 1937, compiling a 5–2 mark on the mound and a .313 average at the plate. But it wasn't good enough to keep him there. Then came the first player to wear the number for an extended period of time.

Righthander **Atley Donald**, known as "Swampy" at a time when nicknames were much more colorful than they are today, pitched credibly for the Yanks as No. 28 from 1938–45. He benefited from great Yankees teams, and his only losing season was his 0–1 mark in his cup of coffee season of 1938. A year later he was 13–3 in 24 games, then 8–3, 9–5, 11–3, 6–4, and 13–10 in 1944. He was never used a lot but always held up his end of the deal. In 1945, he encountered both eye and elbow problems and retired at the end of the season. Swampy had a 65–33 record with the Yanks, good for an impressive .663 winning percentage.

Righty **Spud Chandler** wore No. 28 in 1945, but the star righthander made his reputation as No. 21, which he wore for the majority of his Yankees career. Infielder **Hank Majeski** played for six teams during a 13-year career (1939–41, 1946–55), but his Yankees tenure lasted for just eight games in 1946.

Lefty **Tommy Byrne** wore No. 28 from 1946–54, then switched to No. 23 in 1955, his best season, and kept it through 1957. Another short timer, lefty **Bill Wight**, was given No. 30 for 14 games in 1946, then No. 28 for just a single contest in '47 before he was traded to the White Sox. Righthanded starter/reliever **Tom Morgan** joined the Yanks in 1951 at the age of 21. He started with No. 52, but switched to No. 28 early in the season and wore that number until he left after the 1956 season. Morgan's 9–3 record his rookie year helped the Yanks to a pennant, and he was with three more pennant winners after that. He would later throw for Kansas City, Detroit, Washington, and the Angels before retiring in 1963.

Big **Bill Renna** was an outfielder who wore No. 28 briefly in 1953, staying for just 61 games before being dealt to the A's. After Renna came a couple of pitchers who contributed during the Yankees' dynasty years of the late 1950s and early '60s. They were righthander **Art Ditmar** and southpaw **Bud Daley**.

Ditmar came over from Kansas City in February 1957 and immediately proved a versatile pitcher as the Yanks drove to yet another pennant. He relied on control and changing speeds with his fastball, slider and curve. Ditmar was 8–3 in 46 games in '57, and that included 11 spot starts as well as six saves. By 1959 Ditmar was in the regular rotation and produced two fine years, going 13–9 with a 2.90 ERA and then 15–9 in 1960 with a 3.06 ERA.

By 1961 something had changed. Ditmar just didn't have it. He was only 2–3 with a 4.64 ERA in 12 games when he was traded back to Kansas City that June in return for lefty Bud Daley.

Southpaw Daley took up Ditmar's No. 28 when the two switched uniforms. Daley threw a big roundhouse curse that made it tough for southpaw swingers to hit him, and also mixed it in with a knuckleball. Like Ditmar, he could both start and relieve and had an 8–9 record in just half a season with the powerhouse 1961 Yankees, making 17 starts in 23 appearances. A year later he worked mostly out of the pen, but an arm injury relegated him to just a single game in 1963, and a year later he was just 3–2 in 13 games, the lingering injury leading to his retirement at the age of 31. During his tenure in KC, Bud Daley once threw to catcher Pete Daley, giving birth to the only "Daley Double" in baseball history.

For the remainder of the 1960s and into the 1970s, various No. 28s came and went on a regular basis. Guys like **Gil Blanco**, **Steve Whitaker**, **Andy Kosco**, and **Ron Hansen** all had brief and mostly forgettable Yankees tenures. Southpaw Blanco pitched in 17 games in 1965 before being shipped to Kansas City (the A's again!) in June. Whitaker was a lefty swinging outfielder thought to have some potential, but he left via the expansion draft after 1968. Kosco came in the Rule 5 draft prior to the 1968 season and was traded that December after hitting .240, while Hansen, a former Rookie of the year with the Orioles (1960),

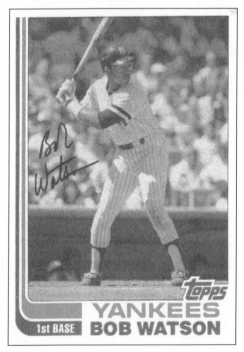

YANKEES
1st BASE BOB WATSON

played just briefly in 1970 and '71 before being released.

After Hansen, Sparky Lyle came on board and wore No. 28 until his trade after the 1978 season. Two years later, it passed on to outfielder/first baseman/designated hitter **Bob Watson**, a very solid player who had a 19-year career in which he hit .295 with 184 homers and 989 RBIs. Known as "The Bull," Watson came to New York as a free agent in 1980. He was 34 years old in 1980 and was mostly a DH for the Yanks, but he was solid. In 130 games he hit .307 with 13 homers and 68 RBIs. A groin injury the next year has tened his demise, and he was traded to the Braves the following April. After retirement, he served as general manager for both the Astros and Yankees, the first African-American to serve in that capacity. Today, Bob Watson works out of the Commissioner's Office.

Say hello to "Bye Bye." **Steve Balboni** was a hulking first baseman, a 6'3", 225-pounder with an abundance of home run power. Balboni came up at the end of Chris Chambliss's time in New York and before Don Mattingly took the first base job, so there was a window of opportunity. Balboni was up and down so often between New York and Triple-A Columbus that it became known as the "Balboni Express." He wore Nos. 66, 36, and 28 between 1981 and '83 before Don Mattingly made him expendable. So it was another kind of bye-bye, off to the Kansas City Royals for a minor leaguer.

Balboni had a couple of pretty good years with the Royals and Mariners, and the Yanks took a second shot with him, trading to get him back in March 1989. He played two years for the Bombers, wearing Nos. 45 and 50. While he got into more than 100 games each year and hit 17 homers twice, his .237 and .192 averages didn't get it done and it was bye-bye for a second time.

If lefthander **Rod Scurry** had a nickname, it might not have been very flattering. The reliever pitched two years for the Bombers, wearing No. 47 in 1985 after a mid-September purchase from the Pirates, and then No. 28 in 1986 when he was 1–2 with a .366 in 31 games. Scurry had a great curve and could have been a very effective reliever had his career not been sabotaged by a cocaine habit, a drug that had crept into major league baseball in the 1980s. Outfielder **Henry Cotto** was a part-timer with the Yanks from 1985–87, wearing No. 46 the first two years and No. 28 in his final season, when he played 68 games and hit just .235. Like so many others, he simply didn't hit enough to be a Bronx Bomber and was traded.

Southpaw **Al Leiter** both started and finished his career as a Yankee, but did his best pitching in between. Leiter compiled a 162–132 record in 19 seasons, but won only 11 in pinstripes. He had his first Bomber audition as No. 56 in 1987 and wore No. 19 when he returned in July of 2005 to go 4-5 in his last ten starts. Today he is a commentator on several networks. His brother, Mark, a righthander, also pitched eight games for the Yankees in 1990.

In the four years between 1988 and 1991, No. 28 became a pass-around again, players slipping in and out of it and changing numbers with those who went up and down between the minors and majors. The players wearing it were **Dale Mohorcic**, **Brian Dorsett**, **Alan Mills**, and **Dave Eiland**. Righthander Mohorcic wore No. 54 for 13 games in 1988 after an August 30 trade from the Rangers. A year later he started as No. 54, then switched to No. 28. Dorsett was a catcher and first sacker who donned No. 56 for eight games in 1989. The next year, he wore No. 28 but hit just .143 in 14 games before a November release. Mills, another righty reliever, wore No. 28 as a rookie in 1990, going 1–5 in 36 games out of the pen. When he was called up the next year, he wore No. 50 and went just 1–1 in six games before going down again. He was traded to the Orioles in the off-season and became a 12-year career reliever.

Dave Eiland came up as No. 52 for three quick games in 1988. Then the dipsy-doodle started. He was No. 28 in 1989 and 1991, No. 58 in 1990. His busiest year was '91 when he worked 18 games, 13 of them starts. But he went just 2–5 with a 5.33 ERA, had some arm problems, and was released after the season. He would return for another four games in 1995, wearing No. 47, his fourth Yankees number in five seasons. Now he's back again, as Joe Girardi's pitching coach, beginning in 2008.

Third sacker **Charlie Hayes** originally joined the Yanks in 1992, coming over from the Phils as a player to be named later after an earlier trade. The Yanks gave him No. 28 and installed him at third, where he had a solid year, but the team didn't protect him and he was picked by the newly formed Colorado Rockies in the 1992 expansion draft. Three years later, the Yankees got him back in an August 30th trade with the Pirates. He only played in 20 games before the end of the 1996 season, hitting .284 and wearing No. 33. Hayes was at third base in the sixth game of the World Series that year with Atlanta, and he caught a foul pop for the final out as the Bombers won their first championship since 1978. Hayes would play one more year with the Yanks, hitting .258 in 100 games before being traded to the Giants.

Pitcher **Scott Kamieniecki** wore No. 28 from 1993–1996, but had No. 40 his first year of 1991 and then No. 22 in 1992. His career was highlighted in Chapter 22. **Ruben Rivera** was No. 17 in 1995, then No. 28 in '96 before he left. Outfielder **Chad Curtis** became No. 28 in 1997 and wore it through '99. He came to the Yanks in a June trade with Cleveland for reliever David Weathers and played well, hitting .291 in 93 games with 12 homers and 50 RBIs. But his power numbers fell off and he was shipped to Texas after the 1999 season and a pair of World Series rings.

The next guy to wear No. 28 certainly could play and for several years was among baseball's best. Outfielder **David Justice** came to the Yanks at the age of 34 on June 29, 2000, when the Indians swapped him for three players. The New Yorkers needed another bat and hitting was Justice's forte. With the Yanks down the stretch, Justice was just what the doctor ordered. In 78 games, he hit .305 with 20 home runs and 60 RBIs, making a huge contribution to the Bombers' winning their fourth division title in five years. His combined totals with the Indians and Yanks in 2000 were a .286 batting average, 41 homers, and 118 RBIs.

But it came apart in a hurry. A persistent groin injury in 2001 limited Justice to 111 games and his production suffered. In December, the Yanks shipped him to the Mets for third sacker Robin Ventura, and a week later the Mets traded him to Oakland, where he played 118 games, hit 11 more homers, and retired.

After that, the number again went into pass-around mode with players coming and going rather quickly. **John Vander Wal**, **Chris Latham**, **Charles Gipson**, **Esteban Loaiza**, **Karim Garcia**, and **Ruben Sierra** gave No. 28 lip service from 2002 to 2005. None distinguished themselves and Loaiza, a former 21-game winner with the White Sox went just 1-2 with the Bombers in 2003 after a July 31 trade for Jose Contreras. Sierra returned to the Yanks for a second time and played sparingly in 2005, his career essentially over.

Centerfielder **Melky Cabrera** could have been the next in line to perhaps give No. 28 a long ride. Melky wore No. 39 in his call-up year of 2005, then switched to 28 the next three years. In 2009, however, he decided to take No. 53, which had been worn by his friend and mentor, Bobby Abreu, before he left as a free agent. Because he hoped to create a legacy with that number, he'll be discussed as 53. Veteran pitcher **Brett Tomko** pitched in 15 games in 2009 wearing No. 28, but was ultimately released and finished the season in Oakland. Outfielder **Shelley Duncan** wore No. 28 briefly in both 2008 and 2009, but the number continues to look for a player to lock it up for more than a year or two.

#29: HUNTING CATFISH

They had called Jim Hunter "Catfish" from his rookie year with the Kansas City A's in 1965. Most fans thought that maybe the North Carolina native was an avid fisherman. It wasn't quite that exotic. When the righthanded Hunter signed for a $75,000 bonus in June 1964, the A's' colorful owner, Charlie Finley, decided he needed a good nickname. Finley came up with Catfish and Hunter complied. "Whatever you say, Mr. Finley, it's OK with me," he supposedly answered.

So Catfish it was. It took him some five years to really find his pitching legs during those seasons in KC and then Oakland (the team moved west in 1968). Hunter was just 55–64. But there were signs of what was to come, such as the game he pitched against the Twins on May 8, 1968. It was a classic, 27 up, 27 down—a perfect game, the first pitched in the American League since 1922. Then, after going 18–14 in 1970, Catfish reeled off four straight 20-win seasons, becoming one of the best pitchers in the league as the A's become the best team, winning three straight World Series from 1972–74. In '74, Catfish went 25–12 with a 2.49 ERA, threw 23 complete games and an ironman 318 1/3 innings. After the season he was named winner of the Cy Young Award, just 28 years old and a pitcher in his prime That's where the story gets interesting. Before the age of free agency, Catfish Hunter became a free agent on a technicality.

CATFISH WRIGGLES FREE

This was one time colorful owner Charles O. Finley outsmarted himself. Hunter's contract with the A's had a clause in which Finley was to pay half of the pitcher's $100,000 salary into a life insurance fund as part of a deferred compensation agreement. Hunter said that because Finley failed to make the payment, he should be declared a free agent. Free agency was just around the corner and that might have had some bearing on this one. That December, arbitrator Peter Seitz ruled that Hunter's contract was void. Catfish was free to entertain any and all offers. It was a precedent-setting ruling and set the stage for the Yankees to become major players in the free agent market for years to come.

That's when George Steinbrenner and the Yankees stepped to the plate. The Yankees were building toward another championship and Steinbrenner wasn't about to be outbid. After 13 days of suspense, Catfish Hunter signed a precedent-setting $3.75-million, five-year contract with the Bronx Bombers. The country boy came to the big city, put on No. 29, and went about his business of earning his money. And that meant winning.

In 1975 he was worth every penny, starting a workhorse 39 times and compiling a 23–14 record with a 2.58 ERA. He led the league with 328 innings pitched and 30 complete games. The next year, the Yanks won their first American League pennant since 1964, but Hunter wasn't quite the same pitcher. Maybe all the innings had taken a toll. He still went 17–15 with a 3.53 ERA, but his run of five straight 20-win seasons was over. The Yanks were swept by the "Big Red Machine" in the World Series and that wasn't good enough. With free agency now officially in swing, owner Steinbrenner went out and signed Hunter's former Oakland teammate, Reggie Jackson, to his group of star players that now included Thurman Munson, Lou Piniella, Graig Nettles, Mickey Rivers, Willie Randolph, Ron Guidry, and Sparky Lyle.

JIM HUNTER

PITCHER **YANKEES**

The Yanks would win it all in 1977 with Jackson the World Series hero on his way to being named "Mr. October." But Catfish was strangely mediocre, finishing the regular season with a 9–9 record and an inflated 4.71 ERA. There were rumors of arm problems, but Catfish wouldn't make excuses. The following March he was diagnosed with diabetes, which could have been a reason for his sub-par season. With that under control, he bounced back to go 12–6 with a 3.58 ERA. Injuries relegated him to 20 starts and just 118 innings, but he was tough down the stretch and went 1–1 in the Series. Then a year later it came apart. He was just 2–9 with a 5.31 ERA and he retired. Catfish was just 33 years old and said he always planned to call it quits when his contract ended. But he also wasn't the same pitcher and there had to be a physical reason—arm and/or shoulder problems.

He finished his career with a 224–166 record and 3.26 ERA. In 1987, his third year of eligibility, he was elected to the Hall of Fame. In deference to both his owners, Charlie Finley and George Steinbrenner, he decided to go into the Hall without a team insignia on his plaque.

Unfortunately, the Catfish Hunter story didn't have a happy ending. Some 10 years after election to the Hall of Fame, Catfish was hunting and found he couldn't lift his shotgun. He also had trouble buttoning his shirts. When the symptoms grew more alarming, he went for tests and learned that he had amyotrophic lateral sclerosis, Lou Gehrig's Disease, the same incurable malady that had claimed the Iron Horse years earlier. He continued to battle the disease, but on September 9,

1999, Catfish died after taking a bad fall at his home and striking his head. He was just 53 years old.

Because Catfish was not a Yankee for that long, his number has never been retired. It continues to be worn today, as it was by various players since 1930, some good, some not-so-good, and many fly-by-nighters who came and went before you could say Jim "Catfish" Hunter.

For instance, does anyone remember **Lou McEvoy**? He was a right-handed pitcher who went 1–3 with a 6.71 earned run average in 28 games in 1930, the first player to wear No. 29. A year later, he slipped into jersey No. 34 for his final six games as a Yankee. **Sammy Byrd's** name has been mentioned in multiple chapters because he wore multiple numbers. In 1931, that number was 29. After Byrd, the number took a decade-long vacation, then was pulled out of mothballs so that righty **George Washburn** could wear it for one game in 1941. Infielder **Oscar Grimes** appeared in Chapter 7 because he wore that number, Mickey's number, from 1944–1946. But in his first year with the club, 1943, he was No. 29. Catcher **Bill Drescher** started with No. 22 in 1944, then switched to No. 29 his final two years with the team.

Righty **Charley Stanceu** threw in 22 games as No. 17 in 1941 only to see his career derailed by World War II. When he returned for just three games in 1946, he was No. 29 before being waived to the Phils in June. Infielder **Johnny Lucadello** didn't get a chance to switch numbers. He played just 12 games as No. 29 in 1947. Young catcher **Sherm Lollar** came up to the Yanks in 1947 at the age of 22, put on No. 29 and caught 11 games to the tune of a .219 batting average. A year later, it was 22 games and a .211 mark. Lollar was a good receiver, but the Yanks had another young catcher named Berra, so he was expendable. He eventually became an outstanding receiver and dangerous hitter, leading American League catchers in fielding four times. Catching for the pennant-winning "Go-Go" White Sox in 1959, Lollar hit .265 with 22 homers and 84 RBIs. The Yanks just couldn't keep all of the good ones.

The backup catcher became **Charley Silvera,** who wore No. 40 for four games in 1948. Then when Lollar left, Silvera took No. 29 and wore it through 1956. Playing behind Yogi, and later Elston Howard, his primary job was warming up pitchers in the bullpen. Silvera was eligible for seven World Series, but played in just one game. His final 57 games were played with the Cubs in 1957.

Even the most diehard Yankee fans probably don't remember **Bobby Richardson** wearing No. 29. He did that in his third season, 1957, after wearing No. 17 his first two years. When he became a regular in 1958, he took over No. 1 and wore it until his retirement in 1966. Infielder **Fritz Brickell** didn't get a chance to pick a longterm number. He was No. 29 for two games in 1958 and 18 more in '59 before being traded to the Angels for pitcher Duke Maas. Lefty **Hal Stowe** was a one-game wonder in 1960. The aforementioned Duke Maas wore No. 24 from 1958–60, then put on No. 29 in his final Yankees season of 1961. The number was having a real nomadic existence.

On June 17, 1961, the Bombers signed veteran first sacker **Earl Torgeson**, who had been a fine player for the Braves in the early and mid 1950s. "Torgy" was really brought on as a player/coach, wore No 29, and got into 22 games. But his .111 batting average showed that, at age 37, he was ready for full-time coaching. **Hector "Skinny" Brown** was another player who had some success elsewhere, came to the Yankees late, and didn't stay long. The righthander, who won 12 games for the Orioles in 1960, was sold to the Yanks on September 7, 1962. Wearing No. 29, he got into just two games, lost one of them, and was sold to Houston before the 1963 season started.

Add **Tom Metcalf, Mike Jurewicz, Bobby Tiefenauer,** and **Bill Henry** to the list of players who were gone almost as soon as they arrived. Between 1963 and 1966, these four players all wore No. 29 for a total of 22 games between them.

Rocco Domenico Colavito could have been a great Yankees hero and that's what he always wanted to be. "Rocky" was perfectly suited for the role. He was tall, handsome, Bronx-born, possessor of a throwing arm the equal of Clemente's, and a bona fide power hitter. In fact, he admitted longing to play for the Yanks all his life. But when it came time to sign, the Indians offered young Rocky $1,000 on signing, another grand if he lasted 30 days, and yet another grand if he survived a month beyond that. In 1950, this was an offer he couldn't refuse. He signed and by 1955 he got his first call-up. A year later, he slammed 21 homers and was off to the races.

From 1958 to '65 Colavito was one of the top sluggers in baseball for Cleveland, Detroit and Kansas City. He had seasons of 41, 42, and 45 homers and as many as 140 RBIs in a season. In 1965, he blasted the 300th homer of his career. At age 31, he was one of the youngest to reach that milestone. But his deterioration came quickly. He hit just .238 in 1966 with 30 homers, but a year later when he split the season between Cleveland and the White Sox, he hit .231 with eight home runs. The Dodgers picked him up in 1968, but he managed just a .204 average with three homers before they released him on July 11. Four days later his longtime dream came true. The Yankees signed him and brought him home to the Bronx.

The pity of it all was that he wasn't the same Colavito. In his only 39 games as a Yankee, Rocky Colavito hit just .220 with five home runs and 13 RBIs. At the age of 34, he was through, and the Yanks released him at the end of the season. As it was, Rocky Colavito hit 374 home runs in a 14-year career. It's just too bad he couldn't have done more as a Yankee.

Like Colavito, lefthander **Mike McCormick** came to the Yankees briefly at the tail end of his career. He pitched for 16 seasons (1956-71), and was a Cy Young Award winner in 1967 but never quite lived up to early expectations. In July 1970, he was traded to the Yanks for southpaw John Cumberland. McCormick was just 31, but didn't have much left in the tank. He pitched just nine games with a 2–0 record and 6.10 ERA. The next year, he threw a few games for Kansas City and retired with a 134-125 record.

A trio of pitchers, righty **Jim Hardin**, southpaw **Wade Blasingame**, and righthander **Tom Buskey,** came next. The Yanks hoped for more for each of them, but didn't get it. Hardin had been 18–13 with Baltimore in 1968, but when he came to the Yanks in a late May 1971 trade with the Orioles, he wasn't completely healthy. He pitched in just 12 games and the next April was released. Blasingame had been 16–10 with Milwaukee in 1965, but never duplicated that season. A fractured finger and sore arm in '66 seemed to derail him. He was just 28 when he pitched 12 games for the Yanks in 1972 before retiring. Buskey, a reliever, threw eight games in 1973 and four more in '74 before being traded to the Rangers.

On June 7, 1973, the Yankees announced that they had purchased the contract of lefthanded pitcher **Sam McDowell** from the San Francisco Giants. "Sudden Sam," was a guy who had struck out 325 hitters in just 273 innings for Cleveland back in 1965. At that time, he was being called the American League Sandy Koufax. Sudden Sam was 6'5", 220 pounds, and had a devastating overhand fastball, which he could mix with a curve and change. In 1970, he would fan 305 hitters in 304 innings as he went 20–12. What no one could know then was that it would be McDowell's last big year, though he was only 27 years old. McDowell himself would later admit why:

"I was the biggest, most hopeless, and most violent drunk in baseball."

There it was. McDowell wasn't the first player to have his career derailed by alcoholism, but he may have been one of the best. By the time he reached the Yankees he was a shell of his former self. He wore both Nos. 29 and 48 in 1973, pitched in 16 games, and went 5–8 with a 3.95 ERA. A year later, he was even worse, logging in at 1–6 with a 4.69 ERA. He simply couldn't do it anymore. On December 20, the Yanks just released him. He would pitch 14 more games for the Pirates the next year and then retire at the age of 32, leaving behind a 141–134 record and 2,453 strikeouts.

It could have been so much more when you consider that between 1965 and 1970, McDowell averaged 275 strikeouts a year. He eventually straightened out his life and has done work for several big league teams as a counselor to drug and alcohol addicted players. Had he remained sober there's no telling how good he could have been.

Righthanders **Casey Cox** and **Dick Woodson** were the last players to wear No. 29 before Catfish came along. Cox threw five games as No. 39 in 1972 and one more as No. 29 the following year before being released. Woodson had an eight-game stay in 1974, going just 1–2. Neither pitcher ever appeared in the majors again. Hunter came along and occupied No. 29 through 1979. Then it was time to start over.

Outfielder **Dave Collins**, a feisty player who had a trio of .300 seasons, signed as a free agent before 1982. He got a 111-game shot and hit just .253 with virtually no power. After the season the .272 lifetime hitter was traded to Toronto. Lefty reliever **Bob Shirley** was the next to wear No. 29 and he hung on to it for five years, through 1987, providing some valuable southpaw help out of the pen. His best year was 1985, when he appeared in 48 games, went 5–5 with a 2.64 ERA, made five spot starts, and had two saves. He was released after 1986, re-signed before '87, pitched 15 more games and was released again on June 5.

Infielder **Randy Velarde** wore No. 29 for part of 1987 but would be remembered as No. 18, which he wore from 1988–95 and again in 2001. Lefty reliever **Pat Clements** was No. 29 at the start of 1987, a year in which he worked in 55 games and had seven saves. He switched to No. 38 before the year was out and wore it again for just six games in 1988. Yet another short-time lefty reliever, **Al Holland**, threw 25 games in 1986 and three more in '87, wearing No. 36 the first year, then No. 29 his final season. Infielder **Paul Zuvella** wore No. 26 in 1986 and No. 29 the following year. His future was decided by batting average of .083 and .176. Yet another infielder, **Luis Aguayo**, had No. 29 for 50 games in 1988, coming over from the Phils on July 15, and getting his walking papers after the season. Lefty **Dave LaPoint** was next, wearing first No. 29 and then switching to No. 42 for 20 games in 1989, going 6–9 with a 5.62 ERA. He kept No. 42 the next season, when he was 7–10 in 28 games, and was released the following February.

Early in 1989, the Yankees had some injuries and began looking for an outfielder. On April 30, they

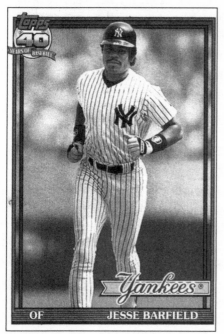

OF   JESSE BARFIELD

made a deal with Toronto for rightfielder **Jesse Barfield,** sending prospect Al Leiter to the Blue Jays. Barfield was an outstanding outfielder with a great arm and a power bat. Three years earlier he hit .289 for the Jays, adding 40 homers and 108 RBIs. He also gunned down 22 runners and won a Gold Glove. Barfield was just 29 years old when he came to New York, took over No. 29, and went to work.

As it turned out, Barfield was still great in the outfield, throwing out 20 runners in 1989 and winning yet another Gold Glove. But he was having problems hitting for average. In 129 games, he batted just .240 with 18 homers and 56 RBIs. He hit 25 homers in 1990, playing in 153 games, but two years later the Yanks phased him out, as he played just 30 games and hit an awful .137. Barfield never really established himself in New York, retiring after 1992 at the age of 32 with 289 home runs in 12 seasons.

Outfielder **Mike Humphreys** was strictly a stopgap who hung in from 1991–93, going up and down from the minors to majors. He played in a total of 54 games in that time and hit below the Mendoza Line. He also had three numbers, wearing Nos. 36, 31 and then 29, a sure sign that he wasn't going to be around long. **Gerald Williams** was a talented outfielder who came up first in 1992. For several years there was a question of whether Gerald or Bernie Williams (no relation) would emerge as the next Yankees' centerfielder. It turned out to be Bernie; Gerald was just a part-time player from 1992–96 and again in 2001 and '02. He wore No. 29 for three years (1994–96) and spent time with Nos. 13 and 36 his first two years and No. 17 his final two seasons in pinstripes. Pitcher **Ricky Bones** wore No. 29 for just four games in 1996, leaving the Yanks with an earned run average of 14.14. Ouch.

Finally, in 1997, No. 29 would find a home with a very successful player, lefty reliever **Mike Stanton**, who became a bullpen stalwart during three Yankees championship seasons. Stanton was with the Bombers from 1997 to 2002, and returned again in 2005. A situational lefty who helped set up for Mariano Rivera, Stanton had a good fastball and a breaking ball, and relied on control to do his job. Manager Joe Torre didn't hesitate to use him. He never pitched in fewer than 64 games during his first Yankees tenure and threw in as many as 79.

That's almost half the games. His best year was 2001 when he was 9–4 with a 2.58 ERA in 76 games, making the All-Star team that year.

From 1997–2002, Stanton also had a 30–12 record out of the pen and never had a sore arm. He would pitch for 19 years, toiling for eight teams and making 1,178 appearances with only one start. He trails only Jesse Orosco (1,252) for the most appearances in big league history. Outfielder **Bubba Trammell** showed some power with San Diego in 2001 and 2002, hitting 42 homers and driving in 138 runs. The Yanks traded for him but the latest No. 29 was only good enough—or not good enough—to play in 22 games and hit an even .200. Goodbye, Bubba.

Switch-hitting first sacker **Tony Clark** has the same résumé as Trammell. He was a guy with power who hit 97 homers and drove in 319 runs for the Tigers from 1997–1999. The Yanks got him in 2004 when Jason Giambi was injured and he played 106 games. Though he hit a few big home runs, his .221 batting average, 16 homers and 49 RBIs made him expendable. In fact, late in the season he was replaced by veteran John Olerud.

From that point, No. 29 again passed into multi-player limbo. Case in point. Pitcher **Tim Redding** came over in a July 2, 2005, trade with the Padres. He pitched in one game, had an ERA of 54.00 and was designated for assignment the next day. Infielder **Felix Escalona** played five games as No. 60 in 2004 and 10 more as No. 29 a year later. Gone. Lefty **Matt Smith** came up to pitch in just 12 games in 2006. Reliever **Octavio Dotel** got a 14-game shot in 2006, two years after saving 36 games for Houston and Oakland. But Dotel was coming off Tommy John surgery and the Yanks couldn't wait. Gone.

No. 29 then passed on to **Kei Igawa**. If his story was made into a TV movie, it might be titled *The Strange Case of Kei Igawa*. Prior to the 2007 season, the arch rival Boston Red Sox went out and signed Japan's best pitcher, righthander Daisuke Matsuzaka. Not to be undone, the Yanks signed southpaw Igawa, who had been his league's strikeout king twice, had a 20–5 record in 2003, and had won his league's equivalent of the Cy Young Award. When the smoke cleared, the Yanks had paid a $26 million posting fee, then signed Igawa to a five-year, $20 million contract.

Whether he was awed by pitching in the majors, or whether his stuff didn't translate well to big league hitters, or whether he just couldn't find his command, Igawa was a bust. He pitched very little for the Yanks in 2007 and '08, spending more time in the minors. During the 2009 season, Igawa pitched at Triple-A Scranton and won ten games. Will the Yanks trade him, give him another shot, or just eat his huge contract? No one seems to know, except that Kei Igawa may have been a $46 million mistake.

Rightfielder **Xavier Nady** wore No. 29 when he came over from the Pirates in July 2008. However, he soon switched to No. 22, which he also wore in 2009. Infielder **Cody Ransom** wore No. 29 in 2008, then switched to No. 12 a year later before being designated for assignment. And finally, in 2009, catcher **Francisco Cervelli** took over the number. Cervelli had a two-game cup of coffee the year before, wearing No. 64, but this time he was pressed into duty when both Jorge Posada and Jose Molina went down with injuries. Cervelli showed everyone he was a first-rate backstop, handling veteran pitchers and throwing very well. And he hit better than anyone expected. Is he the catcher of the future? Only time will tell.

30: TWO TRUE YANKEES

This is a number really dominated by two players. Neither will make the Hall of Fame, but both were extremely talented and made major contributions to the Yankees. It was **Mel Stottlemyre**'s misfortune to come up to the Yankees in the final years of their long dynasty that lasted from 1949–1964 and then collapsed. **Willie Randolph** came in time to help the Bombers to three consecutive pennants and a pair of World Series in the 1970s. He was Mr. Calm and Mr. Consistency on a team dubbed the Bronx Zoo for its collection of characters who often fought among themselves as much as with the opposition. Together, the two wore No. 30 for 24 years, and it was almost consecutive. Just a single season separated Stottlemyre's tenure from Randolph's.

Stott was a righthanded pitcher with a devastating natural sinker and good control. He was called up from Triple-A Richmond in early August 1964 as the Yanks were looking for pitching help to win a fifth straight pennant. He made 12 starts, compiling a 9–3 record with 2.06 ERA and the Yanks won that fifth straight title. And by the time the season ended, many considered the rookie the ace of the staff. He pitched three times in the World Series that October, going 1–1 with a 3.15 earned run average as the Yankees lost to the Cardinals in seven games. Little did he know it then, but it would be his only World Series.

The Yankees' collapse began the very next year as their veterans were aging, injured, and coming to the end of the line. The team plummeted to a 77–85 finish, yet Stottlemyre continued to establish himself

Mel Stottlemyre PITCHER

with a 20–9 record, a 1.63 ERA, and a league-best 18 complete games and 291 innings pitched. But when the team crashed into the basement in 1966, Stottlemyre crashed with them, compiling just a 12–20 mark. That's what can happen when you have very little support. Suddenly, the once great Yankees were a very bad baseball team. But the Yanks slowly rebounded and Stottlemyre became a 20-game winner in 1968 and again in '69.

But it began to get tougher after a 1971 season in which he was 16–12. He went 14–18 and 16–16 the next two years, but he was just 31 years old in 1973 and the team was getting better. There was little reason to think Stott couldn't pitch well for another four or five years.

It didn't happen. In 1974, Stottlemyre suffered a torn rotator cuff and he had to shut down with a 6–7 record. That was it. The shoulder wouldn't get better and he retired with a 164–139 record and a 2.97 ERA. Mel Stottlemyre was a proud Yankee for 11 seasons, wearing No. 30 for all of them. Since that time, he's never strayed far from the game. Two of his sons became big league pitchers and Mel has become one of the most respected pitching coaches in the game, having worked for the Astros, Mets, Yankees, and Seattle Mariners.

Stottlymyre left the Yanks after the 1974 season, and the next year No. 30 remained packed away. But it wouldn't be for long. That December, with the Yanks looking to make a run at the pennant in 1976, the team closed a deal with the Pittsburgh Pirates, trading promising young pitcher Doc Medich to the Pirates in return for three players: veteran pitchers Ken Brett and Dock Ellis and a young second baseman named

WILLIE RANDOLPH

Willie Randolph. The Brooklyn-raised Randolph had played just 30 games for the Pirates in 1975 at the age of 20. His numbers certainly weren't impressive, with a meager .164 batting average. Whether the Yankees scouts had seen something or whether he was a throw-in with Ellis the major piece doesn't really matter now. Randolph won the second base job in spring training, took over No. 30, and would wear it on his back for the next 13 years.

He gave everyone a glimpse of the future immediately. Playing in 125 games as the Yanks did indeed win the pennant, Randolph hit a solid .267 with a homer and 40 RBIs. He also swiped 37 bases and proved himself an outstanding second sacker, with very good range and great effectiveness at turning the double play. As the Yanks won two more pennants and World Series titles in both 1977 and '78, Randolph quickly became not only a staple in the infield, but an amazingly consistent player who provided the same kind of high quality overall performance day in and day out, as well as year to year.

Though the Yanks would only get back to the World Series once more, in 1981, Randolph would continue to play at a high level. He would be a six-time All-Star, a player who almost always hit between the high .270s and .294, though he also hit .305 in 1987. You could wind him up every spring and know exactly what you'd get. He never wavered defensively, even as a parade of shortstops played alongside him, more than 30 of them during his Yankees tenure.

By 1988, Willie was 33 years old and injured much of the year. It was his free agent year, and when the season ended the Yanks didn't offer him a new contract. Willie left his beloved Yankees and signed with the

Dodgers, where he immediately showed his old consistency, hitting .282 in 145 games. Two years later, in 1991, he was with the Brewers and at age 36, hit a career high .327 with 54 RBIs in 120 games. He would play one more year with the Mets and then retire after the 1992 season.

In 18 years, Willie Randolph had a .276 batting average, swiped 271 bases and played consistently outstanding defense. He soon returned to the Yankees as a coach, donning No. 30 again. His hope was to manage the team someday but the offer never came. Finally, he became the Mets manager for several years and remains in baseball today, getting huge ovations at Yankees Old Timers' Days. Because of his long tenure as both a player and coach, no Yankee would wear No. 30 again until 2006.

Before Stottlemyre and Randolph, of course, there were a number of others wearing No. 30, just a couple in the early days. The number wasn't really used regularly until 1940. But there was someone wearing it in 1929, righthander **Gordon Rhodes.** He stayed with the Yanks three more years, wearing No. 19 for two of them and No. 16 his final year of 1932. A lefthander with the strange name of **Bots Nekola** also had No. 30 for nine games in 1929, had no record, and was gone. After that, the number wasn't worn by a player again for 11 years.

When it came out of mothballs in 1940, outfielder **Mike "Shotgun" Chartak** was wearing it. But Shotgun had very little pop in his bat, hitting just .133 in 11 games. A year later, he was up for just five games and wore No. 39. Righthander **Norm Branch** took over the number in 1941 and had a good year, going 5–1 with a 2.87 ERA out of the bullpen in 27 games. Yet a year later he threw in just 10 games, went 0–1, and was out of baseball. After Branch was gone, the Yanks made a July trade with the Cincinnati Reds and acquired a 38-year-old right-handed reliever named **Jim Turner**. It would be the start of a long association with a guy who would become a real pitching guru.

Turner originally joined the Reds in 1937 as a 33-year-old rookie. All he did that year was go 20–11, leading the league with a 2.38 ERA, five shutouts and 24 complete games. By the time he reached the Yanks he was strictly a reliever. He threw in just five games after the trade in

'42 and had a 1.29 ERA. Turner wasn't exactly a workhorse during the war years, but always did well.

With many players returning from the war in 1946, the Yanks had no room for a reliever soon to be 42 years old, so Turner retired with a 69–60 record in nine seasons. Four years later, in 1949, he became the Yanks' pitching coach and stayed for 11 years. He would leave to do the same thing in Cincy from 1961–65, then return to the Yanks in 1966 and stay through 1973. Turner died in 1998 at the ripe old age of 95.

Lefty **Bill Wight** was No. 20 for 14 games in 1946, then switched to No. 28 a year later, but only pitched in one more before being traded to the White Sox. Righty **Dick Starr** has a similar tenure, throwing four games as No. 30 in 1947 and then just a single game as No. 36 a year later. But then came a pitcher who is still remembered fondly by old time Yankees fans, a junkballing lefthander who became part of "The Big Three" during the Yanks' pennant-winning years of the late 1940s and early 1950s. They're normally referred to as Reynolds, Raschi, and Lopat. But **"Steady" Eddie Lopat** usually pitched in between the two fastball-throwing righties, and his tantalizing off-speed pitches often threw batters completely off their games.

Lopat began his career with the White Sox in 1944 at the age of 26. For four seasons, he was essentially a .500 pitcher, going 50–49. After completing a 16–13 season in 1947, the Yankees came calling. In February 1948 he was sent to New York for two lesser players. The Yankees were again on the rise and so was Eddie Lopat. He went 17–11 in '48, benefiting from the big Yankee bats, and a year later, he came under the tutelage of new pitching coach Jim Turner.

In some ways, Lopat was a different kind of pitcher. He had no fastball to speak of and wasn't about to blow hitters away. Steady Eddie tantalized hitters with a variety of slow breaking pitches which he used with guile and great control.

Manager Casey Stengel saw an advantage putting Lopat between his two hard-throwing righthanders, Reynolds and Raschi, and the formula worked like a charm as the Yankees won five straight pennants and World Series from 1949–53. In the pennant-winning years, Lopat had records of 15–10, 18–8, 21–9, 10–5, and 16–4. He was even better in the World Series, going 4–1 with a 2.60 ERA. In the 1951 Series against the Giants, he threw two complete game victories and gave up just one run in 18 innings.

Lopat was 36 years old in 1954. That year the Yanks won 103 games but finished second to a powerful Indians ballclub that won 111. Steady Eddie could still bring it, going 12–4 in 26 games. A year earlier, when he was 16–4 in just 25 games, his 2.42 ERA was the best in the league. Then, in 1955, as the Yanks headed toward yet another pennant, it began to look as if the veteran was slipping. By the end of July, the Yanks decided it was time to add some youth. They traded Lopat to the Orioles for a young pitcher who never panned out. But they made the right call. Lopat went just 3–4 with the O's and retired at the end of the season, leaving a 166–112 record behind.

Lefthander **Rip Coleman** took Lopat's No. 30 for 10 games at the end of the 1955 season, going 2–1 with six saves. That merited him an encore the following year in which he threw in 29 games to the tune of a 3–5 record and 3.67 ERA before being part of an 11-player swap with Kansas City that brought Clete Boyer to the Yanks. That same trade also brought a 5'6", 140-pound lefthander named **Bobby Shantz**. If you look at pitchers today, many of them are a foot taller and 100 pounds heavier than Shantz. But how many of them can brag about a 24–7 season resulting in a Most Valuable Player Award?

When the Yanks got Shantz in 1957 and gave him No. 30, he was 31 years old and coming off four injury-filled seasons that really derailed his career. In late September of his MVP season of '52, his left wrist was broken by a Walt Masterson pitch. The following spring he developed shoulder pain that not only limited his effectiveness, but cost him most of the 1954 season.

But he adjusted and in his first season with the Yanks had an 11–5 record in 30 games with a league-best 2.45 earned run average. He was also versatile, making 21 starts and saving five games with late relief. It was also the first year that Gold Gloves were given for the best fielders at each position and the cat-quick Shantz won it as the league's best fielding pitcher. It would be the first of eight straight, four with the Yanks and four in the National League.

Over the next three years, the little lefty worked increasingly out of the bullpen but contined to do a nice job as the team won two more pennants and a World Series in 1958. By 1960 he was still doing a good job, going 5–4 with a 2.79 ERA in 42 games and leading the club with 11 saves. After the season, he was left unprotected and taken by the new Washington Senators in the expansion draft. They subsequently traded him to Pittsburgh and he spent his final four seasons pitching for the Pirates, Astros, Cardinals, Cubs, and Phils. Shantz retired after the 1964 season with a 119–99 record, one that could have been so much better had he not been injured.

Fastball-throwing **Marshall Bridges** wore No. 30 in 1962 and '63, coming over from Cincy for catcher Jesse Gonder. The southpaw pitched in 52 games in the pennant-winning year of '62 and excelled, going 8–4 with a 3.14 ERA and 18 saves. After the 1963 season, the Yankees sold Bridges's contract to the Senators. After that, No. 30 was monopolized by Stottlemyre and Randolph and it wasn't until 2006 that another player wore it.

That player was pitcher **Corey Lidle**, whose stay with the Bombers lasted for just 10 games. It might have lasted much longer had it not been for a tragic accident after the 2006 season. Lidle, in essence, was a journeyman righthander who was part of the deal that brought Bobby Abreu from the Phils on July 30, 2006. He put on No. 30 and went to work. Lidle had been just 8–7 with the Phils at the time of the trade, and in 10 games with the Yanks had a 4–3 mark with a rather high 5.16 earned run average. In a way it was a typical Lidle year, that of a guy usually just a few games over .500, a number four or five starter.

The Yanks were eliminated by the Tigers in the first round of the playoffs that year and shortly afterward, on the afternoon of October 11, news broke that a small plane had crashed into a building on the Upper East Side of New York City, just off the East River, killing both people on the plane, setting the building on fire, and injuring 21 others, mostly firefighters. It was then learned that the plane was registered to Corey Lidle, who was aboard with his co-pilot/flight instructor. It could not be determined which of the men was flying the the plane at the time of the accident. They had apparently decided to fly up the East

River before heading home to California, and when they made a U-turn they miscalculated and the wind took the plane into the building.

After Lidle's untimely death, No. 30 sat for a year. Then in 2008, two pitchers again wore it, **Scott Patterson** for just one game and then **David Robertson** for 25. Patterson was waived in September, but Robertson was a keeper. The hard-throwing righthander became a bullpen staple in 2009 by pitching in 45 games to a 2–1 record and 3.30 ERA. He got better as the year went on and manager Joe Girardi began trusting him more in key situations. Robertson has a live fastball and sharp curve, surprising many with his ability to strike out hitters. In 43 2/3 innings in 2009, he fanned 63 batters, one of the best strikeout-per-inning ratios in the majors. Will David Robertson be the next to wear No. 30 long term? Only time will tell.

THE COMPLETE GAME SHUTOUT

With relief pitching becoming more and more of a specialty and the quality start now defined as six innings and three runs or less, the complete game is becoming a rarity, the complete game shutout even more unusual. Walter Johnson, who pitched in the first decades of the 20th Century holds the all-time record with 110. Notice the most recent pitcher in the group is Ron Guidry, who pitched in the 1970s and '80s.

Whitey Ford	45
Red Ruffing	40
Mel Stottlemyre	40
Lefty Gomez	28
Allie Reynolds	27
Spud Chandler	26
Bob Shawkey	26
Ron Guidry	26

#31: DON'T CALL HIM MR. MAY

Something strange happened to No. 31 after its debut in 1929, when it was worn for just 18 games by a marginal pitcher named **Roy Sherid**. The number was then put into mothballs, not to be worn by another player for 47 years until it appeared on the back of pitcher **Ed Figueroa**. The third man to wear it took it over in 1981. He was already an established star when he came to the Yankees, and before he was through he would have earned his way into the Hall of Fame. But **Dave Winfield**'s story isn't a simple one, and his Yankee tenure was, in some ways, rather strange.

Winfield was born on October 3, 1951, the very same day Bobby Thomson hit his "Shot heard round the world." That's a good baseball start. He grew up in Minnesota and earned a baseball and basketball scholarship to the University of Minnesota in 1969 and quickly became a star, especially in baseball, where he was an All-American in 1973 and the MVP of the College World Series as a pitcher. The Padres made him the fourth pick in the MLB draft, but that wasn't all. He was also drafted by the NBA's Atlanta Hawks, the Utah Stars of the ABA, and by the Minnesota Vikings of the NFL—even thought he never played football. But that's how great an athlete he was. Fortunately, the 6'6", 220-pound Winfield chose baseball.

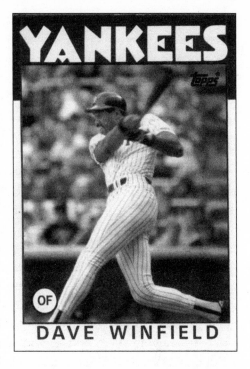

DAVE WINFIELD

The Padres brought him up immediately with not a day spent in the minors and he hit a solid .277 in 56 games before the end of the 1973 season. The next year, he was a starter, but it was really between 1977 and '79 that he fully emerged as a five-tool star. By 1979 he was hitting .308 with 34 homers and a league-best 118 runs batted in. Winfield became a free agent after 1980 and the offers began coming in, including one he felt he couldn't refuse. On December 15, it was announced that Winfield had signed a huge, 10-year, $23-million contract with the New York Yankees. He would be moving onto the big stage and be playing for bombastic owner George Steinbrenner. Though no one knew it at the time, oil was about to meet water and the two don't mix.

The 1981 season was split in half by a players' strike, so Winfield's first Yankee season was just 105 games long. He still hit .294 with 13 homers and 68 RBIs while playing a fine right field. In the first round of the playoffs against Milwaukee, Winfield hit .350 with two doubles and a triple as the Yanks won in five. He was just 2-for-13 in the next round as the Yanks swept Oakland in three straight, and in a six-game World Series loss to the Dodgers, big Dave went into a deep slump and got just one hit in 22 trips to the plate. This was the guy the Yanks were paying all this money? Steinbrenner began to chafe.

Over the next few years, Winfield continued to play at a high level. He would drive in 100 or more runs in six of the next seven seasons, missing by three in 1987. In 1984, he was in a race for the batting title with teammate Don Mattingly. Winfield would hit a career best .340, but Mattingly won it at .343, and many Yankees fans openly rooted for the young first baseman.

With Mattingly becoming the latest home-grown Yankees star, the big guy was often cast as the villain. Then, in 1985, owner Steinbrenner made a remark that would haunt his right fielder. Frustrated by his team's inability to get back to the World Series' Steinbrenner said, "Where's Reggie Jackson? We need a 'Mr. October' or 'Mr. November.' Winfield is 'Mr. May.'" He was alluding to former Yankee Jackson's great clutching hitting in the playoffs and World Series' and still pointing to Winfield's 1-for-22 in the 1981 Fall Classic. There were stories that Steinbrenner tried to trade him but couldn't because Winnie was a five-and-ten man and wouldn't give his consent.

Though he hit .322 with 25 homers and 107 RBIs in 1988, Winfield was experiencing bad back problems and needed surgery. He would miss the entire 1989 season. During Winfield's recovery there were more problems between him and the owner. It all ended early in the 1990 season when Winfield accepted a trade to the Angels in return for pitcher Mike Witt. Winfield slowly regained his form and two years later, playing mostly as a designated hitter for Toronto, batted .290 with 26 homers and 108 RBIs at the age of 40 to lead the Blue Jays to a World Series, which they won. He had finally erased the stigma of Mr. May forever and was now recognized as one of the best all-around ballplayers of his generation.

Dave Winfield would play two years for his hometown Minnesota Twins, getting the 3,000th hit of his career on September 16, 1993, and would finish up with the Indians in 1995 as he approached his 44th birthday. In 22 seasons he batted .283 with 465 home runs, 1,833 RBIs, 223 stolen bases, and 3,110 hits. Those were Hall of Fame worthy numbers and the big guy was inducted in 2001, his first year of eligibility. Finally, in 2008, he made amends with the Yankees and their aging owner by appearing at the last Old Timers' Day and the Final Game ceremony at the old Yankee Stadium. He had continued his philanthropic work since his retirement and has been a role model for current Yankees captain Derek Jeter, who has always admired Winfield for his athleticism and humanitarian efforts and has credited Winnie as an inspiration for Jeter's own philanthropic endeavors. Is there a better testimonial than that?

Compared to the Winfield saga, the story of everyone else is rather tame, and they were all less talented. Pitcher **Roy Sherid** was the first in 1929, but switched to No. 15 his final two Yankee seasons. For whatever the reason, the number didn't appear again until 1976, when righty **Ed Figueroa** donned it after coming over from the Angels in the same trade that brought Mickey Rivers to the Yanks and sent Bobby Bonds to the Angels. If Figueroa was considered a throw-in to the deal, he was one helluva throw-in.

After a 2–8 rookie season with the Angels in 1974, the Puerto Rican-born Figueroa quickly matured to a 16–13 mark and 2.91 ERA the next year. Playing for a powerful Yankees team in '76, Figueroa really came on strong, putting together a 19–10 record with 14 complete games and four shutouts as the Yanks won the pennant before being swept by the Reds in the World Series.

The next two years Figgy was a mainstay, joining Ron Guidry and Catfish Hunter to give the Yanks some great frontline pitching as the Bombers won a pair of World Series. He had records of 16–11 and 20–9, in '78, becoming the first Puerto Rican pitcher ever to win 20. In fact, during the three pennant-winning seasons from '76 to '78, Figueroa won more games than any other Yankees pitcher, including the superstar Guidry.

But Figueroa injured his elbow early in the 1979 season, went just 4–6 in 16 games and

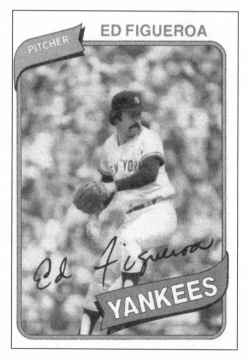

ED FIGUEROA

PITCHER

NEW YORK

Ed Figueroa

YANKEES

never regained his effectiveness. He was 3–3 the next season, when the Yanks sold his contract to Texas on July 28, and he was 0–7 for the Rangers. He pitched just two games for Oakland in 1981, then packed it in. He would pitch in Mexico for a while, but never returned to the majors.

With Figueroa gone, Winfield took back the number until his trade early in 1990. In 1985, the Yanks made a September 15 trade with Houston to bring knuckleballer Joe Niekro to town, where he joined his brother Phil. He pitched in three games before the season ended. For some reason, the team let him wear Winfield's No. 31 for two weeks while Winnie was injured. The next two years, Joe Niekro wore Nos. 47 and 39. He was 40 years old when he came to New York, had a 9–10 season in 1986, and after pitching just eight games in '87 was traded to the Twins that June.

Hensley "Bam Bam" Meulens was given No. 31 in 1990 and wore it for part of three seasons. He also wore No. 57 in 1989 and No. 50 in 1992 when he had little more than a cup of big league coffee. Meulens was one of those guys who would hit a ton in spring training, then fizzle when the regular season began. The 6'3", 215-pound third and first sacker got a 96-game look in 1991, but hit just .222 with six homers. The next year, he played in just two games, then saw action in 30 more in 1993 and hit .170. Bam Bam was more like bing bing, and after 1993 he was released.

For **Bob Wickman** and **Mike Humphreys**, No. 31 was a small part of their Yankee careers. Reliever Wickman wore it in 1992, then switched to No. 27 from 1993–96. Outfielder Humphreys was with the Yanks from 1991–93, and because he was up and down, had more numbers than seasons. He started with No. 36 in '91, went to Nos. 31 and 34 in '92, and Nos. 29 and 39 his last year. Five numbers in parts of three seasons could be a record. When the Yanks took a flyer on southpaw **Frank Tanana** in 1993, they weren't expecting much, and they didn't get it. He came over from the Mets on September 17, went 0–2 and retired at the end of the season. A guy who had a 240-236 record was all but done.

Pitchers **Xavier Hernandez** and **Brian Boehringer** were next. Hernandez lasted for just 34 games in 1994, while fellow righthander

Boehringer wore No. 31 for seven games in 1995, then switched to No. 41 in both '96 and '97, and wore No. 41 again in 2001 when the Yanks brought him back. One reason Boehringer didn't continue with No. 31 in 1996 was because the Yankees made a trade with the White Sox and acquired veteran outfielder **Tim Raines** prior to the 1996 season. Raines, a longtime star in Montreal, took his old No. 31 and wore it for three Yankees seasons.

The solidly built, 5'8", 180-pound Raines was called "Rock," and was long considered the NL equivalent of Rickey Henderson. He was a leadoff man with power who often hit above .300 and was also a dynamic base stealer, leading the National League for four straight seasons from 1981–84, swiping 71, 78, 90, and 75 sacks during those years. Raines was 36 years old when he came to the Yanks but proved a valuable fourth outfielder during the team's dynasty years. He hit .284, .321, and .290 in a part-time role. He also contributed in the postseason and got two World Series rings for his efforts.

After Raines, No. 31 went into pass-around mode once more, starting with reliever **Dan Naulty** in 1999. The righty pitched in 33 games, went 1–0 with a 4.38 ERA and then was traded to the Dodgers. He never appeared in the majors again. Veteran outfielder **Lance Johnson** was 36 years old and basically done when he joined the Yankees in 2000. He managed to hit .330 (9-for-30) in 18 games, was released in June, and retired. Outfielder **Glenallen Hill** came over from the Cubs in July 2000, played 40 games, hitting .333 with 16 homers and 29 RBIs, thereby giving him a career-best 27 for the season. Yet the following March he was dealt to Anaheim for a minor leaguer. Lefty **Ed Yarnall** had two quick cups of coffee, a five-game trial in 1999 as No. 52 and then two more in 2000 when he wore No. 31. That was his final big league appearance.

Reliever **Steve Karsay** had a chance to really make a mark with the Yanks after he signed as a free agent in December 2001. A big, hard-throwing righty, Karsay worked in 78 games in 2002, going 6–4 with a 3.26 ERA and 12 saves. Manager Joe Torre worked him hard, maybe too hard. The latest No. 31 hurt his shoulder in the spring and needed surgery, which cost him the entire season and ultimately his career. He tried to come back in both 2004 and 2005, but pitched in just 13 games before being released.

Another reliever, **Jason Anderson,** pitched 22 games as No. 45 in 2003 before being traded to the Mets. A year later, the Yanks grabbed him off the waiver wire in June, gave him No. 31, but he stayed long enough to pitch in just three games. Once Anderson left, righthander **Aaron Small** switched from No. 50 to No.31. There was a good reason for the switch. A journeyman pitcher who spent many years in the minor leagues, the 33-year-old Small suddenly found some magic when injuries gave him a shot at the rotation. He began to win and didn't stop until the season ended, going a perfect 10–0 in 15 games, nine of them starts. His success earned him a million-dollar contract, his first big payday since he began bouncing around the majors and minors in 1994. But a leg injury in spring training slowed him the next year and he never got in that good rhythm. Used sporadically, he was 0–3 in 11 games with an 8.41 ERA. Granted free agency after the season, he never appeared in the majors again.

As the Yankees continued to be a dominant team toward the end of the first decade of the new century, No. 31 continued to be a number in search of a home. Strong-armed **Jose Veras** wore No. 31 for 12 games in 2006, then switched to No. 41 for his final three years in pinstripes. Reliever **Edwar Ramirez**, one of those guys on the major league-minor league shuttle wore it for 21 games in 2007 without much success. The next year, he switched to No. 36 and pitched in 55 games, going 5–1 with a 3.90 ERA. He kept that number as he bounced back and forth in 2009, pitching in just 20 games to a 5.73 ERA. Journeyman first sacker **Josh Phelps** got a shot in 2007 after making the team in spring training. He played in 36 games as No. 31, hit .263 and was placed on waivers in June.

Young righthander **Ian Kennedy** got a three-game cup of coffee at the end of the 2007 season. Wearing No. 36, Kennedy pitched well, going 1–0 with a 1.89 ERA and showing a lot of poise. The next spring he made a decimated rotation and bombed, going 0–4 with an 8.17 ERA and was demoted to the minors. His number that year, the ill-fated No. 31. He was traded after spending most of 2009 recovering from surgery for an aneurysm in his pitching shoulder. Lefty **Michael Dunn** was a September call-up in 2009, pitched four games to a 6.75 ERA as No. 31, then went to the Braves in the off-season trade that brought Javier Vazquez back to the Bronx.

When diehard Yankees fans think of No. 31, they still think about Dave Winfield. Though Winfield had a fine decade with the Bombers and wound up in the Hall of Fame, the series of strange events culminating in that crazy feud with George Steinbrenner may preclude the number ever being retired in his honor. Whether it is or isn't, one thing is for certain. Dave Winfield was definitely not Mr. May.

#32: YANKEE TRAILBLAZER AND MVP, ELSTON HOWARD

When the legendary Jackie Robinson became the first African American to join a major league team in 1947, it was thought that others would quickly follow. Some teams began signing blacks soon after, but others didn't. In other words, it was more of a steady trickle than a flood. Both the Brooklyn Dodgers and New York Giants integrated quickly, signing star players such as Robinson, Don Newcombe, Roy Campanella, Willie Mays, Monte Irvin and others. In fact, the National League as a whole was more proactive than the American League in scouting and signing African Americans.

But while the Dodgers and Giants, two New York teams, quickly signed some great black players, the Yankees didn't, and still hadn't in the early 1950s. In 1955, amid some criticism for their tardiness, the Yanks finally put an African American player in pinstripes. They gave **Elston Howard** No. 32 and he certainly proved a good choice. Besides being an excellent player for a dozen years, he also became the American League's Most Valuable Player in 1963, the first black to win that award in the junior circuit.

Howard was a catcher by trade, but the Yanks had Yogi Berra firmly entrenched in that position in 1955. Howard wasn't about to replace him, yet because of his talent the Yankees played the rookie in left field and even at first base. And he would spell Yogi behind the plate when the veteran needed a rest. By 1960, he was finally seeing a majority of time behind the plate and Yogi was now seeing more games in left.

The 6'2", 200-pound Howard was a solid hitter with some power, had an excellent throwing arm from the outfield and behind the dish, and was a natural leader. He also became a skillful handler of pitchers, and all the Yankee hurlers had faith in his pitch calling and the way he received the ball. He was also one of the first to use the hinged catcher's mitt, which made receiving easier, and paved the way for the one-hand catching technique of the modern backstops. He fit in with the rest of the great Yankees immediately, hitting .290 with 10 homers and 43 RBIs in 97 games his rookie year. He also homered in his first World Series at bat that year.

By 1958 the Yankees were still in dynasty mode and Howard was a productive member of the team. He hit .314 that year, playing in 103 games and had 11 homers and 66 RBIs, solid pro-

ELSTON
HOWARD
N. Y. YANKEES   CATCHER

duction for the amount of playing time he received. He threw out two runners from the outfield in the 1958 World Series against Milwaukee and won the Babe Ruth Award as the Yanks' outstanding player in the fall classic. In 1961, as the Yankees won yet again, Howard was the catcher and played in 129 games, hitting a career-best .348 with 21 homers and 77 RBIs.

By 1963, Howard was 34 years old and still part of baseball's best team. That year, he hit .287 with 28 homers and 85 RBIs. Beyond that, he provided leadership to a team that saw many of its stars injured during the year. Howard was named the American League's MVP. He showed it was no fluke a year later when he played in a career-high 150 games, and hit .313 with 15 homers and 84 RBIs. He was without a doubt a full-fledged star, a guy who was voted to the All-Star team nine straight seasons beginning in 1957.

The 1964 season, however, was also his last big year. Age was catching up, and his slide coincided with the end of the current

Yankees, dynasty. He hit just .233 in 1965 and .256 the following year while playing 126 games. The Yanks had to retool and on August 3, 1967, he was suddenly traded to Boston for two marginal players. Despite hitting just .147 for the Red Sox, he helped them take the 1967 pennant and earned the respect of his pitchers and the entire team. And he played in all seven games of the World Series. He would return as a part-timer with the Red Sox in '68 and then pack it in.

In 14 seasons, Howard hit .274 with 167 home runs, but his value to the Yankees went far beyond that. They brought him back as a coach in 1969 and he stayed with the club for 11 years. In 1979, he was diagnosed with myocarditis, a rare heart disease that causes rapid heart failure. He was a candidate for a heart transplant but his condition deteriorated too quickly. Elston Howard died on December 14, 1980. Four years later, his No. 32 was permanently retired and a plaque in his honor placed in Monument Park at Yankee Stadium.

Because Elston Howard wore No. 32 for so long, also wearing it as a coach and having it retired soon after his death, a limited number of Yankees have had it on their backs. Add another long-time wearer, third-string catcher **Ralph Houk** and just eight other Yankees ever wore the number, and all came before 1940. **Art Jorgens** was the first in 1929, and if his name sounds familiar, it's because he wore six different numbers in eight years. Lefthander **Frank Barnes** wore it for two games in 1930, while outfielder **Bill Karlon** had it for two games of his own the same year. Pitcher **Ken Halloway** became the

Ralph Houk | MANAGER

third player to wear it in 1930, and he stayed for all of 16 games without winning or losing. Two years later, catcher **Eddie Phillips** pulled it on for just nine games.

Outfielder **Dusty Cooke** managed to last three seasons with the Yanks, from 1930–32, playing three games as No. 32 in 1932. He was No. 6 the previous two seasons before being shipped to Boston. Old Reliable Tommy Henrich wore both Nos. 22 and 32 his rookie year of 1937. This great Yankee also wore Nos. 7, 17, and finally 15, the number for which he is best remembered. Righthander **Steve Sundra** managed to hang around for four seasons. He wore No. 32 in both '38 and '39, but wore No. 24 in '36 and No. 25 in 1940.

Then, in 1947, along came **Ralph Houk**, "the Major," a decorated veteran of World War II. Houk was a catcher who arrived just before Yogi Berra and managed to play in 32 games, starting with No. 50 and then quickly moving to No. 32. He hit .272 but had virtually no power. Once Yogi showed his stuff, Houk was relegated to second string, and finally third string behind Charley Silvera. Yet he stayed with the team through 1954, a good organizational man and someone who could help with the pitchers. Amazingly, he played 10 or more games just twice with a top of 14 in 1948. Houk was in just 91 total games. His lifetime batting average was .272, the same number he reached his rookie year. Yet he had just 158 at bats and never hit a single home run.

But that wasn't the last of Ralph Houk. He was a player/coach in 1953 and '54, still wearing No. 32. Then he left for several years before returning again as a coach in 1958. By then, Elston Howard was wearing the number and Houk switched to No. 35. In 1961, he replaced Casey Stengel at the helm of the team and managed the Yankees to three straight pennants and a pair of World Series triumphs by 1963. The Yanks then moved him upstairs, making him a vice-president and general manager. When the team collapsed in 1965, Houk fired manager Johnny Keane and returned to the field.

Houk stayed at the helm from 1966–73, then left the team when CBS sold it to a group led by George Steinbrenner. He then skippered the Tigers from 1974 to '78 and the Red Sox from '81 to '84. Always a players' manager, he was well-liked despite his toughness because he was always fair. Houk was never fired—a rather unusual circumstance for someone who managed three teams. He managed for 20 years and retired with a 1,619–1,531 record. On August 9, 2009, Ralph Houk celebrated his 90th birthday.

So Houk and Howard were the last two Yankees to wear No. 32. They had the number on the field from 1947–1967, then Howard continued with it as a coach until his death. And then it was retired, one of the 15 Yankees numbers that will never be worn again.

#33: MAKE ROOM FOR BOOMER

Question: What do **Charlie Devens, Pete Appleton, Lee Stine,** and **Doc Medich** have in common? Answer: They all wore No. 33 for the New York Yankees. What they don't have in common, however, is the era in which they donned the same uniform number. Devens, Appleton, and Stine wore No. 33 between 1933 and 1938; Doc Medich, who came next, began wearing it in 1974. That's right. There was a 36-year gap in which No. 33 never appeared on the back of a Yankees player. And who would have thought that the biggest Yankee star wearing number 33 would be an overweight, fun-loving lefthander who just happened to be one helluva pitcher?

David Wells came to the Yanks as a free agent in December 1996. He had come up with Toronto at the age of 24 in 1987, and while he had a 15–10 season in 1991 he was largely erratic and found himself traded to Detroit two years later. At that point in his career, he was considered a journeyman type, a guy who could give you innings but wasn't a big winner. Despite being 10–3 for the Tigers by July 1995, he was suddenly shipped to Cincinnati where he went 6–5 to finish the year at a respectable 16–8. All that earned him was a trade to Baltimore before the 1996 season. Now he was becoming a traveling journeyman. His 11–14 record for the Orioles with a 5.14 ERA that bespoke mediocrity. But one thing Wells had done since coming into the league was pitch

BOOMER WELLS *pitcher NEW YORK YANKEES®*

exceedingly well against the Yanks, so when he became a free agent at the end of the season the Yankees signed him.

The Bronx Bombers were just beginning their latest dynasty, having won the World Series in '96, but even the best teams can never have enough pitching, so they decided to give Wells a shot. He was already 34 years old and a guy who always looked out of shape. Many felt his Yankees career would be a short one. As it turned out, Wells always wanted to play for the Yanks. His all-time favorite player was Babe Ruth and he actually had the audacity to ask for Ruth's No. 3, long retired. Naturally, he was turned down, but he went for the next best alternative. He chose No. 33, which had belonged to third sacker Charlie Hayes the year before. Fortunately, Hayes decided to switch to No. 13, so the man who would become known as "the Boomer" took his double-Babe number and went to work.

With the Yankees, Wells became not only a winner, but a dominant pitcher for the first time in his career. He finished the 1997 season at 16–10 with a 4.21 ERA. The next year he was even better.

Exhibiting almost uncanny pinpoint control and rarely walking anyone, Wells was as close to unbeatable as a pitcher could be. He had a great team behind him in '98, and would go 18–4 with a 3.49

ERA, walking just 29 hitters in 214 innings. He capped his season on May 17, when he threw a perfect game against the Twins at Yankee Stadium. In the postseason that year, Wells was a perfect 4–0 as the Yanks won their second World Series in three years. The Boomer was living a dream, but one that would soon become a nightmare. During the off-season, the Yankees had a unique opportunity.

On February 18, 1999, Wells learned he had been dealt to the Toronto Blue Jays along with Homer Bush and Graeme Lloyd in return for Roger Clemens. The Yanks couldn't

resist the opportunity to land a guy considered the best pitcher of his generation. Though disappointed, Wells didn't sulk. He went north of the border and had records of 17–10 and 20–8 for a team not nearly as good as the Yanks. Yet the Jays shipped him to the White Sox before the 2001 season where back problems held him to a 5–7 record in 16 games. After the season he was a free agent again and despite being 39 years old, the Yankees re-signed him for 2002. Suddenly, he was the old Wells again, compiling a 19–7 record with a 3.75 ERA. A year later, at the age of 40, he was still good enough to go 15–7, giving him four top-tier years with the Yankees. His 15th win was the 200th of his career. In addition, he walked just 20 batters in 213 innings of pitching, an eye-popping number.

When the Yanks didn't offer him a new contract after the season, he signed with San Diego where he went 12–8 before signing with the rival Red Sox in 2005. All he did was give them a 15–7 season at the age of 42. His body might have been breaking down, but not that rubber arm of his. But that would be his last big season.

The Boomer hung on through 2007, when he went 4–1 for the Dodgers after a late-season trade. Though he never formally announced his retirement, he did attend the final Old Timers' Day at the old Yankee Stadium in 2008 and then a year later became a part-time broadcaster. In a 21-year career he was 239–137, with many of those wins coming at an age when most pitchers were already in decline But David Wells was always different and he certainly treated the Yankees and their fans to some outstanding performances and also to his sometimes outlandish personality.

The three early players—Charlie Devens, Pete Appleton, and Lee Stine—barely wore No. 33 long enough to break a sweat. Devens pitched 14 games as No. 33 in 1933 and one game a year later. He also threw a single game as No. 20 in 1932. Appleton was in a single game in 1933 before moving on, while Stine threw just four games with no record in 1938. Both Devens and Stine were out of the majors after finishing their short stints with the Yanks. Then the number went into hibernation for 36 years.

The Yanks brought righthander George Medich up at the tail end of the 1972 season and gave him one start. He gave up two hits and two walks, got no one out, and was done for the year. But if he needed a prescription, he was making sure he could do it himself. The day after his first game he began medical school at the University of Pittsburgh. And from that point on he was known in baseball as "Doc." By 1974 he had switched from both Nos. 50 and 44 to No. 33 and put together a 19-5 season. The 6'5", 227 pounder looked like an emerging ace. He went 16–16 in '75, but his ERA of 3.50 was a bit lower than the previous season and he still threw 15 complete games. There was no reason to believe his days were numbered. But in December, the Yanks suddenly announced they were trading Medich to his hometown Pittsburgh Pirates. One of the three players who came to the Bronx was second sacker Willie Randolph, who would become a longtime fixture at second base.

Whatever the reason, Medich never did become a big star. He bounced around from Pittsburgh to Oakland, then Seattle and the Mets before settling in Texas for nearly five years. In 11 seasons he had a 124–105 record, but never again reached the heights of those early years with the Yankees. He retired after 1982 to practice sports medicine in the Pittsburgh area.

Once again No. 33 took a breather. The trade of Medich gave the number another eight years off until the Yankees swung a November 1981 deal with

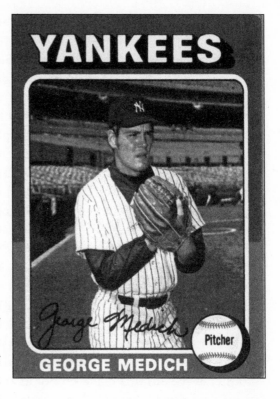

the Reds that brought 32-year-old veteran **Ken Griffey Sr.** to the Bronx in return for a couple of minor leaguers. Griffey had been a mainstay of the Big Red Machine of the 1970s. He was a speedy outfielder who could steal a base and a .300 hitter, though he didn't have a lot of power, unlike his son.

In his first year with the Bombers, Griffey wore No. 6, then switched to No. 33, which he kept until he was traded in June of 1986. But he did a fine job with the Yanks, hitting .300 twice and being very consistent during his tenure

The year after Griffey left the Yankees, they gave No. 33 to a basketball champion. At 6'7" tall and weighing 250-pounds, righthander reliever **Tim Stoddard** looked like, and was, a basketball star, starting on the North Carolina State team that won the National Championship in 1974 with superstar David Thompson leading the way. Stoddard then chose his other sport, baseball. He was drafted by the Rangers, but became a solid reliever when he went to Baltimore in 1978. He eventually signed as a free agent with the Padres and came to the Yanks in July of 1986 for pitcher Ed Whitson.

Stoddard was 33 years old by then, took No. 33, but then switched to No. 43 before the season ended and kept that for the next two years. For the Yanks he did a steady, if not spectacular job, going 4–1 in 24 games in '86, then 4–3 in 57 games with eight saves the next year, often setting up for closer Dave Righetti. In 1986, he regressed, his earned run average ballooning to 6.38, and the Yanks released him in August.

Ron Kittle was a big slugger who clubbed 35 home runs and drove in 100 runs while earning Rookie of the Year honors with the White Sox in 1983. But his career was derailed by low batting averages and injuries. When the Yanks got him in a trade at the end of July 1986, his star had already dimmed. Wearing No. 33, he hit just .238 in 30 games with only four homers. He had been hurt again for a good part of the 1977 season, and when it ended he was released.

Righty **Steve Shields** came on board as No. 33 in 1988, went 5–5 in 39 games and was released. Slugger **Jack Clark** lasted one year, 1988, wearing both Nos. 21 and 33; he was detailed in Chapter 21. Reliever **Scott Neilsen** was another of those multi-numbered guys. He pitched a total of 19 games in 1986, 1988, and 1989, wearing Nos. 41, 47, and 33. Outfielder **Bob Brower** saw action in 26 games as No. 33 in 1989, hitting just .232. Strong armed **Eric Plunk** was originally drafted by the Yanks but went to Oakland in '84 in the trade that brought Rickey Henderson to New York. He returned in 1989 in a trade that saw Henderson returned to Oakland. Plunk went 15–13 in three years, mainly in relief, then was released after 1991.

When the Yanks dealt with the White Sox for righthander **Melido Perez** before the 1992 season, they thought they might have a quality righthander for many years. The brother of talented but flaky southpaw Pascual Perez, Melido was more grounded and had a live arm. He went a workhorse 13–16 as No. 33 in 1992 with a very good 2.87 ERA and 10 complete games. But with the Yankees getting better, Perez got worse. He was just 6–14 in 1993, and arm problems limited him to just 22 games in '94. The next year he pitched in just 13 times and went 5–5. After that, he was out of baseball at age 29.

Charlie Hayes wore No. 33 for 20 games in 1996, caught the final out of the World Series that year, switched to No. 13 in 1997, hit .258, and was traded to the Giants. David Wells took over the number in '97 and '98, then outfielder **Ryan Thompson** wore it for 33 games in 2000. Thompson was an outfielder who seemed to have a ton of talent, but never quite made it anywhere.

What can anyone say about **Jose Canseco** that hasn't already been said? The poster boy for the so-called Steroid Era was actually a Yankee for 37 games in 2000, picked off the waiver wire on August 7 for one reason only... so the arch-rival Red Sox couldn't get him. The 35-year-old Canseco hit .243 in a very limited role, with six homers and 19 RBIs, a far cry from when he was one of baseball's top sluggers. He would play one more year, then retire with 462 home runs. After retirement came his book with all the PED accusations. He was vilified and denounced, but in light of what has happened since, the admitted longtime steroid user is now viewed as perhaps the most truthful player of them all when it came to the widespread use of performance-enhancing drugs.

Second sacker **Alfonso Soriano** wore No. 33 in 2001 after donning Nos. 58 and 54 his first two years. He then switched to No. 12 for his final two Yankees seasons when he was traded for Alex Rodriquez. His story was more thoroughly documented in Chapter 12. After David Wells's second tenure in pinstripes (2002–03), pitcher **Javier Vazquez** took No. 33 with a ton of high hopes. Vazquez had pitched well with some poor Montreal teams and the Yanks traded for the strong-armed righty in December 2003. Vazquez was a winner at 14–10, but his 4.91 ERA didn't impress anyone. So it was one and out, especially when the Yanks had a chance to acquire The Big Unit, Randy Johnson. Vazquez, two other players, and some cash went to Arizona. Ironically, the Yanks made a deal with the Braves that will bring Vazquez back to the Bronx in 2010 after a fine 2009 season in Atlanta.

Jaret Wright was yet another experiment that failed. A promising rookie with Cleveland in 1997, the fastballing righty was 8–3 in the regular season, then showed guts and heart in the playoffs that year. But arm problems followed and he didn't really resurrect until 2004 when he went 15–8 for Atlanta. Sure enough, the Yanks took the bait and signed him as a free agent. But Wright had questionable mechanics and his shoulder flared up again. He went just 5–5 in 13 games with a bloated 6.08 ERA as No. 33 in 2005. He tried to change his luck by switching to No. 34 the next year, but after the season the Yanks swapped him to Baltimore for reliever Chris Britton. They were right to do it. Jaret Wright was 0–3 with the Orioles in just three games. Hurt again, he was forced to retire.

So No. 33 continues to look for a stable new home. Catcher **Kelly Stinnett** wore it for 34 games in 2006, hitting just .228 before being released in July. Reliever **Brian Bruney** was signed at about the same time and took it over, wearing it through 2008 as he looked to be a guy who could play a significant bullpen role with the Yanks. He was 1–1 with an 0.87 ERA in 2006, then used in 58 games the next year, though sometimes hampered by wildness. In 2008, he went 3–0 in 32 games with a 1.83 ERA, and seemed on the brink of getting the prestigious eighth-inning bridge to Mariano Rivera in 2009. He switched to No. 38 that year and was off to a great start when elbow problems shut him down. When he finally returned, he tried to change his luck by wearing No. 99. But control problems surfaced again, and while he went 5–0 with a 3.92 ERA in 44 games, the Yanks deemed him expendable. After the season, he was traded to the Washington Nationals.

And then there's **Nick Swisher**. Before the 2009 season, the Yanks dealt for the switch-hitting outfielder/first baseman, picking him up from the White Sox for Wilson Betemit with the idea of making him the new first baseman. Then a guy named Teixeira came along and Swisher was penciled in as a versatile sub, a fourth outfielder who could also play first. "Swish" had been with the A's for several years, hitting .254 in 2006 with 35 home runs and 95 RBIs.

At the outset of 2009, the newest No. 33 was playing off the bench, backing up Xavier Nady in right. Soon, however, he was getting key pinch-hits and his outgoing, exuberant personality exciting the fans and his teammates. Then Nady went down with a bad elbow and needed Tommy John surgery. Swisher became the everyday right fielder and had a solid year, batting .249 but hitting 29 homers and driving home 82 runs. He became a big part of the Yanks' drive to their 27th championship.

The latest No. 33 may not be a great player, but he's an exciting one and a great complement to the Yanks' cast of superstars and stars.

#34: WHO ARE THESE GUYS?

Talk about an orphan in the storm. No. 34 is one of the few Yankees numbers that simply hasn't been worn by a star, or at least not as a primary, longterm number. It has been more of a way station for players who have come and gone, switched to another number, or made their marks elsewhere after a trade. Some of the names sound familiar, others remain couched in anonymity. All were Yankees, however, and wore No. 34 for better or worse. In this case, though, it was usually for worse. But there's still hope. In 2009, free agent pitcher **A. J. Burnett** took over the number and helped the Yankees to yet another World Series. Time will tell if Burnett will become the man with whom No. 34 is most associated. So let's look at the roster. You'll really need your scorecards for this one.

For example, did you ever think there was a Yankee by the name of **Foster Edwards**? There was, but for just two games in 1930. Why didn't he last longer? In those two games, the righthanded Edwards had an earned run average of 21.60 and never played in the majors again. But he holds the distinction of being the first Yankee player to wear No. 34. He was followed a year later by pitcher **Lou McEvoy,** who wore No. 29 in 1930 before switching. Righty **Ivy Andrews** had two

two-year tenures (1931–32, 1937–38), wearing Nos. 34 and 28 the first two seasons, then No. 24 in the latter pair. Another righty, **Frank Makosky**, wore Nos. 28 and 34 in his only Yankees season of 1937. They were a quartet of strictly forgettable pitchers.

First baseman **Johnny Sturm** played 124 games for the Yanks as a 25-year-old rookie in 1941, wearing No. 34. When Sturm left, the Yanks promptly traded to get first sacker **Buddy Hassett** from Boston.

Hassett had been in the Yankees' system but stuck in the minors while Lou Gehrig manned first base. He would return to play 132 games for the Yanks in 1942, hitting .284 with five homers and 45 RBIs. Hassett, too, would go in the military, and by the time he returned in 1946, the magic was gone and he was released. Backup catcher **Ken Silvestri** wore No. 26 for 17 games in 1941. When he returned from the War, he donned No. 34 for parts of 1946 and '47, playing in just 16 games before leaving.

The 1947 season brought one of baseball's great characters to the Yankees. **Louis Norman "Bobo"** He was 39 years old that season. He'd been pitching since 1929 and would hang around the bigs until 1953 when he was 45 years old. Newsom changed uniforms 15 times in his career, with five separate stints at Washington and three at Brooklyn. Newsom was often plagued by injuries and bad luck, but was definitely talented. He won 20 or more games three times, but also lost 20 on a trio of occasions.

Bobo came to the Yanks on July 11, 1947, when they purchased his contract from Washington. The wily vet pitched in 17 games during the last months of the season, going 7–5 with a 2.80 ERA. The Yanks released him after the season. Bobo would pitch for 20 seasons, missing 1931 and '33 to injury, and spending 1949–51 in the minors before returning for two more years. His record was 211–222, making him one of just two pitchers in baseball history to win more than 200 games but lose even more.

Long, tall **Jack Phillips**, known as "Stretch," had been in the Yanks' minor league system since 1943, and got his chance in 1947, playing in just 16 games as No. 36. A year later, he played in a single game as No. 34, then went back to No. 36 for 45 games in 1949. Though he was batting .308, the Yanks sold his contract to Pittsburgh on August 6. **Bob Cerv** was one of a number of players who wore No. 34 for a single season during a longer career. He donned it in 1952, his second year, then wore No. 41 for three seasons and No. 17 for three years. His career is detailed in Chapter 17. Infielder **Kal Segrist** is another of those forgotten players, and for a good reason. He played just 13 games with the team in 1952 and left with a forgettable batting average of .043. Lefty **Harry Schaefer** was the third player to wear No. 34 in 1952, and had even less of an audition. He lasted just five games.

Yankees stalwarts **Tony Kubek** and **Clete Boyer** both wore No. 34 briefly in the context of their Yankees careers. Kubek wore it in his rookie year of 1957 before switching to his well-remembered No. 10, and Boyer went from No. 59 in 1959 to No. 34 the next two seasons before switching to No. 6. First sacker **Bob Hale** had no such luck. He came over from the Indians during the homer-happy M & M Boys season of 1961, but lasted for just 11 games, hitting .154 before moving on. **Phil Linz** was another story, a utility infielder of some skills who is now more remembered for playing "Mary Had a Little Lamb" on the harmonica than for any big hits or clutch fielding plays.

PHIL LINZ   inf-of

The bespectacled Linz waged a spring training battle with Tom Tresh for the shortstop job in 1962, when the incumbent Tony Kubek went into the Army. Tresh won out because of his power bat, but Linz played well. He wound up hitting .287 in 71 games that year and was a valuable Yankee. Wearing No. 34 again in 1963, he batted .269 in 72 games and then the following year played in 112 games, hitting .250 with five homers and 25 RBIs. But that August there was the harmonica incident that enraged manager Yogi Berra.

Though the Yanks rallied to win the pennant, Yogi was fired after a World Series loss to St. Louis and Linz, switching to No. 12 in 1965, saw his star dim. He played in 99 games, but it was probably his .207 batting average as much as his harmonica reputation that led him to be traded to the Phils for infielder Ruben Amaro.

First sacker **Mike Hegan** wore No. 24 in 1966 and '67, but then donned No. 18 when he returned to the Yanks in 1973 and '74. Infielder **Lenny Randle** came to the Yanks on August 3, 1979, when his contract was purchased from the Pirates. He hits just .179 in 20 games and was sent packing as a free agent. Lefty hit reliever **Dave LaRoche** spent the last three seasons of his big league career with the Yanks from 1981–83. He pitched well the first two years as No. 34, but was released. The Yanks resigned him in July of '83, gave him No. 38, but he lasted just one more game. LaRoche is remembered for a high arching blooper pitch he called a "LaLob" that often drove hitters crazy. He's also remembered as the father of current players Adam and Andy LaRoche.

Shortstop Roy Smalley wore No. 34 his first Yankees season of 1982, then switched to No. 12 the following two seasons and is detailed in Chapter 12. Pitcher **Matt Keough** was assigned No. 34 when he was traded to the Yanks in June 1983 and made 12 starts, going 3–4 with a 5.17 ERA. After the season, he was released. Catcher/outfielder **Scott Bradley** played 28 games in 1984–85 as No. 34. He showed some promise by hitting .286 the first year, then much less by hitting .163 the second, and was traded to the White Sox.

The parade of players continued with the same pattern. Young **Doug Drabek** made the team in 1986, showing a bulldog mentality in 27 games. He started with a high number, 62, but switched to No. 34 before the season ended, indicating he may have found a home. Drabek went 7–8 in 21 starts at age 23, but in November was traded to the Pirates as part of a six-player deal. Drabek had a nice career, going 22–6 for the Pirates in 1990 and winning the National League Cy

Young Award. In 13 seasons, he was 155–134 and probably would have had a successful Yankees career had they kept him.

Mike Easler, the "Hit Man," arrived as No. 17 in 1986, left as No. 34 after 1987, and is detailed in Chapter 17. No such luck for pitcher **Don Schulze**. A two-game audition doesn't get it done. Schulze had his in 1989 before being traded to the Padres with Mike Pagliarulo for pitcher **Walt Terrell** in July. Not surprisingly, the veteran right-hander was given nomad No. 34 and finished the season by going 6–5 in 13 games, all starts. Terrell had won, 15, 15, and 17 games for Detroit from 1985 to 1987, but apparently the Yanks didn't think he could do it in New York. He was granted free agency in November.

Righty **Bob Davidson** became the third pitcher to wear No. 34 in 1989. Davidson lasted just a single game, gave up two runs in one inning, and left with an ERA of 18.00.

Before the Yankees got Melido Perez in 1992, they had his brother Pascual, a kind of wild and crazy guy who had talent and also a bad shoulder. Righty **Pascual Perez,** rail thin at 6'2", 163 pounds, always put on a show. But he could pitch. Perez was 15–8 and 14–8 with the Braves, but his shoulder betrayed him and his wild personality didn't help, either.

The Yanks signed him as a free agent in November 1989, gave him No. 34, but he wasn't the old Pascual. Injuries limited him to just a 1–2 record in three games with a 1.29 ERA in '90, and the next year he was just 2–4 in 14 games. That would be his final year in the majors.

Then came a trio of forgettables once again. Lefty **Jerry Nielsen** lasted 20 games in 1992 before going to the Angels a year later. **Sam Militello** threw from the right side, wore No. 43 for nine starts and a 3–3 record in 1992, then switched to No. 34 for three more games in '93 before his big league career ended. And righty **Andy Cook** also wore the number in 1993, lasting all of four games before his baseball days were done. Lefty **Sterling Hitchcock** had a longer Yankees career (1992–95, 2001–03), but wore No. 34 only in 1993 after starting as No. 54 a year earlier. Hitchcock is remember as No. 41 by many fans and will be detailed in that chapter.

Then we come to one **Greg. A. Harris.** The middle initial is necessary to differentiate him from Greg W. Harris. Both were righthanders whose careers somewhat overlapped. Unfortunately, Greg A.'s Yankees career lasted just three games in 1994. He was signed July 3 and released July 13. But a year later, the final season of his career, he made history. You see, Greg A. Harris could pitch with either hand. He was a natural righty, but on September 28, 1995, in his second to last game with Montreal, he became the first pitcher of the modern era to pitch with both his right and left arms. And he got the side out.

Oddly enough, the Yankees now have a "switch pitcher" in their minor league system. Pat Venditte was drafted in 2008 and pitched at the Class A level in 2009. He throws both ways every game. Whether he makes it to the majors or not remains to be seen.

No. 34 continued to be mostly a pitcher's number and the pitchers it was assigned to didn't last very long. Lefty reliever **Rob Murphy** was with the team for three games in 1994, coming off waivers in August and being released in October. **Rob McDonald**, another lefty, did a bit better. He had a 33-game stay in 1995. Then came **Sean Henn**, another southpaw and one thought to have some real potential. Like so many up from the farm system, Henn wore No. 58 for a three-game cup of coffee in 2005, then No. 62 for a four-game cup the next year. In 2007, he stuck and was given No. 34. That year he got into 29 games, and went 2–2, but his bloated, 7.12 earned run average was enough to end it. On May 9, 2008, he was plucked off waivers by the Padres, his Yankees career over.

Big righthander **Phil Hughes** wore No. 34 briefly in 2008. Otherwise, he has worn No. 65 for most of his three year Yankees stint (2007–09) and that seems to be the number he wants to keep. We'll visit him there. Lefty reliever **Damaso Marte** has also gone away from No. 34. He wore it in his first Yankees season after coming over from Pittsburgh with Xavier Nady in 2008. The next year, he switched to No. 43 and spent the first half of the season rehabbing a weakened shoulder. In the regular season he was awful, but in the playoffs he seemed to rediscover the reason the Yankees wanted him in the first place, shutting down lefthanded hitters with regularity. He also excelled in the

World Series and was especially effective against the two top Phillies hitters, Chase Utley and Ryan Howard. He pitched in four games, threw 2 2/3 innings, gave up no hits, and fanned five. The Yanks expect big things from Marte in 2010. When healthy, he's an outstanding situational reliever.

And that brings us to the latest player to wear No. 34. Righthander A. J. Burnett has the opportunity to give a real face to a number that has been searching for one. The 32-year-old, 6'5", 205-pound hurler was signed to a huge, five-year $82.5-million contract following an 18–10 season and a league-leading 231 strikeouts with Toronto in 2008, a year in which he seemingly dominated the Yankees every time he pitched against them. Burnett has stuff as good as anyone in the league. He can throw a 95-mph fastball with seeming ease and has a big breaking curve that handcuffs hitters when it's working well. Yet he's had some strangely mediocre seasons since joining the Marlins in 1999 at the age of 22. Burnett had Tommy John surgery in 2003, yet returned the next year to throw a fastball at 102 mph. In 2005, his fastball averaged 95.6 mph, best in the league.

Despite all his talent, his best years were 12–9, 10–8, 10–8, that is until his breakout season with Toronto. His first year with the Yanks was strangely inconsistent. He finished 13–9 with a 4.04 ERA. He tended to get wild at times and his curve was sometimes so sharp that it would result in a wild pitch. But he showed enough flashes of dominance and helped the Yanks win the pennant and World Series. It was the old cliché: when he was good, he was very, very good. When he was bad, you know the rest.

Yet A. J. Burnett should be in his prime for several more years and has a chance to be a dominant pitcher for a great team. That's what the Yankees expected when they signed him for the big bucks and that's what Burnett hopes to deliver. No. 34 could certainly use it, a Yankee to finally call its own.

#35: THE MOOSE; A FREE AGENT SIGNING WELL WORTH IT

How many times in recent years has a team given a free agent a long-term, big-bucks contract only to be ultimately disappointed by the returns? This is especially true of pitchers because you never know when the next pitch will result in shoulder or elbow injury. But among the biggest free agent success stories you'll find **Mike Mussina**, one of the most consistent winning pitchers in baseball history. After spending the first 10 years of his career winning 147 games for the Baltimore Orioles, Mussina signed a six-year, $88-million contract to join the Yankees. He spent the next eight years in the Bronx, winning another 123 games and finishing his career at the age of 39 with his first ever 20-win season. No wonder why "Moose," as he was called, put his own Yankees stamp on No. 35.

The righty Mussina wasn't a big man by today's standards at 6'2", 185-pounds, but was already a fine pitcher when he graduated from Stanford University with a degree in economics and All-American honors. The Orioles drafted him in 1990, and two years later in his first full major league season he went 18–5 with a 2.54 ERA, and was off to the races. With the O's he'd win 19 games twice, 18 twice, and have only one losing season (11–15 in 2000), when he led the league in innings pitched. The very next year he was a Yankee.

Early in his career, Mussina had a live, mid-90s two-seam fastball, slider, changeup, and a knuckle curve. Later, when he began losing velocity off his fastball he added a splitter. An extremely bright and cerebral player, he always found ways to adjust as his physical skills changed. In his first three Yankees seasons, he showed he was earning his keep by winning 17, 18, and 17 games, helping the Yanks reach the World Series twice (2001, 2003), though they lost both times.

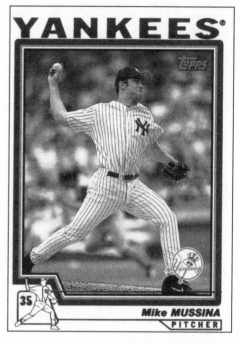

Mussina continued to pitch well, though the erstwhile Bronx Bombers didn't have the firepower to reach the World Series again after 2003. But the team was happy with his performance, and when his original contract was up he signed a two-year extension prior to the 2007 season when he'd be 38 years old. That year he struggled. His velocity was down further and his command was spotty. He was even pulled from the rotation at one point, and it took three late-season wins to give him a winning record of just 11–10. The Yanks had a new manager in 2008 as Joe Girardi replaced longtime skipper Joe Torre, and some wondered what would be in store for Mussina. But once the season was underway it soon became apparent that Mussina had adjusted again. He was changing speeds more and working both sides of the plate as never before. He was the Yankees' best pitcher and finally won that elusive 20th game in his final start of the season.

While the Yanks made it known that they'd like Mussina to return in 2009, he had other ideas. Shortly after the season ended, he announced his retirement, saying that he wanted to go home to Pennsylvania and spend more time with his wife and children. Eighteen big league seasons had been enough. And while the Yanks, the pitching bolstered by the additions of CC Sabathia and A. J. Burnett in 2009, moved toward yet another World Series, Mike Mussina said he had no regrets about not returning. He refused to look back.

In 18 seasons Mike Mussina had a record of 270–153 with a 3.68 earned run average and 2,813 strikeouts. He is only the ninth pitcher in history to win more than 100 games with two different teams and he also won seven Gold Gloves for his fielding excellence. His strikeout total is 19th best all-time and he was the first pitcher since Sandy Koufax in 1966 to retire after a 20-win season.

The biggest question with Mussina is whether he's a Hall of Famer. There are many pitchers in the Hall with fewer victories. One criticism had been that he never won 20 games, but he managed to do that his final season. Besides, he pitched in an era where getting 20 wins is more difficult than ever and he did win 19 twice and 18 three times. Only time will tell if the voters feel he is worthy, but Mike Mussina certainly made himself a valuable and popular Yankee, and was worth every penny of his free agent contract. As No. 35, he made the pinstripes proud.

Before Mussina, there were a couple of other star players who wore No. 35, but not for a long period of time. When a young **Dixie Walker** became the first to wear it in 1931, it was the highest number on the team. Walker, of course, quickly switched to No. 27 before being traded and becoming a star in Brooklyn. Six years passed before the number was issued again. Star righthander **Spud Chandler** wore it his rookie year of 1937 before switching to No. 21, the number he wore while becoming a star. Again, it was the highest number on the team back then.

Flash forward to the war year of 1945. No. 35 made a two-game return on the back of 42-year-old pitcher **Paul Schreiber**, who last appeared in the big leagues 22 years earlier. How did that happen? Schreiber, who had a two-year pitching career with the Dodgers, was a Yankees coach in 1945, and with the pitching staff depleted by WW II, was called out of his two-decade retirement to throw 4 1/3 innings in relief. Catcher **Aaron Robinson** was one of those number changers, wearing No. 35 briefly in 1946. In four years (1943, 1945–47), he wore five different numbers. **Yogi Berra** wore No. 35 his rookie year of 1947 before making the permanent transition to No. 8.

Between 1948 and 1955, No. 35 was worn by a succession of forgettable players who appeared in pinstripes very briefly or without special distinction. It began with pitcher **Red Embree**, who came over from the Indians in 1948 and pitched in 20 games, making eight starts. Embree went 5–3 with a 3.76 ERA, but all it earned him was a trade to the St. Louis Browns after the season. For infielder **Mickey Witek**, his Yankee career lasted all of a single game in 1949.

Righthander **Duane Pillette** started his career with the Yanks in 1949, throwing in just 12 games and going 2–4. After just four games the following year, he was shipped to the Browns in June. Lefty **Joe Ostrowski**, called "Specs" like so many players who wore glasses then, was a 31-year-old rookie with the Browns in 1948. He came to the Yanks when Pillette was sent to the Browns. Taking over No. 35 from Pillette, the bespectacled southpaw did a nice job, his best being in 1951 when he was in 34 games with a 6–4 record, a 3.49 ERA and five saves. The Yanks used him in just 20 games the next year and then he retired.

Another lefty, **Johnny Schmitz**, lasted a total of eight games in 1952 and '53. He wore No. 40 in '52, but when Ostrowski retired got No. 35 for all of three games in 1953 before being traded to Cincinnati in August for Ewell Blackwell. **Steve Kraly** was the second southpaw to wear No. 35 in 1953. Unlike Schmitz, his big league career lasted five games and was over. The last of this group was catcher **Lou Berberet**, who played in five games as No. 49 in 1954 and two more as No. 35 in 1955.

After Berberet left, No. 35 went on a 22-year hiatus, returning to action when the Yanks signed free agent pitcher **Don Gullett** in 1977. He was part of the first class of free agents and, after helping the Reds win the 1976 World Series, Gullett signed a six-year deal with the Yankees valued at nearly $2 million, which for those days was enormous. But unlike the signing of Mike Mussina years later, this one was a perfect example of what could go wrong.

Gullett came up to the Reds at the age of 19 in 1970, going 5–2 in 44 games, mostly in relief. A year later he was in the rotation and compiling an impressive 16–6 record. His speed impressed everyone. After a subpar 1972 (9–10), Gullett became one of the National League's best, running up records of 18–8, 17–11, 15–4, and 11–3 through 1976. But there were already some ominous signs. Gullett seemed to have bad luck. He lost time to hepatitis in 1972, back problems in '74, a broken thumb in '75, and a pinched nerve in his neck that limited him to 23 starts in 1976.

But the Yanks laid out the bucks and Gullett went to work for a very talented New York team in 1977. When he pitched, he usually won, but he began having shoulder problems. He would go 14–4 in his first season in the Bronx, but the balky shoulder limited him to 22 starts and 158 1/3 innings. A year later, the free agent nightmare came to pass. Gullett could only pitch in eight games before the shoulder went. He won as usual, going 4–2, but the diagnosis was a torn rotator cuff. At any rate, Dr. Frank Jobe operated on the lefty and found the damage extensive and beyond repair. Gullett was done at the age of 27.

A pair of veteran pitchers were both short-timers with the Yanks and took No. 35 back into limbo. Righty **Bill Castro** signed as a free against prior to the 1981 season and worked in just 11 games before being traded to the Angels for third baseman **Butch Hobson**. Hobson was also about done at age 30; he wore No. 35 for a few games before switching to No. 24 for the remainder of his 30-game, .172 Yankees tenure. Another righthander, **Roger Erickson**, then took over No. 35 for 16 games in 1982 and another five the following year. Erickson had been Rookie of the Year with the Twins in 1978 but faded quickly and 1983 proved to be his final season.

What are the odds of the Yankees signing a 45-year-old pitcher and getting two solid years of production from him? Whatever the odds, it happened—but only because that pitcher was **Phil Niekro**, one of the best ever at throwing the elusive, hard-to-hit knuckleball. Niekro had been with the Braves since 1964; when the Yanks signed him prior to the 1984 season, he was already a star. His first big year came in 1969, when he was 30 years old. Niekro was 23–13 that year and then was 20–13 in 1974.

In 1982, he was 17–4 as the knuckler really danced all year. Two years later, he decided to test the free agent market and landed in New York.

"Knucksie" was already gray-haired when he joined the Yanks. But he could still throw that pitch and went 16–8 in '84 with a 3.09 ERA, an amazing season at his age. A year later, he made 33 starts and finished at 16–12. And these were not great Yankees teams then. On the final day of the 1985 season, he won the 300th game of his career.

PHIL NIEKRO

He moved on to Cleveland the next year, was traded to Toronto in 1987, then released at the end of August. The Braves signed him so he could pitch his final game with the team that started it all. In 24 seasons, Phil Niekro was 318–274 with a 3.35 ERA and 3,342 strikeouts. He was elected to the Hall of Fame in 1997, and combined with his brother, Joe, won more games than another other brother tandem in big league history.

Young **Bob Tewksbury** followed ancient Phil Niekro, but he never had the chance to realize his potential with the Yankees. Tewks was a 25-year-old rookie fastballer in 1986 and showed immediate promise with a solid 9–5 record in 23 games. But when he faltered the next year with a 1–4 and 6.75 ERA in eight games, the Yanks moved him in July, sending the righty to the Cubs for southpaw **Steve Trout**. Tewksbury later became a sports psychologist working with the Boston Red Sox.

Steve Trout was the son of former pitcher Dizzy Trout, who won 170 games in a 15-year career. This was one case where the son didn't surpass the father. Steve had a 13–7 season with the White Sox in '84, but by the time he came to the Yanks he had pretty much lost it. He was winless in four decisions in 1987 with a 6.60 ERA and gone after the season, traded to the Mariners for lefty **Lee Guetterman** in a five-player deal. His 12-season record was just 88–92.

A 6'8" southpaw, Gutterman took Trout's No. 35, would wear it for five seasons (1988–92), and he was pretty much a workhorse out of the pen. From 1989 to '91 he appeared in 70, 64, and 64 games, with a combined record of 19–16 with 21 saves. In June 1992, he was traded to the Mets.

Veteran lefty **Curt Young** was signed as a free agent in mid-June of 1992. The 32-year-old lefty, who spent most of his career with Oakland, went 3–0 in 13 games but was granted free agency after the season. Infielder **Andy Stankiewicz** hit .268 in 116 games as a hustling rookie in 1992 when he wore No. 17. As No. 35 the next year, he played in just 16 games and failed to get a hit. After spending most of the year in the minors, he was shipped to Houston. Lefthander **Paul Gibson** was signed as a free agent in June 1993 and went 2–0 with a 3.06 ERA in 20 games. The next year, his ERA ballooned and he was sent to the Brewers in late August. He got another shot in 1996, lasted just 45 days as No. 39 and was released.

Then No. 35 got lucky again. It landed on the back of **John Wetteland**, a righthanded reliever who became the Yankee closer after being traded to the Bombers from Montreal in April 1995. Wetteland began his career as a starter but just didn't seem to have the calm temperament needed for the job, but as a closer he was a guy who wanted the ball every day. Within two years, he had become an All-Star.

With the Yanks, Wetteland saved 31 games in 1995, then hit his stride the next year as the Bombers drove toward their first championship since 1978. Once again the big righthander was the go-to guy finishing the regular season with 43 saves. He was even better in the playoffs, named World Series MVP for saving all four Yankees victories against the Braves. With his newfound stardom, he decided to test the free agent market and signed with Texas, pitching for four more years and saving more than 40 games for the Rangers twice. He retired after the 2000 season with 330 saves and the distinction of being named Rolaids Reliever of the Decade. Today, John Wetteland is the bullpen coach of the Seattle Mariners.

The infamous **Hideki Irabu** wore No. 35 in his first Yankee season of 1997, but is now remembered (not always fondly) for wearing No. 14 in his final two seasons in the Bronx. The last player to wear No. 35 before Mike Mussina came along was infielder/outfielder **Clay Bellinger,** who somehow lasted three years while struggling to hit above the Mendoza Line. A year later, in 2001, Mussina came in and took over No. 35. Bellinger wore No. 12 in his final 51 games as a Yankee and he hit .160.

Then Mike Mussina took care of the rest.

YANKEES IN THE HALL

In this chapter we've met a Hall of Fame pitcher in Phil Niekro and another who has a chance to make it, Mike Mussina. Andy Pettitte is another Yankee who may merit consideration before he's through, Alex Rodriguez, Derek Jeter, and Mariano Rivera are sure shots, and perhaps Jorge Posada will make it. And if Mark Teixeira continues to play as he has, he, too, may someday enter the hallowed halls of Cooperstown.

If any or all of them make it, they'll have plenty of company as the Yankees are well represented. Here's a look at all the Yankees who have earned their way to baseball immortality. A couple of names you may not recognize, since they played before 1929, didn't wear a number, and thus are not represented in this book. And some of the players made their marks with other teams. But all were Yankees at one time or another. Here's the list in alphabetical order:

Frank "Home Run" Baker, Yogi Berra, Wade Boggs, Frank Chance, Jack Chesbro, Earle Combs, Stan Coveleski, Bill Dickey, Joe DiMaggio, Leo Durocher, Whitey Ford, Lou Gehrig, Lefty Gomez, Goose Gossage, Joe Gordon, Clark Griffith, Burleigh Grimes, Bucky Harris, Rickey Henderson, Waite Hoyt, Miller Huggins, Catfish Hunter, Reggie Jackson, Wee Willie Keeler, Tony Lazzeri, Bob Lemon, Mickey Mantle, Joe McCarthy, Bill McKechnie, Johnny Mize, Phil Niekro, Herb Pennock, Gaylord Perry, Branch Rickey, Phil Rizzuto, Red Ruffing, Babe Ruth, Joe Sewell, Enos Slaughter, Casey Stengel, Dazzy Vance, Paul Waner, and Dave Winfield.

36: CONEY: MR. PERFECT

There was a time when some people called **David Cone** a mercenary, a gun for hire, a rent-a-player. In other words, he was a guy who was often available at the trade deadline to help a team try to make the playoffs and hopefully go far beyond that. In reality, that scenario happened just twice, first in 1992 when Coney went from the Mets to the Toronto Blue Jays on August 27, and then again in 1995, when he was dealt by the Blue Jays to the Yankees on July 28. Neither move was David Cone's doing. He was simply part of a trade that would hopefully benefit both teams. David Cone was a superb pitcher and ferocious competitor who loved the big stage and wanted the ball in difficult situations and important games.

By the time he reached the Yankees in 1995, he was an established winner, including an amazing 20-3 record with the 1988 Mets, and the Yanks were betting he would continue his winning ways with a team on the brink of making the playoffs. Sure enough, Cone was great in the Bronx, going 9–2 down the stretch with the Yankees as they made the playoffs. Cone was pitching well again as the 1996 season began, but he then started feeling some numbness in his pitching hand. An examination showed he had developed an aneurysm in his shoulder and he needed immediate surgery to repair it. He didn't return until September, but when he did he promptly threw seven no-hit innings against Oakland before leaving the game due to his pitch count. He finished the year at 7–2 with a 2.88 ERA, then won his only start in the 1996 World Series as the Yanks topped Atlanta.

Cone was 12–6 in 29 starts in 1997, but the following year regained his top form and was a 20-game winner for a second time (20–7) as the Yankees won 114 regular season games and another championship. Then there was his July 19, 1999, start against the Montreal Expos at Yankee Stadium. The Yanks were celebrating Don Larsen's perfect game in the 1956 World Series that day and—as Larsen and his catcher Yogi Berra watched the from the stands—David Cone retired all 27 Expos to face him, throwing his own perfecto. Though Cone didn't pitch exceptionally well the rest of the season (12–9), he won a pair of games without a loss in the playoffs to help the Bombers win yet again. Then a year later, in 2000, he seemed to lose it, compiling a 4–14 record

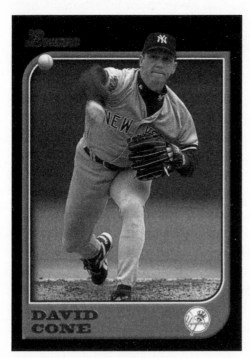

with a 6.91 ERA for a team that once again won its division and a championship, the Yanks fourth in five years.

When the season ended, the Yanks granted Cone free agency and he surprised everyone by signing with the rival Red Sox. He went 9–7, but it was a last hurrah. He was forced to sit out the 2002 season with injuries, tried to come back with the Mets a year later, but after going 1–3 in just five games, he said he couldn't continue. He left with a 194–126 record in 17 seasons, striking out 2,668 hitters. Not quite Hall of Fame numbers, but David Cone was an outstanding pitcher who made No. 36 memorable, especially on that July day in 1999 when he was absolutely perfect.

Beyond David Cone, No. 36 has an interesting history. It didn't debut until 1942 and had the usual variety of short-time players and also multiple-number guys who wore it along with several others during their Yankees days. Pitcher **Mel Queen** was the first to wear No. 36, followed in succession by obscure names such as **Bill Drescher, Al Lyons, Jake Wade, Jack Phillips, Dick Starr**, and **Jack Madison**. No Monument Park candidates in this group.

Then, in August 1949, along came big **Johnny Mize**. A 6'2", 215-pound first sacker, Mize was 36 years old when he joined the Yanks and had been playing since 1936, when he was a rookie with the St. Louis Cardinals. He was traded to the Giants in 1942, then lost three seasons to the war only to return with a bang in 1946. Anyone who looked at his stats back then knew that the Yankees were getting a possible future Hall of Famer, and a guy who was still dangerous with a bat in his hands.

As a rookie, Mize hit 329 with 19 homers and 93 RBIs. Over the next three seasons, he sported batting averages of .364, 337, and a league best .349 in 1939. Though he's been described as slow and lumbering, he actually led the NL in triples with 16 in 1938. In 1940, he was both the home run (43) and RBI (137) leader. With the Giants after the war he continued his great slugging. In 1947, he tied with Ralph Kiner for the home run lead with 51 and drove home a league-best 138 runs, and a year later he and Kiner deadlocked again with 40 homers and big John drove home 125. Then came his trade to the Yanks.

Aging and a bit heavier, Mize could still play a solid first. He couldn't be intimidated and despite his slugging totals, rarely struck out. There was no denying his all-around talent.

The Yanks got Mize as they were about to embark on a run of five straight pennants and World Series titles. Mize was there long enough to play just 13 games during the regular season in '49. The next year he was in 90 games, hitting .277 with 25 homers and 72 RBIs. After that he began showing his age, but still collected timely hits. In the 1952

World Series, he slammed three home runs, drove home six, drew three walks, and hit an even .400. He retired after the 1953 season with a .312 career average and 359 home runs. In addition, Mize fanned just 524 times in 1,884 trips to the plate. He was elected to the Hall of Fame in 1981.

The Yanks tried to duplicate the success they had with Mize by trading for another veteran first sacker. Thirty-four year old **Eddie Robinson** came over in a 10-player deal with the Philadelphia A's. He was given Mize's No. 36 and the same part-time role, but didn't have quite the same impact. He had just three homers in 85 games in 1954, then showed some pop with 16 dingers in 88 games the following year, but his batting average plummeted to .208. By June 1956, he was traded back to the A's, who were now in Kansas City.

Outfielder Norm Siebern wore No. 36 in his first season of 1956, but switched to No. 25 his last two New York years before he was traded. Then came yet another veteran, **Harry "Suitcase" Simpson**, who arrived in June 1957. Simpson was coming off a 1956 season that saw him hit .293 with 21 homers and 105 RBIs, but he wouldn't get a chance to play regularly in New York. He hit .250 in 75 games the second half of 1957, adding seven homers and 39 RBIs, a solid contribution. But the next year he was dealt back to KC in yet another June trade.

Infielder **Hal Lanier** finished his career with the Yanks, wearing No. 36 in 1972 and No. 22 the following year. In mid-1973, the Yanks made a deal with the Braves, bringing righthander **Pat Dobson** to the Bronx. Dobson, a curveballer, was one of four Baltimore pitchers to win 20 or more games in 1971. A year later, he was then dealt to the Braves and in turn traded to the Yanks. Dobson went 9–8 the remainder of the '73 season, then had a big year in '74, going 19–15 in 39 games as the team finished second. But when he fell back to 11–14 in 1975, the Yanks cut bait and traded him to the Indians for Oscar Gamble.

When the Yankees traded with the Pirates in December 1975, the object of their affection was supposedly young second sacker Willie Randolph, who turned out to be a star for well over a decade. But also coming to the Bronx with him was a righthanded pitcher named **Dock Phillip Ellis**. Yep, Dock was his given name and he was colorful, controversial, talented, and ultimately close to unmanageable. Ellis took over No. 36 and, like so many controversial players, showed both his talent and his torment in just a little over a year.

He was a guy good enough to go 19-9 with the Pirates in 1971, and throw a no-hitter and later say he did it while under the influence of LSD. Those were the two sides of Dock, and he never changed. He once hit the first three Cincinnati batters, then threw behind the next two before he was removed from the game.

Though his teammates liked him, management had just about enough. After an 8–9 season in 1975, he was shipped to the Yankees. As the New Yorkers headed to their first pennant since 1964, Dock Ellis became a mainstay. He finished the year at 17–8 with a 3.19 ERA, won a game in the ALCS and lost one in the World Series sweep by the Reds. After the season, he was named Comeback Player of the Year, and No. 36 seemed to have found a home. That home lasted only three games into the 1977 season. Dock was 1–1 with a 1.83 earned run average when he was sent to Oakland on April 27, with two others, as the Yanks acquired righthander Mike Torrez.

Why the Yanks dealt him so quickly was never completely clear. They probably knew about his penchant for self-destruction. Ellis would pitch only two more seasons before retiring. After his retirement he finally sought help for his drug and alcohol problems, eventually becoming a counselor and helping others. The Yankees hired him in the 1980s to speak about substance abuse to minor leaguers. Unfortunately, the effects of his old lifestyle

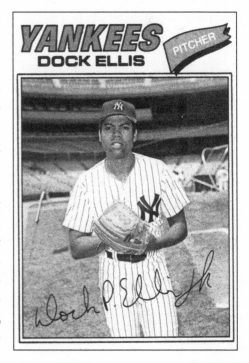

caught up with him. Dock was diagnosed with cirrhosis of the liver in 2007 and died on December 19, 2008, while awaiting a possible liver transplant.

The mixture of young and old continued. When Ellis left in 1977, righty **Stan Thomas** had No. 36, for all of three games. Veteran **Paul Lindblad**, who would pitch for 14 seasons, was a Yankee for seven games in 1978, his final season. The Yanks signed free agent reliever **Rawly Eastwick** before the 1978 season, the same year they got Goose Gossage. Eastwick, a righthander, had been a rookie sensation with the Cincinnati Reds in 1975 and the Fireman of the Year in 1976. But instead of getting another star, the Yanks got a reliever who had lost the magic. After just eight games and a 2–1 record, Eastwick was traded on June 14 to the Phils for outfielders Bobby Brown and Jay Johnstone.

Lefty **Paul Mirabella** pitched for the Yanks in 1979, his second season in the bigs, and lasted 10 games before moving on. **Jim Kaat**'s Yankee career may have spanned just 44 games, but his career covered a quarter century, from 1959 to 1983. A 6'4", 217-pound southpaw, Kaat

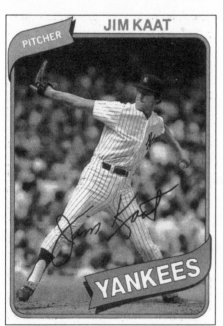

pitched for five teams and won 283 games. Purchased from the Phils in May of '79, Kaat pitched in 40 games for the Yanks wearing his favorite No. 36 and did a nice job. It was the first time in his career he relieved more than started and it paved the way for him to pitch through 1983, when he was 44 years old. He threw just four games in 1980 wearing No. 36 before being sold to the Cards on April 30. After retiring, Kaat was the pitching coach of the Reds and then became a highly respected broadcaster.

Kaat's departure paved the way for another veteran star. Righthander **Gaylord Perry** was traded to the Yanks on August 14, 1980. Perry was 41 years old at the time and had been pitching since 1962. He was also a five-time 20-game winner, twice for the Giants and Indians and once with the Padres.

DID HE OR DIDN'T HE?

Despite his great talent and winning ways, Gaylord Perry was constantly embroiled in a did-he-or-didn't-he drama. For most of his career, he was suspected of throwing the illegal spitball, and he reveled in the accusations because it felt it gave him an edge. Perry would fidget incessantly on the mound, going to his brow, his cap, the back of his head, making the batter wonder if he was loading up. But he was never caught. Just for the record, the spitball was outlawed in 1920, and the only pitchers allowed to keep throwing it were those who used it as the major part of their repertoire. Burleigh Grimes, who pitched for the Yanks, was the last of the legal spitballers. But without a doubt the pitch has since been used by many, including Perry. Sometimes it's just as effective to make the batter think you're throwing it. How much Perry actually did load up we'll never know.

With the Yanks he only threw 10 games in the last month and a half of 1980, going 4–4 with a 4.44 ERA, eight of his games starts. After the season, he was granted free agency and moved on. He would retire after the 1983 season with a career mark of 314–265, an earned run average of 3.11, and 3,534 strikeouts. He is the only pitcher to win the Cy Young Award in both leagues and was elected to the Hall of Fame in 1991.

Steve "Bye Bye" Balboni, the big first baseman, wore No. 36 during the 1982 season, but also wore Nos. 66, 28, 50, and 45 in his part time appearances over five seasons. He appears first in Chapter 28. Then came another group of pitchers starting with **Mike Armstrong**, a righthander who wore No. 36 from 1984–86 and was used the most in '84 (36 games). He pitched just 16 times the final two seasons and was released. Lefty **Al Holland** wore No. 36 in 1986 when he pitched in 25 games, but switched to No. 29 in 1987, pitched three more times, and was gone. **Brad Arnsberg** went from No. 62 in 1986 to No. 36 the next year, but pitched just eight times in two seasons and was off to Texas. Outfielder **Jeff Moronko** broke the pitching hold on No. 36 when he wore it for seven games in 1997, but his .091 batting average was his ticket out of town.

Righty **Richard Dotson** had gone 22–7 for the White Sox in 1983 and came to the Yanks five years later in a trade for outfielder Dan Pasqua. Dotson pitched in 32 games in 1988 and had a 12–9 record with a 5.00 ERA. But the next year his ERA went even higher, and after a record of just 2–5 in 11 games, he was released. The team had high hopes for pitcher Mike Witt, who wore No. 22 in his first year with the Yanks (1990) and that's where he's detailed. He also wore No. 36 in '91 and No. 39 the next year before he retired. Outfielder **Mike Humphreys** lasted parts of three seasons (1991–93), wearing Nos. 36, 31, and 29. His numbers went down and so did his stock with the Yankees. Righty **Shawn Hillegas** lasted from April 9 to August 22 of 1992. He wore No. 36 and left it with a 1–8 record in 21 games.

Into the 1990s, the Yanks started building toward their next dynasty but that didn't stop the parade of marginal players amid the stars. Righty **Russ Springer** threw 14 games his rookie year of 1992. That December he was ticketed to the Angels in the trade that brought Jim Abbott to the Bronx. Reserve outfielder **Gerald Williams** was with the Yanks for parts of six seasons. He wore No. 36 his first year of 1993. But since he wore No. 29 for three years (1994–94), he's detailed in that chapter. David Cone then took over and wore No. 36 from 1995 to 2000, covering the dynasty years and bringing the number into the new century.

The first player to wear No. 36 after Cone left was catcher **Bobby Estalella**, who lasted all of three games in 2001. First baseman **Nick Johnson** got his first look in 2001 wearing No. 60. He hit just .194, but the Yanks switched him to No. 36 the next year and turned him loose to play in 129 games. He hit .243, but whacked 15 homers and drove home 58. The next season he was up to .284 in 96 games with 14 homers, but by then the Yanks had Jason Giambi ensconced at first and Johnson became expendable. He was sent to Montreal. Though injury prone, Johnson has proved a professional hitter and good player with a high on-base percentage, so good that the Yanks signed him to be their designated hitter in 2010.

Tom Gordon was another veteran who did No. 36 proud for several pinstriped years. "Flash" came to the team as a free agent in December 2003, was 36 years old, and had been pitching in the bigs since 1988 as both a starter and reliever. He had a 17–9 record for the Royals back in 1989 both starting and coming out of the pen. The Red Sox made him a closer for the first time in 1998 and he responded by saving a league best 46 games. When the Yanks needed an eighth-inning guy, a solid bridge to closer Mariano Rivera, they signed Gordon.

Still able to throw hard and with a disarming curveball, Flash made 80 appearances in 2004, going 9–4 with a 2.21 ERA and four saves when Mo wasn't available. A year later he was almost as good, appearing in 79 games with a 5–4 record, a 2.57 ERA, and a couple more saves. Not sure how long he could handle a big workload, the Yanks let him become a free agent and he signed with Philly. Flash pitched into 2009 when injuries shelved him once more. Whether he'll try to come back again at the age of 42 is doubtful, but his 21-year career has produced a 138–126 record to go along with 158 saves.

Submarine-throwing lefty **Mike Myers** wore No. 36 in both 2006 and 2007. Perhaps the quintessential situational lefty, Myers was often used to get a single lefthanded batter. He appeared in 62 games for the Bombers in 2006, yet pitched just 30 1/3 innings. After using him in 55 games in 2007, the Yankees released him in August.

Pitcher **Jim Brower** wore No. 36 for three games in 2007 after Myers left but was himself released on August 31. Pitching prospect **Ian Kennedy** took No. 36 when he was called up at the end of the season and pitched well. Then he switched to No. 31 the following year, and that's where he's discussed. And reliever **Edwar Ramirez** also wore the number for a time in both 2008 and 2009. But because Ramirez wore No. 31 when he first arrived in 2007, he is also discussed in that chapter.

No. 36 does have an interesting Yankee history. A couple of future Hall of Famers wore it, albeit not for long, and then there was David Cone's perfect game. You can't get any better than that.

#37: THE OLD PERFESSOR

If it wasn't for **Gus Niarhos** and manager Bucky Harris, the No. 37 would have been worn by only a single New York Yankee, and he wasn't even a player. That's because **Casey Stengel** took the number when he became the team's manager in 1949, wore it until he was fired in 1960, and then saw it retired 10 years later in honor of his leading the Bombers to 10 American League pennants and seven World Series triumphs. Who, then, is Gus Niarhos?

Niarhos was a 25-year-old catcher when he joined the Yanks in 1946 and became the first player ever to wear No. 37. Gus was six feet tall and weighed only 160 pounds, making him an unusual candidate to catch. Most backstops in those days tended to be on the short and stocky side. But Gus could hack it defensively and played 37 games that year, hitting just .225 with no home runs and only two runs batted in. He was often used as a late-inning defensive replacement and had just 40 at bats. He lasted until 1950, when he played just a single game before being waived to the White Sox.

By that time Casey Stengel was the manager and had appropriated No. 37, a number that would become closely associated with him in New York. After his tenure with the Yanks ended, he would wear it again as the first manager of the expansion New York Mets from 1962 until he fell and broke a hip during the 1965 season. As a manager in New York he often entertained the fans and media with his own special use of language dubbed *Stengelese*. He was funny and longwinded, and sometimes you had to listen hard to understand him. But as far as baseball was concerned, Stengel was crazy like a fox.

A baseball lifer, Ol' Case had been a big leaguer from 1912–1925, an outfielder who hit .284 for his career and couldn't learn enough about the game. He played for Brooklyn, the Giants, Pittsburgh, Boston, and Philadelphia, all in the National League. He especially loved playing under John McGraw with the Giants in the early twenties because he could learn a ton of baseball, both strategy and the handling of players from the fiery and successful Giants manager.

His first managerial job came with the Dodgers from 1934–36. He was just 208–251 with Brooklyn before being canned. Then the Braves came calling and he skippered them from 1938 to 1943 with even less luck, his teams going just 373–491. After that it was back to the minors until 1949 when the baseball world did a double-take. Why would the mighty New York Yankees call upon Stengel, who had done nothing but lose at other managerial stops?

CASEY STENGEL
MANAGER • NEW YORK

As it turned out, Casey was simply a good manager in search of a team, and the Yankees provided just that. He was the first manager to platoon players extensively. While competitors like Hank Bauer and Gene Woodling hated it, many of Casey's left-right switches worked to perfection. He also reshaped the team in the early fifties to revolve around a trio of superstars—Mickey Mantle, Yogi Berra, and Whitey Ford—using talented role players to man many of the other positions. But Casey wasn't averse to using any of the Big Four starters—Ford, Vic Raschi, Allie Reynolds, and Eddie Lopat—in relief if the situation called for it.

His Yankees won five straight championships from 1949–53, and two more in 1956 and 1958. They lost in the Series in 1955, '57, and '60. It was that 1960 defeat to the Pirates that was especially tough to take. And that's when management decided to make a change, the implication that Casey was now too old to handle the team.

"I'll never make the mistake of being seventy again," the Old Perfessor quipped.

After the Yanks canned him, Casey wasn't out of baseball for long. In 1962, the New York Mets were born, replacing the departed Giants and Dodgers, and the 72-year-old Stengel was chosen as their first manager. The most inept Mets team of all would lose 120 games that year, and Case was heard to quip, "Can't anybody here play this game?"

But he lasted until 1965, when he fell and broke a hip. Yet it's often said that Stengel, not any of the players, was the team's first superstar, and he brought his own brand of color to the nascent organization. The Yankees retired Casey's No. 37 in 1970, four years after he was elected to the Baseball Hall of Fame. The Mets would also retire his No. 37, further immortalizing it in New York. Once asked to sum up his career, Casey Stengel replied in the true spirit of Stengelese.

"There comes a time in every man's life and I've had plenty of them."

TOP MANAGERS

Casey Stengel became a legend managing the Yankees from 1949–60, following another legend, Joe McCarthy (who never wore a number). But both were eventually eclipsed in total wins by Joe Torre. Here are the five top Yankees managers and their records.

Joe Torre 1,173–767

Casey Stengel 1,149–696

Joe McCarthy 1,460–867

Miller Huggins 1,067–719

Ralph Houk 944–806

#38: A NUMBER IN SEARCH OF A STAR

In the early days of the game the higher numbers weren't used that often. Witness that no Yankee wore No. 37 until Gus Niarhos in 1946. There were enough numbers to give the minor leaguers and marginal players who often came and went during the course of a season. Number 38 was similar in that it wasn't worn until 1942. But unlike its predecessor, no single player came along right after that to immortalize it and send it onto the wall at Monument Park. In fact, while there were a number of players who wore No. 38 for multiple seasons, not one single high-profile superstar has even been issued it as a Yankee. So, in that sense, No. 38 is still a number very much in search of a star. Let's look at those who aspired, but never quite made it.

In addition to not having a glut of big names, No. 38 was also worn by a large number of players who switched to other numbers during their Yankees tenures. Pitcher **Hank Borowy** was the first to wear the number in 1942, but switched to No. 15 the next three years. Another pitcher, **Mel Queen**, wore it for part of 1946, but then switched to No. 17, which he continued to wear in 1947. He also wore No. 36 in 1942 and No. 16 in 1944. The one and only **Yogi Berra** even had a turn as No. 38 his rookie year of 1946 before moving to No. 35 the next year, and then his now retired No. 8. So the number was off to a real transient start.

That tradition, if you could call it one, continued with pitchers **Frank Hiller** and **Karl Drews**, and catcher **Gus Niarhos,** until first baseman **Johnny Hopp** stabilized it to a small degree. Righty Hiller wore it in 1946 for three games, then returned as No. 39 in 1948 and '49 before being sold to the Cubs. Drews had four numbers in three years. Niarhos wore No. 38 from 1948 to 1950, when he left. Hopp, however, a backup first sacker from 1950–52, kept No. 38 from the time he was purchased from the Pirates on September 5, 1950, right up until his release on May 26, 1952.

It was a little different story in the 1950s and into the '60s. A couple of players stayed with the number, but they weren't exactly front liners. Third sacker **Loren Babe** wore No. 38 for 12 games in 1952 and another five a year later. Lefty reliever **Art Shallock** wore No. 38 from 1953–55, but also wore No. 20 in 1951 and '52. It took a third-string catcher with some pop in his bat to put the number on and not take it off for awhile.

Johnny Blanchard got a one-game cup of coffee in 1955, wearing No. 38. He wouldn't return to the big club for four years, but when he resurfaced in 1959 he was sporting the same number and would wear it until he was traded in May 1965. Blanchard was a lefty swinger and the Yanks always liked guys who could reach that short right field porch. But he was also a poor defensive catcher and stuck behind both Yogi and Elston Howard. His best year was 1961, when the Yanks clubbed a then record 240 home runs. Blanchard's contribution was a .305 batting average, 21 homers, and 54 RBIs in a limited role. He would play the same role through early 1965 with varying degrees of success. He was then traded to Kansas City and later to Milwaukee that year before retiring.

Then the same pattern emerged. Catcher **Doc Edwards** caught 45 games in 1965 but hit below the Mendoza Line at .190. Young **Frank Fernandez** also tried to fill that role from 1967–69, wearing No. 38 the first two years and No. 10 the third. He, too struggled to get past the .200 mark. It was the same story with second sacker **Len Boehmer,** 45 games in 1969 as No. 38 and three games the following year as No. 25. Then in 1970, 22-year-old righthander **Steve Kline** switched from No. 42 to No. 38, and he would wear it through early April 1974.

Kline was a control pitcher, but one with good stuff who seemed to be a coming star when he went 16-9 with a 2.40 ERA, 15 complete games, and four shutouts in 1972. But early the next season came the pitcher's bane, an arm injury. Kline was never the same. He was 4–7 that year and just 2–2 early the next season before he was traded to Cleveland.

Hall of Famer George Brett's big brother, southpaw **Ken Brett**, pitched just two games for the Yanks in 1976, then was shipped to the White Sox in May for outfielder **Carlos May**. May tried, but couldn't sustain. He took over No. 38 and hit .278 with three homers and 40 RBIs in 87 games in 1976. When he didn't hit in a part-time role the next year, his contract was sold to the Angels in September.

Catcher **Jerry Narron** continued the tradition of poor hitting backstops when he batted an anemic .171 his rookie year of 1979 before a November trade to Seattle. Another disappointment was pitcher **Tom Underwood**, who came in the trade that brought catcher Rick Cerone from Toronto and sent first sacker Chris Chambliss north of the border. Underwood was one of those guys with a world of potential and also a world of inconsistency. As No. 38 in 1980, he was 13–9 with a 3.66 ERA. But a 1–4 start and 4.41 ERA in '81 prompted a trade to Oakland.

Outfielder **Dave Stegman** and infielder **Barry Evans** both wore No. 38 the same year, 1982, and were gone almost as soon as they arrived. Lefthander **Dave LaRoche** wore No. 38 in 1983, his last year with the Yanks after throwing his LaLob pitch as No. 34 his first two seasons (1981–82). Pitcher **Jose Rijo** was a hard-throwing righty who went just 2–8 with a 4.76 ERA in 24 games his rookie year of 1984. After the season, he was dealt to Oakland in the trade that brought Rickey Henderson to the Yanks. Rijo won 78 games for Cincinnati between 1988–93 and looked like a coming star until arm problems derailed him.

Then came the curious case of **Ed Whitson**, one of the first examples of a guy they said just couldn't pitch in New York. Whitson was a righty with sometimes electric stuff. After he went 14–8 with a 3.24 ERA for the Padres in 1984, the Yanks signed him as a free agent, gave him good old No. 38, and sent him out to the mound. It proved a lonely place. Whitson wasn't horrible in 1985, but he wasn't real good, either. His 10–8 record and 4.88 ERA brought out the boo birds, especially every time he left the mound in the middle of an inning. The next year it got worse. His record in 14 games was 5–2, but his 7.54 earned run average told another story, and the boos seemingly never stopped. On July 9, the Yanks cut bait, sending him back to San Diego for reliever Tim Stoddard.

More deals that didn't work followed, as No. 38 seemed to be given to all the test cases who had the odds stacked against them. Infielder **Leo Hernandez** came over from Baltimore, played seven games, and was released. Lefty **Pat Clements** came from Pittsburgh and went 3–3 out of the pen in 55 games during 1987. A year later, the Yanks sent him to San Diego. Righthander **Clay Parker** came from Seattle in December 1987, spent a year in the minors, then got into 22 games

EDDIE WHITSON

in '89, going 4–5 with a 3.68 ERA. A year later, he followed the same pattern as Clements and was traded to the Tigers for catcher **Matt Nokes**.

Nokes was a below-average receiver, but he had some pop in a lefthanded bat. In 1987, he hit .289 for the Tigers with 32 homers and 87 RBIs and the Yanks envisioned those numbers at the Stadium. But in the second half of 1990, he hit just .238 with eight homers. The next year he was the regular catcher and, in 135 games, hit .268 with 24 homers and 77 RBIs. But he never reached that level again. He batted just .224 in '92 and a year later he found the seats on just 10 occasions. He played sparingly in 1994, and at the end of the season was granted free agency. Another No. 38 passed into history.

More quickies. **Josias Manzanillo**, **Jeff Patterson**, **Matt Howard**, and **Scott Pose** all wore No. 38 briefly between 1995 and '97, at the time when the Yankees were once again becoming a dynasty. None stayed very long. Utility infielder **Homer Bush** lasted parts of 1997 and 1998, then reappeared for a brief time in 2004. He wore No. 37 in '97, then Nos. 22 and 18 the other two years and has been mentioned previously. Outfielder **Ricky Ledee** wore No. 38 in 1998, but switched to No. 17 the next two years and is discussed in Chapter 17.

Jason Grimsley was a pitcher of some talent, but wound up a player smack in the middle of the steroid era controversy. He signed with the Yanks as a free agent before the 1999 season and would wear No. 38 for two pretty good years. He was 7–2 with a 3.60 ERA and a save the first year, then 3–2 in 63 games with a 5.04 ERA in 2000. But the Yanks apparently saw a regression and released him in November. It later came to light that Grimsley had failed a drug test in 2003, and he later admitted he began using performance enhancing drugs when he was sent to the minors in 1998 and feared he wouldn't make it back.

Pitcher **Jake Westbrook**'s Yankee career lasted all of three games in 2000. The Yanks knew the righty had talent, but used him as a chip to get slugger David Justice from Cleveland in June. Lefty sidearmer **Randy Choate** was the next to wear No. 38, the reliever taking it on in 2001 after wearing No. 58 the season before. Choate showed some effectiveness out of the pen and the Yanks used him 37 times in 2001, but the next two years he was hit harder, and in December of 2003 he became part of the deal with Montreal that brought Javier Vazquez to the Bronx.

Next is the case of the All-American quarterback who preferred baseball and lost two careers in the process. **Drew Henson** was a star at Michigan, the guy who beat out Tom Brady—yes, *the* Tom Brady—for the Wolverines' QB job his junior year and was projected as a Heisman Trophy candidate the next season. Instead, he signed with the Yankees in July 1998. He didn't develop in the minors and the Yanks dealt him to Cincinnati in July 2000, then got him back in a swap the following March. A third baseman, Henson got two cups of coffee, a three-game shot in 2002 as No. 57, and a five-game trial a year later as No. 38. It didn't work. He finally gave up baseball and returned to football, bouncing around the NFL, notably with Dallas and Detroit, but he was ultimately released.

Pitcher **Bret Prinz**, first baseman/outfielder **Travis Lee**, and pitchers **Buddy Groom** and **Kris Wilson** all had brief trials with the Yankees without much success. What they all had in common was No. 38. **Ramiro Mendoza** was a valuable relief pitcher from 1996–2002 before arm trouble reared its ugly head. He returned for one game in 2005, at which time he wore No. 38. But he spent 1997–2002 as No. 55, and will be discussed in that chapter. No. 38 continued to be worn by marginal players. Pitchers **T. J. Beam**, **Chase Wright**, and **Dan Giese** followed each other as No. 38 from 2006 to 2008. None showed enough to remain in pinstripes but at least they can tell their grandchildren they once pitched in Yankee Stadium.

Catcher **Chris Stewart** was a one-game wonder in 2008, having signed as a free agent and spent most of the year in the minors before being let go. The last player to wear No. 38 was reliever **Brian Bruney** in 2009. But Bruney tried to change his luck by switching to No. 99 before the year was out, and had spent his first couple of seasons as No. 33, the chapter in which he's discussed. So No. 38 is still on a mission to find that special player. But then again, as you get into the higher numbers, the special players who take them seem to thin out. As we'll see, however, there are always exceptions to the rule.

LONGTIME YANKEES

Most of the players in their middle chapters weren't with the Yanks for long. There are a few exceptions, but numbers from the upper 20s to low 40s mostly feature players who come and go quickly, sometimes several players a year wearing the same number. Not so with the players listed below. These are the top 10 Yankees in games played, with Mickey Mantle heading the list but Derek Jeter gaining rapidly. Jeter should be the top guy once his career ends. Here's how the list stands as of 2009.

Mickey Mantle.............................2,401

Lou Gehrig	2,164
Derek Jeter	2,138
Yogi Berra	2,116
Babe Ruth	2,084
Bernie Williams	2,076
Roy White	1,881
Bill Dickey	1,789
Don Mattingly	1,785
Joe DiMaggio	1,736

#39: THE STRAW MAN: WHAT COULD HAVE BEEN

ALL TIME NO. 39 ROSTER

Player	Year
Rollie Hemsley	1942
Mike Chartak	1942
Tommy Byrne	1946
Frank Hiller	1948–49
Wally Hood Jr.	1949
Harry Schaeffer	1952
Bob Wiesler	1954–55
Ted Gray	1955
George Wilson	1956
Darrell Johnson	1957
Jim Coates	1959–1962
Steve Hamilton	1963–70
Gary Jones	1970–71
Rob Gardner	1971
Casey Cox	1972
Wayne Granger	1973
Jim Magnuson	1973
Larry Gura	1974–75
Gene Michael (coach)	1976
Mickey Klutts	1977
Ron Davis	1979–1981
Mike Morgan	1982
Larry Milbourne	1983
Otis Nixon	1983
Don Cooper	1985
Joe Niekro	1986–87
Bobby Murcer (coach)	1987
Roberto Kelly	1987–92
Mike Witt	1993
Donn Pall	1994
Dion James	1995–96
Darryl Strawberry	1996–99
Roberto Kelly	2000
Mark Wohlers	2001
Ron Coomer	2002
Chris Hammond	2003
Andy Phillips	2004
Melky Cabrera	2005
Shawn Chacon	2005–06
Craig Wilson	2006
Chris Britton	2007–08
Ross Ohlendorf	2008
Richie Sexson	2008
Anthony Claggett	2009
Mark Melancon	2009

In some ways, **Darryl Strawberry** is one of baseball's tragic figures, though he's never asked for sympathy and has always accepted responsibility for the mistakes he's made. He came to the Mets in 1983 with a rather unfair label. They were calling him "the black Ted Williams." Imagine being a 21-year-old kid and who's already compared with one of the greatest hitters the game has ever known. But for a while, "the Straw Man" looked as if he might land somewhere in the vicinity of the hype. Then came the drugs and alcohol, and ultimately a career torpedoed. By the time he came to the Yanks he was 33 years old, but the ball still jumped off his bat and the fans still loved him. Just when it looked as if he was all the way back, he had to battle yet another adversary, one that wasn't of his making. Yet even today, a decade after his retirement, Yankee fans remember and cheer for Darryl Strawberry, No. 39.

The Straw Man came up a Met and, if circumstances had been different, might have been a Met for life. His natural talent level may have merited it. But like teammate Doc Gooden, Straw reached a level and just couldn't sustain it. As a 21-year-old rookie in 1983, he slammed 26 homers and drove in 74 runs and was named National League Rookie of the Year. At 6'6", 200 pounds, he was tall and wiry, and very strong. Batting from the left side with a high kick and long swing, the ball jumped off his bat and traveled long distances.

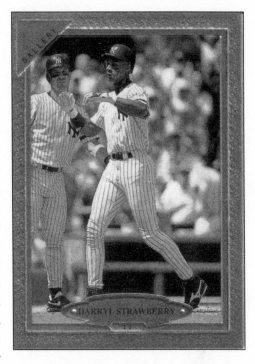

By 1986 the Mets had become World Champions, with Straw contributing 27 homers and 93 RBIs. Over the next few years, the Mets remained one of baseball's best and Strawberry was becoming one of the league's top sluggers. He hit 39 homers the next two seasons and then in 1990 hit 37 more to go with a .277 average and 108 RBIs. But by then the Mets must have known something. The Straw Man was a free agent and the Mets let him sign with the Dodgers, allowing him to return to his home town of Los Angeles. In 1991 with the Dodgers, Straw hit .265 with 28 homers and 99 RBIs. Not bad, but not near what had been expected of him. He was 29 years old and played in 139 games that year. He never reached the 100-game mark again, except in 1998 with the Yanks, his second to last year in the majors. The combination of injuries and personal problems were now on the way to derailing a potentially great career.

After two more years with the Dodgers, he was released on May 26, 1994, without playing a game. The rival Giants signed him, but he played just a handful of games that year and after the season was released. By then Straw had failed a drug test for cocaine and was suspended. He wouldn't be able to play until late in the 1995 season. In anticipation of his return, the Yankees signed him on June 19. He joined the team to play in 32 games at the end of the season, hitting .276 with just three homers and 13 RBIs. That year he wore No. 26. A free agent again, he wasn't signed and went to play for the St. Paul Saints in the independent Northern League. On June 2, the old Darryl emerged and he belted a tape measure homer measured at 522 feet. A month later, on July 4, the Yankees signed him for a second time, this time giving him No. 39, which he would wear for the remainder of his Yankees career.

By then it was apparent he would never be the same player. His value now was strictly as a part-timer and designated hitter. But he played in 63 games for the Yanks in '96 and hit 11 home runs, driving in 36 runs with a .262 batting average. He more than earned his keep in the ALCS against Baltimore that year, hitting three homers, driving in five runs, and batting .417. And he got to play in yet another World Series. Injuries relegated him to just 11 games in 1997, but a year later, as the Yankees rolled to 114 regular season wins, Darryl Strawberry once again became one of the toasts of New York.

He played in 101 games that year, the ball jumping off his bat as it did in his heyday with the Mets. Though he batted just .247, he hit 24 home runs and drove home 57 runs in just 295 at bats. He also walked 46 times and was a big part of the Yankees' great season. But toward the end he wasn't feeling well and was losing weight. On October 1, before the playoffs began, it was learned that Darryl had been stricken with colon cancer. He had surgery to remove a tumor and 24 inches of his colon. After that he had to undergo debilitating chemotherapy. The Yanks won another World Series, and the next year the Straw Man was well enough to play in 24 games, hitting .327 with three homers and six RBIs. His final hurrah came in the division and league championship series as he homered in each and got one final hit in the World Series.

By then Straw was 37 years old, and the combination of injuries, alcohol, drugs, and finally, cancer had taken its toll. He retired with a .259 average, 335 home runs, and an even 1,000 RBIs. But oh what could have been. And it wasn't over yet. His retirement was filled with more problems, charges over delinquent child support, more drug arrests and rehabs, divorce, and a recurrence of cancer necessitating a second surgery in July of 2000.

Yet Darryl Strawberry has prevailed. He remarried, and with his wife, Terry, has founded the Darryl Strawberry Foundation dedicated to children with autism. And the fans in New York have never forgotten him. Both the Mets and Yankees view him as one of their own. He's also the only player to have spent his entire career with only the two present and two former New York teams (Mets, Dodgers, Giants, and Yankees). Despite all of his problems, the memories of the ball jumping off his bat as it only does with those special few are still fresh in the minds of all who saw him.

Let's see who else wore No. 39. It began with veteran catcher **Rollie Hemsley**, who came to the Yanks in July 1942 at the age of 35. Hemsley stayed three years, but only wore No. 39 the first year. He then switched to No. 27 for his final two Yankees seasons. Outfielder **Mike Chartek**, called Shotgun, didn't have much time for the fans to learn his nickname. He played 11 games as No. 30 in 1940 and five more two years later when he wore No. 39. Lefthander **Tommy Byrne** was a more recognizable figure but also a multi-numbered player who started with No. 11 in 1943, and wore both Nos. 39 and 28 in 1946, after the war, but is best remembered as No. 23, which he wore in his second stint in pinstripes and in his best season of 1955. Righty **Frank Hiller** wore No. 38 in 1946, then switched to No. 39 the next two seasons before leaving.

Righthander **Wally Hood Jr.** wore No. 39 for just two games in 1949. Lefty **Harry Schaeffer** went Hood three games better. He lasted five games in 1952. Southpaw **Bob Wiesler** had three cups of coffee, four games as No. 53 in 1951, six in 1954, and 16 more in '55 when he wore No. 39. Then it was off to Washington. Pitcher **Ted Gray** was a veteran who would spend nine seasons in the bigs. His Yankee tenure? One game in 1955 in which he wore No. 39. A year later, outfielder/first baseman **George Wilson** lasted for all of 11 games and endeared himself with a .167 average.

Darrell Johnson was part of a long tradition of catchers who could handle the glove, but not the bat. He was a Yankee for a total of 26 games in 1957 and '58 wearing No. 39, then No. 22. In six big league seasons, he hit just .234. Pitcher **Jim Coates** came up for two games in 1956 wearing No. 52. When he returned for good in 1959, he became the first player to make No. 39 somewhat memorable. Coates had talent and a nice three-year run during the late 1950s and early 1960s. At 6'4", 192 pounds, the tall righthander looked almost skeletal and was nicknamed "The Mummy" because of "a funereal visage on the mound."

In 1959, Coates pitched mainly out of the pen and went 6–1 with a 2.87 earned run average. A year later, he was in 35 games with 18 starts, and finished at 13–3 with a 4.28 ERA. And in '61, the year of the M & M Boys and the 240 team homers, he was 11–5 in 43 games, with a 3.44 ERA and five saves. When his performance lagged in 1962, the Yanks decided to make a trade. In April 1963, they dealt him to Washington for lefty reliever **Steve Hamilton**.

The guy he was traded for was even taller. Steve Hamilton stood 6'7" and weighed just 195 pounds. He took over No. 39 in 1963 and would wear it through 1970. Hamilton was fun to watch. He had a nasty slider which he threw with a three-quarter sidearm motion and it simply froze lefthanded hitters. He also developed a blooper pitch, delivered with a hesitation step—he called it the "Folly Floater." For the Yanks, he was a very successful reliever, even when the team started to crash after the 1964 season.

In the last two pennant years of 1963 and '64, Hamilton was a combined 12–3 with eight saves. By 1968, with the team struggling, Hamilton became the closer and registered a 2.13 earned run average with 11 saves in 40 games. He was 34 years old in 1970, still good enough to appear in 35 games with a 2.78 ERA, but that September he was waived to the White Sox.

After Coates and Hamilton monopolized No. 39 for an even dozen years, the lesser names began appearing once more. Lefty **Gary Jones** had the number for two games in 1970 and 12 more in '71. Lefty **Rob Gardner** came to the Yanks from Cleveland in June of '69 but didn't pitch for the big club until 1970, when he wore No. 43, and that was for just a single game. He switched to No. 39 the next two years, went back to No. 43 in '73, and was traded to Oakland.

Righty **Casey Cox** came to the Yanks in late August 1972, wearing No. 39 for five games. He started the next year as No. 29, pitched in a single game, and was released. Veteran reliever **Wayne Granger** arrived in an August 1973 trade with the Cards. The righthander had a big run with Cincinnati from 1968–71, pitching in 90, 67, and 70 games with 73 saves. That could have worn him out. With the Yanks he lasted seven games, went 0–1, but with an impressive 1.76 ERA. But after looking at him in the spring, the Yanks released him released him. Lefty **Jim Magnuson** presented no such problem. It was eight games and out in 1973.

Southpaw **Larry Gura** was one guy the Yanks may have been wrong about. He started as a reliever with the Cubs, went to Texas briefly, and the Rangers shipped him to the Yanks in May 1974. The crafty Gura was 5–1 in eight starts with a 2.41 in '74. The next year, he went 7–8 in 26 games, 20 of them starts. The following May, the Yanks sent him to Kansas City for catcher Fran Healy. Gura proved a late bloomer, winning 18 games twice for those good Royals teams of the early '80s, and he went 16–4 another year.

Utility infielder **Mickey Klutts** played all of eight games in three years (1976–78) and wore three different numbers (20, 39, 24) before being traded. Bespectacled reliever **Ron Davis** had a cup of coffee in 1978, wearing No. 53 for four games. The next year he began an effective three-year run as No. 39 and as a set-up man for closer Goose Gossage. A 6'4" fastballer, Davis pitched in 44 games in 1979, impressing with a 14–2 record, 2.85 earned run average, and nine saves. He was 9–3 the next year in 53 games and then 4–5 with a 2.71 ERA in '81.

Davis wanted to close, and in April 1982 the Yanks traded him to Minnesota for shortstop Roy Smalley. He proceeded to save 22, 30, 29, and 25 games over the next four years but then, as his fastball lost velocity, he lost effectiveness.

Righty **Mike Morgan** became a Yankee in 1982, his third big league season. He pulled on uniform No. 39 and worked in 30 games, 23 of them starts, going 7–11 with a 4.37 ERA. That December, the team traded him to Toronto. Morgan would be the ultimate journeyman, pitching for 22 seasons with 12 different teams.

Infielder **Larry Milbourne**, outfielder **Otis Nixon**, and pitchers **Don Cooper** and **Joe Niekro** all spent short times in pinstripes and

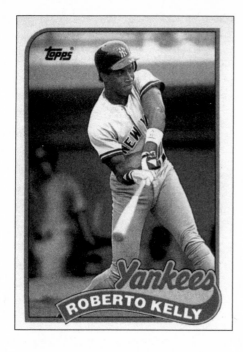

wore No. 39 at some point. By the time **Roberto Kelly** arrived in 1987, No. 39 was a uniform looking for a long-term home.

Kelly was a very good center-fielder, solid hitter, aggressive baserunner, and all-around fine ballplayer. He patrolled center from 1987–92 and was probably just a cut below being a real star. Becoming a regular in 1989, Kelly batted .302 that year with nine homers. By 1991 he was up to 20 homers and 69 RBIs, and the next year he was an All-Star. But sometimes you have to sacrifice a very good player in order to make your team better.

In November 1992, the Yankees dealt Kelly to Cincinnati in return for right fielder Paul O'Neill. They also had Roberto's replacement waiting in the wings in young Bernie Williams. Kelly went on to become an All-Star with the Reds in '93 and again with the Braves in '94. He was the first player to be chosen for three straight All-Star Games with three different teams. And while he had a .290 average for 14 seasons, he was never again a regular on any one team again.

Believe it or not, Kelly's departure in 1992 marked the final time No. 39 would be worn by a regular or long-time player. After that it once again began scorecard jumping with a variety of youngsters, stop-gaps, and fading veterans. Pitcher **Mike Witt** was the first, spending his final three years with the Yanks (1990–91, 1993) and wearing Nos. 22, 36, and 39, one for each season. He was followed by righty **Donn Paul**, who threw 26 games as No. 39 in 1994 before being released that July. Outfielder **Dion James** was with the Yanks twice, from 1992–93 and again from 1995-96. See more about him in Chapter 19. **Matt Luke** played one game in 1996 before being waived and giving No. 39 over to Darryl Strawberry, who had it through 1999.

Mark Wohlers was a veteran closer who came to the Yanks in July 2001, threw 31 games to a 4.54 ERA, and was let go. When he pitched for the Yankees, he was just a year away from retirement.

The versatile **Ron Coomer** could play both the infield and outfield, as well as DH, but all that got him with the Yanks was 55 games as No. 39 in 2002. Coomer, who had several solid years as Minnesota, hit just .264 with three homers and was gone. Middle reliever **Chris Hammond** did his job well in 2003. But he was also 37 years old, and that December was traded to Oakland. Utilityman **Andy Phillips**, a fan favorite, wore No. 39 briefly in 2004 and '05, but also wore Nos. 14 and 18, then settled on No. 12 in 2006 and '07. Read about him there. Outfielder **Kevin Reese** wore No. 39 after a call-up in 2005, then No. 27 when he was summoned from the minors in 2006.

Centerfielder **Melky Cabrera** wore No. 39 when first called up in 2005, then settled on No. 28 for the next three seasons before switching to No. 53 in 2009. Pitcher **Shawn Chacon** probably wishes he could have remained a Yankee. He was summoned in a late July trade with the Rockies in 2005, and the curveballer helped the Yanks to the division title. Put in the rotation due to injuries, the righthander went 7–3 in 14 games, 12 of them starts, with a 2.85 ERA. Unfortuately, injuries slowed him the next year and he was just 5–3 with a 7.00 ERA when he was traded to Pittsburgh on July 31.

First baseman/outfielder **Craig Wilson**, pitcher **Chris Britton**, first baseman/outfielder **Richie Sexson**, and pitcher **Ross Ohlendorf** complete the roll call of No. 39. Wilson was the guy the Yanks got from Pittsburgh in the Chacon trade, but he bombed out by hitting just .212 in 40 games. Reliever Britton was up and down several times in 2007 and '08, wearing No. 39 for four games in '07, then Nos. 39, 38, 47, and 69, and he bounced like a pogo stick between the Yanks and Triple-A Scranton in 2008. Sexson came as a free agent in July 2008 after his release by the Mariners. He was a guy who had 45 homers twice and 39 with 121 RBIs as recently as 2005. But with the Yanks he hit just one in 22 games and was released in mid-August.

The cerebral Ohlendorf, a Princeton graduate, threw just six games in 2007 as No. 60, then switched to No. 39 in 2008 when he appeared in 25 games and went 1–1. The Yanks felt he had an upside but dealt him to Pittsburgh in July in the trade that brought Xavier Nady and Damaso Marte to the Bronx. Righty **Anthony Claggett** threw two games in 2009, had a 33.75 ERA, and was also off to Pittsburgh. Another righty reliever, **Mark Melancon**, pitched in 13 games to a 3.86 ERA and also might have a future with the team.

So No. 39 remains something of a giveaway, one of those digits that require a new scorecard each year. But you never know. Someday a player may just come along who wears it, likes it, has talent, stays around, and makes it memorable.

#40: SUPPORTING PLAYERS NEED ONLY APPLY

It may not be quite as bad as the title implies, but as the numbers rise, there are fewer superstars and impact players. Sure, there are a few on the way, like Reggie Jackson at No. 44 and Ron Guidry at No. 49, just to name two, but as a rule, there are more marginal and short-term players issued the high numbers. While there are some familiar names who have worn No. 40 on their backs at Yankee Stadium, there's also a run of guys who came, saw, and surely didn't conquer.

It begins with the unlikely name of **Herb Karpel**. His name certainly won't be at the end of a list that starts with Ruth, Gehrig, DiMaggio, and Mantle, but in 1946, pitcher Karpel became the first Yankee to wear No. 40. It stayed with him for just two games and then he left baseball. The high numbers were also worn by players who soon switched to something lower. Backup catcher **Charlie Silvera** wore both Nos. 46 and 40 in his first season of 1948, then switched to No. 29, which he kept for the next eight seasons through 1956.

Golden Boy **Jackie Jensen** wore No. 40 his first year of 1950, then switched to No. 27 the following year and finally No. 25 in 1952 before he was traded. Lefty **Bob Wiesler** was assigned No. 40 in 1951, then returned in 1954 and '55 as No. 39. Righty **Billy Hogue** broke the mold when he kept No. 40 for seven games in 1951 and 27 more the following year. Pitcher **Johnny Schmitz**, like some of the others, wore No. 40 for five games in 1952, then switched to No. 35 for just three games the next year.

The next guy had to be very intriguing to the Yankees. They traded with Cincinnati for him on August 28, 1952. He was 6'6", 195-pound righthander **Ewell Blackwell**, a thin sidearmer with a delivery that made the ball seem as if it was exploding at righthanded hitters from third base. He had the appropriate nickname of "The Whip," and had compiled a 22–8 record for Cincy back in 1947. That year, he set a record for righthanded pitchers by winning 16 straight games and came within two outs of tying Johnny Vander Meer's record of two consecutive no-hitters. That's how good he was.

The downside? Arm problems. Blackwell first experienced them in 1948 and wasn't close to his old self until 1950, when he went 17–15. But in the first half of the 1952 season, he was just 3–12 and the Reds pulled the trigger on a trade to the Yanks. Blackwell threw in just five games the remainder of the season but was effective. He won one and had a 0.56 ERA. At the age of 29 there was hope could come back. It wasn't to be. The next year, he was 2–0 with a 3.66 in just eight games before shutting it down. He sat out the 1954 season and in March 1955, the Yanks gave up and sold his contract to Kansas City. The A's took a look, let him pitch twice, and released him on April 30.

Infielder **Tom Carroll** played 14 games for the Yankees in 1955 at the age of 18 and another 36 the next year, wearing No. 40 each season. He had just 23 at bats in two years. Only then was he sent to the minors and on April 12, 1959, Carroll was traded to Kansas City where he played 14 games, hit .143, and was released. Carroll was a victim—if you want to call it that—of the old, antiquated "Bonus Baby" rule, which began in 1947.

If a team signed a player for more than $4,000, it had to keep him on the 40-man roster for two years or lose his rights to the waiver wire. In other words, the Yanks couldn't send bonus baby Carroll to the minors to get the seasoning he needed. The rule, with several variations, lasted until 1965, when it was finally, and rightfully, abolished.

Pitchers **Gabe Gabler** and **Jack Cullen** were both multiple-number guys who played very few games for the Bombers, while veteran outfielder **Lou Clinton** got a one-season look and was gone early the next. A couple of seasoned veterans followed. Unfortunately, pitchers **Bill Monbouquette** and **Lindy McDaniel** came to the Yankees just after the latest dynasty ended. So they worked the Bronx during some tough years. "Monbo," a righty who threw a no-hitter in 1962 and went 20–10 for the Red Sox in 1963, was signed as a free agent on May 31, 1967. Wearing No. 40, Monbouquette had a good year, working 33 games with 10 starts and finishing 6–5 with a 2.36 ERA. That's a valuable pitcher. But the next year, the Yanks decided to make a change, especially after Monbo's ERA went up to 4.43 after 17 games. On July 12, he was traded to the Giants for veteran reliever McDaniel.

Taking over No. 40, Lindy McDaniel came on with a bang. Pitching in 24 games the balance of the '68 season, he went 4–1 with a 1.75 ERA and 10 saves. Tall and durable, a very consistent control pitcher, McDaniel began his career with the Cardinals in 1955 at the age of 19. He was a starter then, but by 1960 had become a top closer. When he joined the Yanks at age 32, he had slipped a notch to journeyman status, but he came back to have a great season in 1970, working 62 games, and going 9–5 with a 2.01 ERA with 29 saves.

McDaniel continued to pitch well through 1973. That December the Yanks were retooling, putting together the team that would dominate from 1976–78, so they dealt McDaniel to Kansas City in order to get Lou Piniella. McDaniel pitched two more years, giving him a total of 987 games. At that time, only Hoyt Wilhelm had worked more. Today, McDaniel stands at number 14 on the all-time list.

Rick Sawyer was one of those guys who borrowed numbers. The righty threw one game as No. 40 in 1974 and just four more as No. 41 the next year before being shipped to the Padres in July. Not so for Tippy Martinez. Fans tend to forget that the longtime Orioles reliever began as a Yankee. The slick southpaw wore No. 40 from 1974–1976 before he was dealt to Baltimore. But because he also wore No. 18 during part of the 1976 season, he was discussed in that chapter.

Catcher **Fran Healy** came to the Yankees in the May 1976 deal that sent pitcher Larry Gura to Kansas City. Healy was 6'5", and very fast for a catcher. When he batted .252 with nine homers, 53 RBIs and 16 stolen bases in 1974, he looked like a coming star. But a shoulder injury the next year affected his overall play. He essentially backed up Thurman Munson from 1976–78, but after playing just one game in 1978, Healy was released and subsequently retired. He later became a well-known broadcaster in the New York area.

Three young pitchers came next, followed by a veteran whose tenure with the Yanks was somewhat disappointing. Righty **Bob Kammeyer** pitched in seven games in 1978 wearing No. 40. When he was recalled the next year, he donned No. 53, pitched in a single game, got hammered and was yanked from the game and from the Yanks. **Larry McCall** was typical of a very marginal player. The righthander had three numbers over two seasons that encompassed just seven total games. He started as No. 51 in 1977, then wore both No. 53 and No. 40 a year later. **Steve Shields**, the third righty of the trio, actually lasted for 39 games in 1988. He was 5–5 with a 4.37 ERA before being traded to the Twins the following March.

ANDY HAWKINS

The veteran pitcher was **Andy Hawkins**, a big righty the Yanks hoped would also be a big winner when they signed him as a free agent in December 1988. The latest No. 40 was a workhorse in '89, going 15–15 with a 4.80 ERA. A year later, he was just 5–12 with a 5.37, and in '91 seemed to lose it all. After four games, an 0–2 record, and a 9.95 ERA he was released.

Pitcher **Scott Kamieniecki** was No. 40 his first season of 1991, but is remembered as No. 28, which he wore from 1993–96. Righthander **Darren Holmes** was signed as a free agent in December 1997 and pitched during the 114-win season of '98. He worked 34 games, went 0–3 with a 3.33 ERA and two saves. Holmes was traded to the Diamondbacks before the next season began. Three more pitchers followed, as No. 40 suddenly seemed to go to the guy out on the mound. Lefty **Gabe White**, righty **Dan Miceli**, and southpaw **C. J. Nitkowski** all wore No. 40 between 2003 and 2004.

The tradition of giving No. 40 to a pitcher continued in 2005, only this pitcher was different—a guy with a chance to become a big star. It was righthander **Chien-Ming Wang**, a native of Taiwan who was signed by the Yanks in May 2000 when he was just 20 years old. Wang pitched in the minors, represented his country in the 2002 Asian Games and 2004 Olympics, and did well. By the time the Yanks brought him up for an 18-game trial in 2005, he looked ready. He went 8–5 with a 4.02 ERA, and by the start of the 2006 season he earned a spot in the rotation. For the next two years, it was the top spot.

Wang was a sinkerball pitcher with an edge. He threw the ball in the mid-90s, making it a hard sinker and difficult to hit except on the ground. He also used an occasional slider and change, and even had a splitter. But that hard sinker was his bread and butter and he threw it up to 90 percent of the time. The results were a 19–6 season in 2006 and a 19–7 mark the following year.

Then came 2008. By the end of April, Wang was 5–0 and seemingly on his way to another great year. By June 15, Wang was at 8–2 and pitching in an interleague game in a National League park. So he had to run the bases and while racing home to score, he came up lame. He had torn the Lisfranc ligament in his right foot and had a partial tear of the peroneus longus in the foot. It was a serious injury that would cost him the remainder of the season and require extensive rehabilitation. The injury would prove more costly than that.

Wang struggled at the outset of the 2009 season. His velocity was down and he was being hit very hard. He went on the DL to strengthen his hip muscles and then, when he seemed to be getting it back, hurt his shoulder and needed surgery. After the season he was allowed to become a free agent. Whether he resigns with the Yanks or goes to another team is still up in the air.

#41: A NOT SO BIG UNIT

Ever since the Babe and his big bat officially put the Yankees on the map, the team in the Bronx has been a team of prominent names and great players, as witnessed by the 16 players who have had their numbers retired. Since free agency began, the New Yorkers have been in the mix almost every time a great or potentially great player comes onto the open market. And don't forget trades. Every now and then there's still something akin to a blockbuster. So it wasn't surprising when the Yanks had a chance to deal for one of the greatest pitchers of his era—a sure first-ballot Hall of Famer—and one of the great strikeout pitchers of all-time. On January 11, 2005, it was announced that the Yanks had sent pitcher Javier Vazquez and two prospects to the Arizona Diamondbacks in return for **Randy Johnson.** The news spread quickly. The pitcher known as "The Big Unit" was coming to New York, even though he was 41 years old.

Johnson was already a legend, a 6'10" southpaw with a blistering fastball and hard-biting slider. One of the tallest pitchers ever, it took him a few years to put it all together—arms, legs, mechanics—but once he did he was almost unstoppable By the time he reached the Yankees, he had already achieved a number of amazing milestones. He was a nine-time strikeout king, five in the National League, four in the American. He fanned more than 300 batters in a season five times, with a high of 372 with Arizona in 2001. He was a three-time 20-game winner and five-time winner of the Cy Young Award. He had seasons of 18–2, 20–4, 21–6, and 24–5. In other words, when he was on his game he didn't lose much. He struck out 20 Cincinnati Reds in 2001, threw a no-hitter with Seattle, and then hurled a perfect game against the Braves on May 18, 2004. At 40 years of age, he was the oldest pitcher ever to achieve perfection. And then he came to New York.

With Randy Johnson, who quickly took his familiar No. 41, the expectations were exceedingly high. His bottom line in 2005 was 17–8 with a 3.79 ERA and 211 strikeouts in 225 2/3 innings. On the surface, not bad. But he was inconsistent for much of the season and sometimes hit hard. He gave up 32 homers, the most of his career. His only redemption was that he beat the rival Red Sox five times.

Randy Johnson

The next year it got worse. It was soon apparent that Johnson didn't really like pitching in New York and the fans let him know their feelings. He had a 17–11 record in 2006, and his earned run average ballooned to 5.00 while his strikeouts dipped to 172. In the postseason, he faltered again, giving up five runs to the Tigers in 5 2/3 innings. He wasn't helpd by a herniated disk in his back that was causing him to stiffen up, but it was apparent that this was a marriage destined to end. And that it did, on January 9, 2007, when he was dealt back to the Diamondbacks for four players. The Big Unit had won 34 games for the Yanks in two years, but in the eyes of most New Yorkers he simply wasn't as big as he once was.

In 22 seasons through 2009, Randy Johnson has a 303–166 record with a 3.29 ERA and 4,875 strikeouts, second only to Nolan Ryan all time. Unfortunately, the Yankees and their fans never quite saw the real Randy Johnson. Had Johnson come to New York 10 years earlier, No. 41 might be destined for Monument Park with a plaque in his honor. But that didn't happen.

Before Johnson arrived, the number had the same kind of checkered history that many of the higher numbers have with a variety of players coming and going and only a handful becoming staples of the team. It began with **Steve Souchock**, an outfielder/first baseman who was given No. 41 in 1946, the first Yankee to wear it. He played in 47 games, then wasn't with the big club in 1947, but came back again the next year to hit just .203 in 44 games. Boom. Traded to the White Sox. Like many players of the day, Souchock had his career disrupted by World War II. He returned decorated for his heroics during the epic Battle of the Bulge.

First sacker **Joe Collins** spent his entire career (1948–57) with the Yanks, wearing No. 42 his rookie year, then No. 41 from 1949–52. But because he wore No. 15 from 1953–57 he was detailed more in that chapter. The same with the next two guys, outfielder **Bob Cerv** and first sacker **Marvelous Marv Throneberry**. Cerv, a part time player in his Yankees years, started with No. 7 in 1951, then went to No. 34 the next year before settling on No. 41 from 1953–56. He was traded away but returned from 1960–62, at which time he wore No. 17, where he is also discussed. Throneberry, he of the stone hands at first, was No. 41 in 1955, then No. 20 in '58 and '59 before he was traded. So look for more in Chapter 20.

Catcher **Jake Gibbs** was the first player to spend significant time with No. 41. He donned it during his entire career from 1962–1971. Gibbs was an All-American quarterback at the University of Mississippi and led the Rebels to a 10–0–1 record his senior year. He was then drafted by both the Houston Oilers of the old American Football League and the Cleveland Browns of the NFL, but he never signed. That's because the Yanks swooped in and offered him $105,000 to become a bonus baby. That meant he had to spend at least two years with the big club before going to the minors. Gibbs stayed 10 years.

The young catcher played just nine games in three years before he finally began seeing action behind Elston Howard in 1965. He would never be a solid hitter and didn't have power, though he was a good defensive catcher when healthy. Though he played in more than 100 games in both 1967 and '68, he hit just .233 and .216. Surprisingly, the Yanks kept him three more years. His best season was 1970, when he hit .301 in 49 games with eight home runs. But a year later he was back to .218 and retired, going back to his alma mater to coach baseball.

Outfielder/first baseman **Fran Tepedino** was with the Yanks part of five seasons. He wore No. 41 his final New York season of 1972 and No. 47 his first (1967), but wore No. 21 in three other seasons. Catcher/outfielder **Duke Sims** played four games in 1973 and five more in '74 before being traded to Texas. Lefty **Mike Wallace** had a real reversal of fortune. He came to the Yanks in May 1974 and went 6–0 in 23 games with a 2.41 ERA. A year later the newest No. 41 pitched three times, had an earned run average of 14.54 and was sold to the Cards in June. Pitcher **Rick Sawyer** wore No. 40 in 1974 and No. 41 a year later and threw in a total of six games.

Whenever he is introduced at Old Timers' Days, the same word is used before his name. Welcome back, **"Big" Cliff Johnson**! Big Cliff was also called by the nickname "Heathcliff," but he was a big man, standing 6'4" and weighing 225 pounds. He started out as a catcher with Houston and struggled behind the plate. To know how much, you only have to hear one stat—in 1976 he led all major league catchers in passed balls yet he was behind the dish in only 66 games. But Big Cliff could hit. In 1975, he batted .276 with 20 homers and 65 RBIs in just 340 at bats. The Yankees got Heathcliff on June 15, 1977, for a player to be named later. He came to the team just as they were driving toward a pennant and World Series.

Wearing No. 41, Johnson caught a few games, was the DH in even more, and played some first base. And, of course, he quickly became a dangerous and reliable pinch-hitter. In 56 games, he hit .296 with 12 homers and 31 ribbies. He then hit .400 in the ALCS against Kansas City, with six hits and homer, and he eventually got a World Series ring.

The next year Cliff inexplicably tailed off at the plate, hitting just .184 in 76 games with six homers. He started to come back the following season year, hitting .266 in 28 games when he made a big mistake, getting into a locker room fight with the team's superstar closer, Goose Gossage. When Gossage emerged with ligament damage in his thumb and had to go on the DL for some two months, it sealed Johnson's fate. On June 15, the big guy was traded to Cleveland for a pitcher named Don Hood. He would play until 1986, finishing with the most pinch hit homers (20) in major league history.

With Johnson gone, the Yanks took a flyer in August on veteran first sacker **George Scott**, who had spent most of his career with the Red Sox. Just four years earlier, in 1975, Scott has his best season, hitting .285 with 36 homers and 109 RBIs as the Bosox won the pennant. But Scott had gone downhill quickly, and he played in 16 games as No. 41 the balance of the year. He managed to hit .318, but the power that produced 271 "long taters" in his career was all but gone. He hit his final home run with the Bombers and eventually retired.

Pitcher **Joe Cowley** was one of those baseball mysteries. Why does a guy who looks so good suddenly lose it and look like he doesn't belong at all? The 6'5", 210-pound righty spent eight years in the Atlanta Braves, organization with only a cup of coffee call-up in 1982. Two years later, the Yanks signed him as a free agent. As No. 41, he had seasons of 9-2 and 12-6, but during the off-season the Yanks traded him to the White Sox for pitcher Britt Burns. Cowley went 11–11 for the Pale Hose, with his final victory of the season coming on a no-hitter September 19. At the end of spring training the next year, the White Sox sent him to the Phils and Cowley imploded. He was hard-pressed to get an out or throw strikes and in five games had an ERA of 15.43. He was sent home in July, his career over. Yet Joe Cowley does hold an unusual distinction. He is the only pitcher in baseball history to never win another game after pitching a no-hitter.

After Cowley, there continued to be a parade of pitchers wearing No. 41, starting with the multi-numbered **Scott Nielsen**, who went from No. 41 to No. 47 then back to No. 33 in 1986, and 1988–89. Righties **Charles Hudson, Lance McCullers, Wade Taylor**, and **Tim Burke** followed, all donning No. 41. None stayed for long and none distinguish themselves.

The righty mold was broken by southpaw **Sterling Hitchcock**, a pitcher the Yankees thought could be a solid middle-of-the-rotation guy. After cups of coffee as No. 54 and No. 34 in 1992 and '93, Hitchcock took on No. 41 and began pitching more often in 1994. The next year, he was in the rotation and went 11–10 with a 4.70 ERA. With his value as high as it had been, the Yanks shipped him to Seattle in a deal that brought first sacker Tino Martinez and reliever Jeff Nelson to the Bronx. That was a trade that would pay dividends for the Yanks over the next five years. As for Hitchcock, he pitched well for both the Mariners and Padres, then returned to the Yanks in 2001, working mainly in relief until dealt to the Cardinals in August of 2003. Hitchcock wound up with a 74–76 record over 13 seasons and never quite became the lefthander the Yanks thought he would.

Righty **Brian Boehringer** relieved for the Yanks in parts of four seasons, starting off as No. 31 in 1995, moving to No. 41 the next two years and again when he returned in 2001. Another righthander, **Jorge DePaula**, threw a total of 11 games from 2003–2005, going up the ladder from No. 41 to 43 and then 61 in each succeeding season. Finally, the pitching logjam was broken by infielder **Miguel Cairo**, a utility player who rightly earned the moniker of super sub. Cairo was extremely valuable in 2004, when he played in 122 games, and hit .292 with six homers and 42 RBIs. He left the next year, but returned in 2006 and '07, playing less frequently but always counted on to do a solid job. Cairo wore No. 41 his first and last season with the Yanks, and No. 14 in the middle year of 2006.

The last player to wear No. 41 was something of an enigma. Righthander **Jose Veras** could have electric stuff when he was on his game, blowing away hitters with a mid-90s fastball and a deep, late-breaking slider. Veras first appeared on the scene for 12 games in 2006, wearing No. 31. He upped it to No. 41 the next year, but an arm injury relegated him to nine games. Then in 2008 he emerged, working in 60 games and going 5–3 with a 3.59 ERA. He also fanned 63 hitters in just 57 2/3 innings. At times, he looked like a potential closer. But in 2009 he was erratic and wild, walking too many and giving up key hits. With the team retooling the bullpen for the second half, Veras' contract was sold to the Indians in late July.

WORKING MEN

Randy Johnson has been a workhorse pitcher, a guy who has piled up the innings, has more strikeouts than anyone except Nolan Ryan, and has won more than 300 games. He's a Hall of Fame lock someday. But he didn't do it with the Yankees, pitching in pinstripes only two years. When it comes to innings and games pitched, the Yankees round up the usual suspects.

Games Pitched		Innings Pitched	
Mariano Rivera	917	Whitey Ford	3,170 1/3
Dave Righetti	522	Red Ruffing	3,168 2/3
Whitey Ford	498	Mel Stottlemyre	2,661 1/3
Mike Stanton	456	Bob Shawkey	2,488 2/3
Red Ruffing	426	Andy Pettitte	2,406 2/3

#42: THE BEST CLOSER EVER

He's the best at what he does, period. As of 2009, no one in baseball will argue that. Not only is he the best of his generation—he's the best ever. Never before in the long history of the game has a late-inning pitcher, a closer, been as dominant for so long a period as **Mariano Rivera**. When opposing teams see the slim righthander jogging in from the bullpen, they pretty much know their chances of rallying or winning are slim to none. "Mo" is simply the best at shutting the door. He began doing it as a set-up man for John Wetteland in 1996, became the closer the next year, and has been doing it ever since, including the 2009 postseason when he was the only closer in the entire play-offs who didn't blow a save as the Yanks won their 27th world title. Mo finished the season as good as ever, as dominant as ever, as intimidating as ever. And he did it just a few weeks shy of his 40th birthday.

Where does a once-in-a-lifetime player come from? In Mariano's case, Panama. He grew up in the fishing village of Puerto Caimito playing more soccer than baseball. But soon baseball became his sport. Though he started as a shortstop, it was his fine throwing arm that drew attention. The Yanks signed him in 1990 and he began working in the minors. By 1992 his career came to a halt when he needed elbow surgery, but it turned out to be relatively minor. He finally made the Yanks in 1995 as a starter, and in his first game was shelled as the team lost, 10–0. There was even some talk of trading him to the Tigers that year for David Wells, but then the coaches noticed his velocity had increased to the mid-90s and he stayed. He was just 5–3 with a bloated ERA of 5.51 that year, starting 10 times in 19 games. But when he returned the next year, things had changed.

Mo was put into the set-up role in front of closer John Wetteland. Suddenly he was all but unhittable, often pitching two or three innings with Wetteland throwing the ninth. He pitched in 61 games that year, going 8–3 with a 2.09 earned run average, five saves, and 130 strikeouts in 107 2/3 innings.

He was mostly using his electric fastball and pinpoint control to dominate. The Yanks won the World Series that year and then Wetteland left to test the free agent waters, signing with Texas. Mo became the closer, and that year he developed what would become his trademark pitch, the cut fastball. The cutter is thrown in the mid-90s and has a late and sharp break, boring in on the hands of lefthanded batters and away from righties. Mariano learned to vary the movement of the cutter by adjusting the pressure on the ball with his middle finger. Soon, he became a master.

His first year as the closer he pitched in 66 games, had a 6–4 record, a 1.88 ERA, and 43 saves. He was off to the races and hasn't looked back since. Compare that with his pitching line in 2009. In 55 games, he was 3–3 with a 1.76 ERA and 44 saves. That's 13 years apart and the numbers are close to identical. Look at the rest. Mo has had nine seasons in which his earned run average was under 2.00. He's a 10-time All-Star. He finished the 2009 season with 526 saves, second only to Trevor Hoffman, but virtually no one thinks of the highly effective Hoffman as the superior closer. He has had 50 or more saves twice, in 2001 and 2004, but his best season might have been 2005, when he was 7–4 in 71 games with a minuscule 1.38 ERA and 43 saves. He was second in the Cy Young voting that year.

And then there are the playoffs. Because he's been with the Yankees during their dynasty years, he has a postseason record second to none. In 88 games, he has an 8–1 record, 39 saves, and an earned run average of 0.74. Talk about pitching well when the stakes are high. Being human, Mo gives up the occasional home run, but many of the hits off him are bloops and broken bat base hits.

Mariano Rivera

Off-season arthroscopic surgery in 2008 to scrape away some calcification didn't slow him. He seemed as good as ever in 2009 as he approached his 40th birthday and was, by far, the best closer in the playoffs. The cutter still has its bite and his control is usually impeccable. His ability to repeat his delivery is another of the secrets of his success. On the mound he is always calm and composed, even in the toughest situations, and longtime teammate Derek Jeter calls him the "most mentally tough teammate I've ever played with." Others have called him the most valuable of all Yankees from 1996 through 2009, and the most important player on the team.

In some ways, he seems like the perfect player. He never pumps his fist, or screams, or points to the heavens like so many closers, and he doesn't outwardly show up the opposition. He just does his job, then does it again, and again. In between, he's made numerous philanthropic contributions, especially in his native Panama, and enjoys universal respect. Slugger Jim Thome has called his cutter "the single best pitch ever in the game." But perhaps it was Dennis Eckersley, the game's top closer in the 1980s and early 90s and a Hall of Famer, who best summed up No. 42, Mariano Rivera.

"He's the best ever," Eckersley said. "Of that there is no doubt."

Before Mo, there weren't a lot of Yankees wearing No. 42, with just a few recognizable to Yankee fans. For openers, the number wasn't worn until 1947, when war veteran **Butch Wensloff** put it on. Wensloff had shown promise as a 27-year-old rookie in 1943, wearing No. 14 and going 13–11 with a 2.54 ERA. But when he returned from military service his arm was dead.

Outfielder **Bud Stewart** lost five years to the war, not appearing in the majors between 1942 and 1948. In '48, he played six games for the Yanks as No. 42 before being traded to Washington. First sacker **Joe Collins** wore No. 42 as a rookie in 1948, then wore No. 41 between 1949–52 and No. 15 from 1953 to '57, and that's where he is discussed. Then came second sacker **Jerry Coleman**, a player old-time Yankee fans will readily identify by the number 42, which he wore from 1949–57, the length of his Yankees career.

Coleman looked like a coming star his first two years. As a rookie he hit .275 and he led all AL second baseman in fielding. A year later, he batted .287 with six homers and 69 RBIs and was named the 1950 World Series MVP. Aninjury slowed him in '51,and then came the Korean War. Coleman was a Marine aviator who had flown combat missions in World War II. He missed most of the next two seasons doing the same thing in Korea. When he returned, he had flown a total of 120 combat missions in two wars and received two Distinguished Flying Crosses.

Unfortunately, he never quite regained the magic he had before going back into the service. He hit just .217 in 107 games in 1954 and was just a part-time player over the next three years, though he ended his career in a big way by hitting .364 in the 1957 World Series. He later became a broadcaster for the Yankees, the Angels, and the San Diego Padres, and even left the booth to manage the Padres for a short time. He continues to broadcast in San Diego as of 2009 and is always a favorite when he returns to Yankee Stadium.

Once Coleman left, No. 42 sat in a box for six years until it was given to infielder **Pedro Gonzalez** in 1963. Essentially a second sacker, Gonzalez came at the time when Bobby Richardson was ensconced at second and was traded to the Indians in May 1965. The trade of Gonzalez brought first baseman **Ray Barker** in return, so he took over No. 42. Barker simply went on a downward spiral with the Yanks, culminating with an .077 mark in 17 games in 1967. He couldn't go much lower than that so he was gone.

After pitcher **Steve Kline** wore No. 42 briefly in his rookie year of 1970 before switching to No. 38, rookie outfielder **Charlie Spikes** claimed it in 1972. Spikes played in just 14 games hitting only .147 before being traded to the Indians that November. Pitcher **Doc Medich** was another who wore the number briefly. He started with No. 50 in 1972, switched to No. 42 the next year, then settled on No. 33 in his best Yankee seasons before he was traded. Pitcher **Ken Wright** wore No. 42 for just three games in 1974 before being sent to the Phils on May 3, and he never pitched in the majors again.

The Yanks bought the contract of outfielder/infielder **Bob Oliver** from the Orioles in December 1974. Oliver was a competent power hitter, but with the Yanks he lasted just 18 games as No. 42 in 1975 and was released on July 15. After Oliver, no one claimed, or was given No. 42 until 1989, when the team signed veteran lefty Dave LaPoint. He switched from No. 29 to No. 42, then wore it again in 1990.

Righthanders **John Habyan** and **Domingo Jean** were the final players to wear No. 42 before Mariano Rivera came along. Habyan came over from the Orioles in late July 1989. He was rehabbing that year and didn't pitch. In '90, he wore No. 61 and threw in just six games. A year later, he switched to No. 42, which he would wear the next two and a half seasons before being shipped to Kansas City in July of 1993. As for Domingo Jean, he pitched just 10 games in 1993, his only year in the majors.

So the last two Yankees to wear No. 42 have pitched in a total of 927 games through 2009, 10 for Domingo Jean and 917 for Mariano Rivera. If you want to talk about a living legend, then Mo is your man. Aside from Jackie Robinson, he will certainly be the most memorable player ever to wear that magic number. Or to put it another way, a number that both Robinson and Rivera have made into magic by virtue of their great talent and character.

THE MAGIC 100-WIN MARK

Mariano Rivera is all about winning, and so are the Yankees. Mo has saved games in five seasons that have resulted in 100 wins or more during the regular season. But there have been others, as well, more than any other franchise. Here's the list of the Yanks 18 100-win seasons, the team's record, and the manager who helped guide them there.

1927	110–44	Miller Huggins
1928	101–53	Miller Huggins
1932	107–47	Joe McCarthy
1936	102–51	Joe McCarthy
1937	102–52	Joe McCarthy
1941	101–53	Joe McCarthy
1942	103–51	Joe McCarthy
1954	103–51	Casey Stengel
1961	109–53	Ralph Houk
1963	104–57	Ralph Houk
1977	100–62	Billy Martin
1978	100–63	Billy Martin/Bob Lemon
1980	103–59	Dick Howser
1998	114–48	Joe Torre
2002	103–58	Joe Torre
2003	101–61	Joe Torre
2004	101–61	Joe Torre
2009	103–59	Joe Girardi

Note: The only time the Yanks won 100 games or more and didn't win the pennant or division was 1954. That year, they finished eight games behind a Cleveland Indians team that won 111 games.

#43: A BUNCH OUT OF THE BULLPEN

What do the names Rob Gardner, Rudy May, Ken Clay, Doug Bird, George Frazier, Rich Bordi, Tim Stoddard, Paul Assenmacher, Jeff Nelson, and Scott Proctor have in common? They've all come out of the Yankee bullpen wearing No. 43. Though no one player has stepped forward to make No. 43 his own—as Mariano Rivera has done with No. 42—there has been a group of relievers who have stepped forward to help the Yanks win during their various dynasty years, and even in years when they weren't baseball's best.

In fact, the first player ever to wear No. 43 was a pitcher, and a very good one. **Vic Raschi**, the "Springfield Rifle," wore the number briefly in 1947, his second season. But before the year was out he switched to No. 17, the number he wore the remainder of his Yankees career. Though Raschi got the ball rolling, no one would pick up on it for six more years, to 1953, when outfielder/first baseman **Art Schult** wore it for seven games, but never got a chance to bat.

After Schult there was yet another gap and the number returned to mothballs. It wasn't brought out again until the Yankees called up a 6'3" outfielder named **Roger Repoz** in 1964. Tall and fleet of foot, Repoz had the look of a star and was quickly touted as the heir apparent to the aging Mickey Mantle. But Repoz was just another pretender, as he hit only .220 with 12 homers in 1965. A year later, he got into 37 games and didn't hit a single home run. That June, Mantle's "successor" wound up in Kansas City.

Third sacker **Mike Ferraro** wore No. 43 briefly in 1966 and then No. 26 two years later. He never cleared the Mendoza line. Then some of the pitchers began to emerge, beginning with **Dale Roberts**, **Rob Gardner**, and **Terry Ley** between 1967 and '71. None made much of a mark and were soon gone.

When the Yankees bought the contract of third baseman/outfielder **Jim Ray Hart** in April of 1973, they were taking a flyer on a fading veteran. Hart had set a Giants rookie record by belting 31 home runs in 1964, and between that year and 1968 he averaged almost 28 homers and 90 RBIs a year. But a shoulder injury in 1969 stripped him of his power and he was pretty much a part-time player after that. As a Yankee, he played in 114 games in '73, exclusively as a DH or pinch-hitter. Wearing No. 43, Hart batted .254 with 13 homers and 52 RBIs. But by the next year he had pretty much lost it, and after hitting just .053 in 10 games was released.

HELLO TO THE BIG LEAGUES

Jim Ray Hart had one of the more unusual welcomes to the big leagues back in 1963. First, Bob Gibson said hello by breaking his shoulder blade with a fastball to the back. A few days after he returned to the lineup, he was beaned by Curt Simmons and missed the rest of the season after playing just seven games. That would make almost anyone want to quit. But Hart didn't mind standing in against the top pitchers of the day. What bugged him the most was playing third base. "Too damned close to the hitters," he once quipped.

After Hart was released, catcher **Jim Deidel** wore No. 43 for just two games and two at-bats. But when lefthander **Rudy May** showed up in the second half of the year, the Yanks got a pitcher who would spend nearly seven seasons in pinstripes during two separate tenures. His first lasted from from 1974–76, wearing No. 43, and when he returned from 1980–83, he would wear No. 45.

He came over in June of '74 when his contract was purchased from the Angels, stepped into the rotation, and went 8–4 with a 2.28 ERA. The next year, he was 14–12 with a 3.06 in 31 starts. May was just 30 years old at the time and it would seem he might be set to stay a while. But after going 4–3 in 11 starts in '76, he was packaged into a deal with the Orioles that netted the Yanks very little. The Yanks re-signed him as a free agent in November of 1979.

Though he missed the World Series years, he returned to go 15–5 with a 2.46 ERA in 1980 as he pitched in 41 games with 17 starts and even three saves. It was his last outstanding year. He struggled after that and retired at the end of the 1983 season.

After May, the parade of pitchers wearing No. 43 really began. **Jim York**, **Ken Clay**, **Doug Bird**, and **George Frazier** were the quartet who followed. York was a short-timer, a guy who was gone after three games in 1976. The righty Clay got a longer look, pitching mostly out of the pen from 1977–79. It was back to the minors in 1980, until he was traded in Texas that August for veteran Gaylord Perry.

Doug Bird was a veteran who spent two years (1980–81) in the Bronx and he did well, throwing in 39 games over two seasons with a combined 8–1 mark and an ERA just under 2.70. He was traded to the Cubs in June of 1981. Righty George Frazier came over from the Cardinals on June 7, 1981, and promptly impressed the Yanks by pitching to a 1.63 ERA in 16 games with three saves. Though he got bombed in the 1981 World Series, losing three games, he pitched well out of the pen for two more years until he was traded to the Indians.

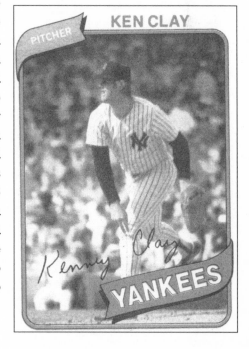

Another four hurlers followed as the tradition of No. 43 became more established. **Rich Bordi, Tim Stoddard, Jeff Robinson**, and **Jeff Johnson** pitched mostly out of the pen with varying degrees of success. Bordi came in a 1985 trade with the Cubs, then was dealt to Baltimore in '86 and returned as a free agent the following April, but after just 16 games and a 7.64 ERA in 1987 he was released. Stoddard was a solid reliever and had some good moments for the Yanks from 1986–88. Because he wore No. 33 briefly before switching to No. 43, he has already been discussed. Righty Robinson came over from Pittsburgh in December of '89 and had a pretty decent season, but then he, too, was released. Johnson, a southpaw, saw action in parts of three seasons (1991–93), always had a high ERA, and was also released.

The string of mediocrities and lesser lights continued. Infielder **Torey Lovullo** broke the string of pitchers wearing No. 43 when he played in 22 games in 1991, batting .176. Gone. Righty Sam Militello appeared in Chapter 34, the number he wore in 1993. The year before, he donned No. 43. Southpaw **Paul Assenmacher** was a different story. He was one of those lefties who always seemed to find another job. He was with the Yanks for just a single season, pitching in 26 games in 1993, but he had a big league career of 14 years.

Once righthander **Jeff Nelson** took over No. 43, the Yankees had found a real difference-maker. The 6'8", 235-pound Nelson came to the Yanks from Seattle in December 1995, the same trade that brought Tino Martinez. He joined with lefty Mike Stanton to form nearly the perfect bridge to closer Mariano Rivera. Nelson threw a hard-breaking slider with tremendous late movement and a hard cut fastball that gave righthanded hitters fits. He worked in a high of 77 games in 1997 and probably had his best Yankee season in 2000, going 8–4 with a 2.45 ERA in 73 games. He also pitched well in the post-season, to the tune of a 2.65 ERA in 55 games.

"Nellie" tested the free agent waters after the 2000 season and returned to Seattle, where he had another outstanding season, holding opposing hitters to just a .136 average. Two years later, the Yankees got him back via an August 6 trade. Returning to the scene of his greatest triumphs, Nelson pitched in 24 games, went 1–0 with a 4.58 ERA, and picked up one save before moving on again.

Until the arrival of Jose Molina in 2007, the Yanks had a shuttle of backup catchers moving in and out of the Bronx while incumbent Jorge Posada held court. **Todd Greene** was the temp in 2001, catching 35 games as No. 43. Like most of the others, he was a competent receiver and weak hitter (.208). Pitcher **Christian Parker** had a one-game major league career and it came with the Yanks in 2001. When the Yanks traded to get **Raul Mondesi** in July 2002, they were once again taking a gamble that a veteran player could regain his former skill level. Mondesi was the Rookie of the Year for the Dodgers in 1994 and a two-time Gold Glover with a throwing arm that was compared with Roberto Clemente's. Though he had some fine seasons, Mondesi never quite cut it with the Yanks. He hit .241 for the balance of the 2002 season and .258 in 98 games the next year before being traded to Arizona.

Pitcher **Jorge DePaula** wore No. 43 in 2004, one of four numbers in three years. Because he wore No. 41 the year before, he's discussed in that chapter. Righthander **Scott Proctor** might be an example of a pitcher who was overused. Proctor had a live arm, and once he learned to off-set his fastball with breaking pitches became an effective reliever. He wore Nos. 56 and 57 in 2004, his first year with the Yanks when he was in just 26 games. A year later, he switched to No. 43 and pitched in 29 games and finally found it in 2006 to became one of Joe Torre's go-to guys out of the pen. Suddenly, Proctor found himself pitching in 83 games. He was 6–4 with a 3.52 ERA and a save.

A year later, he was being worked hard again. By July 31, he already appeared in 52 games when the Yanks decided to trade him to the Dodgers for infielder Wilson Betemit. Proctor continued to pitch well and often, fell off in 2008, and then needed Tommy John surgery a year later.

The last player to wear No. 43 is another, you guessed it, relief pitcher. Damaso Marte came over in July 2008 and wore No. 34 that year. His Yankees tenure is profiled in Chapter 34. Suffice to say that after an injury-filled 2009 Marte emerged in the playoffs and was one of the heroes in the World Series. Is there any other way to earn your (pin)stripes as a New York Yankee?

#44: REGGIE! REGGIE! REGGIE!

Here's a number that almost doesn't have a history beyond the man who immortalized it. When fans think of No. 44, just a single name goes through their minds. Reggie. That's how strong the name is identified with one player—**Reginald Martinez Jackson**. Of course, you can also call him "Mr. October" for his postseason heroics, but no matter what you call him, Reggie Jackson was a winner. Reggie today is considered a true Yankees icon, a Hall of Famer and World Series hero, and a powerhouse slugger who loved the spotlight and seemed to thrive in it. Yet this Yankees hero was only in pinstripes for five of his 21 seasons in the bigs.

Reggie came to the Yanks as a free agent before the 1977 season, cashing in on players being freed up to make their own deals. "Jax" signed for five years at $2.96 million. That might seem like chump change today, but back then it was the jackpot. But Reggie certainly had the résumé that made him seem suited for the Bronx. He started with the A's when they were still in Kansas City in 1967 and moved with them to Oakland the next year. Then, in 1969, Reggie Jackson hit the news when he went on a tear from Opening Day on. By July 29, he already had 40 home runs. He slowed after that and finished with 47 homers and 118 RBIs.

Three years after that, the A's began their run of three straight world championships. Reggie was the AL MVP in 1973 and the World Series MVP as well. In 1975, he led the AL with 36 homers and then was packaged off to Baltimore, where he had another solid season. Then free agency came calling and so did the Yankees.

The Yanks already had a diverse group of explosive personalities, and it didn't help when Reggie told the press that he "was the straw that stirs the drink," basically saying that he was going to be the Yanks' main man. The remark didn't sit well with the surly Thurman Munson, the team leader, so the marriage got off to a rocky start.

But toward the end of June, Reggie went on one of his patented tears that could carry a team and the Yanks rolled, winning 100 games and the pennant. Reggie finished the regular season at .286 with 32 homers and 110 RBIs. But the best was yet to come.

It happened in Game Six of the World Series against the Dodgers. The Yanks had a 3–2 lead in games and Reggie had homered in both the fourth and fifth contests. The Dodgers had a 3–2 lead when Reggie came up for the second time against righty Burt Hooton, with a runner on. He promptly drove Hooton's first pitch into the rightfield seats to give the Yanks a 4–3 lead. The next two times up, against Elias Sosa and then Charlie Hough, he also homered on the first pitch. Three homers on three pitches against three different pitchers. He also became the only player besides Babe Ruth to hit three homers in a World Series game and set a record all his own with five home runs in the Fall Classic. He batted .450 in the Series with five homers and eight RBIs. Needless to say, he was the Series MVP. And soon after, he got the nickname of "Mr. October" for his fine postseason play.

THE REGGIE BAR

Before coming to the Yanks, Reggie once remarked that if he played in New York they would name a candy bar after him. He may have been under the mistaken impression that the Baby Ruth candy bar was named after the Babe, when in truth it was named for the daughter of President Grover Cleveland. But sure enough, when the Yanks took the field for their home opener in 1978, all the fans were given a complementary Reggie Bar. It was a square bar of chocolate and peanuts, with a likeness of Reggie swinging a bat on the front. And when Reggie hit a three-run homer his very first at bat, the fans went wild. It started with one and grew to thousands. Fans began throwing the Reggie Bars like frisbies and they came raining down on the field in a tribute to the Yanks' hero, while creating a mess for the grounds crew.

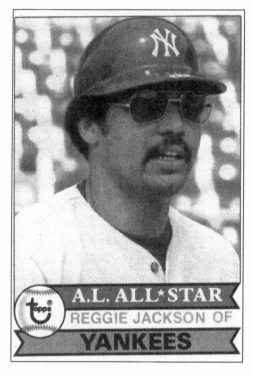

A.L. ALL★STAR

topps

REGGIE JACKSON OF

YANKEES

Reggie helped the Yanks win another World Series in '78 (hitting .391 with two more homers and another eight RBIs). In 1980, he led the American League in home runs with 41, batted an even .300, and drove home 111 runs. With his contract up in 1981, the Yanks let the 35-year-old Jackson test the free agent waters and he wound up signing with the Angels. His Yankees career was done after five years.

Reggie would play through 1987, when he was 41 years old. He returned to Oakland for his final season and hit his 563rd and final home run there. On the negative side, he struck out 2,597 times, still the most in baseball history, but Reggie was always going for the downs with that big swing.

In addition to being a 14-time All-Star, he was on 11 division winners, six pennant winners, and five world championship teams. In five World Series, he batted .357 with 10 homers and 24 RBIs in 27 games. As for Mr. October, he earned it. Reggie was voted into the Hall of Fame in 1993, his first year of eligibility, the same year the Yankees retired his No. 44. Today, he's a special advisor to the team and appears at Yankee Stadium for most special occasions.

Because no Yankee wore No. 44 until 1953 and there were some gaps between the times it was issued, only five different players wore the number before Reggie came along. Let's take a look at the orphan five, guys who few remember today as having worn the number shared by Reggie with fellow Hall of Famers Henry Aaron and Willie McCovey.

It started with shortstop **Frank Verdi** in 1953, but you had to look quickly to see him. Verdi was a one-game wonder who never even got to bat in the majors. Two years later, No. 44 went to another phantom player, outfielder **Dick Tettelbach**, who played all of two games before being shipped to Washington. In 1959, outfielder **Ken Hunt** came up with the Bombers and played two games. A year later, he appeared in 25 games before being drafted by the expansion Angels.

Infielder/outfielder **Bill Sudakis** and outfielder/DH **Terry Whitfield** were the final two Yankees to wear No. 44 before Reggie. Sudakis was a switch hitter with some pop in his bat, but had trouble hitting for average. The Yanks purchased his contract from the Rangers before the 1974 season. But Sudakis hit just .232 in 89 games with seven homers and was traded to the Angels.

Whitfield started his career with the Yanks in 1974, wearing No. 51 for two games. The next two seasons, he wore No. 44 but didn't get much of a chance to show it off. His 28-game audition in '75 produced no homers. After one game in '76, he spent the rest of the year in the minors and then was traded to the Giants.

That did it for No. 44 until Reginald Martinez Jackson came along. In a sense he came, he saw, he conquered . . . and then he left. But what he left has never been forgotten, and to Yankees fans he will always be known as Mr. October.

THE RUN PRODUCERS

Reggie Jackson was a great RBI man. And had he driven in all his runs with the Yankees, he would stand in third place on their all-time list with 1,702. But Reggie didn't play that long in New York and these pinstripers did. Here's the top ten RBI producers in Yankees history.

Lou Gehrig 1,995
Babe Ruth 1,975
Joe DiMaggio 1,537
Mickey Mantle 1,509
Yogi Berra 1,430
Bernie Williams 1,257
Bill Dickey 1,209
Tony Lazzeri 1,154
Don Mattingly 1,099
Derek Jeter 1,068

#45: PITCHERS AND SLUGGERS

This is a number pretty much bereft of real stars, at least when they were in their prime, and has its share of guys who came and went with hardly a notice. But there are also those who contributed to Yankees pennant and World Series winners and produced some fond memories for fans who remember them.

No. 45 didn't make its pinstriped debut until 1951 with catcher **Clint Courtney**. It then hibernated for another two years before it became visible once again. For a good part of the time it was the domain of pitchers, but in later years it also became a number worn by aging sluggers who came to the Yankees with their best days behind them. Courtney, whose Yankees career lasted just one game, has the distinction of being the first catcher to wear eyeglasses while behind the mask. He would catch for 11 seasons and was one of the most combative players in the game.

Three one-season guys followed between 1953 and 1959, the six-year gap showing that there was still little need for this number in the 1950s. First sacker **Don Bollweg** had the longest tenure, 70 games in 1953. Outfielder **Lou Skizas** and pitcher **Mark Freeman** had even shorter tenures. Skizas played six games in 1956, hit .167, and was put on the Kansas City shuttle in June, while Freeman threw in just one game in 1959.

In 1961, young righthander **Rollie Sheldon** became the first player to give No. 45 some real identity. He got a shot in spring training of 1961and made the team, winding up in the rotation and going 11–5 in 35 games. At age 24, it appeared the 6'4", 190-pounder had a future.

But then he went backwards, to 7-8 in '62 before missing the '63 season with arm problems. He was just 5–2 when he returned for part of 1964, and three games into the 1965 season he was traded to Kansas City (where else?).

After Sheldon left, it wouldn't be that long before an even more successful pitcher came along. Before he did, however, pitcher **Jack Cullen** and first baseman/outfielder **John Miller** had temporary possession of No. 45. Cullen threw two games as No. 40 in 1962, then pitched 17 more in '65 and '66 wearing No. 45 before leaving the majors. Miller came up for just six games in 1966 and left a batting average of .087, with just two hits in 23 trips to the plate.

In 1966, the Yanks also brought up a young pitcher for a four-game cup of coffee. Righty **Stan Bahnsen**, wearing No. 49, went 1–1 with a 3.52 ERA and a save. Two years later he was back, this time wearing No. 45 and pitching in the starting rotation. All he did this time was go 17–12 with a sparkling 2.05 ERA and 10 complete games to become the American League's Rookie of the Year. Bahnsen's Yankees career would last another three seasons at a time when the New Yorkers were trying to rediscover their championship magic. After a sophomore slump that saw him go 9–16, he rebounded with a pair of 14-win seasons in '70 and '71. That winter, in need of a third baseman, the Yankees surprised a lot of people by dealing Bahnsen to the White Sox for Rich McKinney. Bahnsen continued to be a workhorse but not quite the coming star he looked like as a rookie. He would pitch for 16 seasons and finish at 146-149.

It was a continuing pattern, a few short timers and then some talented pitchers. The short timers were pitchers **Larry Gowell** and **Rich Hinton**, along with catcher **Ed Herrmann**. None of the three stayed in pinstripes for long. Gowell had a two-game career in 1972, while Hinton pitched just seven games for the Yanks that same year. Hermann was in 80 games in 1975 before his sale to the Angels.

Pitcher **Jim Beattie** was given every chance to make it with the Yanks and even threw the game of his life, but it wasn't enough. The 6'6" righthander came up to a great Yankees team in 1978 and made 22 starts in a pennant-winning year. He showed promise, going 6–9 with a 3.73 ERA. Then came the World Series against the Dodgers. Beattie got the start in Game Five and looked like Bob Gibson. He threw the first complete game of his career, giving up just two runs and fanning eight.

The next year, Beattie divided his time between the majors and minors, pitching in only 15 games and going 3–6 with a 5.21. In November, he was dealt to Seattle. Beattie became a journeyman after that, but he'll always have that great World Series game.

Lefty **Rudy May** was the next pitcher to wear No. 45. He took the number during his second tenure with the Yanks from 1980–83. Since he had worn No. 43 from 1974–76, he was discussed in that chapter. After May, another lefty came along who looked like he might be special. Big **Dennis Rasmussen** was pitching for the Yanks in the minors when he was sent to San Diego in September 1982. After pitching his first four big league games for the Padres at the end of the 1983 season, he was sent back to the Yanks the following March.

At 6'7", 230 pounds, Rasmussen was an imposing presence on the mound. He went a solid 9–6 as a starter in 1984 and a not-so-solid 3–5 the following year. But in 1986 he broke out, going 18–6 with a 3.88 ERA. When he regressed to 9–7 by late August of the 1987 season, the Yanks decided to cut bait. They traded Rasmussen to the Reds for the erratic **Bill Gullickson**. As for Gullickson, he threw in just eight games before the end of the 1987 season, went 4–2 with a 4.88 ERA, and was granted free agency.

You can't say the same for "the Candy Man." **John Candelaria** loved to pitch and couldn't help loving the Bronx. That's because the 6'7" southpaw with talent was born in New York City. He had to be overjoyed when the Yanks signed him as a free agent in January 1988. The Candy Man was 34 years old then, having come up with the Pirates as a 21-year-old in 1975. A year later, he was 16–7 and the year after that 20–5 with a league-best 2.34 ERA. In 1976, he threw the first ever no-hitter by a Pirates pitcher in Pittsburgh. Candelaria commanded the mound with a variety of stuff and great control, all thrown from a three-quarter delivery. The only thing, it seemed, that would stop him was injuries; unfortunately, he had plenty.

Though the Candy Man had just one losing season from 1975–88, injuries, including a chronic back problem, were taking a toll. Yet he was the Yanks' best pitcher in 1988, the latest No. 45 putting together a 13–7 record and a 3.38 ERA in 25 games. Not surprisingly, he went on the DL late in the season, this time with knee problems. It was more of the same in '89, and on August 29, the Yanks officially gave up on the Candy Man. He was just 3–3 in 10 games when they traded him to Montreal. Though he would pitch until 1993, he never won more than seven games in a season again and wound up with a 177–122 record for 19 injury-filled seasons with eight teams. Had he stayed healthy, John Candelaria could have been a potential Hall of Famer.

DANNY TARTABULL
YANKEES

Though No. 45 had been worn mostly by pitchers, the transition to some sluggers was close. Lefty **Kevin Mmahat** threw just four games in 1989. The toughest thing about him was probably spelling his last name, which began with a double-m. Slugger Steve "Bye Bye" Balboni wore No. 45 in 1990, his final Yankees season. But since he also wore a number as low as 28, he's been discussed earlier. Then righthander **Rich Monteleone** came along and wore No. 45 for just one of his four years in pinstripes. The reliever had the number in

1991, but donned No. 55 in 1990 and again in '92 and '93. He would later return as a coach.

The first of the real sluggers to wear No. 45 was **Danny Tartabull**, who joined the Yanks as a free agent prior to the 1992 season. The son of Jose Tartabull had come up with Seattle in 1984, them went to the Royals in '87, and that year batted .309 with 34 homers and 101 RBIs. By 1991, he was established as a top slugger and that's when the Yanks shelled out big to get the 29-year-old outfielder. "The Bull" had 25 homers and 85 RBIs in 123 games in his first year in pinstripes, then in '93 belted 31 and drove in 102 runs.

But his production began to drop in 1994, the strike year. Tartabull hit just .256 with 19 homers and 67 RBIs in 104 games. When he was hitting just .224 with six homers and 28 RBIs by July of '95, the Yanks once again got impatient and sent Tartabull to Oakland for another veteran slugger, Ruben Sierra.

Between Tartabull and another slugger, **Cecil Fielder**, catcher **Joe Girardi** wore No. 45 for part of 1996, but he soon changed to No. 25, opening the door for Fielder, who came over in a July 31 trade with Detroit. At 6'3", 240-pounds (or more), Fielder looked the part of the big slugger and his power could be awesome. All he did with Detroit in 1990 was blast 51 homers and drive in 132 runs, leading the league in both categories. Not only that, but he became the first player to reach the 50-home run mark since the Reds' George Foster in 1977. He led again the next year with 44 and 133, then hit 35 in 1992 and once again led the league with 124 RBIs. Between 1990 and 1995, Fielder had 219 home runs, most in the majors during that period.

After 107 games in 1996, he was having another big year with 26 homers and 80 RBIs. Suddenly, at the July 31st trade deadline, the Tigers sent him to the Yankees for Ruben Sierra and a minor leaguer. The Yanks were driving toward a pennant and figured Fielder's big bat could only help. It did, as he hit 13 more and drove home 37 runs in 52 games as No. 45 for the Yanks. That gave him 39 homers and 117 RBIs for the year. He was just 32 years old, so there was no reason to believe he didn't have three or four prime years left.

But in 1997 it started to go south. Fielder missed time to injury and played just 98 games, hitting .260 with 17 homers and 68 RBIs. At season's end, the Yanks granted him free agency and he signed with the Angels. As it turned out, the Yanks were right. That would be the big guy's final season. In 2007, his son, Prince, belted 50 homers for the Milwaukee Brewers, making them the first father and son to both reach the 50-home run mark.

With Fielder gone, the Yanks began looking for another slugging designated hitter type in 1998 and they signed 38-year-old **Charles "Chili" Davis**, a switch-hitter who had been in the bigs since 1981. Chili was a fine player, a cut below superstar level, but a productive hitter. He had a career-high 112 RBIs with the Angels in 1993 and his best home run season with 30 as a Royal in 1997, when he was 37 years old.

Never a great defensive player, Chili also had chronic back problems since 1990, so he spent most of his time at designated hitter. His back flared up again in '98 and he played in just 35 games, though he hit well in the postseason. In 1999, he was the DH in 146 games, hitting .269 with 19 homers and 78 RBIs in what would be his final season. His career home run total (350) was surpassed by only three switch-hitters: Mickey Mantle, Eddie Murray, and Chipper Jones.

A young outfielder and a veteran shared No. 45 in 2000 but didn't approach the productivity of Tartabull, Fielder, or Davis. **Felix Jose** had been out of the majors since 1995, playing in South Korea and other places. He was a good player in the early '90s, but his Yankees career lasted just 20 games for a .241 average. **Ryan Thompson**'s Yankee career spanned just 33 games, yet he wore two numbers, 33 and 45.

Once again No. 45 was being passed around, as outfielder **Henry Rodriguez**, pitcher **Jay Witasick**, and catcher **Albert Castillo** all wore it in 2001 and 2002, proving that even the top teams have transient players. All three had better years elsewhere and never did much in the Bronx.

Southpaw **Ted Lilly** didn't get a full shot with the Yanks and has done his best work elsewhere. He was with the New Yorkers from 2000–2002, wearing No. 56 the first year, No. 61 the second, and finally No. 45 the last year. After a seven-game trial in 2000, Lilly made 21 starts the next year and was 3–6 with a 3.40 ERA in 16 games in 2002 when he was traded to Oakland as part of a three-way deal with Detroit that brought Jeff Weaver to the Yanks. As of 2009, Lilly has won 10 or more games for seven straight seasons, with a best of 17–9 for the Cubs in 2008. His career mark is at 103–84 after 11 seasons and counting.

More pitchers followed from 2003–2005. **Felix Heredia**, **Jason Anderson**, and **Armando Benitez** all got looks of various lengths and none made it work. Heredia was picked off waivers in late August of 2003 and threw 12 games to the tune of a 1.20 ERA. He got another 47 chances in 2004 as a situational lefty, but his 6.28 ERA pointed to more failures than successes and he was gone. Anderson, a righty, pitched in 22 games in 2003 before being traded to the Mets for Benitez on July 16. In June 2004, he was plucked off waivers and had a second chance as No. 31. After three games, it was over.

Benitez was another story. A righthander with electric stuff, he didn't always control it and sometimes couldn't keep his emotions in check. Yet he was a successful closer in some seasons. He threw nine games for the Bombers after coming over from the Mets on July 16 and wasn't bad, going 1–1 with a 1.93 ERA. But on August 6, the Yanks decided to ship him to Seattle to get back Jeff Nelson, who had pitched for them before.

And that brings us to the man who wore No. 45 from 2005 to 2008. He came to the Yanks off an 18–8 season with the Marlins and signed a four-year deal worth approximately $40 million. Before he left, the New York media had dubbed him with the unflattering nickname of "American Idle." Look again. That's *Idle*, not *Idol*. **Carl Pavano** got the name because he rarely pitched. For $40 million dollars, Pavano had a four-year Yankees mark of 9–8. The guy was paid more than $4 million a win! That's because the injuries came (see sidebar) and Pavano didn't always handle them well.

ANATOMY OF A BAD INVESTMENT

When the Yanks signed Carl Pavano, they thought they were getting a big winner. Here's what they got instead. In 2005, he debuted with seven quality starts in his first 10 outings. Then he injured a shoulder in June and went on the DL. He made just seven more starts and finished with a 4–6 record and a 4.77 ERA. Bring on 2006. It came and went and Pavano didn't pitch. During spring training he bruised his buttocks and was out several months. By early August he was making rehab starts in the minors. Then on August 15, he was in an auto accident and broke two ribs. The problem was that he didn't tell the Yankees until August 28, the day the team told him he was coming off the DL. Season done.

In early 2007, Mike Mussina voiced what many thought—Pavano had to prove he wanted to pitch again for the Yanks. Then a hamstring injury to Chien-Ming Wang made the reluctant righty the team's Opening Day starter. Pavano pitched pretty well, but by April 15, was on the DL once again with an elbow strain. On May 23, he opted for Tommy John surgery and was out for the year. His slate for 2007, a 1–0 record in two games. In 2008, he made his first start on August 23; by September 14 he was walking off the mound with a hip injury. His final tally in '08, a 4–2 record in seven games, with a 5.77 ERA. It was no surprise when the Yanks let him go to free agency. Talk about bad luck.

The last player to wear No. 45 was another pitcher coming off Tommy John surgery. The Yanks signed righty **Sergio Mitre** in November 2008, knowing he was rehabbing from surgery. Manager Joe Girardi knew Mitre when he managed at Florida and liked his natural sinker, so the team took a flyer. Mitre came back to pitch in 12 games during 2009, going 3–3 but with a high 6.79 ERA. The Yanks hope to find out if he can return to being a solid pitcher in 2010.

#46: ANDY PETTITTE, ACTS I AND II

There's little doubt that Andy Pettitte has become a full-fledged Yankees icon. Now known as one of the "Core Four," along with Derek Jeter, Jorge Posada, and Mariano Rivera, Pettitte has been part of all five Yankees championships since 1996. He's also now the winningest postseason pitcher in baseball history and further cemented his place in Yankees lore when he won the deciding game in the Division Series, the ALCS, and then the World Series in 2009. The crafty southpaw, who has worn No. 46 since the beginning, is so entrenched in recent Yankees history that some tend to forget that he left the team after 2003 and pitched for his hometown Houston Astros for three seasons before returning in 2007 for his second go-around with the Bronx Bombers. Though he was born in Louisiana and grew up in Texas, the common perception was that when he came back to the Yanks he was returning home.

By coming home, Andy Pettitte sent a message that really said, "I'm sorry I left in the first place." As a 23-year-old rookie in 1995, he showed his grit and willingness to battle deep into games. He went 12–9 with a 4.17 ERA as the Yanks made the playoffs for the first time since 1981. A year later, he began creating his New York legacy when he compiled a 21–8 record and helped pitch the Yankees to the World Series.

He continued as a mainstay of the staff as the Yanks won four Series in five years, culminating the run with a five-game victory over the

Andy Pettitte

Mets in 2000. And he continued to pitch well in the regular season, winning 18 games in 1997, 19 in 2000, and another 21 in 2003. And that's when Yankees fans got a shock. Both Pettitte and teammate (and fellow Texan) Roger Clemens were free agents and decided to sign with the Houston Astros.

So this lifetime Yankee was suddenly gone. Andy was injured in 2004 and needed elbow surgery, limiting him to just 15 games, but a year later he bounced back to a more Pettitte-like 17–9 mark and helped the Astros into the World Series. A year later, he went just 14–13 and was a free agent once more. He soon signed a $16 million one-year deal to return to the Yanks. At age 35 he was still essentially the same Andy, going 15–9 and leading the league with 34 starts. A year later, now on another one-year deal, he was pitching well until the end, when a barking shoulder caused him to slump and finish at 14–14. Would the Yanks want him back again at the age of 37?

The off-season signings of CC Sabathia and A. J. Burnett gave the Yankees two potential aces at the top of the rotation, and a third big money signing, first baseman Mark Teixeira, seemed to drain the budget. For a while, it looked as if Andy wouldn't return. But at last an agreement was reached, a one-year deal for $5.5 million plus incentives. But before the season was done, the man who at first was an afterthought was again one of the most important cogs in the Yankees' machine, going 14–8 in the regular season and a perfect 4–0 in the playoffs, including two wins in the World Series. And, sure enough, he signed another one-year deal to return again in 2010.

As a pitcher, Andy Pettitte has never been overpowering. But he has the whole arsenal—fastball, curve, cutter, sinker, and change. He's relied more on his cutter in later years, as well as on control and a competitive fire that still burns brightly. In addition, he's got the best pickoff move in the game. Runners on first beware. Through 2009, Pettitte's record is 229–135; it's not quite Hall of Fame, but add his 18–9 post-season mark and you're getting close.

Other than Pettitte, the best players to wear No. 46 have been those who donned it early in their careers before switching to other numbers. It's a number that wasn't worn regularly until the 1970s. The first guy to wear it was backup catcher **Charlie Silvera** in 1948, his rookie year. But Silvera soon switched to No. 29, which he wore until 1956. As for No. 46, it was then put on the shelf for a dozen years until lefty **Bill Short** took it in 1960. Short had a short Yankees career lasting 10 games before he went to Baltimore as a Rule 5 draft pick. Then another 10 years passed before a fan at Yankee Stadium saw No. 46 again. Guess what? Another 10 games and gone. This time outfielder **Bobby Mitchell** wore it and hit .227 before being returned to the minors. A year later, righthander **Roger Hambright** had the number, pitched in 18 games and never appeared in the bigs again.

When catcher **Rick Dempsey** was given No. 46 in 1973, he might have thought he was getting a jinxed number, especially as he got to play in just six games and hit .182. Dempsey then backed up Thurman Munson for the next three seasons. He didn't have much of a stick but was a good catcher with a quick throwing arm.

In June of 1976, the Yanks dealt Dempsey to Baltimore, where he became a fixture for 11 years. Though never much of a hitter, Dempsey became a popular, sometimes flaky player and one heck of a catcher. Dempsey would play for 24 seasons, until he was 42 years old.

Next came another succession of short-term players, followed by a group who wore No. 46 but switched to a different number before they made their mark. It began with outfielder **Gene Locklear**, who played 13 games in 1976 and just one the following year before leaving the game. **Mike Heath, Don Hood, Joe Lefebvre**, and **Gene Nelson** all wore No. 46 for a single season or part of a season. Catcher Heath played 33 games in 1978, hit .228, and was traded to the Rangers. Lefty Hood came in a June 15, 1979, trade with the Indians for Cliff Johnson, pitched in 27 games, and went 3–1 with a 3.07 ERA. But he was granted free agency at season's end.

Outfielder Joe Lefebvre (pronounced luh-FAY) homered in each of his first two games with the Yankees in 1980, tying a major league record. It didn't help in the long run. In March 1981, he was traded to the Padres. Righthander Nelson was the youngest player in the majors when he came up with the Yanks at age 20 in 1981. He made seven starts, went 3–1 with a 4.81 ERA. At his age, that's pretty good. But the Yanks traded Nelson to Seattle before the 1982 season.

How about those guys who wore, but didn't keep, No. 46? Leading off that list is none other than **Don Mattingly**, the future captain, who wore No. 46 in 1982 and '83 before cutting the number in half and putting on No. 23. Pitcher **Shane Rawley** came to the Yanks in 1982 and wore No. 46 until he switched to No. 26 later in the year, then wore it the following two seasons. Third sacker Mike **Pagliarulo** had No. 46 his rookie year of 1984, then dropped to No. 6 the following year and finally to his more familiar, pre-Alex Rodriguez No. 13, which he wore through 1989. Part time outfielder **Henry Cotto** had No. 46 in 1985 and '86, then was issued No. 28 in his final Yankees season of 1987.

The same pattern continued, the number given to players who didn't last or to those who wore it and then went lower. Infielder **Jerry Royster** joined the Yankees in August of 1987, when he was 34 years old. He lasted just 18 games, despite hitting .357 (15-for-42). Pitcher **Rich Bordi** went the opposite way, wearing No. 43 in 1985, then taking No. 46 when he returned briefly two years later. Lefty **Hipolito Pena** threw 16 games for the Yanks in 1988, his third and final year in the majors. Infielder **Randy Velarde** wore Nos. 29 and 46 in 1987 and '88 before the fine utility infielder switched to No. 18, which he wore through 1995 and again when he returned in 2001.

Terry Mulholland pitched in the majors for 20 years, but his Yankees career lasted all of 24 games in 1994. This was a guy who started and relieved for 11 teams over the years, proving the old adage that there's always a job for a competent lefty. The year after Mulholland left, Pettitte arrived and occupied No. 46 through 2003. When he left for Houston, the Yanks wasted no time issuing the number to others.

Another lefty, **Donovan Osborne**, wasn't as lucky as Mulholland. His career was shortened by a succession of injuries, including shoulder problems. The Yanks signed him in February 2004 and released him May 27. He threw just nine games, the final nine of his career. Lefty **Darrell May** also pitched for the Yanks in his final season. But he lasted just two games in 2005.

Alan Embree and **Scott Erickson** were both veterans with some good seasons behind them, yet they didn't remain with the Yankees long. Embree, a hard-throwing lefthander, signed as a free agent on July 30, 2005, after the rival Red Sox released him. He was 35 years old and threw 24 games before the end of the year, going 1–1, but with an unacceptable 7.53 ERA the Yanks granted him free agency. Righty Erickson went 20–8 for the Twins back in 1991, when they won the World Series. He was trying to make a comeback with the Yanks at the age of 38 in 2006, but after nine games and a 7.94 ERA he was released.

Outfielder **Aaron Guiel** was the last player to wear No. 46 before Andy Pettitte returned for Act II. Guiel was plucked off waivers from Kansas City on July 5, 2006, and played in 44 games, hitting .256 with four homers. The Yanks granted him free agency after the season and he never hooked up with another team. Then Pettitte returned, reclaimed the No. 46 and proceeded to build on his own legend.

PETTITTE MOVING UP THE LADDER

Andy Pettitte has been a Yankee moundstay since 1995 with the exception of his three years in Houston. Not surprisingly, he's high on the list of all-time Yankees winners.

Whitey Ford........................ 236

Red Ruffing 231

Andy Pettitte...................... 192

Lefty Gomez....................... 189

Ron Guidry 170

Bob Shawkey 168

Mel Stottlemyre.................. 164

Herb Pennock..................... 162

Waite Hoyt......................... 157

Allie Reynolds.................... 131

Note: The irony of this list is that with all their success and 27 World Championships, the Yankees have never had a 300-game winner. And, as you can see, no one is close. With more players changing teams and pitchers coming and going as free agents, there's a chance the Yankees will never have a hurler who wins that many games.

#47: NO. 47: IN MOTHBALLS UNTIL 1955

No. 47 is unusual for two reasons. One, it wasn't issued to anyone for the first 26 years numbers were worn. And when a player finally claimed it in 1955, it wasn't a guy who was up for just three games, a veteran on his last legs, or someone who would wear two or three other numbers before his Yankees career was done. The first player to wear it would keep it for more than four years and, for a time, looked as if he was poised to become a real star.

That guy was pitcher **Tom Sturdivant**, a righthander who was 25 years old when he was called up for the first time in 1955 and given No. 47. Sturdivant had an unusual assortment of pitches. He had the usual fastball and slider, but also mixed a knuckleball into his repertoire. Working almost exclusively out of the bullpen his rookie year, he pitched in 33 games and went 1–3 with a 3.16 ERA. But the next year, he made 17 starts in 32 appearances and began to flourish, finishing at 16–8 with a 3.30 ERA. Besides his starts, he found time to get five saves and quickly became a valuable member of Casey Stengels's pitching staff as the team won another World Series

When Sturdivant went 16–6 with a 2.54 ERA in '57 as a full-time member of the rotation he looked like a coming star with the best team in baseball. But then came the dreaded sore arm. Sturdivant threw just 15 games in 1958 and was 3–6 with a 4.20 ERA. He never

LUIS ARROYO
Pitcher

New York
Yankees

regained the magic. He was 0–2 with a 4.97 ERA in seven games in '59, when the Yanks traded him with Jerry Lumpe to Kansas City for Hector Lopez and Ralph Terry on May 26.

Less than a year would pass before a second memorable pitcher would pull on uniform No. 47. Reliever **Luis Arroyo** put together one of the greatest seasons ever out of the pen before falling victim to the same malady as Sturdivant—the dreaded arm injury. Before he arrived, righty **Eli Grba** was No. 47 for 19 games in 1959, switching to No. 18 the next year, then going to the Angels in the 1960 expansion draft. Bobby Shantz's younger brother, catcher **Wilmer "Billy" Shantz**, was with the Yanks for a single game early in the 1960 season. Then on July 20, with the Yanks heading for another pennant, they purchased Arroyo's contract from the Reds.

Arroyo was a 28-year-old rookie with the Cards in 1955 and produced an 11–8 year, mostly as a starter. But when he was dealt to Pittsburgh and moved to the bullpen, he struggled. When the Yanks got him from the Reds, they didn't know quite what to expect. At 5'8" and a pudgy 190-pounds, the lefty-throwing Arroyo didn't look like much. But once he unleashed an effective screwball on American League hitters, he found success. For the balance of 1960, he went 5–1 in 29 games, with a 2.88 ERA and seven saves.

The 1961 season was a magical one. The Yanks would not only win another pennant, but as a team would hit a then record 240 home runs. On the mound, Whitey Ford had the greatest season of his career, going 25–4, and he had plenty of help from Arroyo. One lefty often relieved the other, and Luis relieved a lot of other starters as well. He pitched in 65 games that year, had a 15–5 record, a 2.19 ERA, and 29 saves. So Arroyo had a direct hand in 44 of the Yanks' 109 regular season victories, an All-Star year if there ever was one for the first Puerto Rican born player ever to appear in pinstripes.

Arroyo was 35 years old in 1962, but that wasn't the problem. An injured arm was. He was only able to pitch in 27 games, went 1–3 with a 4.81 ERA, and posted seven saves. But he couldn't pitch in the World Series and the next year was even worse. He worked just six games with a 13.50 ERA and was done.

The assigning of No. 47 to some interesting, if not great, pitchers would continue. Utilityman **Frank Tepedino** had the number in 1967, but then switched to No. 21 for his final three partial seasons in pinstripes. Then, in 1972, a righthander named **Fred Beene** was given No. 47. At 5'9", 160 pounds, Beene was always told he was too small, and that made him more of a competitor and fighter. But like so many others, he wasn't immune to arm problems.

"Beeney" did a nice job for the Bombers, pitching in 29 games to a 2.34 ERA and three saves. The next year, he was even better, though his season was cut short by more arm problems. In the 19 games he pitched, he was a perfect 6–0 with an impressive 1.68 earned run average. Opposing batters just weren't hitting him. But in late April 1974, the Yanks packaged Beene with three other pitchers and sent them to Cleveland.

Marginal outfielders **Larry Murray** and **Kerry Dineen** were temporary tenants of No. 47. Murray had it for eight games in 1976 after wearing No. 52 two years earlier and No. 18 in 1975 for a total of 12 games. Dineen played seven games as No. 49 in 1975 and another four with No. 47 the following year. Then two years later, the Yankees purchased the contract of a player who helped change the face of baseball. In 1975, pitchers **Andy Messersmith** and Dave McNally decided to test baseball's reserve clause by playing the season without contracts in their option years. Their claim was it would free them from their contracts, and that the reserve clause would bind them to their teams for the option year, but no further. The owners said the reserve clause kicked in automatically and was perpetually renewed. When an arbitrator ruled in favor of the players, free agency was born.

The righthanded Messersmith had a track record, going 16–11 and 20–13 for the Angels in 1969 and '71, then 20–6 and 19–14 for the Dodgers in '74 and '75. When the ruling went in his favor, he signed with the Braves for $1.75 million. He was not only one of the first free agents, but one of the first free agent disappointments, going just 11–11 with the Braves in '76. Then the injury jinx hit. That December, the Braves sold his contract to the Yankees. He had an impressive spring for the Bombers, looking like his old self, but the week before the season began he injured his shoulder in a fall while covering first. He was 0–3 in just six games all year, was released after the season, pitched a few games for the Dodgers the next year, and then retired.

After Messersmith, No. 47 took on the varied look of many other numbers in the 40s. Catcher **Bruce Robinson**, for example, caught a total of 10 games in 1979 and '80. Righty **Curt Kaufman** threw 11 games in 1982 and '83 combined, wearing No. 47 the first year and No. 55 the second.

Southpaw **Ray Fontenot** caught a break in 1983 when he was inserted into the rotation to replace an injured Ron Guidry. Fontenot made 15 starts and went 8–2 with a 3.33 ERA. A junk thrower who counted on control, he had another pretty good year before the Yanks moved him to the Cubs, and he ran into a series of injuries. Lefty reliever **Rod Scurry** wore No. 47 for five games in 1985, then switched to No. 28 the following year. Drug problems curtailed his career. Another lefty, **Alfonso Pulido**, came over from Pittsburgh and lasted just 10 games as a Yankee in 1986 before handing the number over to veteran knuckleballer Joe Niekro. Because he wore No. 31 in 1985 and No. 39 in 1987, his Yankees career has already been documented.

Lefty **Pete Filson** was another short timer, working just seven games in 1987 Infielder **Alvaro Espinoza**, pitcher **Scott Nielsen**, and infielder **Dave Silvestri** were all guys who changed numbers during their stay in pinstripes. Espinoza wore No. 47 his first Yankees season of 1988, then No. 20 the next three seasons. Nielsen had it when he returned to the Yanks in 1988. He had been around briefly as No. 41

in 1986 and then wore No. 33 in 1989, one of the many number-a-year guys. Silvestri, in parts of four seasons (1992–95), went from No. 56 to No. 47 twice and No. 43 his last year.

Then in 1993 the Yanks made a late-season pickup as they battled Toronto for the division title, dealing to get reliever **Lee Smith** from the Cardinals on August 31. The 6'6", 265-pound Smith was an intimidating presence on the mound, especially when he unleashed his 95-mph fastball. One of the best closers of his generation, two years earlier he had saved a National League record 47 games with the Cardinals. He could still throw hard, though he was 35 years old by the time he pulled on the pinstripes and No. 47.

Smith did his job, pitching brilliantly, giving up nothing in eight games and saving three. The problem was that the Yanks as a team went into the tank and Toronto pulled away to win easily. Instead of re-signing Smith, the Yanks let him go to free agency, and he moved on to the Orioles. Smith would pitch for 18 seasons, working for eight teams and saving what was then a record 478 games. He's since been passed by Trevor Hoffman and Mariano Rivera.

Righty **Dave Eiland** was another pitcher whose career was dampened by arm problems, though he spent parts of five seasons (1988–91, 1995) with the Yanks. One of the number jumpers, Eiland began with No. 52, went to 28, then 58, back to 28, and finally No. 47 when he returned in '95. He's presently the Yankees' pitching coach. Veteran lefty **Rick Honeycutt** came to the Yanks at the tail end of the 1995 season. He wore No. 47, just a bit higher than his age of 41, and lasted all of three games, posting a 27.00 ERA. He left in December.

Pitcher **Dave Pavlas** and and outfielder/first baseman **Ivan Cruz** were caretakers of No. 47 during 1996 and '97. Pavlas threw four games as No. 56 in 1995 before pitching in 16 more as No. 47 the next year, while Cruz lasted for all of 11 games in '97. In 1998, the Yanks brought up a stocky outfielder late in the season who showed everyone how to become a hero overnight. His name was **Shane Spencer**, but the way he played at the end of the 1998 season, some of his teammates began calling him Roy Hobbs, the name of the protagonist in the novel and movie, *The Natural*.

Spencer was 5'11", 225 pounds and had a powerful righthanded stroke. Whether pinch-hitting or getting spot starts in the outfield, he seemed like Johnny-on-the-spot as the Yankees rolled toward 114 regular season wins. In 27 games, Spencer batted .373, hit 10 home runs, and drove home 27 runs. Three of his home runs were grand slams and he homered at the rate of one every 6.7 at bats. At the age of 26, he had been waiting for his chance and seemed determined to make the most of it.

But Shane Spencer wasn't the first, or the last, player to look like an All-Star the first time around the league. In 1999, he played in 71 games and hit just .234 with eight homers and 20 runs batted in. More time, less production. For the next three years, Spencer had his chances and couldn't make it work. His production continued to go downward and he struck out too much. After the 2002 season, the Yanks just let him to to free agency and he signed with Cleveland.

After Spencer departed, No. 47 has gone strictly to the pitchers, with a group of youngsters and veterans wearing it, none staying very long or really excelling. Veterans **Al Reyes** and **Jesse Orosco** were the first two, both wearing No. 47 for a short part of the 2003 season. The righty Reyes, who would pitch for 13 seasons in relief, worked 13 games, and was released in July. Orosco, who had a long, 24-year career, came to the Yanks in a July 22 trade with the Padres and was dealt in turn to the Twins on August 31.

The arms continued to come, starting with **Bret Prinz** and going to **Colter Bean**, **Felix Rodriguez**, **Ron Villone**, **Chris Britton**, and **Sidney Ponson**. Prinz threw for parts of 2003 and 2004, wearing No. 38 the first year and No. 47 his final year. Bean was brought up three times, wearing No. 58 in 2005 and '06, and finally No. 47 in 2007. He pitched in a total of six games and was gone. Rodriguez was a veteran who came from the Phils in December 2004 and pitched in 34 games with no record and a 5.01 ERA. Then it was off to free agency.

Ron Villone was from New Jersey and always wanted to pitch for the Yanks. The Marlins traded the hard-throwing lefty to New York in November 2005, and he was used extensively during the 2006 season, pitching in 70 games with a 3–3 record and 5.04 ERA. The next year, he was in just 37 games with no record and a 4.25 ERA. The Yanks had apparently lost confidence and let him leave via free agency.

Not the same with Chris Britton. A portly righthander, he came over from the Orioles for Jaret Wright and pitched sparingly in 2007 and '08, wearing both No. 39 and 47 before being granted free agency. Sidney Ponson has always been a starter, and in 12 years has been with seven teams to the tune of a 91–113 record. The Yanks got him as a fill-in for injured pitchers in both 2006 and 2008. He was No. 24 the first time around when he pitched just five games, then was given No. 47 in his second tenure, which was somewhat more successful. Ponson threw 16 games and went 4–4 with a 5.85 ERA. When you're hired as a stopgap, going .500 isn't too bad a job. With Ponson leaving, utilityman **Freddy Guzman** wore No. 47 briefly at the end of 2009, so the question remains, who'll be the guy who really puts a stamp on it? It hasn't happened yet.

#48: THE PLAYERS DWINDLE DOWN

Start with the names **Frank Colman**, **John Gabler**, and **Elvio Jimenez** and you might have an idea of the direction No. 48 has taken. As we begin entering the numerical stratosphere, recognizable players become scarcer.

As for Colman, Gabler, and Jimenez, none of them wore No. 48 for very long. Outfielder Colman was the first, wearing it for 22 games in 1947 after taking the field for just five games a year earlier with No. 8 on his back. Gabler, a righthander, was given No. 48 in 1959 and pitched in three games. When he threw in 21 games the following year, he donned No. 40, but his mediocre performance earned him a trip to Washington. Jimenez, an outfielder, was one of the many one-game wonders who've passed through the Stadium on their way in and out of the league. His game came in 1964.

Long-time Yankees outfielder **Roy White** wore No. 48 for three-plus years, from 1965 through the middle of 1968 when he switched to No. 21. Firmly established by then, White took No. 6 in 1969 and wore it for the next 11 years. Righty **Cecil Perkins** had the number for two games in 1967, and then southpaw **"Sudden Sam" McDowell** wore it in 1973 and '74. But since McDowell wore No. 29 when he first arrived in '73 before switching, his sometimes meteoric career was discussed in that chapter. And that leads up to one of the most one-dimensional players of all-time, the well-traveled **Dave Kingman**.

At 6'6", 210 pounds, the lanky Kingman had a big, long swing and could hit the ball as far as anyone in the game. No wonder his nickname was "King Kong." But he also struck out a lot, hit for low averages, and would never win a Mr. Popularity contest. Kingman came to the Yanks at the tail end of the 1977 season, via a September 15 trade with the Angels for a minor leaguer. The Yanks were driving toward a division title and looking for a bat. He did his job, hitting .250 in eight games, but driving four balls out of the park. Because he arrived after September 1, he wasn't on the playoff roster, and after the season he left as a free agent.

Playing the Mets in 1982, Kingman led the National League in homers with 37 while hitting just .204. That's .204! It was the lowest average ever for a home run champion. In 16 seasons with seven teams, Dave Kingman blasted 442 homers to go with a lowly .236 batting average. Hall of Famer? Never happen.

Had pitcher **Mike Torrez** not switched numbers, Dave Kingman couldn't have worn No. 48. Torrez came to the Yanks early in 1977

and was instrumental in their championship season. But Torrez decided to take No. 24 some time after arriving, making No.48 available once again. After Torrez and Kingman, the number went into mothballs for six years until relief pitcher **Dale Murray** took it and kept it from 1983 to early in the 1985 season.

Murray was an outstanding rookie with the Montreal Expos in 1974, pitching in 32 games with a 1.03 ERA and 10 saves. A big righthander, he had an exploding fastball and diving forkball, more than enough of an arsenal for a short reliever. By the time the Blue

Jays traded Murray to the Yanks in December 1982, he had thrown a lot of innings. The word was that overwork had taken some of the bite out of his fastball. The Yanks used him in 40 games in 1983, and the next year Murray was only in 19 games, losing some time to injury. He was released the following April 29 after pitching just three games.

Reliever Neil Allen pitched for the Yanks in 1985 and then again in 1987 and '88. He was a multiple number guy, wearing Nos. 53 and 26 his first year, No. 48 in 1987, and finally No. 27 in 1988. Obviously, he's been mentioned already. After Allen came seven more quickies, players even the most diehard of Yankees fans would have difficulty remembering: Catcher **John Ramos**, outfielder **Robert Perez**, infielder **Scott Seabol**, lefthander **Randy Keisler**, righties **Jay Tessmer** and **Brandon Knight**, and outfielder/first baseman **Fernando Seguignol**. All wore No. 48.

The final four players to wear No. 48 were all pitchers. First there was **Paul Quantrill**, a righthander who helped coin the term "inning eater." He was essentially a middle reliever who could pitch and pitch often. In fact, in the three years before Quantrill came to the Yankees he was considered one of the best at his role. No wonder the Yanks went out and signed him in December 2003.

One of the few knocks against Joe Torre when he managed the Yanks was that he tended to burn his bullpen, but with Quantrill he probably felt he didn't have to worry. As a result, the reliever with impeccable control was called to the mound another 86 times in 2004, once again leading the league in appearances. In 2005, it was clear that Quantrill wasn't the same pitcher. He was hampered by a bad knee and being hit regularly. He appeared in just 22 games by July 2, with an inflated 6.75 earned run average, when the Yanks surprised everyone by trading him to San Diego.

When Quantrill left, southpaw **Wayne Franklin** was called up for just 13 games, but his 6.39 ERA didn't cut it and he was granted free agency at season's end. That December, still looking for the right set-up man for Mariano Rivera, the Yanks signed 6'4", 220 pound **Kyle Farnsworth** to a three-year, $17-million deal. The enigmatic righthander had electric stuff, including a fastball that could sometimes touch 100 mph, and a sharp slider. But the story was that he passed up opportunities to close and would rather set-up, which made some wonder about his ability to pitch in tough situations.

In two-plus seasons, "Farnsy" became the pitcher fans at Yankee Stadium most liked to boo. He had some successes, but his failures always seemed more glaring, especially when he would lose his command and then get hit. He seemed to have dominating stuff, yet rarely dominated. By 2008 the Yankees were getting tired of watching history repeat itself. Even though he had his ERA down to 3.65 in 45 appearances, the Yankees traded him to Detroit on July 30 for catcher Pudge Rodriguez.

In 2008, young lefthander **Phil Coke** became the latest to wear No. 48. Coming up late in the season, Coke showed promise, pitching in 12 games and going 1–0 with an impressive 0.61 earned run average. Mixing a live fastball with a slider, Coke seemed to have the right mentality for a short reliever. In 2009, he became one of manager Joe Girardi's dependable relievers. Then, after the season, he was included in a trade with Detroit that brought outfielder Curtis Granderson to the Bronx.

#49: LOUISIANA LIGHTNING

He stood just 5'11" and 160 pounds, not the kind of guy expected to throw a 95-mph fastball and a hard slider with a devastating downward bite. But he did. And when he combined that with a fierce competitiveness and tremendous all-around athletic ability, southpaw **Ron Guidry** pitched himself into Yankee history and onto the wall at Monument Park. He was the ace of the staff in the pennant and World Series years from 1976–78, and into the early 1980s he remained guy who always brought excitement to the mound and the game. He started off as No. 49 during his first of two cups of coffee years in 1975 and he stayed with it, making it as synonymous with him as his nicknames, "Gator" and "Louisiana Lightning." No other Yankee wore No. 49 from the time Guidry retired in 1988 until it was retired in his honor in 2003. And very few wore it before him.

The Yankees signed him in 1971 but he spent nearly five full years in the minors because no one thought the slim lefthander with the Cajun drawl would be a star. When he was finally called up in 1975, he had a bad outing and then spent 46 straight days in the bullpen without getting the call again. But he used his time well. He watched the Yanks' star reliever Sparky Lyle throw his highly effective slider and noticed how he threw it so it would break down instead of across the plate. Two years later, when Guidry made the rotation, he not only had a crackling fastball, but a slider that left hitters swinging at air.

Louisiana Lightning was 16–7 with a 2.82 ERA in '77, helping the Yanks win their first World Series since 1962, but that still didn't prepare anyone for what would happen the following year. To put it bluntly, in 1978, Ron Guidry had one of the greatest seasons ever by a pitcher. He was as close to unhittable, winning his first 13 decisions, including a game against the Angels on June 17, in which he tied a then Amer-

ican League record with 18 strikeouts.

In fact, it was Ron Guidry's magnificent pitching that kept the Bombers close enough to rally and then win in a one-game playoff, 5–4, when Bucky Dent hit his big, three-run homer at Fenway. The winning pitcher: Ron Guidry.

That was Guidry's 25th victory of the year. His final line was 25–3 with a league best 1.74 ERA, nine shutouts, and 248 strikeouts. He was a runaway Cy Young Award winner and helped the Yanks win a second straight World Series. His two-year playoff record in '77 and '78 was a perfect 4–0. No one, of course, expected him to duplicate that kind of season, but he continued as one of the AL's best, winning 18 and 17 games the next two years. In 1983, he was 21–9, and two years after that, adding a curveball to his repertoire, he was 22–6.

What people didn't know what that starting in 1981 (when he was just 11–5 in 23 games) Guidry had to deal with periodic arm problems. After his big season in 1985, the 35-year-old Guidry wasn't the same pitcher. He went 9–12, 5–8, and then just 2–3 in 12 games in 1988. He could no longer compensate for the aching arm. He finally underwent surgery after the 1988 season and when he didn't respond the following spring, he retired.

Ron Guidry pitched 14 seasons for the Yankees, going 170–91 with a 3.29 ERA, 95 complete games, and 26 shutouts. But he really had nine peak seasons if you subtract the cups of coffee in '75 and '76, and those last three seasons when he pitched with a bad arm. But during those nine years he was as good as they come—an exciting, dynamic pitcher whose wiry body unleashed a fastball and slider that made him the league's best and one of the Yankees' best of all-time. He may not have Hall of Fame numbers, but during his peak years it was hard to find someone better.

Guidry's No. 49 was retired on August 23, 2003, at ceremonies held on "Ron Guidry Day." His plaque in Monument Park reads, "A dominating pitcher and a respected leader. A true Yankee." That he was. And, oh yes. Here's a bit of Ron Guidry trivia. Louisiana Lightning was a good amateur drummer and once accompanied the Beach Boys during a post game concert at Yankee Stadium.

Because No. 49 was not worn until 1954 and then worn only intermittently until Guidry came along, not a lot of other Yankees are really remembered for the number. Catcher **Lou Berberet** was the first in 1954, catching just five games. A year later he caught two more, but as No. 35. A righthanded pitcher named **Jim Bronstad** was next, and his Yankees career lasted all of 16 games in 1959. Lefty **Bob Meyer** worked in just seven games in 1964, while Stan Bahnsen wore No. 49 during his cup of coffee year of 1966. When he returned two years later, he took on No. 45, which he wore through 1971.

Charlie Sands, **Loyd Colson**, and **Kerry Dineen** were the final three players to wear No. 49 before Ron Guidry put his stamp on it. Catcher Sands had a one-game Yankees career in 1967, while Colson, whose first name was indeed spelled without the second "l," pitched a single game for the Yanks in 1970, his only appearance in the bigs. Dineen, an outfielder, wore No. 49 in 1975 when he was in seven games. A year later, he played just four games but wore No. 47. That's because Ron Guidry had already taken over the number and no Yankees fan will ever forget what happened next. Louisiana Lightning struck—and hitters struck out.

K IS FOR STRIKEOUT

Ron Guidry wasn't the typical strikeout pitcher. With his thin frame, he almost looked like some of the junk throwers of an earlier time. But he could bring the heat and his slider was a devastating strikeout pitch. He's now second on the all-time Yankee list with Andy Pettitte poised to pass him in 2010.

Whitey Ford 1,956
Ron Guidry 1,778
Andy Pettitte 1,772
Red Ruffing 1,526
Lefty Gomez 1,468
Mike Mussina 1,278
Mel Stottlemyre 1,257
Bob Shawkey 1,163
Al Downing 1,028
Roger Clemens 1,014

Note: Sitting in 11th place is Mariano Rivera with 1,006 whiffs. He should move into ninth or tenth in 2010, an amazingly high ranking for a relief pitcher, especially a closer.

#50: GET ME A SCORECARD

ALL TIME NO. 50 ROSTER

Player	Year
Ralph Houk	1947
Billy Bryan	1967
Bill Burbach	1969–71
Alan Closter	1971–72
Doc Medich	1972
Dave Pagan	1973
Ken Clay	1977
Roger Slagle	1979
John Pacella	1982
Lynn McGlothen	1982
Jay Howell	1984
Marty Bystrom	1985
Phil Lombardi	1986
Chris Chambliss	1988
Steve Balboni	1989
Oscar Azocar	1990
Alan Mills	1991
Ed Napoleon (coach)	1992–93
Robert Eenhoorn	1994–95
Chris Chambliss (coach)	1996–97
Don Zimmer (coach)	1998–2000
Todd Erdos	2000
Matt Lawton	2005
Larry Bowa (coach)	2006–07
Bobby Meacham (coach)	2008
Mick Kelleher (coach)	2009

When the numbers reach 50 and above, people begin thinking football. Baseball, traditionally, has been a game of lower numbers, and why not. The first numbers corresponded with the batting order, one through nine. Now it isn't unusual for young up players from the minors to wear a number in the 50s and even the 60s. If the player doesn't make it, no harm done. If he does, chances are he'll switch to a lower number. There are those players, of course, who begin with a high number, have immediate success, and decide to keep it. But here at the half century mark, you'll really need to pay attention. Most of the players who had the number came and went quickly, while a few hung onto it for a couple of years, and some quickly jettisoned it for something else. Here's the roster.

A familiar name is in the leadoff spot. Backup catcher **Ralph Houk** became the first Yankee to wear No. 50 his rookie year of 1947. Before the year was out, however, he dropped down to No. 32, which he wore during the rest of his Yankee years as a player. And a pattern was established, albeit one that wouldn't be repeated for awhile, because no player donned the number for some 20 years. In 1967, catcher **Billy Bryan** was No. 50 for just 16 games. He actually reversed the pattern. The year, before he was No. 23 for 27 games.

Pitcher **Bill Burbach** was another guy who broke the mold. He wore No. 50 from 1969–71, though in the latter two seasons he appeared in just six games. Lefty **Alan Closter** also wore No. 50 during 1971 and

'72, pitching 14 games the first year and just two the next. Righty Doc Medich wore the number for one game in 1972. He then went to No. 42 the following season and then No. 33 his final two years before being traded.

Dave Pagan, another righthander, took the opposite approach. He wore No. 50 in 1973, when he appeared in just four games. A year later, despite pitching more, he went up to No. 53, which he kept through June 1976 when he was traded to Baltimore. Righty **Ken Clay** was No. 50 in 1977 before switching to No. 43 his final two Yankees seasons, while righty **Roger Slagle** wore it for his one-game major league career in 1979. Another righty, **John Pacella**, did Slagle three better. His Yankee career lasted for a trio of games in 1982.

No. 50 continued to be a pitcher's number. The same year Pacella came and went, **Lynn McGlothen** also pitched three games, his 0–1 record and 7.20 ERA earning him a quick trip out of town. That same year, the Yanks brought up righty **Jay Howell** and it finally looked like they had a keeper. Howell was given No. 53 in 1982, working just six games. He kept the number the next year, but when the team switched him to No. 50 in 1984 and made him a short reliever, Howell hit his stride. In 61 games, he had a 9–4 record, a 2.69 ERA and seven saves. That year the hard-throwing righthander struck out 109 batters in just 103 2/3 innings.

But that December, the latest No. 50 bit the dust when the Yanks had one of those deals they had to make. Howell was sent to Oakland as part of the deal that brought Rickey Henderson to New York. Howell would go on to a 15-year career as a short reliever and closer.

Like Jay Howell before him, righty **Marty Bystrom** wore No. 53 in his first Yankee season of 1984 and then No. 50 the year after that. The problem was that he only pitched in 15 total games as a starter and was just 5–4.

The pitching monopoly ended when catcher/outfielder **Phil Lombardi** was given No. 50 in 1986, playing in 20 games and hitting .278. But the next year, he was brought up as No. 61, got in five games with a .125 average, and found himself traded to the Mets after the season. First sacker **Chris Chambliss** never had to worry about a

STEVE BALBONI

job. He wore No. 10 during his successful Yankee years from 1974–1979. In 1988, he became the Bombers' hitting coach and a player shortage resulted in him being activated for one game. He fanned in his only at bat wearing No. 50.

Steve "Bye Bye" Balboni has already been mentioned several times because he was a number switcher. The big slugger, who had two Yankees tenures, wore Nos. 66 and 36 between 1981–83, then Nos. 50 and 45 when he returned in 1989 and 1990. Outfielder/first sacker **Oscar Azocar** was No. 50 in 1990 when he played in 65 games, a solid trial, and hit .248 with five homers. A year later, he was playing in San Diego. Righty **Alan Mills** had a 36 game audition in 1990 as Nos. 69 and 28. His 1–5 record earned him only a six-game encore the next year, as he wore No. 50. He was subsequently traded to Baltimore.

The saga of No. 50 was almost at an end. Infielder **Robert Eenhoorn** wore it in both 1994 and '95, playing in a total of eight games. When he returned in 1996 he was wearing No. 20, but his .071 average sealed his Yankees fate and he was waived to the Angels in September. Righty **Todd Erdos** was typical of the fringe player, wearing No. 54 for brief trials in 1998 and '99, then dropping down to No. 50 for 14 games in 2000 before being waived to San Diego in July.

Veteran outfielder **Matt Lawton** was the last player to wear No. 50 when the Yanks acquired him from the Cubs in late August 2005. Though he was a proven veteran who had hit .305 for the Twins with 13 homers and 88 RBIs in 2000, the Yanks probably didn't consider him a long-term acquisition, hence the high number. Lawton proved them right, hitting just .125 in 21 games before being granted free agency that October.

#51: BERNIE, JUST BERNIE

In the beginning, **Bernie Williams** had his doubters. Sure, he looked like a ballplayer, standing 6'2" and weighing 205 pounds, but when he first came up in 1991 to replace an injured Roberto Kelly in centerfield, the Yankees weren't even sure if that was his best position. He could run balls down, but had a below average throwing arm. He had natural speed, but wasn't a good baserunner. He could hit from both sides of the plate, but there was a question about his power. And when he batted .238 in 85 games in '91, with just three homers and 34 RBIs, nobody thought he was a guy who would ever become a Yankee legend. And, hey, the guy was wearing No. 51. They don't give stars numbers like that.

Not only did Bernie Williams stick with the Yankees, he also stuck with No. 51 for 16 seasons. The highlights of his career are almost too numerous to mention. He became the full-time centerfieder in 1993, and two years later he began to show the kind of ballplayer he really was. That year, 1995, he batted .307 with 18 homers and 82 RBIs. Suddenly, he was becoming a run producer with some real pop in his bat. That was the beginning of eight straight, .300 seasons that included batting averages of .342, .339, .333, and .327. He also drove in more than 100 runs in five different seasons with a high of 121 in 2000. While he was never a big home run hitter, he did slam 30 of them in 2000 and had 25 or more three other times. And he was as good a clutch hitter as the Yankees had during those years, the years that saw four World Series titles in five years and a trip to the playoffs every season starting in 1995.

His postseason was almost another season in itself. Bernie played in 121 playoff games, hitting .275 with a record 22 home runs and 80 RBIs. In 1998, for example, he became the first player ever to win a batting title (.339), a Gold Glove, and a World Series ring all in the same year. Along with teammates Derek Jeter, Mariano Rivera, Jorge Posada, Andy Petitte, Paul O'Neill, and Tino Martinez, he was an integral part of a great team that sustained its excellence for nearly a full decade.

After his great 1998 season, Williams' contract was up and there were rumors that the archrival Red Sox were going to make him an offer. The Yanks swooped in and gave him a new, seven-year pact worth $87.5 million, making him one of the highest paid players in the game. His string of .300-plus seasons ran out in 2003 when he batted just .263 in 119 games, losing time to injury. Time was catching up to him. When his average dropped to .249 in 2005, the team went out and signed centerfielder Johnny Damon to a four-year deal. Bernie wasn't yet ready to pack it in, and the Yanks finally offered him a one-year deal at just $1.5 million. It was a huge comedown, and Bernie was considered the fourth outfielder going into the season.

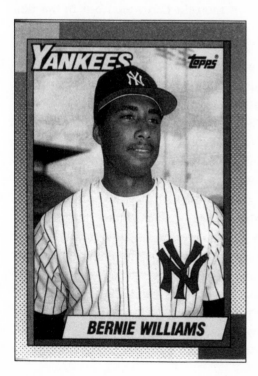

BERNIE WILLIAMS

It didn't turn out that way. Due to injuries Bernie played more than expected, 49 games in right, 23 in center, five in left, and 30 as the designated hitter. He also pinch-hit and he produced, batting .281 with 12 homers and 61 RBIs in 420 at bats. And, as usual, he hit in the clutch, making him still a valuable member of the team. But what happened next wasn't pretty. With everything else, baseball is a business, and when Bernie indicated he wanted to play again in 2007, the Yankees didn't offer a contract. Instead, they said he could come to spring training as a non-roster invitee, but Bernie wanted a guaranteed pact and declined the invitation.

After 16 seasons, a .297 average, 287 homers, and 2,336 hits, he was suddenly gone. It just wasn't a good way to have it end. The Yankees went on, as all teams must, and Bernie disappeared from sight. Finally, on September 21, 2008, he returned to the Stadium for the first time to take part in the final game ceremonies marking the end of the old Yankee Stadium. He was the last player introduced and got a huge standing ovation from the capacity crowd.

Bernie Williams has always had a second love besides baseball. He studied classical guitar as a youngster and took it up again during his final years with the Yanks. He has performed frequently and how has two albums to his credit. The second, *Moving Forward*, was released in April 2009 and has been very successful.

The Yankees have yet to retire his No. 51, but they also haven't issued it to anyone since he left in 2006 and the speculation is that it will be retired someday. Who would have thought that a number in the 50s would ever be immortalized?

Beyond Bernie, the pickings at No. 51 are slim. The number began with first sacker **George McQuinn** in 1947. McQuinn was in his final two seasons but still a solid ballplayer. So before the year was out he switched to No. 9, which he continued to wear in 1948. The next player to wear it was **Frank Leja** in 1954. Leja was one of those bonus babies, signed for $45,000 out of Holyoke High School in Massachusetts. A 6'4", 205-pound first sacker, the Yanks were hoping he'd grow into a bona fide power hitter. But there was one problem.

The Bonus Baby rule of the day stated that players had to remain on the roster for two full years before going to the minors. Leja was barely 18 when he joined the Yanks, thrown in with the likes of Mantle, Berra, Ford, and all the great Yankees of the day. He became the youngest player ever to put on a Yankees uniform and got into 12 games in '54 with a single in five at-bats for a .200 average. The next year, he failed to get a hit and at season's end was finally sent to the minors. Whether those two years hurt him or not is hard to say, but Leja never really developed. He was finally traded to the Cards in the fall of 1961, then moved on to the Angels. By 1962 he was done.

After outfielder **Gordie Windhorn** went 0-for-11 in seven games as No. 51 in 1959, the number took a five-year rest until sinkerballer **Pete Mikkelsen** showed up in 1964 and made the team. For a rookie to make a major contribution to a top Yankee team is unusual, but the 6'2", 220-pound righthander was suddenly pitching in all kinds of important situations as the Yankees moved toward their fifth straight pennant. Mikkelsen got the call 50 times, and finished the season with a 7–4 record, a 3.56 earned run average and 12 saves.

A year later, as the Yankees went into a sudden eclipse, Mikkelsen went just 4–9 with one save, and even got three starts. But much of that could be attributed to the Yanks going from a 99-win team to a 77-win team in '65. Mikkelsen's earned run average of 3.28 was actually lower than the previous season. Then in December, the Yankees made a surprising trade, sending Mikkelsen to the Pirates for aging starter Bob Friend.

American Somoan-born first baseman **Tony Solaita** wore No. 51 for just a single game as a Yankee in 1968. Nothing to write home about. In fact, he'd stay in the minors until the Yanks finally traded him to Pittsburgh in February 1973 and he didn't appear in the majors again until 1974 with Kansas City. But there's a little more to the story than that. At six-feet, 215 pounds, the lefty swinging Solaita was considered one of the strongest men in the league

To find success, the big Somoan went to Japan in 1980 and played four years, belting a total of 155 home runs. He just couldn't quite do it in the majors.

Veteran pitcher **John Wyatt** wore No. 51 for just seven games in 1968, having been purchased from the Red Sox on May 17, and was then sold to Detroit on June 15. Another hurler, **Ron Klimkowski**, wore No. 51 for three games in 1969, but changed to No. 24 the next year, left for Oakland for one season, and then returned as No. 22 in 1972. Outfielder **Terry Whitfield** played for parts of three seasons (1974–76), but switched from No. 51 his first year to No. 44 the final two. And pitcher **Larry McCall**, who was with the club for just seven games in 1977 and '78, wore No. 51 his first year and No. 53 the next.

Righty **Cecilio Guante** pitched in 1987 and '88 and kept No. 51 both years. He was traded to Texas in August of the latter season. That brings us to **Chuck Cary**, a lefthanded pitcher who may someday end up a trivia question. He was the last player to wear No. 51 before Bernie Williams came along. Cary was signed as a free agent in January of '89, pitched fairly well, then regressed and was finally sent back to the minors early in the 1991 season. About that same time, Bernie Williams came up to replace Roberto Kelly, pulled on uniform No. 51, and kept it on for the next 16 years.

ANOTHER DOUBLE FOR WILLIAMS

There's little doubt about Bernie Williams' contributions to the Yankees. He'll be remembered as one of their finer center fielders, a clutch hitter, and a winner. He also loved to hit doubles as shown by his spot on the all-time list, where he sits in second place behind the legendary Lou Gehrig.

Lou Gehrig 534
Bernie Williams 449
Don Mattingly 442
Derek Jeter 438
Babe Ruth 424
Joe DiMaggio 389
Mickey Mantle 344
Bill Dickey 343
Jorge Posada 342
Bob Meusel 338

#52 & 53: CC AND THE ROAD TO ABREU AND MELKY

Time for a two in one. As the numbers get higher, the rosters get shorter and the repetitions and uniform changes rise. We'll begin with a player who just may make No. 52 very memorable and end with the two players who followed each other with No. 53, the second wearing it as a tribute to the first.

The player beginning his Yankees career did so in 2009 after signing the biggest contract ever given to a pitcher: **CC Sabathia**. (And yes, there are no periods after the two Cs; he dropped them in 2009.) The free agent contract he signed with the Yanks was for $161 million over seven years. At 6'7" and weighing upward of 300 pounds, Sabathia is a top-of-the-rotation horse, a hard-throwing southpaw who not only gives his team innings, but wins. There was a harbinger of things to come in 2001, when as a 20-year-old rookie with the Indians, Carsten Charles Sabathia went 17–5, finishing second in the Rookie of the Year balloting to Ichiro Suzuki of the Mariners. That was the beginning of Sabathia's winning ways.

He had a strong career in Cleveland, winning in double figures each year, culminating in a 19–7 season in 2007 and a Cy Young Award for his efforts. Sabathia was viewed as one of the top pitchers

Ken Holtzman	1977–78
Larry McCall	1978
Ron Davis	1978
Bob Kammeyer	1979
Ray Burris	1979
Tim Lollar	1980
Jerry Walker (coach)	1981
Jay Howell	1982–83
Lee Walls (coach)	1983
Marty Bystrom	1984
Neil Allen	1985
Orestes Destrade	1987
Bob Geren	1989–91
Glenn Sherlock (coach)	1992
Mark Hutton	1993
Neal Heaton	1993
Jose Cardenal (coach)	1996–99
Mike Thurman	2002
Don Zimmer (coach)	2002–03
Luis Sojo (coach)	2004–05
Larry Bowa (coach)	2006
Bobby Abreu	2006–08
Melky Cabrera	2009

in baseball. He got off to a slow start in 2008, his free agent year, and on July 7, the Indians traded him to Milwaukee for prospects, knowing they couldn't afford to re-sign him at the end of the year. He was 6–8 when he left the Indians, but caught fire in Milwaukee, going 11–2 with a 1.65 ERA down the stretch and pitching the Brewers into the playoffs. When the season ended he filed for free agency and the Yankees, a team that in 2008 had missed the playoffs for the first time in 13 years, came calling. The result was his record-breaking contract.

Sabathia took his spot at the top of the Yanks rotation in 2009 and quickly made No. 52 one Yankees fans were glad to see. He not only had a great 19–8 season, but had a 3–1 record in the playoffs as the Yankees won their 27th World Championship. CC has a repertoire consisting of a fastball, slider, cutter and change—all of which he can throw for strikes. Like many great pitchers before him, he often gets stronger in the late innings and has thrown 28 complete games in his career, unusual in this day and age.

The big lefty has already passed some milestones. He is the first southpaw to start his career with six straight seasons of double-digit wins. In 2005, his fastball averaged 94.7 mph for the season, tops in the majors. His seven-year deal will give him plenty of opportunity to cement a Yankees legacy, and barring unforeseen injury, there's a good chance he'll finish his career in New York.

While CC is the latest to wear No. 52, the guys before him were not quite so celebrated. It began in 1947 with a second sacker named **Johnny Lucadello**. He didn't get much of a chance, playing just 12 games and hitting .083. Outfielder **Jim Delsing** also had a short Yankees career as a guy who jumped around the higher numbers. He wore No. 52 for nine

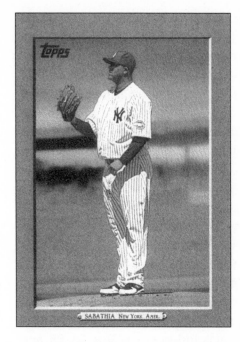

SABATHIA New York Amer.

games in 1949 and then No. 54 for 12 more games in 1950.

Add **Wally Hood Jr.** to the quickie category. He pitched in just two games as No. 52 in 1949, while reliever **Tom Morgan** wore the number in 1951 before switching to No. 28 for the next four years.

That's the pattern that continued. Reliever **Jim Coates** was No. 52 in his cup of coffee year of 1956. When he returned from 1959–62, he wore No. 39. Same with southpaw **Fritz Peterson**. A few might remember him as No. 52 in his rookie year of 1966, but most recall him as No. 19, which he wore from 1966–74. Pitcher **Joe Verbanic** came to the Yanks before the 1967 season. He was given No. 52 and kept it until a sore arm permanently sidelined him in 1970.

Outfielders **Larry Murray** and **Otto Velez** didn't play much as Yankees, but did some number switching. Murray played a total of 22 games in three years (1974–76), first as No. 52, then as 18, and finally No. 47. Velez, once considered a hot prospect, lasted parts of four years (1973–76) and wore No. 52 in 1975. The other three years he was No. 24. And then we come to the enigmatic **Doyle Alexander**, a righthander of some talent who lasted 19 seasons in the bigs and was pretty much disliked wherever he went. "Dour Doyle" drifted between eight teams during his career, which included two trips to New York.

Alexander began with the Dodgers in 1971 at the age 20. A year later, he was moved to Baltimore but in the early years was pretty much mediocre, both starting and relieving. The Yanks got him from Baltimore in June 1976, Wearing No. 52, Alexander pitched well, going 10–5 with a 3.29 ERA in 19 games, helping the Yankees win the pennant. He then signed with Texas as a free agent. He went 17–11 in 1977, but after two mediocre years moved on to Atlanta, where he went 14–11 in 1980, and then to the Giants the next year when he finished at 11–7. Then in March 1982, he was traded back to the Yankees, where he again put on No. 52. This time his trip to New York was a disaster.

In 1982, he was 1–7 with a 6.08 ERA in just 16 games and a year later he was 0–2 with a 6.35 ERA in eight games before being unceremoniously released on May 31.

Mostly pitchers continued to wear No. 52. **Dave Rajsich** lasted all of four games in 1978. The most interesting thing about the 6'5", 175-pound southpaw was his nickname. Because he was so tall and thin, they called him "The Blade." Righty **Mike Griffin** wore No. 52 from 1979–81, pitching a total of 18 games before being dealt to the Cubs for Rick Reuschel. Catcher **Juan Espino** broke the pitching monopoly briefly. He only played 24 games in four seasons (1982–83, 1985–86) and wore No. 52 only in '85. Current Yankees pitching coach Dave Eiland wore No. 52 in 1988, then gravitated between Nos. 28, 58, and 47 (1989–91, 1995).

Australian-born righthander **Mark Hutton** got a lot of press because of his country of origin, not a place where baseball is played much. Unfortunately, he didn't garner raves for his pitching. Wearing No. 53, he threw seven games in 1993 to a 5.73 ERA, then switched to No. 52 for a two-game trial the following year and a final 12-game audition in 1996. Again his ERA was over five, and he was traded to the Marlins.

When the Yanks traded Hutton on July 31, 1996, the Marlins sent righty reliever **David Weathers** to New York. Wearing No. 52, the results were not good. Weathers pitched in 21 total games in 1996 and '97, going 0–3 with an ERA approaching 10.00. He was moved to the Indians in June of '97 for outfielder Chad Curtis, but he has endured. In 19 seasons through 2009, Weathers is 73–88 with a 4.25 ERA and 75 saves. Another longtime reliever, **Joe Borowski**, had similar luck with the Yankees. He pitched and lost one game in 1997 as No. 52, then threw in eight more the next year wearing No. 57. His ERA was 6.52.

Then there was "Inky." Not the kind of nickname you'd expect for a 6'1", 230-pound slugger. But it was a play on **Pete Incaviglia's** last name and it stuck. Incaviglia played his college ball at Oklahoma State University, was drafted by Montreal in 1985, traded to Texas, and then promoted to the majors without having playing a single day of minor league ball. Inky hit the ground running, playing 153 games as a rookie. He hit just .250, but blasted 30 home runs and drove in 88. On the negative side, Incaviglia struck out 185 times, most in the majors. From there it was a repetition of homers, too many strikeouts, and low batting averages. The Yankees signed him on July 25, 1997, just 11 days after the Orioles released him. But there'd be no magical resurrection. Inky was done. He played just five games for the Yanks, didn't hit a homer, and was released on August 15. Two years later he was gone. In 12 seasons, he hit .246 with 206 homers.

After Incaviglia, No. 52 again became the domain of the pitchers. Two easily forgotten names, **Mike Buddie** and **Ed Yarnall**, came next, followed by a guy who arrived with great fanfare and left with little, Cuban defector **Jose Contreras**. Buddie arrived in 1998 and worked 24 games as No. 52. The next year he was No. 41, but after two games he was gone. Yarnall, a lefty, went from No. 52 in 1999 to No. 31 in 2000. Same result. Five games the first year, two the second, and out. Contreras, however, was a different story. The big righthander was one of Cuba's greatest pitchers and a star of their famed National Team, as well as Cuban Athlete of the Year three times. His last season in Cuba (2001–02), he was 13–4 with a 1.76 ERA and 149 strikeouts. He defected in October 2002. The Yankees aced out the Red Sox and signed him to a four-year deal that December.

Many felt that Contreras would be even better than countryman Orlando "El Duque" Hernandez. But he also had trouble adjusting to the majors. In 2004, the Yanks used him both as a starter and out of the pen with mixed results. He finished the season at 7–2 with a 3.30 ERA in just 18 games (9 starts), and 72 strikeouts in 71 innings.

Somehow, Contreras and the Yanks never quite worked. He pitched another 18 games in 2004 and was 8–5, but with a 5.64 ERA by July 31. That's when he was surprisingly dealt to the White Sox for veteran Esteban Loaiza. His 15-7 record with the White Sox in 2005 was a high point. Two years later he was 10–17 and has been a mediocre pitcher ever since.

Righthander **Luis Vizcaino** became the last Yankee to wear No. 52 before the arrival of CC Sabathia. Vizcaino, a workhorse reliever, came to the Yanks in January 2007. He did his usual thing, working in 77 games with an 8–2 record, but a mediocre 4.30 ERA. Because so many of these middle relievers are interchangeable the Yanks let him go via free agency at season's end.

The move from No. 52 to No. 53 certainly isn't a quantum leap. The names may change, but the type of players wearing these higher numbers remains pretty much the same. And, of course, many of them change numbers if they stay on more than one season. That was the case of lefty **Bob Wiesler**, the first Yankee to wear No. 53 in 1951. Wiesler pitched in just four games that year, starting three and bombing with a 13.50 ERA. But he returned in 1954 and '55 for another 22 games wearing No. 39. Then it was off to Washington.

Bill "Moose" Skowron wore No. 53 his rookie year of 1954, then switched to the more familiar No. 14, which he kept until he was traded after 1962. After that, the number got its first long-term recipient, pitcher **Johnny Kucks**, a righty who looked very promising but never quite reached the heights some predicted for him. Kucks was called up in 1955, a decade in which the Yankees won almost every year, so he had a great team behind him. The 6'3" hurler was mainly a sinkerballer and just 21 when went 8–7, starting 13 games in 29 appearances.

It all came together in 1956. As the Yanks rolled toward yet another pennant, Kucks emerged as a pitching star, compiling an impressive 18–9 mark with a 3.85 ERA and three shutouts. It would be, however, the last winning season for this No. 53. Kucks was mediocre the next two years and saw it all come apart in 1959. He was just 0–1 with an 8.64 ERA when he was traded to Kansas City on May 26.

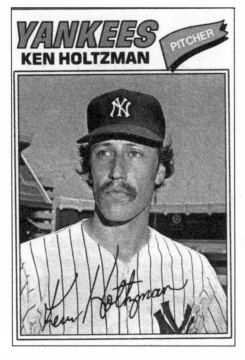

Kucks pitched just two more years and was done, going 54–56 in his career with a third of his victories coming in one season. You have to suspect arm problems as the reason. Trivia question: Who was the last pitcher to ever face Jackie Robinson in a big league game? Answer: Johnny Kucks.

Outfielder **Ross Moschitto** got his chance in 1965 at the age of 20. He appeared in 96 games, mostly as a late-inning defensive replacement, but hit just .185 in 27 at bats. Two years later he was back, again wearing No. 53, but only playing in 14 games and hitting .111. Gone. Outfielder **Otto Velez** and pitcher **Dave Pagan** were already mentioned since they wore both Nos. 52 and 53. Then, in June 1976, the Yanks made that awful, oft-mentioned trade with Baltimore, and one of the players they received was lefthander **Ken Holtzman**.

Ten years earlier, in 1966, the 20-year-old Holtzman was dubbed "The New Koufax" when he made the Cubs' starting rotation. That's quite a burden to bear. Holtzman pitched for the Cubs through 1971, going 9–0 in 1967 while spending much of the season in the National Guard, then won 17 games twice, and pitched a pair of no-hitters before being shipped to Oakland.

He then joined a great Oakland team that would win three straight World Series from 1972–74. During those years, Holtzman won 19, 21, and 19 games, becoming one of the best pitchers in the league. In 1975, he was packaged in a deal with Reggie Jackson and sent to Baltimore. That June, the Orioles shipped him to the Yanks and he started

21 games before the end of the season, going 9–7 with a 4.17 ERA. But Holtzman didn't pitch in the postseason and he pitched even less in the World Series year of 1977, working only 18 times and going 2–3 with a 5.78 ERA.

Finally, on June 10, 1978, and with just a 1–0 record in five games, he was returned to his first team, the Cubs. But he no longer had his best stuff and was 0–3 for the Cubs the rest of the way. He pitched one more year, went 6–9, and called it quits. His final record was 174–150, not bad but not nearly as good as some thought he would be.

Set-up man **Ron Davis** came to the Yanks in the Holtzman deal and wore No. 53 for the remainder of 1978. But he then switched to No. 39 and pitched well for the Yanks through 1981. Righty **Bob Kammeyer** started as No. 40 for seven games in 1978, then took No. 53 for a single game in '79 before disappearing. Better things were expected from righty **Ray Burris** when he was acquired from the Cubs in late May 1979 for pitcher Dick Tidrow. By the time Burris had thrown 15 times, the Yanks had seen enough. His 1–3 record and 6.18 ERA weren't enough to keep him in pinstripes and he was waived to the Mets on August 20. The pitchers wearing No. 53 continued with rookie **Tim Lollar** in 1980. He was up long enough to pitch 14 games and go 1–0 with two saves. The following March, he was sent to the Padres

One guy they were wrong about was reliever **Jay Howell**, who wore No. 53 in both 1982 and '83. His later successes were detailed in Chapter 50. Two more pitchers followed who wore multiple numbers. Righties **Marty Bystrom** and **Neil Allen** both wore No. 53 their first season in New York (1984 and '85, respectively), then switched to lower numbers before being dealt. First sacker **Orestes Destrade** had the number in 1987, played in nine games, and hit .263 before being sent to Pittsburgh the following year.

Backup catcher **Bob Geren** debuted in 1988, wearing both Nos. 57 and 58, and then settled in as No. 53 for the next three seasons. He didn't hit much, but got into 110 games in 1990. He was waived to San Diego in December of '91. Australian-born pitcher Mark Hutton wore No. 53 in 1993, then No. 52 in short call-ups in 1994 and 1996. Lefty **Neal**

Heaton was another of those pitchers who got a last-ditch chance with the Yankees. He was signed in February 1993, pitched in 19 games, and was released on July 27, the end of a 12-year career in which he went 80–96. That scenario was repeated with **Mike Thurman**, who pitched the final 12 games of his career with the Yanks in 2002. Same number (53), same result.

Now we come to two players who were more than window dressing when they put on No. 53, **Bobby Abreu** and **Melky Cabrera**. On July 30, 2006, the Yanks announced a trade with the Philadelphia Phillies in which they acquired rightfielder Abreu and pitcher Cory Lidle for four minor leaguers. Abreu would stay for three seasons and prove to be the same consistent ballplayer he had been with the Phils, a guy who performed at a high level, maybe just a cut below that of a superstar.

After two part-time seasons in Houston, the Venezuelan-born Abreu came to the Phils in 1998. A year later, he had the first of what would become a typical Abreu season, hitting .335 with 20 homers and 93 RBIs. By 2001 his line was .289, 31, 110 and in 2005, the year before he came to the Yanks, he was at .286, 24, 102. That's consistency. The lefty swinging Abreu was a patient hitter who worked deep in the count, took a lot of walks, and never considered himself a power hitter. He had good speed, was an outstanding baserunner, and a fair decent outfielder with a strong throwing arm.

With the Yanks, he continued to produce. He batted .330 after coming over in 2006, his first taste of the American League. A year later, he was at .283, 16, 101 and a fan favorite. He also rarely missed a game. And in 2008, he was at .296, 20, 100. Unfortunately, the Yanks didn't win the World Series during his tenure, and in New York that's always considered a failure. Abreu made $16 million in 2008 and after the season the Yanks granted him free agency. He was looking for a three-year deal but the Yanks knew they were going to go after some big free agents (think CC Sabathia, A. J. Burnett, Mark Teixeira), so Abreu was cut loose. He wound up signing with the Angels for just $5 million and proved to be worth every cent, hitting .293 with 15 homers and 103 RBIs.

Abreu is just one of six players in the history of baseball to have more than 250 homers, 2,000 hits, 1,000 runs scored, 1,000 RBIs, and 300 stolen bases. The others are Willie Mays, Barry Bonds, Rickey Henderson, Craig Biggio, and Joe Morgan.

Young centerfielder Melky Cabrera, a native of the Dominican Republic, was trying hard to stake out a Yankees legacy. He came up for six games in 2005, when injuries depleted the team, and appeared overmatched. But he was just 20 years old then, licked his wounds, and made the team the next year, playing in 130 games, and hitting .280 with seven homers and 50 RBIs. He also showed he could play all three outfield positions, seeing a lot of time in left, as Johnny Damon patrolled center, and exhibiting an outstanding throwing arm. Melky had worn No. 39 in 2005, then switched to No. 28, which he would wear through 2008. When Abreu left, Melky requested No. 53 in tribute to his friend and mentor.

Melky's tenure with the Yanks has had its share of ups and downs. A switch-hitter with decent power, he's never shown real consistency at the plate. In 2007, he played in 150 games, had eight homers and 73 RBIs, becoming a major contributor. But the next year he slumped, losing his job after midseason and even being sent to the minors for a period of time. In 2009, Brett Gardner was named the Opening Day centerfielder. Melky was a fill-in and pinch-hitter, and suddenly he was getting a brace of big hits, including several walk-off game winners. When Gardner slumped, Melky took over the centerfield job once again.

He wound up playing 154 games, hitting .274 with 13 homers and 68 RBIs. It was a solid season but still not quite what the Yankees expected from him. In December, he was traded to the Braves for pitcher Javier Vazquez. The acquisition earlier of centerfielder Curtis Granderson made him expendable. Now Melky will have to show the Yanks they made a mistake by dealing him. He's still young enough to do it.

SINGLE SEASON LEADERS

Up to now there have been numbers showing the all-time Yankee lists. But here, close to the end, it might be interesting to see what the Yankee hitters have accomplished in a single season. Here are the leaders in a number of batting categories.

At Bats	Alfonso Soriano	696	(2002)
Batting Average	Babe Ruth	393	(1923)
Hits	Don Mattingly	238	(1986)
Doubles	Don Mattingly	53	(1986)
Triples	Earle Combs	23	(1927)
Home Runs	Roger Maris	61	(1961)
Runs Scored	Babe Ruth	177	(1921)
Runs Batted In	Lou Gehrig	184	(1931)
Total Bases	Babe Ruth	457	(1921)
Bases on Balls	Babe Ruth	170	(1923)

#54: THE GOOSE: A HALL OF FAMER AT LAST

He was the prototypical closer of his time—big, strong, intimidating, never hesitating to back a hitter off the plate or plunking him if necessary, possessor of a vicious fastball that he could spot with accuracy, and a guy capable of pitching multiple innings to end a game. For all those reasons and more, **Rich "Goose" Gossage** is in the Hall of Fame and remains a beloved former Yankee who is always greeted with cheers when he returns to Yankee Stadium. Gossage loved to pitch. Even when his closing days were over he continued coming out of the pen for several teams, spending 22 seasons in the majors and not retiring until he was 42 years old. During his six years as a Yankee, he made fans look with anticipation for No. 54 to emerge from the bullpen.

The nickname Goose came about as a play on his last name. This Goose grew to 6'3" and 220 pounds and joined the White Sox when he was just 20 years old in 1972. He did the job from the outset, going 7–1 that year in 36 games, all but one out of the pen. At that time he was still trying to get that big fastball under control. By 1975 he had hit his stride, coming out of the pen 62 times, going 9–8 with an impressive 1.84 ERA and 130 strikeouts in 141 2/3 innings. At a time when closers weren't at a premium and not used the way they are today, he also led the league with 26 saves. A year later, the Sox got a bright idea and made Gossage a starter. He threw 224 innings in 29 starts, relieving only twice, but it didn't work out well. He was 9–17 with a 3.94 ERA. That fall, the Sox traded him to Pittsburgh.

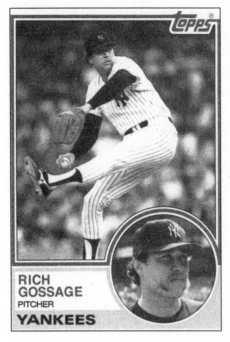

RICH
GOSSAGE
PITCHER
YANKEES

One year with the Pirates was enough to convince the Yankees he was someone worth pursuing. A free agent after the season, he signed with the Yankees, baseball's reigning World Champions. The problem was that the Yankees already had an All-Star closer in lefty Sparky Lyle, one of the heroes of the 1977 championship season. But as the 1978 season progressed, it was soon apparent that the Goose had taken over as the main man out of the pen late. That year the Bronx Zoo Yankees chased and caught the Red Sox, necessitating a one-game playoff for the division title. That was the game of the Bucky Dent home run, but it was the Goose who closed it out by getting Carl Yastrzemski to pop up to Graig Nettles with two on and two out in the ninth. The Yanks won, 5–4, and went on to a second straight World Series triumph.

After the season, the Yanks traded Lyle, and the Goose was the main man. He was slowed in '79 by a thumb injury, the result of a clubhouse fight with Cliff Johnson, but came back to have a great season in 1980, leading the league with 33 saves and finishing third in the balloting for both the Cy Young Award and Most Valuable Player. In the shortened split season of 1981, he had a minuscule, 0.77 ERA and 20 saves as the Yanks went to the World Series again, this time losing to the Dodgers.

The Goose stayed with the Yanks through 1983. He was 13–5 that year with a 2.27 ERA and 22 saves, as good as ever. But the Yanks were rebuilding and allowed Gossage to sign with the Padres as a free agent. He remained a closer through 1988, his first year with the Cubs, and then pitched another five years as a set-up man, missing the

1990 season to injury. He even returned briefly to the Yanks in 1989, picked up on waivers from the Giants on August 10. He pitched in 11 games, won one and saved one, but he wasn't the same pitcher. After the season, he moved on once again.

Gossage's achievements are numerous. He is third all-time in games pitched with 1,002, third in relief wins with 115, and third in innings pitched in relief with 1,556 and 2/3. He has a lifetime mark of 124–107 with a 3.01 ERA and 310 saves. His election to the Hall of Fame in 2008 was fully merited. Today, the Goose lives in Colorado Springs, Colorado, and has created the Rich "Goose" Gossage Youth Sports Complex, which has five fields that youngsters can use to play both baseball and softball.

TALK ABOUT COINCIDENCE

More than any other sport, baseball is a game of numbers and statistics. There are certainly plenty of them in this book. But sometimes those numbers create almost implausible, coincidental circumstances. Here's one that involved Goose Gossage. Late in his career on July 23, 1991, while pitching for Texas, Goose came in to save a game for the Rangers. When he recorded the final out he had saved his 308th game. The coincidence involved the guy he saved it for. It was the great Nolan Ryan and it turned out to be the 308th win of his long career. As the old Yankees announcer Mel Allen would say, "How about that?"

Outside of the Goose, one of the few players to latch onto and keep a high number, the other Yankees players wearing No. 54 are pretty much what you'd expect. It began with outfielder **Jim Delsing** in 1950. Since Delsing wore No. 52 the year before, he's already been mentioned. Third sacker **Andy Carey** was given No. 54 in his rookie year of 1952, then switched to No. 6, which he wore through 1960. Pitcher **Thad Tillotson** wore the number for two years (1967–68), and was gone from the majors. Veteran **Ken Johnson**, who once pitched a no-hitter and lost, threw 12 games for the Yanks during a two-month stay in 1969 before being sold to the Cubs.

The list leading up to Gossage continued with **Gary Waslewski**, **Steve Blateric, Jim Roland**, and **Dave Bergman**. The first three were hurlers while Bergman was an outfielder/first sacker who played briefly with the Yanks in 1975 and '77, at the beginning of a 17-year career. None made a mark in pinstripes.

Gossage came next and wore No. 54 from 1978–1983. In 1985, the Yanks gave Goose's number to another big righthanded reliever, rookie **Brian Fisher,** who surprised everyone by appearing in 55 games, going 4–4 with a 2.38 ERA and 14 saves. He looked like a coming star. But following the 1986 season, the Yanks included Fisher in a trade along with starter Doug Drabek, sending them to Pittsburgh in the deal that brought pitcher Rick Rhoden to the Yanks. Fisher was never again quite the same pitcher.

Righty **Brad Arnsberg** was another No. 54 stopgap. He wore it in 1987 for just six games after appearing as No. 62 the season before in which he worked only twice. Another short-time player followed, but this is a guy the Yankees might have regretted dealing. He was outfielder **Jay Buhner,** who came up as a 22-year-old rookie in 1987 and played just seven games, hitting .227. The following July, the Yanks dealt the young outfielder to Seattle for veteran first sacker Ken Phelps. Buhner would stay with the Mariners through 2001, becoming one of the top sluggers in the American League. From 1995–1997, he had 40, 44, and 40 homers, topping 100 RBIs each year with a high of 138 in 1996. The righty swinger was also a good outfielder with a strong throwing arm. He retired after 15 seasons with a .254 average and 310 home runs. He's one guy who got away and sure would have looked good in pinstripes.

Marginal pitchers **Cecilio Guante** and **Dale Mohorcic** have both been mentioned earlier because of number changing. Guante wore Nos. 54 and 51 in 1987 and then No. 51 again in '88, while Mohorcic was No. 54 in 1988 and then both 54 and 28 the following year before being released at season's end. Then there was **Tim Leary**, a big righthander who started with the Mets, hurt his arm, then became

Comeback Player of the Year with the Dodgers in 1988 by going 17–11 with a 2.91 ERA and six shutouts. The Yanks picked him up from Cincinnati in December 1989 in return for Hal Morris.

Leary had the misfortune of joining a Yankees team in 1990 that would bottom out at 67–95 and have one of the worst starting rotations in years. The righty became the poster boy for the team's futility, going 9–19 in 31 starts with a 4.11 ERA. Leary would pitch two more seasons for the Bombers before being shipped to Seattle in August, ending the agony.

Lefty **Sterling Hitchcock**, remembered as No. 41, the number he wore in 1994 and '95, and then again from 2001 to 2003, actually wore No. 54 his rookie year of 1992, then had a short stop at No. 34 the following year. Rookie **Bobby Munoz** was No. 54 in 1993 when he pitched in 38 games and went 3–3 with a 5.32 ERA. That February, he was shipped to Philadelphia for veteran Terry Mulholland. Another righty, **Joe Ausanio**, had some moderate success in 1994 and '95, going 4–1 out of the pen, but his ERA of 5.57 didn't cut it, and when the Yanks dropped him he couldn't find another big league job.

Jeff Reardon was one of the better closers in the 1980s and early 1990s, but when he arrived at Yankee Stadium he was 38 years old and in his final season. He pitched 11 times and won a game, but his 8.38 ERA proved he was done. He was released in May, but don't sell him short. Reardon retired with 367 saves, had 40 or more saves in three different seasons, and was nicknamed "The Terminator." Righty **Jim Mecir** was a career reliever who never started a game in 11 seasons. He was a two-year Yankee, wearing No. 54 in 1996 and '97 after coming from Seattle in the same deal that brought Tino Martinez and Jeff Nelson to the Bronx. Mecir had his chance, getting the call 26 times the first year and 25 the next, but his ERA of more than 5.00 sealed his fate. He was dealt to the Red Sox in September.

Young righty **Todd Erdos** was No. 54 in 1998 and '99, then switched to No. 50 in 2000. But he threw a total of 20 games in parts of three seasons and was waived to San Diego in July of 2000. And the final Yankee to wear No. 54 was none other than **Alfonso Soriano**, who donned the number in 2000 before becoming a regular. Soriano then wore No. 33 the following year and No. 12 in his final two Yankees seasons before being traded to Texas for Alex Rodriguez.

Does that fact that no Yankee has worn No. 54 since 2000 mean that it will soon be retired in honor of Goose Gossage? Perhaps. Now that Gossage is in the Hall of Fame and recognized as a great Yankee, it's certainly possible.

#55–57: GODZILLA HITS THE BRONX

Here we go, three for the price of one. This chapter will cover the uniform numbers 55–57 and will feature many players spoken of earlier because they dropped down to lower numbers at some point. But there is a major star lurking here, as well as a player who shone brightly for a couple of seasons, was injured, and later made news with a ground-breaking, tell-all book. We're talking about **Hideki Matsui** as the star and pitcher **Jim Bouton** as the pitcher-author. So they get the leadoff spots here.

Hideki Matsui came to the Yankees from Japan, saw the major leagues and conquered, quickly becoming one of baseball's best all-around hitters. A lefty swinger who was one of Japan's best ever sluggers, "Godzilla" didn't become a 40–50 home run hitter with the Yanks, but he became a run producer with power, a great situational hitter, and a lefty swinger who hit lefthanded pitchers as well as any player in the league. He was with the Yankees seven years (2003–2009) and drove in more than 100 runs in four of the five seasons that he stayed healthy.

Matsui played 10 years for the Yomiuri Giants of Japan's Nippon Professional Baseball League, where he was a three-time Most Valuable Player and an All-Star for nine straight seasons. He virtually

Rick Down (coach)	2002–03
Scott Proctor	2004–05
Tanyon Sturtze	2005–06
Tony Pena (coach)	2007–09

#57

Art Lopez	1965
Roy Staiger	1979
Dennis Sherrill	1980
Tucker Ashford	1981
Bobby Ramos	1982
Ray Fontenot	1983
Bob Geren	1988
Hensley Meulens	1989
John Habyan	1991
Steve Howe	1991–1996
Joe Borowski	1998
Jay Tessmer	1999–2000
Jeff Juden	1999
Carlos Almanzar	2001
Erick Almonte	2001
Drew Henson	2002
Karim Garcia	2002
Michel Hernandez	2003
Juan Acevedo	2003
Alex Graman	2004
Scott Proctor	2004
Brad Halsey	2004
Neil Allen (coach)	2005
Joe Kerrigan (coach)	2007
Mike Harkey (coach)	2008–09

never missed a game, had a .304 batting average, and belted 332 home runs, becoming Japan's biggest star along the way. Like other top Japanese players, Matsui decided to test himself against the best—and play for the best—so he signed with the Yankees. His fans in Japan were so overjoyed that they had a parade in his honor in Tokyo just to celebrate his signing.

After the grand slam, Matsui went through a period of adjustment, but by the second half of the season he was one of the Yanks best hitters. He finished the season with a .287 average, 16 homers, and 106 RBIs. Though the Yankees lost the World Series to the Marlins that year, Matsui became the first Japanese player to homer in the Fall Classic. And when he followed that up with a .298, 31, 108 season in 2004, he firmly established himself as a real deal. In addition, he was an ironman, playing in every game after having played in 1,250 straight in Japan. Though just an average left fielder, he rarely hurt the team on defense, being steady if not spectacular.

It was the same the next season, maybe his best, a .305 average, 23 homers, and a high of 116 RBIs. Matsui was 31 years old and obviously in his prime as he once again played every game. Then there was a roadblock. Trying to make a diving catch early in the 2006 season, he broke his left wrist and needed surgery. He returned on September 12 and in typical Matsui fashion, he went 4-for-4 that day. For the season he was limited to 51 games and still hit .302. But his combined (Japan and MLB) consecutive game streak was over at 1,768 games.

THE PERFECT DEBUT

In his very first game ever at Yankee Stadium, Hideki Matsui got the winning hit. That in itself is always news. But this one wasn't just a single. It happened on April 8, 2003, the Yanks, home opener against the Twins on a cold, 35 degree afternoon. Matsui came up in the fifth inning with the sacks jammed facing righthander Joe Mays. With the count full, Yanks' announcer Jim Kaat said that Matsui, "with his rock star persona," could well do something special here, and seconds later the lefty swinger belted a grand slam home run to the delight of a packed house. Matsui became a true Yankee in his first time at the Cathedral that was the old Yankee Stadium, and the first Yankee in history to hit a grand slam in his first game at the Stadium. But judging from what Matsui had done in Japan, the Yankees were expecting just that, a fully mature star.

After that it became more difficult. He bounced back to have a .285, 25, 103 season in 2007, but manager Joe Torre began giving him days off from time to time. Still, on August 5, he reached another milestone by becoming the first Japanese player to hit 100 home runs in the Major Leagues. Then in 2008, knee problems surfaced. He was limited to just 93 games and needed surgery after the season. By 2009, Matsui

Hideki Matsui

was 35 years old and because both knees were now troublesome, the Yankees decided to use him exclusively as a designated hitter. He accepted the role without complaint, hitting .274 with 28 homers and 90 RBIs in 142 games, some of them as a pinch hitter. But his clutch hitting was as good as ever and he proved it again in the World Series when he led the Yanks to their first championship since 2000 by hitting .615 (8-for-13) with three homers and eight RBIs. Six of his runs batted in came in the final game, when he slammed a homer and two doubles and was named the World Series MVP.

With the Yanks looking to get younger and feeling Matsui could no longer play the outfield, the team didn't offer him a new contract for 2010. Instead of waiting, he signed a one-year deal with the Angels and will be moving on. But his Yankee legacy has been cemented in big hits. In seven seasons, he had a .292 batting average, has hit 140 homers and has driven in 597 runs. He has also hit .312 in the post season, with 10 homers and 39 RBIs in 56 games. As we said, the guy is clutch. And without the injuries, the numbers would have been even more impressive.

As of 2009, Hideki Matsui was the last player to wear No. 55. Let's look at the first player to wear No. 56. After three seasons in the majors, **Jim Bouton** looked like a coming star. A righthander with a crackling fastball and sharp breaking ball, he had a herky-jerky, violent delivery that often resulted in his cap flying from his head when he threw. Bouton joined the Yanks in 1962 when he was 23 and went 7–7 in 36 games, 16 of them starts. A year later, he emerged as a star with a 21–7 record in 40 games. He had a sparkling 2.53 ERA, made 30 starts, and threw six shutouts. A year later, when he went 18–13 with a 3.02 ERA, he looked as if he was settling in as a mainstay of the staff. Though the Yanks lost the World Series that year to the Cardinals, Bouton was 2–0 with a 1.56 ERA in the fall classic.

But pitching can be a very tenuous profession. In 1965, the Yanks as a team crashed and so did Bouton. He hurt his arm, lost his fastball, and plunged to a 4–15 record. He stayed with the Yanks three more years and went a combined 5–9 before being purchased by the late lamented Seattle Pilots. Bouton retired in 1970, but worked at developing a knuckleball. He made it back to the majors with Atlanta in 1978, pitched in five games, went 1–3 and retired again.

But that isn't the finale the story. At the end of his career, Jim Bouton was working on a book he called *Ball Four*. Its publication in 1970 caused a stir throughout the sports world. Not only did it chronicle his 1969 season with the Pilots, but it was also a recollection of his Yankees years, a *real* recollection. It was perhaps the first sports book to break what was called the sanctity of the locker room, revealing the personal lives of players, including the drinking habits of Mickey Mantle and his pals, the wholesale use of amphetamines by ballplayers, as well as stories of widespread womanizing. Commissioner Bowie Kuhn said the book was detrimental to baseball—of course, it became a huge bestseller.

In a sense, *Ball Four* was really Jim Bouton's legacy. It opened the door to more candid books about sports and sports heroes. The book has almost made people forget that for two years Jim Bouton, No. 56, was one of the best pitchers in the game. Besides writing a couple of additional books, Bouton became a sportscaster and a frequent guest on sports talk shows.

Now let's look at the rest of the cast in this three-for-one chapter. The first Yankee to wear No. 55 had a career that somewhat paralleled Bouton's, early success followed by arm problems. He was righthander **Bob Grim**, who came on the scene as a 24-year-old rookie in 1954 and promptly won 20 games. Grim pitched in 37 games, made 20 starts, and won eight of his games in relief. He also threw eight complete games and had a 3.26 ERA. He did it with a blazing fastball and biting slider, and was equally effective starting and relieving. The Yanks thought they had yet another star.

But the lights dimmed quickly. Grim seemed to suffer what they used to call the sophomore jinx his second year, then went 6–1 the following season with a 2.77 ERA and five saves, but his arm was already bothering him and he was now mainly a reliever. A year later, he pitched in 46 games, all in relief and led all AL relievers with 12 wins, going 12–8 with a 2.62 ERA and a league-best 19 saves. Good season, but the last good one. A year later the arm problems worsened and on June 15,

Grim was traded to Kansas City. He hung on for three more years, but was mediocre at best, retiring with a 61–41 record and 3.61 ERA, and probably thoughts of what could have been.

After Grim, players wearing No. 55 began coming and going quickly, though the number did get put in mothballs for a couple of decades. Pitcher **Zach Monroe** started the parade, throwing 21 games in 1958 and just three the following year. Then no one wore the number until 1969, when first sacker **Dave McDonald** donned it for just nine games and hit .217. Another decade passed until the number was given to lefty **Paul Mirabella**. He came from Texas in the Sparky Lyle trade, lasted 10 games (0–4, 8.79 ERA), and was sent to Toronto.

Roger Holt, a second baseman, had a two-game big league career with the Yanks in 1980, and righty **Gene Nelson** lasted all of eight games in his rookie year of 1981. Infielder Andre **Robertson** wore No. 55 for ten games in 1981, then switched to No. 18 during his next four years with the team. The same occurred with veteran shortstop **Roy Smalley**. He wore No. 55 for a short time after joining the team in 1982, switched to No. 34 before the year was out, and then wore No. 12 his final two seasons with the team. Righty **Curt Kaufman** was another with two numbers, wearing No. 47 in 1982 and No. 55 in '83.

Stan Javier was a veteran outfielder who would play for 17 years with moderate success for eight teams. His Yankees tenure lasted for just seven games in 1984, as he hit just .143 before going to Oakland that December. Outfielder **Victor Mata** wore No. 55 for 30 games in 1984, hitting .329. A year later, he was given No. 17 before the bubble burst. Infielder **Juan Bonilla** played eight games as No. 55 in 1985, hit .125, and was shipped to Baltimore. He returned in 1987 as No. 57, hit .255 in 23 games and left the majors. Righty reliever **Rich Monteleone** wore No. 55 in 1990, 1992 and '93, but because he took No. 45 in 1991 he's discussed in that chapter. Another pitcher, **Wally Whitehurst**, didn't have the same luck. He pitched just two games for the Yanks in 1996, the last of his seven seasons in the majors. Nobody today thinks of **Jorge Posada** as No. 55, but he wore it in 1996 after wearing No. 62 briefly the year before. By 1997 he was No. 20, the number he continues to wear as of 2009.

When Posada went from No. 55 to No. 20 in 1997, reliever **Ramiro Mendoza** took over No. 55 after wearing No. 57 the season before. The righty would wear it through 2002 and play a big role in three Yankees championship teams. Never a big star, the Panamanian-born Mendoza could pitch both long relief and close if necessary, and he could start when called upon. In 1998, for example, he pitched in 41 games, starting 14, and had a 10–2 record, a 3.25 ERA and one save. In 2001, the Yanks summoned him 56 times with two starts. He had an 8–4 mark, a 3.75 ERA and six saves. That's the kind of pitcher he was.

After working in 62 games in 2002 and doing his usual fine job, he left the team via free agency, signing with Boston, where he won another World Series ring in 2004. He returned to the Yanks in 2005, but needed shoulder surgery. He would pitch in just one game as No. 38 before realizing it was over. Then along came Hideki Matsui to put his own personal stamp on No. 55, and Bouton to lead off with No. 56.

After Bouton left in 1968, another run of the same kind of in-and-out players followed. Lefty **John Cumberland** wore No. 56 for parts of three seasons (1968–70), appearing in a total of 18 games (15 in 1970) before being traded to the Giants in July for hurler Mike McCormick. Dave Righetti, who became a Yankee star wearing No. 19, actually wore No. 56 in his debut season of 1979, while outfielder **Ted Wilborn** had the same number for just eight games in 1980 before leaving the majors. Pitcher **Mike Patterson** worked a total of 15 games in 1981 and '82, his only two years in the majors, while veteran reliever **Bill Castro** lasted all of 11 games in 1981, yet had a 10-year career.

Infielder **Bert Campaneris** played 60 games at both second and third in 1983, signed as a free agent after playing the previous season in the Mexican League, but his story is a lot more interesting than that. He joined the A's in 1965 as a speedy shortstop and hit the very first pitch he saw in the bigs for a home run, adding a second one later in the game. That September, as part of a Charles O. Finley publicity stunt, the versatile Campy played one inning at every single position in the field, including pitcher and catcher. After that he became one of the keys to Oakland's three time World Champs in the early 70s, a six-time stolen base champ, and a fine shortstop. By the time he came to the Yankees he was 41 years old.

Yet Campy still played very well. In fact, he finished the year with a .322 average in 143 at bats, the highest batting average of his 19-year career. With the Yankees as a player past his 40th birthday, he was far from an embarrassment. After the season, he retired with 649 stolen bases among his many accomplishments.

Infielder **Rex Hudler** played the first two years of a 13-year career with the Yanks. As No. 56, he hit just .143 in nine games in 1986 and .157 in 20 games the following year. No wonder the Yanks dealt him to Baltimore. Lefty **Al Holland** is another of those players previously mentioned since he wore No. 29 in 1987 after wearing No. 56 the year before. Same with catcher **Brian Dorsett,** who wore No. 56 in 1989, then dropped down to No. 28 the following year before being traded to Cincinnati.

The Yanks also had a brother act in the Leiters, though neither did their best work in the Bronx. Southpaw Al wore No. 56 in his first season of 1987, switched to No. 28 the next two years, was traded, then wore No. 19 when he returned to the Bronx briefly in 2005. Righthander **Mark Leiter** pitched just eight games for the Bombers in 1990, wearing No. 56 as a 27-year-old rookie. He went to Detroit the next year. The parade continued with **Dave Silvestri**, **Dave Pavlas**, **Dale Polley**, **Ted Lilly** and **Todd Williams**. Infielder Silvestri wore No. 56 for seven games in '92, then switched to No. 47 for two years and No. 43 in '95, his last Yankees season. Pavlas pitched in parts of two seasons, wearing No. 56 in '95 and No. 47 the next year. Polley threw in 32 games as No. 56 in 1996 and never pitched in the majors again. Lilly wore No. 56 in 2000, switched to No. 61 a year later, then No. 45 in 2002 before being traded. Williams, a righthander, pitched in just 15 games in 2001 before leaving as a free agent.

Outfielder **Juan Rivera** was considered a prospect when he was brought up for three games in 2001. He wore No. 56 that year, then switched to No. 59 the next two years. By 2003 he was in 57 games, hit .266 with seven homers and 26 RBIs. In December of 2003, the

Yanks felt they had to part with him, along with Randy Choate and Nick Johnson in order to get pitcher Javier Vazquez. Rivera ended up with the Angels where he became a solid power hitter. Reliever **Scott Proctor** was another who switched numbers and thus has been mentioned previously. Proctor wore No. 56 his first year of 2004, went from No. 57 to 43 the next year, and kept it through 2007.

Big righthander **Tanyon Sturtze** was a favorite of manager Joe Torre after he joined the Yanks in a deal with the Dodgers in May 2004. The 6'5" Sturtz could both start and relieve, though the Yanks used him mainly out of the pen. After going 6–2 with a 5.47 ERA in 28 games after joining the team, Torre called on Sturtze 64 times in 2005. Sturtz was 5–3 with a 4.73 ERA with one start and one save. But the next year he had arm problems and had to shut it down after 18 games, then underwent surgery for a partially torn rotator cuff which would end his career.

After Sturtze, the last Yankee to wear No. 56, came a group of guys wearing No. 57 who are tough to remember. If began with outfielder **Art Lopez**, went to infielders **Roy Staiger**, **Dennis Sherrill**, and **Tucker Ashford**, and catcher **Bobby Ramos**. They donned the number between 1975 and '80 and didn't really contribute to the cause.

The next five players have all been mentioned previously due to number switching. Pitcher **Ray Fontenot** wore No. 57 in 1983 and No. 47 the next year before departing to the Cubs. Infielder **Juan Bonilla** went from No. 55 in 1985 to No. 57 in '87. Then gone. Catcher **Bob Geren** wore both No. 57 and 58 in two call-ups in 1988, then wore No. 53 for the next three seasons. **Hensley "Bam Bam" Meulens** got five short tries to make it from 1989 to '93 and his numbers went from 57 to 31 twice, to 59 and back to 31. Pitcher **John Habyan** started off as No. 61 in 1990, dropped to No. 57 the next year, and finally changed to No. 42 his last two Yankees seasons.

And then we come to **Steve Howe**, arguably one of the most talented players to throw away a career to alcohol and drug problems. The southpaw closer was the National League Rookie of the Year with the Dodgers in 1980, when he saved 17 games. For another two years, he continued to look like a coming star, a talented closer with ice water in his veins when the game was on the line. Turns out it was things other than ice water. In 1983, he checked himself into a substance abuse clinic for the first time. It didn't work. He failed another drug test and was suspended for the entire 1984 season. It would be the first of an incredible seven suspensions in his career.

Howe was suspended again in 1986, pitched for Texas in 1987, then was suspended from 1988–1990. That's when the Yankees picked him up, signing him prior to the 1991 season. Though he hadn't pitched in the majors since 1987, he looked good in a set-up role, working in 37 games with a 3–1 record and a 1.68 ERA. Now if he could only stay clean. He couldn't. After 20 games of the 1992 season, in which he was 3–0 with a 2.45 ERA and six saves, Howe failed another test and was suspended for life, the second player ever to receive that penalty for violating the league's drug rules. But he appealed successfully and returned to pitch in 51 games that year with limited effectiveness.

Then in 1994 he had his last outstanding season. At the age of 35 he pitched in 40 games, had a 3–0 record, and posted a 1.80 ERA. He saved 15 games and showed that from a talent level, he was still one of the best. He would pitch 56 times in 1995 and go 6–3, but his earned run average was up to 4.96. The next year it ballooned to 6.35 after 25 games, and the Yanks had seen enough. They released Howe on July 24, and his career was over. In 12 years, he had a 47–41 record with a 3.03 ERA and 91 saves. But it could have been much more.

After retirement, Howe became a framing contractor in California. On April 28, 2006, he was driving alone in Coachella, California, when he rolled his pickup truck and was killed. Toxicology results showed he had methamphetamine in his system at the time of his death. Steve Howe was one of baseball's tragedies, a guy who just couldn't get the monkey off his back. At the time of his death, he was just 46 years old.

Pitchers **Ramiro Mendoza**, **Joe Borowski**, and **Jay Tessmer** were all number switchers. Mendoza began as No. 57 in 1996, then went to No. 55, which he wore for the remainder of his first successful tenure with the Yanks. Borowski went from No. 52 in 1997 to 57 a year later, while Tessmer wore No. 62 in 1998, No. 57 the next two years, and then No. 48 when he returned for two games in 2002. Righty **Jeff Juden** didn't have a chance to switch; he was No. 57 for just two games in 1999. Juden was a team-a-year guy, pitching for eight different teams in eight seasons. **Carlos Alexander**, a righthander, pitched in 10 games as No. 57 during the 2001 season after coming over from the Padres.

Shortstop **Erick Almonte** played in eight games as No. 57 in 2001. A year later, wearing No. 60, he replaced an injured Derek Jeter for 31 games and hit a credible .260. Yet when Jeter returned, he was sent down, eventually played for three other organizations, and never made the majors again. **Drew Henson,** the former Michigan all-American quarterback was No. 57 for three games in 2002 and then No. 38 for five more the following year. Read more about his exploits in Chapter 38. Outfielder **Karim Garcia** also switched, going from No. 57 in 2002 to No. 28 in 2003. Catcher **Michel Hernandez** played in just five games as No. 57 in 2003 before being waived to the Red Sox the following January.

The final players to wear No. 57 were **Juan Acevedo, Alex Graman, Brad Halsey**, and the aforementioned **Scott Proctor**. Acevedo, a right-hander, got a 25-game audition in 2003, but his 0–3 record and 7.71 ERA led to a June 10 release. Lefty Graman pitched three games in 2004, then two more in 2005 wearing No. 58. With earned run averages of 19.80 and 13.50 his fate was sealed. Halsey, another lefty, went 1–3 with a 6.47 ERA in eight games during 2004. Proctor, remembered more as No. 43, wore No. 57 in 2005.

That's the three-in-one. It's almost amazing to see the number of players who have passed through the Yankees, organization so briefly, sometimes barely getting a real chance. But even with these higher uniform numbers you find a combination of a real star (Matsui), a con-troversial figure (Bouton), as well as a tragic one (Howe). That's what makes it interesting.

#58–61: WHO GETS THE REALLY HIGH NUMBERS?

These are the numbers that baseball players rarely wore years ago. After all, when numbers began Yankees fans looked at the Babe and Lou, Nos. 3 and 4, and later DiMaggio and Mantle, Nos. 5 and 7. In fact, almost all the great players from earlier days wore low or relatively low numbers. When you had a Jackie Robinson wearing No. 42, it was almost an aberration. No one certainly looked for a star wearing No. 59 or 60. Today there are a few exceptions. So checking out Yankees who wore the numbers 58–61 is like looking for a needle in a haystack, trying to find a gem or two who might have stayed with the number.

Ironically, the first Yankee to wear No. 58 looked like he might be a coming star. He was **Horace Guy Womack,** known as "Dooley" to his teammates and fans. Womack was a 26-year-old righthanded relief pitcher who had toiled for some seven years in the minors when he unexpectedly made the team in 1966. The latest Yankees dynasty had ended in 1964, and this was not a good New York team. With a depleted bullpen, Womack suddenly found himself getting the call 42 times, and he responded with a 7–3 season, a 2.64 ERA, and four saves. A year later he showed he wasn't a fluke, pitching in 65

Brett Jodie	2001
Erick Almonte	2003
Brandon Claussen	2003
Sam Marsonek	2004
Felix Escalona	2004
Wil Nieves	2005–06
Ross Ohlendorf	2007
Rich Monteleone (coach)	2007–08

#61

Marshall Brant	1980
Jim Lewis	1982
Phil Lombardi	1987
John Habyan	1990
Jim Bruske	1998
Ted Lilly	2001
Juan Padilla	2004
Brad Halsey	2004
Jorge De Paula	2005
Darrell Rasner	2006
Matt DeSalvo	2007
Billy Traber	2008

games with a 5–6 record, but a fine 2.41 ERA and 18 big saves.

But the Yanks have never been a patient bunch. It's produce or go elsewhere. After Womack fell off to 3–7 with a 3.21 ERA and just two saves in 1968, he was shipped to Houston for a marginal player named Dick Simpson. Just two years later, he suffered the dreaded torn rotator cuff and his career was over.

Following Womack, No. 58 went to a whole series of players who either switched to a lower number were discussed in earlier chapters or were with the club only long enough to grab a sandwich and cup of coffee. Outfielder **Bobby Brown**, for instance, was with the team from 1979–81, wore No. 58 his first year, then No. 13 the next two. Catcher **Bruce Robinson** was given No. 58 also in 1979, then No. 47 the following year. He played a total of 10 games. Pitchers **Andy McGaffigan** and **Dave Wehrmeister** both wore No. 58 in the same season, 1981, McGaffigan lasted two games with the Yanks, 11 in the big leagues; Wehrmeister lasted all of five games in New York.

The pattern continues. Career backup catcher **Mike O'Berry** played 13 games for the Yanks in 1984 wearing No. 58, while catchers **Juan Espino** and **Bob Geren,** pitchers **Dave Eiland** and **Randy Choate**, and the one-and-only **Alfonso Soriano** all wore No. 58 at one point, then went lower. Pitcher **Mike Jerzembeck** threw just three games as No. 58 in 1998, had an ERA of 12.79, and was out of the majors.

A quartet of pitchers will close out No. 58. Righty **Colter Bean** wore it in both 2005 and '06 before switching to No. 47 in 2007. His total number of appearances, six. Lefty **Sean Henn** got more of a chance between 2005–07 but didn't make it. Alex Graman was No. 57 in 2004 and No. 58 the following year. Gone. Righty **Jeff Karstens** wore No.

58 in 2006 and part of 2007 before moving to No. 17. Didn't help. He pitched in a total of 15 games before being sent to Pittsburgh.

The first Yankee to wear No. 59 was outfielder **Dell Alston** in 1977, but the pattern continued when he swiched to No. 27 the following year, pitched in three games, and was off to Oakland. Infielder **Damaso Garcia** was mentioned way back in Chapter 23, the number he wore in 1978. When called up for 11 games the following year, he wore No. 59 and was shipped to Toronto. Outfielder **Ted Wilborn** actually wore two numbers, 56 and 59, for just eight games in 1980, while lefty **Steve Adkins** pitched in five games as No. 59 in 1990. **"Bam Bam" Meulens** is another guy who was all over the place since he wore Nos. 57, 31, and 59 in parts of five seasons, while lefty **Billy Brewer** wore just No. 59 because he only got to pitch in four games in 1996. Righty **Ryan Bradley** was No. 59 for just five games in 1998, went 2–1 with a 5.68 ERA, and was out of the majors. And Juan Rivera wore No. 59 in 2002 and '03 after wearing No. 56 in 2001.

The list of forgotten names continues. Try **D'Angelo Jimenez**, **Donzell McDonald**, **Hipolito Pena**, and **Darrin Chapin** on for size. Infielder Jimenez got a seven-game trial as No. 59 in 1999, was shipped to San Diego in 2001. Outfielder McDonald had the same number, but only for five games in 2001. He managed to hit .333 but it wasn't good enough. He played 10 more games in Kansas City and was done. Pena, a lefty, pitched just 16 games in 1988 but wore both Nos. 60 and 46. He was 1–1 with the Yanks, pitched two years in Pittsburgh and went 0–6. His distinction: the first Yankee ever

J.T. SNOW
YANKEES

to wear No. 60. Chapin, a righty, only got a three-game look as No. 60 in 1991, went to Philadelphia for just one more game in '92, and was gone.

First baseman **J. T. Snow** was definitely one who got away. The son of former Notre Dame and NFL All-Pro wide receiver Jack Snow, J. T. opted for baseball and got a seven-game look with the Yankees in 1992 as No. 60. The Yanks still had Don Mattingly then (though his best years were already behind him), yet elected to trade Snow that December to the Angels for pitcher Jim Abbott. What happened? J. T. Snow became a solid hitter and one of the finest fielding first basemen in the majors, the winner of six Gold Gloves. He also drove in more than 100 runs twice and had a high of 28 homers for the Giants in 1997. He also played for the Giants and in 16 seasons batted .268 with 189 home runs.

Utilityman **Tim McIntosh** didn't get the same chance. He played just three games in 1996 wearing No. 60 and was dealt away. Then came the second one to get away, third sacker **Mike Lowell**, who wore No. 60 for just eight games in 1998 before being traded to the Florida Marlins. By 1993, Lowell put together a .276, 32, 105 season in Florida. Later, he went to Boston and was even better. In 2007, he hit .324 with 21 homers and 120 RBIs; in 2009, at the age of 35, he hit .290 with 17 homers and 75 RBIs. He's also been a Gold Glove third baseman and a top clutch hitter with 218 career home runs so far.

First sacker **Nick Johnson**, another good hitter, was also dealt because there was no place for him. Johnson wore No. 60 in 2001, but because he switched to No. 36 the following two years his story has already been told. He will be returning to the Yankees in 2010. Righty handed pitcher **Brett Jodie** doesn't have much of a story, pitching one game as No. 60 in 2001 and then being traded. Infielder **Erick Almonte** wore No. 60 in 2003, but started with No. 57 two years before and has been mentioned previously.

As for lefthander **Brandon Clauseen**, his full name was longer than his Yankees career. Wearing No. 60, Brandon Allen Falker Clausen pitched exactly one game in 2003 before being traded to Cincinnati. **Sam Marsonek** is another of those names. Like Claussen, he pitched just a single game in 2004, just two innings, and was gone from the majors. Infielder **Felix Escalona** had a previous mention since he went from No. 60 in 2004 to No. 29 the following year. Two more number jumpers close out No. 60. Catcher **Wil Nieves** wore No. 60 in 2005 and '06, then switched to No. 26 in his final Yankees season of 2007 before being shipped to Washington. And pitcher **Ross Ohlendorf** was No. 60 in 2007 before dropping down to No. 39 the following year. Then it was off to Pittsburgh.

You can tell when the numbers are getting into new territory. No. 61 was not worn by a Yankee player until first sacker **Marshall Brant** appeared with it in 1980. He didn't leave much of an impression after playing just three games before departing for Oakland in 1983. **Jim Lewis**, a righty, wore No. 61 for a single game in 1982. Catcher **Phil Lombardi** and pitcher **John Habyan** have both been previously mentioned.

Since lefty **Ted Lilly** had three numbers (56, 61, and 45) in three years (2000–02), his story has already been told. Still, a good pitcher who could have been a winning Yankee. Righty **Juan Padilla** was another one-year less-than-wonder. He wore No. 61 for six games in 2004, had no record and a 3.97 ERA before being shipped to Cincy. Southpaw **Brad Halsey** has been mentioned because he had two numbers while pitching in just eight games, 57 and 61, in 2004. **Jorge DePaula**, another righthander, went up the ladder, wearing Nos. 41, 43, and 61 from 2003–05. **Darrell Rasner** got three chances from 2006–08 and, like so many others, had three numbers, 61, 27, and 43. He ran the gamut, then went to Japan.

Southpaw **Billy Traber** was the last player to wear No. 61, donning it for 19 games in 2008. Traber was brought on board to be a situational lefty and get some key outs primarily against lefthanded hitters. He didn't do it, and was quickly exiled from New York.

#62–99: YOU SURE THESE AREN'T FOOTBALL PLAYERS?

At left tackle, No. 76... Well, it isn't quite like that, but there was a time when baseball numbers just weren't supposed to go into the 60s and 70s. And the 90s? That was even a bit high for football. While there aren't a slew of players wearing the numbers between 62 and 99, and while every single slot is not filled, there are nevertheless a number of players given those high numerals. There are even two present day pitchers, both highly touted as potential stars, who have now worn numbers in the 60s for several years as their careers with the Yankees build. So let's lead off with No. 62, **Joba Chamberlain** and No. 65, **Phil Hughes**.

Ever since his dramatic debut back in 2007, Joba Chamberlain has been in the high beam headlights. It seems as if his every move is scrutinized, analyzed, second-guessed, and debated. Should he be a starter or short reliever? Did the "Joba Rules" that limited his innings in 2009 hurt or help him? Will the Yankees deal him if they have a chance to pick up an established star pitcher? With Joba, it seems to never end.

A burly, 6'2", 230-pound righthander with a blazing fastball and biting, late-breaking slider, Joba was raised by his wheelchair-bound father, Harlan, a Native American of the Winnebago Tribe.

#69
Alan Mills   1990

#72
Juan Miranda   2009

#75
Ben Ford   2000

#76
Craig Dingman   2000

#77
Humberto Sanchez   2008

#91
Alfredo Aceves   2008–09

#99
Charlie Keller   1952
Matt Howard   1996
Brian Bruney   2009

The 41st pick in the 2006 draft, he ripped through the minors in 2007, advancing quickly from Single-A to Triple-A, blowing away hitters along the way. On August 7, the Yanks brought him up to fortify the bullpen, specifically the bridge to closer Mariano Rivera. They wanted Joba to be the eighth-inning guy but no one expected what they would get—a poised and cool 21-year-old with electric stuff and outstanding control. He struck out the first hitter he faced and took off from there. The fans loved him. When he got a key strikeout with men on base to end an inning, he'd screamed and pumped his fist and no one would argue with the results. In 19 games, Joba went 3–0 with a minuscule 0.38 earned run average. He fanned 34 hitters in 24 innings and walked just six.

His one hiccup came in the playoffs when a swarm of bugs and midges disrupted his concentration during Game Two of the ALDS in Cleveland. Still, it looked as if a star had been born.

Though Joba began 2008 in the pen, he was sent down to the minors in May to stretch his arm out in preparation to joining the rotation. The Yanks always envisioned him as a starter. He made his first start on June 3, losing to Roy Halladay and the Blue Jays. But by July 25, he threw seven shutout innings against the Red Sox, giving up just three hits and striking out nine as the Yanks won, 1–0. Then in early August, he had to go on the DL with shoulder tendinitis and when he returned finished in the pen. For the year he was 4–3 in 42 games, 12 of them starts, and had an ERA of 2.60. Though he fanned 118 in 100 1/3 innings, he wasn't quite as dominant as the year before.

In 2009, the Yanks again made him a starter, only this time they said they would try to limit his innings, fearing another arm injury if he

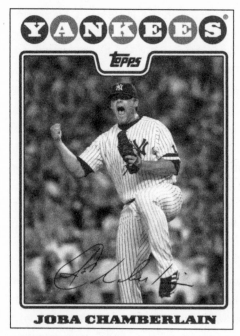

JOBA CHAMBERLAIN

pitched too much. They tried it in several ways, stretching out the days between starts, then pulling him from games early after he reached a set pitch count. All of this seemed to take away his confidence. He was often inconsistent and didn't even seem to throw as hard. When the season ended. he was 9–6 with a 4.75 ERA in 31 starts, this time fanning 137 in 157 innings. He no longer appeared dominant. Because the Yanks went to a three-man rotation in the playoffs, Joba returned to the pen and again showed some of the magic and electricity of 2007, igniting the debate once more.

Will he be a starter or a reliever? Joba has said he'll do whatever the team wants. Yankee brass seems to still envision him as a starter. Many observers, however, feel his temperament is more suited to short relief, where he can feed off the emotion of the moment and just let it all loose. He should be, many say, the heir apparent to Mariano Rivera. So the jury is still out. The talent is obviously there and 2010 could be crucial. And he continues to wear No. 62, a number he's already made his own. He may just keep it.

Phil Hughes has also sparked a kind of debate about his ultimate role, though it only cropped up for the first time in 2009. A 6'5", 220-pound righthander, Hughes was the Yanks' first round draft choice out of Foothill High in Santa Ana, California, in 2004. By 2006, he was considered not only the Yanks' best minor league prospect by *Baseball America*, but the best pitching prospect in the minor leagues. Possessor of a mid-90s fastball and knee-buckling curve, Hughes held opposing hitters to just a .179 batting average in 2006. When he was called up in 2007, the 21-year-old was the second youngest player in the majors.

He made his debut on April 26, going 4 1/3 innings and giving up four runs. Then in his second start against Texas on May 1, Hughes had it all going. He was pitching a no-hitter through 6 1/3 innings when he pulled his left hamstring while delivering an 0–2 curveball to the Rangers' Mark Teixeira. He went on the DL and didn't return until August 4. He finished the year with a 5–3 record and 4.46 ERA, and a ton of potential.

Plugged into the rotation in 2008, Hughes saw his season turn into a disaster. First of all, he had worn No. 65 the season before but now switched to No. 34, his high school number. He was ineffective early and on April 30, strained an oblique muscle and cracked a rib. He didn't return until September 13, at which time he returned to No. 65. But he ended his season with a disappointing 0–4 mark and 6.62 ERA in just eight games. What was next?

Though Hughes pitched well in spring training, he returned to the minors at the beginning of the 2009 season because there wasn't room in a rotation that featured new acquisitions CC Sabathia and A. J. Burnett, veterans Andy Pettitte and Chien-Ming Wang, and Joba. But when Wang went on the DL, Hughes returned and went into the rotation. He was a bit inconsistent, but on May 25 threw eight scoreless innings against the Rangers. When Wang returned in early June, the Yanks decided to move Hughes to the bullpen instead of sending him down again.

Suddenly he began establishing himself, and soon he took over the eighth-inning role, Joba's old role, and did it exceedingly well. His presence stabilized the bullpen and he helped the Yanks run away with the division. He finished the regular season with an 8–3 record, a 3.03 ERA, and three saves. His ERA as a reliever was much lower. His role for 2010 also remains unclear. He's again projected as a starter, as is Chamberlain, but if the need arises in the bullpen, one of them could fill it, especially since the Yankees traded for Javier Vazquez to fill the fourth slot in the rotation.

By the way, Phil Hughes had a reason for choosing No. 65. He said he always wanted a number ending in 5. When he joined the Yanks, they were all taken or retired: DiMaggio retired No. 5, Munson retired No. 15, Jason Giambi had No. 25, Mike Mussina had No. 35, Carl Pavano had No. 45, and Hideki Matsui had No. 55. That left No. 65 and Phil Hughes grabbed it. Yankee fans would love to see him grab 15 or 20 wins next season.

Other than Chamberlain and Hughes, these ultra-high numbers contain a variety of players, usually marginal players who quickly went to a lower number. Let's take a look at these last-inning guys, starting with outfielder **Brian Dayett**. Dayett got a shot during 1983 and '84 when the team was down. Wearing No. 62, he played 11 games in '83 but then got a 64-game audition the following year. It didn't work out and he was traded to the Cubs.

Pitcher **Doug Drabek** wore Nos. 62 and 34 in 1986, his only year with the Yanks, and has been discussed previously. Same with **Brad Arnsberg**, **Hal Morris**, **Jorge Posada** (a no-brainer), and **Willie Banks**. All wore No. 62 before switching, and with the exception of Posada, had very short Yankee careers.

It continued with **Jay Tessmer**, **Brandon Knight**, and **Sean Henn**. All had No. 62 at one point and then another number. Infielder **Jim Walewander** played in nine games as No. 63 in 1990, his only year with the Yanks, hitting just .200. Catcher **Mike Figga** was No. 63 in 1997, then switched to No. 13 for parts of the next two seasons. His total Yankees career—eight games.

Righty **Danny Rios** wore No. 63 for two games in 1997. In 2 1/3 innings he gave up five runs for a 19.29 earned run average and was sent to Kansas City. Lefty **Randy Keisler** went from No. 63 in 2000 to No. 48 the following year, was traded, and had just a 4–4 record in parts of six seasons. Big righthander **Jonathan Albaladejo** has been up and down several times in 2008 and '09, wearing No. 63 both years. In 2009, he threw in 32 games and went 5–1, but with a 5.24 ERA. He's got a live arm, but needs consistency.

Righty **Bill Fulton** was the first Yankee to wear No. 64 in 1987, but was one of those guys whose stay in the majors was painfully short. He pitched in three games and was gone. Infielder **Steve Kiefer** saw action in just five games in 1989, wearing No. 64, and hit a not-so-robust .125

before departing. For outfielder **Bronson Sardinha**, No. 64 was on his back for just 10 games in 2007. For the Hawaiian-born Sardinha, the most fascinating thing was his middle name. It's Kiheimahanaomaulakeo. And that's no lie. Try putting that on the back of a uniform.

Catcher **Francisco Cervelli** wore No. 64 for three games in 2008, then No. 29 a year later when he played in 42 games and hit .298. At age 23, he has a chance to be the catcher of the future. Another backstop, **Juan Espino**, was the first player to wear No. 65 back in 1983. Righty **Adrian Hernandez** was No. 65 in both 2001 and '02, pitching in a total of eight games before moving to Milwaukee for a few more in 2004. Lefty **Jim Deshaies** was the first to don No. 66 in 1984. His Yankees career lasted just two games as he lost one and had an 11.57 ERA. Many players with those numbers quickly disappear, but Deshaies went to Houston, wound up pitching 12 years for six teams, and went 84–95, all as a starter.

The oft-mentioned **Steve Balboni** wore No. 66 in 1981 and again in '83. But he also wore Nos. 36, 28, 50 and 45 in two Yankee tenures lasting a total of five years. Righty **Clay Christiansen** was the first to wear No. 67, getting an 11-game shot in 2000, not winning or losing while posting a 3.55 ERA and then leaving the majors. Another righty, **Alan Mills,** stuck around 12 years, but only two were with the Yanks, 1990 and '91s, wearing No. 69 and then No. 50. In 2009, first base prospect **Juan Miranda** wore No. 72 during a September call-up. But with Teixeria firmly entrenched at first, Miranda may soon wind up traded.

Righty **Ben Ford** was No. 75 for four games in 2000 as the numbers dwindle down to a precious few. Righty **Craig Dingman** topped Ford's tenure at No. 75, throwing 10 games in 2000 with an ERA of 6.55. Big **Humberto Sanchez** wore No. 77 for just two games in 2008. The 6'6", 270-pound righty came to the Yanks from Detroit, when Gary Sheffield left New York, and was considered a prospect, but he was rehabbing from Tommy John surgery and the Yanks just ran out of patience.

Alfredo Aceves may be a keeper. A versatile righthander out of Mexico, he joined the Yanks in 2008, wearing No. 91, and went 1–0 with a 2.40 ERA in six games. Making the club again in 2009, he stayed with his unusually high number and proceeded to become an integral part of the staff. Aceves can start or relieve, go long or go short; he's a guy who just knows how to pitch. Manager Joe Girardi used him 43 times and he compiled a 10–1 record with a 3.54 ERA.

And now we come to No. 99. Can you get any higher than that? No so far. The first to wear it was longtime star Charlie "King Kong" Keller. He returned to the Yanks in 1952 to play two games at the end of his career. He had been with the Yanks from 1939–1949, then spent two years with the Tigers. He returned to retire as a Yankee and wore both No. 28 and No. 99 for those two games. He's remembered more as both No. 9 and No. 12. Infielder Matt Howard actually wore No. 99 early in the 1996 season, then switched to No. 38 as he played in 35 games, hit .204, and was soon out of the bigs.

And finally there was reliever **Brian Bruney**. From 2006–2008, the hard-throwing righthander wore No. 33. In 2009, he began as No. 38, was the eighth-inning set-up guy early and ran into elbow problems. He had two stints on the DL, and when he returned late he suddenly appeared as No. 99, hoping to change his luck. Though he pitched fairly well at the end, his luck didn't change. In early December, it was announced that the Yanks had traded him to the Washington Nationals for a player to be named later.

So that's it, No. 1 to No. 99, all the Yankees since 1929. Perhaps the most surprising thing is that with all the winning, the 27 World Championships, and all the huge stars from the Babe to Derek and A-Rod, so many players passed through Yankee Stadium and so many had very short stays. But that's the nature of the game. The scouts are always looking, the minors are always filled, and many players try to make the big club. But with their traditional emphasis on winning and the success they've had, the Yankees aren't always the most patient of organizations. Players have to deliver and do it quickly in most cases. The only thing they have in common is uniform numbers. Everyone has to have one but, hey, that's why scorecards were invented.

DECEMBER MOMENTS

December is the final month of the year and this is the final chapter of the book, but that doesn't mean nothing happens. In fact, the Yankees have seen many significant events occur in December. Here are some of them:

On December 8, 1939, Lou Gehrig was elected to the Hall of Fame in a special vote by the Baseball Writers' Association.

On December 18, 1956, Phil Rizzuto joined the broadcast team of Mel Allen and Red Barber. The Scooter would stay in the booth for the next 40 years.

On December 17, 1966, Mickey Mantle told the Yankees he'd be willing to move from center field to first base if it would help the team and help his legs hold up longer.

On December 14, 1980, Yankee great Elston Howard died in New York at the age of 51; and on December 14, 1985, home run king Roger Maris died in Houston, also at the age of 51.

On December 25, 1989, Billy Martin died in an automobile accident at the age of 61. His plaque in Monument Park at Yankee Stadium reads, "Casey's Boy. A Yankee forever. A man who knew only one way to play—to win."

And that's pretty much what the New York Yankees have done down through the years. Win.

ACKNOWLEDGMENTS

The author would like to cite both baseball-almanac.com and baseball-reference.com, two exceptional baseball websites that provided a wealth of information and easy access for the large amount of research that was needed for this book. A special thanks to my editor, Mark Weinstein, for enduring some unforeseen delays and then working overtime to help get a rather large manuscript ready to go. There were a lot of pinstriped players down through the years.

ABOUT THE AUTHOR

Bill Gutman is a freelance author of more than 200 books for both children and adults, including *What if the Babe Had Kept his Red Sox?, It's Outta Here! The History of the Home Run from Babe Ruth to Barry Bonds, Parcells: A Biography*, and *Twice Around the Bases*, written with Kevin Kennedy. A lifelong Yankees fan, he lives in upstate New York.